The best treatise on development in existence ... Thorough, well written and easy to read ... a professional masterpiece.

Professor Karsten Laursen

John Martinussen's work ... distinguishes itself from all previous introductions to development [by virtue of] its comprehensiveness and multi-disciplinarity.

Associate Professor Jorgen Dige Pedersen

A particular strength of this book is that it ... combines discussion of development economics with theories concerning political and cultural conditions.

Hans Peter Dejgaard

Probably the first book to deal with all the important contributions to theory concerning development in the Third World.

Klaus Winkel

This comprehensive introduction to development theory will without doubt provide the baseline for research and teaching in the field well into the next millenium.

Professor Bjorn Hettne

Awesome in its coverage and imaginative sweep. It not only portrays vividly the plurality of approaches to development issues in the Third World but also sets out a convincing case for discarding any mono-economic or, for that matter, mono-statist or mono-societal perspective on the complex and challenging problems facing the majority of mankind at the close of the 20th century. It should serve as an advanced undergraduate text or a text for beginning graduate students in the disciplines of economics, political science, sociology and as a foundation course in development studies. The multi-disciplinary approach of the book and its lucid analysis of the rival perspectives would be a great help to both the clarity of perception and imagination of the serious student of development studies. I do not know of any other book which can serve as an alternative text in the areas indicated.

Professor Amiya Kumar Bagchi, Director, Centre for Studies in Social Sciences, Calcutta

John Degnbol Martinussen has written an extremely wide-ranging survey of development concepts, theories and strategies. His extensive knowledge and his skills of concise explanation make him a trustworthy guide for both students and general readers. His text will be praised for its valuable treatment of the social, political and international dimensions of development thought, as well as the economic aspects.

Professor John Toye, Director, Institute of Development Studies (IDS), Sussex

About the Author

Professor John Degenbol Martinussen has had a distinguished career in development studies. He is currently study director for International Development Studies at Roskilde University in Denmark. He is also a former chairman of the Danish Social Science Research Council and a former president of the Danish Association for International Cooperation (Mellemfolkeligt Samvirke). He is currently chairman of the Council for International Development Cooperation in Denmark.

Over the years he has acted as a consultant to various international organisations, including the UNDP. South and South East Asia have been his primary geographical regions of specialisation and his research interests revolve around, *inter alia*, a reappraisal of the role of the state in development, as well as appropriate methodological approaches and the growth of theory in development studies.

His recent books in English include:

Pluralism, Competition and Choice: Emerging Local Self-Government in Nepal, New Delhi: Sage Publications, 1995.

The Theoretical Heritage from Marx and Weber in Development Studies (edited), Roskilde: International Development Studies, 1994.

New International Economics and their Applicability in a Third World Context (edited), Roskilde: International Development Studies, 1993.

Transnational Corporations in a Developing Country: The Indian Experience, New Delhi: Sage Publications, 1988.

Society, State and Market

A guide to competing theories of development

JOHN MARTINUSSEN

Zed Books Ltd
LONDON & NEW JERSEY

Fernwood Publishing
HALIFAX, NOVA SCOTIA

HRSC
RGN
PRETORIA

Society, State and Market: A guide to competing theories of development was first published in English by Zed Books Ltd, 7 Cynthia Street, London N1 9JF, UK, and 165 First Avenue, Atlantic Highlands, New Jersey 07716, USA, in 1997.

Published in Canada by Fernwood Books Ltd, PO Box 9409, Station A, Halifax, Nova Scotia, Canada, B3K 5S3.

Published in South Africa by Human Sciences Research Council, PO Box 5556, Pretoria 0001.

Originally published in Danish under the title *Samfund, stat og marked: En kritisk gennemgang af teorier om udvikling i den 3. verden* by Mellemfolkeligt Samvirke, Borgergade 14, DK 1300 Kobenhavn K, Denmark, in 1995.

Copyright © Mellemfolkeligt Samvirke, 1995
Copyright © John Martinussen, 1997
Translation and revision © John Martinussen, 1997

Cover designed by Andrew Corbett
Set in Monotype Garamond by Ewan Smith
Printed and bound in the United Kingdom by Redwood Books Ltd, Kennet House, Kennet Way, Trowbridge, Wilts BA14 8RN

The right of John Martinussen to be identified as the author of this work has been asserted by him in accordance with the Copyright, Designs and Patents Act, 1988.

A catalogue record for this book is available from the British Library

Library of Congress Cataloging-in-Publication Data
Martinussen, John.
    [Samfund, stat og marked. English]
    State, society, and market: a guide to competing theories
of development / John Martinussen.
        p.   cm.
    Includes bibliographical references and index.
    ISBN 1-85649-441-1 (hb). — ISBN 1-85649-442-X (pb)
    1. Developing countries—Economic policy.   2. Development
economics—Developing countries.   3. Developing countries–
–Dependency on foreign countries.   I. Title.
HC59.7.M326   1997
338.9'009172'4—dc20   96-24005
                                                          CIP

Canadian Cataloguing in Publication Data
Martinussen, John.
    Society, state and market
    Includes bibliographical references and index.
    ISBN 1-895686-72-5
1. Economic development.   I. Title.
HD75.M37 1997   338.9

ISBN 1 85649 441 1 hb
ISBN 1 85649 442 X pb
South Africa ISBN 07969 1795 7
Canada ISBN 1 895686 72 5

Contents

Tables and Figures

Tables

Figures

Preface

This book is addressed to readers interested in a comprehensive introduction to development theories and international debates on development, mal-development and underdevelopment in Asia, Africa and Latin America over the last 40 years. It is written especially with two target audiences in mind. One comprises students at university level and others who for study purposes wish to delve into the subjects of development research and the associated theories of why development or underdevelopment occur in different societal settings. For this group of readers, the book provides a thorough and extensive introduction, together with guidance on how one can work further with the various themes and theories.

The other primary target audience comprises administrators, decision makers, journalists, practitioners in international development work and others who wish to delve into the book's themes out of a general interest. Common for this reader group is a need to acquire an overview and general knowledge of issues, approaches, concepts, theories and strategies which, combined, can contribute to a better understanding of what is happening in Asia, Africa and Latin America and how dynamics in these parts of the world interact with developments in the highly industrialised countries. This group of readers may ignore the several references to the literature given in the text and concentrate on the review of the various concepts, approaches, modes of reasoning, theories and strategies presented.

There is no consensus on what should be understood by 'development'. Neither is there agreement on how development can best be brought about nor why it has proved so difficult for most of the poor countries in the Third World to achieve any kind of major improvements for the large majority of their citizens.

The book therefore reviews a multiplicity of conflicting and competing conceptions and views on all these issues. However, to facilitate the forming of a general view and the acquisition of a broad understanding of the subject matter, emphasis has been given to revealing patterns and stages in both theory building and the international debates. The book further tries to trace the theoretical origins within the social sciences with a view to identifying the more basic positions and intellectual similarities and differences. Particular attention is given to describing different conceptions of development and underdevelopment. The underlying objective here is to add to the understanding of where, more exactly, genuine disagreements occur in the development debates and, at the same time, facilitate a more considered and substantiated stance on the issues involved.

In selecting theories and strategies for closer scrutiny, a number of criteria have been used. First, views and theories which have strongly influenced practical development co-operation or the international development debate are included. Since these views have changed significantly over the last 40 years, the book also gives an insight into these changes.

Second, theories are included which deal explicitly with power relations and political aspects of the development process. In this way the book contributes to a broader understanding of development problems than that contained in the more traditional economic theories.

Third, theories have been chosen which place the individual Third World country's own traditions and inherited social and political structures centrally in the understanding of the development process and in the elaboration of development strategies. Much space is given to theories which acknowledge the dissimilarities between Third World countries. Furthermore, theories and discussions on the importance of ethnic, religious and other socio-cultural relations have been included.

Fourth, importance is placed on including the global connection. Both the developing countries and the other nations of the world are part of a comprehensive and multifarious network of international and transnational relations, which in the case of developing countries have colossal importance for their development opportunities.

Fifth, theoretical and strategic contemplations that try to draw in the environmental problems are included – in recognition that the natural environment sets limits for growth, and moreover has significant influence on the course of the development process in the longer term.

Sixth, especially towards the end of the book, theories that can particularly contribute to adding new people-centred perspectives to the development debate are examined.

Throughout the book, the theories and strategies are put into the geographical, historical and broader theoretical contexts in which they have been formulated. This implies that many lines have been drawn backwards to the theories of earlier times. However, the emphasis is on the theoretical and strategical debates of the last 20 years. As a consequence, considerable attention is given to themes such as: state versus market, human development, democracy, and security and aid policy issues following the dismantling of the Eastern Bloc – in addition to the previously mentioned environmental problems. It should be noted, however, that high priority has been given to what could be termed the theoretical mainstreams within development studies, because they have had a strong impact upon strategy elaboration, and because they have provided conceptual continuity and a framework – even for alternative approaches that have challenged the conventional wisdom.

Most of the theories presented and discussed were originally formulated by scholars from the highly industrialised countries. This is not an attempted bias but rather a reflection of the actual state of affairs in development research and theory construction. However, this bias has been reduced as much as possible by including Third World contributions wherever feasible.

In some cases, theories and strategies are presented separately. This is done when they have played independent and leading roles in theory formation, or in development co-operation and the ensuing debates. In other cases, the theories and strategies are treated as parts of thematic analyses of selected development issues.

In the course of the presentations I have added some of my own contributions to theory building within the field of development studies. In addition, I have added personal assessments and considerations in order to highlight where I see the strengths and weaknesses of the various theories and strategies. The assessments are based primarily on documented experience and the development trends and patterns which can be observed over the last 40 years. I have tried, naturally, to separate my own evaluations from the presentation of others' views and arguments, but in recognition of how difficult this may sometimes be, it must be remembered that no discussion of social and cultural relations can be entirely value-free. The reader is referred to Chapter 25 for a discussion of these matters.

The approach and mode of presentation applied in the book implies that it may be read both as a presentation of the different theories and main concepts, and as a comprehensive introduction to development and underdevelopment problems and issues. In the latter connection the individual theories and thematic discussions function as pieces in a mosaic depicting the developing countries' basic structures, their previous achievements, and their contemporary development options and obstacles.

An earlier version of this book was published in Danish in 1994, addressed to Scandinavian readers. It was published in both Denmark and Norway. The present version in English has been thoroughly revised with an international readership in mind. The issues and themes dealt with are essentially the same, but most specific Scandinavian contributions have been left out and some recent theories and international discussions have been added.

I must take full responsibility for any possible misinterpretations or lack of proportion embodied in the presentation. On the other hand, many others have contributed valuable elements to the book. This applies first and foremost to my colleagues at the Department of Geography and International Development Studies at Roskilde University, Denmark. But it also applies very much to colleagues abroad, particularly in India and the UK. The Library of the Danish Association of International Co-operation (Mellemfolkeligt Samvirke) in Copenhagen and Roskilde University Library have given me excellent help in connection with literature searches and requisitions. Ms Anette Feldbæk and Ms Kenja Henriksen have assisted me in translating parts of the original Danish version of the book into English.

I expect there to be a need for a revised edition of the book in the coming years. It was no easy task to cover theory formation and the international development debates so extensively. Therefore, much can undoubtedly be improved in future editions, and I would be grateful for any form of criticism, not least from students and others who will come to work more intensively with the text.

John Martinussen
Roskilde University, Denmark

TO VIBEKE

PART I

Introduction

CHAPTER I

Development Studies as a Subject Area

There is no consensus on what the subject of development research covers. In fact there is not even agreement that development research is a distinct subject with its own approaches, methods and theories. Furthermore, many researchers have claimed that development studies in the last decade have been caught in a serious crisis, because mainstream theories have not been able properly to explain the patterns of transformation and stagnation in the developing countries. Moreover, there is disagreement on just how large a part of the world development research can or should cover – and in connection with this, to what extent it still makes sense to talk about a Third World, or about developing countries as a special category of countries.

It is necessary to examine these issues in order to outline a framework for a review of the various development concepts, theories and strategies. This is what the present chapter is about. A separate section of the chapter describes the method of analysis and presentation applied in the book.

What is development research?

It is common in international development co-operation to regard development research as synonymous with developing country research, i.e. a collection of all types of research which have to do with developing countries – regardless of subject area. Based on this conception, botanical studies in tropical areas, for instance, becomes developing country research and thus development research.

A different, though not necessarily opposing concept, is found among many representatives of basic research, especially within economics. They take their starting point in the established disciplines and claim that the methods and theories of these disciplines are essentially valid for all societies throughout the world. They thereby dismiss theory and method which give developing countries or the Third World a separate status. To them there is no development economics or any other form of theory construction with special validity for what others call developing countries, the Third World, or peripheral societies (in this regard, see also Chapter 2 below).

In itself it is understandable that the aid agencies – the multilateral as well

3

as the bilateral – in a pragmatic way choose to regard development research and developing country research as the same subject area. This follows logically from the geographic areas of particular interest to these organisations. Problems arise, however, when the aid agencies' work and strategy recommendations are based on the assumption that the theories, methods and strategies that have been shown to be useful in highly industrialised countries can be applied, without modifications, to countries with totally different structures, internal conditions, and relations to the international system.

These are exactly the differences one would expect to be discussed thoroughly in basic research at universities, in connection with determination of the area of validity of the theories. Unfortunately this is not always the case. On the contrary, there is a widespread tendency to assume a kind of universal applicability and validity, again especially within economics. Views like these seem open to criticism and they appear as ethnocentric, because they a priori give precedence to methods and theories which are developed with empirical foundations in Western societies and culture.

Evidently, other societies in the world may develop and change under different conditions and according to other 'laws of motion' than those which apply to the highly industrialised societies. This could be the case for Third World countries or different categories within that group. The same could apply to the previously centrally planned economies of Eastern Europe and the former Soviet Union. These possibilities are ignored if it is asserted at the start that theories and methods based on experiences from the North-Western region of the world, in Europe and North America, are applicable and valid everywhere. It is thereby also asserted, albeit implicitly, that the developing countries' own traditions and inherited economic, social and political structures and institutions are of little importance as determining factors for their societal development.

It seems more reasonable, as a starting point for defining the core areas of development research, to proceed from the hypothesis that the special features of the developing countries are of critical importance – until the opposite has been shown to be the case. This forms the basis in the present account, which more precisely defines the subject area of development studies and research as *the societal reproduction and transformation processes of the developing countries, in conjunction with the international factors that influence these processes.*

This definition does not necessarily embody an assertion that the conditions and laws governing development and change in Third World countries differ qualitatively from those which apply to the highly industrialised countries. But the definition does imply a need to be aware that the geographic and cultural foundations of the existing theories may reduce or even eliminate their applicability to societies outside the North-Western region. That the methods and theories of the established disciplines within the North-Western region may be relevant and valuable in the various parts of the Third World is not precluded, but the suggested definition underlines that it remains an open and empirical question just how far and in what respects this is the case. The same reasoning can be applied to theories with empirical foundations in the Second World – the former centrally planned economies.

The suggested definition, at the same time, implies a narrowing or focusing of perspective, namely by putting emphasis on *societal* factors and consequently on social science theories and methods. This further entails that culture studies and other disciplines of the humanities are centrally positioned in many areas, because they have so extensively inspired and supplemented large parts of social science research. On the other hand, natural science, medical science and technical science approaches are only included in those cases – and to the extent – to which they are necessary for the understanding of societal processes. This could be the case, for instance, in connection with development problems like deforestation, desertification and technological maladjustment. The point is that research in the Third World becomes development research only when expressly related to societal conditions and processes.

The delimiting of the subject area of development research implied here forms the basis for the presentation in this book.

Development research is more than economics

For many years there was a widespread tendency to reduce the problems of developing countries to economic problems. This applied also to development research as it was conducted in the 1950s and the following couple of decades, albeit to a decreasing extent.

Many of the original theories of development were first and foremost theories of economic growth and economic transformation. They revolved around conditions that researchers thought promoted or obstructed economic progress – with or without a social dimension. Correspondingly, discussions on development strategies were mostly concerned with economic issues. This very much applied to the international debates of the previous decades on aid and development co-operation.

In the beginning, development theories rarely concerned themselves with political or cultural considerations. On the one hand they did not raise questions about the extent to which political or cultural factors influenced economic development. On the other hand they did not, as a rule, concentrate on describing what actually happened to political or cultural life when a developing country went through an economic crisis or experienced rapid economic growth.

From the start there were, as we shall later see, theories which did concern themselves with politics and culture, but the majority of these theories were weak when it came to economic analysis. Therefore, they too failed to give a comprehensive picture.

The strategies, based on the economic theories, which the International Monetary Fund, the World Bank and other organisations recommended the developing countries to follow, were similarly devoid of politics and culture. They paid very little attention to prevailing power relations or other political preconditions for economic reform. They rarely concerned themselves with the political institutions through which policies were to be implemented. This meant, among other things, that they normally failed to consider whether the governments concerned had even the administrative capacity or the political will to implement the suggested strategies. Finally, understanding of the developing countries' own, often vigorous and significant, social and cultural values was often lacking.

Surprisingly, this underemphasising of non-economic conditions was also embodied in the majority of strategies that were drawn up by the developing countries' own authorities. Not even in the otherwise comprehensive five-year plans did one find serious discussion of political or cultural conditions.

It was hardly a coincidence that both development research and the international debate about the problems of developing countries were characterised by these biases in the first decades after the Second World War. The theories themselves often argued in favour of stressing economic aspects with reference to the fact that the developing countries were primarily poor in the economic sense, and that so many people in these countries were without the most basic material necessities. Therefore, it seemed natural to start here, both with the analyses and the strategies. The problems arose when this – in itself a reasonable and convincing starting point – was combined with the assumption that if they succeeded in initiating economic growth and change processes then the other aspects of societal life would automatically follow and adjust.

The dangers in attributing the dominant role in societal development to economics was not so conspicuous in the industrialised countries, where the theories and strategies were first worked out. In the North-Western region neither political nor cultural considerations blocked the way for economic progress and social reforms. In fact, there was not much that obstructed economic progress during the long period of growth that continued until the end of the 1960s. Therefore, this period was also characterised by widespread optimism and a belief that economic progress would lead to better quality of life in every respect.

This attitude affected the discussion on the developing countries' conditions for development. Because of this, many took it for granted that the poor countries could make good use of the experience of the more developed countries – again, in itself, a reasonable assumption. Meanwhile, in practice, it was found that this assumption shifted, almost naturally, to the more ideological conviction that the more developed countries constituted ideal models for development even in the Third World. The specific models proposed varied, but the same basic ideological conception characterised – explicitly or implicitly – most theories which were elaborated in the North-Western industrialised countries and in the USSR and Eastern Europe for many years after the Second World War.

As a consequence of the dominance of the highly industrialised countries – the First and Second Worlds – within research as well as economically, these distortions and ideological conceptions came to characterise the developing countries' own research and self-understanding for several years.

There has, however, always existed a significant opposition to the prevailing theories and strategies. Researchers, politicians, and planners around the world have consistently tried to reach a broader and deeper understanding of the problems facing developing societies. Many examples can be given of theories and strategies which assumed such broader perspectives, but it is only in more recent years that the mainstream of development research has seriously started to analyse the development processes as both economic and politico-cultural processes.

In keeping with the above outlined main stages in the intellectual history of development research, the chapters in the following parts of this book are arranged to provide, first, an introduction to economic growth and development theories and, second, a review and discussion of political and sociological theories. Only after that – as a reflection of today's prevailing research priorities and emphases – will we turn to the multidisciplinary approaches and theories.

As far as the strategies are concerned, there is still a long way to go before the non-economic factors can be said to have been systematically integrated in mainstream thinking, but the tendencies here are in that direction, both with regard to the recommendations of the World Bank and in the new approaches adopted in international development co-operation.

Along with the increased attention to non-economic conditions, we have also observed over the last 20 years more interest in the special circumstances prevailing in the individual developing countries; more awareness about specific local conditions; and better understanding of the importance of changes over time, both in the individual countries, and in their relationship to the world market and world society as a whole. Moreover, increased attention has been given to social and cultural differentiation, including gender differentiation. Finally, the interaction between societal development and ecological conditions has increasingly been brought into the theory construction process, as well as into the debate on development strategy.

All these trends towards a broadening of the perspective, and the concurrent trend to focus on selected constituent problems, are reflected in this book in that the further one progresses through the text, the broader is the perspective. At the same time, however, individual sections of the various chapters concentrate on a particular area, reflecting the changes in the theory construction process away from grand theories towards middle-level and thematic theories – like those on the role of transnational corporations, democratisation, or gender-specific issues.

The concluding chapter (Chapter 25) takes up for discussion the outlined trends and patterns in theory construction. Further, factors which have influenced extensively the profiles and accentuations of development research are dealt with in that chapter.

Is there a crisis in development research?

During the last decade much has been written on crises in development research (e.g. Hettne, 1990: Ch. 1). In this connection, it has to be acknowledged that the earlier so dominant grand theories – Marxist as well as liberalist – have not been able to provide adequate explanations for the different kinds and patterns of development and underdevelopment which have occurred in the Third World. In addition, these general theories have often resulted in incorrect predictions. Parallel to this, the strategies worked out on the basis of these theories have frequently been shown to give unintended results or no results at all.

All this reflects a crisis for the earlier predominating theories and strategies. At the same time, it can be seen as a crisis for development research in the wider perspective, in the sense that no sustainable alternatives have yet been elaborated.

It is somewhat disturbing to have to acknowledge that so many years of working with theory construction and strategies concerning the developing countries have brought about such modest results. On the other hand this acknowledgement has formed the starting point for a very fruitful discussion in both the industrialised countries and the Third World – a discussion which is far less fettered and much less dogmatic than it used to be. There is now a greater openness and determination to look more closely at the actual conditions obtaining in the developing countries and the global system. The result can only be better theories and more adequate and effective strategies.

One of the purposes of this book is to present some of the more open theories, especially the theories that are based on concrete insight into the developing countries' actual problems and opportunities. This cannot, however, be done in isolation from the earlier predominating theories – partly because the new theoretical contributions borrow a lot of ideas and concepts from them; partly because, to a large extent, they are formed as a criticism of the older theories. In addition, the older theories cannot be justifiably rejected in their entirety. In some areas they give still relevant and valuable descriptions, interpretations and explanations. The book therefore comprises a review and discussion of the older theories, along with an underlining of both their weaknesses and their strengths.

Does the Third World still exist?

Part of the criticism against development economics and other kinds of development research is that there is no unambiguous research field in the geographical sense. The view is that the Third World, or the so-called developing countries, do not exist at all as a homogenous group which is different from the rest of the countries in the world. This criticism is important, because it raises the question about whether or not it is meaningful and appropriate to work with generalisations and theories for developing countries as a special group of countries and societies. No attempt will be made here to answer the question with a simple 'yes' or 'no'. On the other hand, it can be useful to try to differentiate the whole debate a little, and point out the main perceptions which are found in the literature, and also to outline the arguments put forward for the contradicting viewpoints.

The first step to differentiating the debate is to emphasise that we are actually facing two separate questions. The first question can be put: 'Are the societies in the so-called developing countries qualitatively different from other societies in the world? Are these societies organised in a way that is essentially different from societies in the First and the Second World? Are they subject to profoundly different conditions and laws of development and change?' The second question can be summarised as: 'Is it meaningful and appropriate to group together all developing countries into one category? Does it make sense to lump together the problems and circumstances of Asian, African, and Latin American societies as those of the Third World? Do these societies share the same basic features and are they subject to essentially uniform conditions of development and transformation?'

To these questions can be added a time dimension by asking if any significant changes have occurred since the 1950s, especially after the dismantling of the Eastern Bloc and the break-up of the Soviet Union into a number of independent states.

Broadly speaking, three different answers have been suggested to the first question: (a) the developing countries are not qualitatively distinct from other societies in the world; (b) the developing countries are distinct from the fully developed market economies, i.e. the highly industrialised members of the Organisation for Economic Co-operation and Development (OECD), but they have many features in common with the earlier centrally planned economies in the East; and (c) they are qualitatively distinct.

The first notion can be found, for instance, among the neo-classical economists, whom John Toye has described as the counter-revolutionary group of economists (Toye, 1987). One of these economists, P. T. Bauer, has advanced the opinion that the only thing that the Third World and all its synonyms – such as developing countries, underdeveloped countries, the South, and so on – have in common is that they request and receive development aid. 'The Third World is the creation of foreign aid: without foreign aid there is no Third World.' (Bauer, 1981: p. 87). As a consequence, says Bauer, the developing countries and their problems must be subjected to analyses using the same theoretical tools that economists utilise in the countries of the OECD (cf. Chapter 18 below).

Bauer's opinions are grounded in neo-classical economic theory. Corresponding theoretical foundations probably cannot be found for the second notion that 'developing countries', as a category, should include all the former centrally planned economies. However, it is noteworthy that the World Bank in its latest publications has quite simply located these countries in its tables according to their per capita income (see, for example, World Bank, 1994). They all appear in the categories 'lower middle-income economies' or 'higher middle-income economies'. In keeping with this lumping together of the formerly Communist-led states with the Third World countries, the Bank, along with other national and international aid organisations, have altered their loan and aid policies so that the former Eastern Bloc countries can be treated on a par with developing countries within the equivalent income bracket.

Opposing these notions, most development researchers maintain that the societies of the Third World are qualitatively different from those of both the Second and the First Worlds and must be examined and treated accordingly. There are minor variations in the exact demarcation of the Third World and significant variations with respect to the employed criteria – stretching from per capita incomes, through industrial production per capita and industrial export per capita, to more theoretically grounded criteria concerning production structure and dependency relationships. However, the result is that in most cases development researchers count as the Third World – or whatever other label that might be used – the countries which neither belong to the OECD nor formerly belonged to Comecon. Israel and South Africa, who would qualify by this definition as Third World countries, are left out because they are considered by most to be special cases. Mexico, although now a member of the OECD, is regarded by most as a Third World country.

It is worth noting that the South Commission, under the chairmanship of Tanzania's former president, Julius Nyerere, in its report from 1990, put great emphasis on the Southern countries' special character and common identity: 'What the countries of the South have in common transcends their differences; it gives them a shared identity and a reason to work together for common objectives' (South Report, 1990: p. 1).

By stressing both the unique and the common features – despite differences in many respects – the South Commission took a position on the second of the above two questions. The Commission's reason for grouping together all Third World countries into one category was, however, not theoretical but more an expression of a fundamental, politically motivated wish to unite them in joint efforts for a new and better world order. The Commission did mention instances of actual political co-operation between the countries of the South, for example the formation and expansion of the Group of 77 – a loose alliance within the United Nations Conference on Trade and Development (UNCTAD), which originally (in the 1960s) consisted of 77 member countries and has since grown to more than 120 countries, all from the Third World. But neither this reference nor other notions in the report can substitute for substantial arguments for lumping together the countries of the South with a view to further elaborating theory.

Substantial arguments within a theoretical framework can be found in the development literature, as will be shown later in this book. However, on this point there are great differences between old and more recent contributions to the debate. In the literature from the 1950s and 1960s there was a tendency to look at the developing countries as so fundamentally similar that it was deemed reasonable to generalise about them as one type of society. This is no longer the dominant conception. On the contrary, the predominant notion today is that the developing countries have always been too different – and subject to such great variation with regard to their internal as well as external development conditions – for them to be treated as a homogenous group in theory building and strategy formulation. Further the current prevailing opinion today is that the dissimilarities have been continuously accentuated by the very different patterns of development and stagnation which have occurred. Correspondingly, the differentiation in the Third World has increased considerably. High-growth middle-income economies in the Far East and extremely poor countries with negative growth in Africa constitute extreme cases in this differentiation process. As a result great caution is exercised now when considering the relevance and validity of all-embracing generalisations.

On the other hand, there are few development researchers who would go as far as, for example, Nigel Harris, who has declared the Third World as a dead concept with reference precisely to the marked differences between the newly industrialised countries and other developing countries (Harris, 1987). Most researchers instead maintain that it can be fruitful to compare and contrast development experiences from various countries and regions within the Third World – though without assuming that these countries are more alike than they really are (cf., for example, Worsley, 1984; Hettne, 1990). Continued attention to the Third World as a particular group of countries is regarded as an appropriate basis for forming systematic descriptions of the great variety of basic problems facing the developing countries. It is further claimed to be a suitable approach to evolving theories (in the plural) on the reasons for the very different patterns of change and stagnation observed in the Third World over the last 40 years.

In this book, we assume that it is meaningful to compare descriptions, interpretations and explanations concerning societal development in Asia, Africa and Latin America. However, we do not conceive of the Third World as a homogenous group of societies that can be understood and theoretically reconstructed within one and the same conceptual framework. Rather, it is taken for granted that a number of conceptual frameworks and theories will be required to cover the variations. Consequently, we shall frequently add to the conceptual examination of the various theories particular references to the countries or regions to which we believe the specified theories have greatest relevance. Certain theories may be useful tools for describing and explaining growth and social transformation in Far Eastern high-growth economies, while we may need completely different approaches in relation to stagnating economies in Sub-Saharan Africa. Some theories may be particularly relevant for explaining democratisation in Latin America, while at the same time they may have little to offer in relation to autocratic rule in Africa.

Possibly, some of the Far Eastern societies like South Korea and Taiwan have been transformed to such an extent that they can no longer be treated as part of the Third World, but this does not preclude their past experiences being dealt with in the context of conventional development theories.

Before we leave the question of the Third World's separate existence in the present context, it should be noted that criticism can be directed against mainstream development research for even using legally defined countries as the principal units of analysis. By doing so, the researchers may ignore or grossly underestimate the importance of internal differences. They may further disregard the significance of transnational processes which introduce dynamism into only certain sectors and segments within the individual countries, while at the same time excluding others. This could apply to transnational corporations which bring about significant industrial growth within certain geographical enclaves and concomitant income growth for population segments within those enclaves, while at the same time excluding or maybe actually damaging the conditions in other areas and for other population groups (see Chapter 9).

The method of analysis

This book is not meant as an independent contribution to theory formation. It contains first and foremost a presentation of partially opposing conceptions and theories, competing to give the best descriptions, interpretations and explanations. However, at the same time the theories are discussed as pieces in a mosaic, where every piece contributes to an overall understanding of the circumstances affecting and determining development and underdevelopment in Asian, African and Latin American countries. The aim throughout the book is to add to the understanding of what has happened in the Third World, especially over the last 40 years – and why.

Some of the guiding questions that form the basis for our discussion of the various theories can be summarised as follows:

- How have the developing countries changed according to the theories? What has happened, and what is about to happen in these countries internally, and in their relationship to the rest of the world and the international system – again, according to the theories?

- What conditions are particularly crucial for the kinds of changes that may be called 'development'? What type of development concept is contained in each of the theories?
- What explanations do the theories offer for development, maldevelopment or underdevelopment and stagnation? In addition to economic factors, do they include also political, social, cultural and ecological factors and, if so, how?
- How do the theories take into consideration internal differentiation within individual societies?
- What development strategies are suggested in the various theories? Do the suggestions take into account the economic, political and cultural realities? Do they incorporate environmental or security problems and, if so, how?

The method of analysis used in the book implies that the individual theories are introduced and discussed only in contexts where they offer particularly interesting or important answers to the questions raised. The focus is on the main ideas embodied in each of the theories presented. However, for the most interesting and for the most influential (not necessarily the same) theories, a more comprehensive introduction is provided. This includes a review of their conception of development, their perspective, method, central concepts, essential hypotheses and derived strategies. Throughout the text, references are given to relevant original literature, where the interested reader can delve more deeply into selected theories.

In order to provide an overview of the many different theories and strategy proposals, we have grouped the various contributions into a few main traditions and theoretical schools of thought. These groupings should be treated with caution. Development research is not – unlike the natural sciences – characterised by a few explicitly and well-defined paradigms in the sense proposed by Thomas Kuhn (cf. Kuhn, 1972). Rather, what we may identify are research programmes and profiles which, to a certain extent only, resemble paradigms in that they contain certain characteristic constellations of value premises, preconceived opinions and assumptions that, together with a set of propositions and methods, form the intellectual framework for empirical studies of development processes and issues.

It should be stressed that it is not an aim in itself to assign labels to the different theorists and their work. This is done, as mentioned above, merely to facilitate the overview and to reveal the more fundamental lines of conflict in the international development debate. Or in other words: to identify substantial differences which are more interesting to compare than terminological or other minor differences.

As part of the identification of the major traditions, Chapter 2 contains a brief summary of the theoretical heritage in a long-term perspective. As an extension of this, a number of critical issues are highlighted. Development researchers have been, and continue to be, in disagreement on how to deal with these issues. The list of controversial issues can – together with the chapter's overview of a number of opposing conceptions – provide the reader with some useful tools or benchmarks which may be valuable while reading the rest of the book.

Another tool is introduced below: the set of distinctions between development concept, theory, and strategy. Much of the debate on development has been characterised by an obscuring and rather confusing mixing of various dimensions of the issues. Values and individual preferences, in particular, have been mixed up with observations and analyses – to the detriment of the latter. The alternative to this is not to avoid value premises and other normative elements; this is by the very nature of social science research impossible (cf. Myrdal, 1959). However, it can be more explicitly stated when, and in what respects, interpretations and conclusions arrived at depend primarily on value premises and preferences rather than on empirical analyses. For this purpose, we shall employ throughout the book a now widespread set of distinctions between (a) development concept (or development objective), (b) development theory, and (c) development strategy.

A *development concept* contains the answer to what development is. This answer can never be value-free; it will always reflect notions of what ought to be understood by development. These notions can be formulated as development objectives, either in terms of particular conditions which must be achieved or in terms of a certain direction of change (Riggs, 1984).

To illustrate: a development concept – like the one embodied in modernisation theory – may claim that the large industrialised countries, for example the USA, are developed, that is they have achieved certain, positively evaluated conditions. According to this conception, changes in Third World countries towards increasing similarity with these industrialised countries are regarded as development. Other changes are not regarded as such. The dynamic change processes through which a country moves towards greater resemblance with the developed countries is called the *development process*, according to this notion.

Other concepts of development focus more on the given conditions in Third World societies and define development in terms of bringing out, unfolding, what is potentially contained in these societies. In this sense, these concepts come closer to the original meaning of development as the opposite of enveloping. Often, emphasis is given here to increasing the capacities for taking and implementing decisions in accordance with nationally or locally perceived priorities. Notions like these are also normative, albeit in a different manner to that in the above.

Development theory seeks to answer questions such as the following: How can chosen and specified development objectives be promoted? What conditions will possibly obstruct, delay or detract progress towards the objectives? What causal relationships and laws of motion apply to the societal change processes? What actors play dominant roles, and what interests do they have?

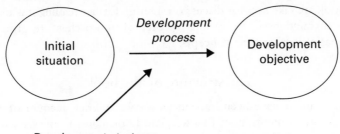

Figure 1.1 Development objective (concept), theory and strategy

How do the changes affect various social groups and various geographical regions?

Questions like these are not value-neutral, but they set the stage for expounding, unlike a development concept, how social reality is actually structured – as opposed to how it ought to be structured. Theories thus contain significant normative elements, but can none the less be subjected to validating or invalidating tests through empirical analyses of the actual conditions and historical experiences. While value premises of a particular researcher may be understood by others, but not accepted or endorsed by them, the testing of theories must ideally follow transparent and universally accepted procedures which produce conclusions other researchers have to accept as valid.

Development strategy as an abstract notion refers essentially to the actions and interventions that can be appropriately used to promote strictly defined development objectives. Once again the basis is heavily value-loaded in that there are 'chosen' development goals. But there is – at least in principle – the possibility of a matter-of-fact weighing of which strategies are the most effective and least costly to promote the established objectives. In practice, though, decision makers as well as researchers often have had too little insight into the relevant contexts and causal relationships to ensure indisputable strategy choices. These are, therefore, in many cases more reflections of prejudices, ideologies and personal preferences. This book will attempt to reveal how several development strategies are partly reflections of such normative premises rather than being solidly based on empirical analyses and theoretical insights.

The abstract interrelationship between development objective (development concept), development process, theory and strategy may be depicted as shown in Figure 1.1.

With the above definitions in mind, Chapter 3 provides a brief presentation of some of the prominent development concepts with emphasis on concept definition, though also with reference to the theories and strategies that later in the book are taken up for discussion. During further reading it is important to keep in mind how the various theoretical approaches are grounded in certain basic development concepts.

The structure of the book

Chapters 2 and 3 have been introduced above. A brief account of the rest of the book's contents now follows. The book consists of six parts. The first part, of which the current chapter is a component, gives a general introduction. The sixth part rounds off the account with some general considerations on development research and its theories. The several chapters in between – the main substance of the book – contain a review and discussion of a large number of theories. There is no chronological order to their presentation, rather an analytical structure.

Briefly stated, Part II contains the theories which chiefly focus on economic conditions, that is production, market and the organising of economic activities within companies. National and international perspectives are applied, and theoretical propositions regarding the economic foundation of social classes are included. Environmental issues are also taken up in this part, based on the observation that these issues, to a large extent, deal with economic development with limited natural resources.

Part III contains theories which primarily concern themselves with politics and the state, including systems of government and their interaction with social power structures and pressure groups.

Part IV presents and discusses the theories which, in one way or another, have tried to comprehend and explain both economic and political conditions and change processes. In this context, the role of the state in societal development is examined in greater detail, and the debate on state versus market is reviewed. Chapter 19 concludes this part, looking at the interplay between national security issues and development in a holistic way.

Finally, the theories in Part V shift attention away from the state, the market and the large companies, to civil society, i.e. the life of the citizens and their interactions within households, local communities and the various other forms of social organisation which lie outside the formal political system and the corporate economy. Chapter 23 is devoted to theories about ethnic identities, nationalities and conflict.

Figure 1.2 – with its references to parts and chapters – may provide an overview of the different perspectives applied in the various parts of the book. The figure is based on the assumption that, in any modern society, we will find at least four different types of structures, institutions and dynamics of social behaviour and practice, corresponding to the four boxes shown. In

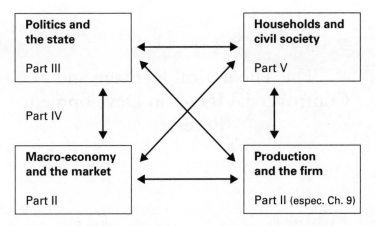

Figure 1.2 The structure of the book

addition, several processes of interaction between the four societal components may be identified, as illustrated by the double arrows. The parts and chapters referred to in the boxes deal primarily with conditions and processes internal to the respective components of society, but some of them also address interaction processes involving the other components. As for extra-societal relations, these are included throughout the book – providing the theories reviewed themselves include these relations. This is the case particularly with regard to the theories dealt with in Parts II and IV.

The abstract conception of society depicted by Figure 1.2 is inspired by some of the approaches and theories presented later in this book, including the otherwise very different conceptual frameworks of historical materialism and new institutional economics. Other ways of presenting the diverse perspectives are reviewed later in the book.

In the first chapter of each part, there is a more elaborate introduction concerning the perspectives applied and how the subsequent chapters are organised, together with reference as to how the chosen perspectives relate to other parts of the book. In addition, the contents list may be used to acquire a preliminary understanding of the structure of the book.

CHAPTER 2

The Theoretical Heritage and Controversial Issues in Development Research

Studies of Third World societies date back to the earliest European colonisations of Latin America, Asia and Africa. A large number of these studies, however, at least up to the middle of the nineteenth century, were so preoccupied with the unique that one must describe them as atheoretical and ideographic. Their aim was not to identify patterns and general determinants of people's behaviour and societal development, but rather to describe local conditions without a theoretical framework, without a systematic comparative perspective, and without trying to generalise. Consequently, studies of this kind did not form schools of thought for method and theory construction. It should be added, though, that in much of the historical writings about the colonies, and in many of the older ethnographic and socio-anthropological descriptions, one can find a wealth of detailed information which has since been used extensively for re-analyses within subsequently elaborated theoretical frameworks.

Methodologically conscious and generalised approaches to studies of societies emerged primarily in Europe, and in connection with studies of European societies, rather than their colonies. It is these approaches that form the major part of the theoretical heritage of present-day development research and theory construction.

Development research embraces, as was stressed in the previous chapter, many social science disciplines and additional elements from the humanities, in particular. The delineation of disciplines, like economics or political science, is of recent date. The breaking-up of all-embracing society studies into mono-disciplinary studies came about only in the twentieth century, primarily in the period following the Second World War. This specialisation did not characterise the earliest and school-founding theorists of the nineteenth century. None the less, it is a characteristic of the modern disciplines that each has reconstructed its own theoretical heritage with emphases assigned to particular classical theorists. Therefore, it will be appropriate to divide the present review into at least two main streams of thinking: development economics and socio-political development theories. These are the two major traditions from which contemporary development research has drawn considerable inspiration.

Theoretical origins of development economics

Development economics first appeared as a distinct subject area during the 1940s and the beginning of the 1950s, concurrently with the political de-colonisation of Asia, the Middle East and, later, Africa. The main interest of development economics was from the outset to uncover the causes for continued poverty and underdevelopment or stagnation in the Third World. At the same time, the emerging analytical perspective drew attention to the opportunities and preconditions for economic growth in the former colonies. Hence, from the very outset close linkages were established between theory and strategy.

Development economics emerged as a special perspective and later as a sub-discipline within the field of economics. The focusing of development economics on the sources of, and obstacles to, long-term economic growth separated the subject area from the neo-classical mainstream which, since the turn of the twentieth century, had been increasingly taken up with short-term economic equilibrium analyses and maximising of efficiency in resource allocation.

However, economics in general as well as development economics have common roots in the so-called *classical political economy* of the eighteenth and nineteenth centuries, represented primarily by Adam Smith (1723–1790), Thomas Robert Malthus (1766–1834) and David Ricardo (1772–1823). To this group could later be added John Stuart Mill (1806–1873).

Adam Smith placed himself at the centre of the debate towards the end of the eighteenth century with his major work, *Wealth of Nations* (1776). In it he underlined the critical role of the market mechanisms, operating – as it later became known – as 'the invisible hand' which ensured that production in society was (in most cases) organised in the best interests of all. Smith's central argument can be summed up in one sentence: there may be producers who will try to sell inferior goods at high prices, but if the producers are competing they will all eventually be forced to deliver proper goods at reasonable prices.

Another important role the market played, according to Adam Smith, was that of a growth source. The reasoning in this context was that when the market expanded as a result of population growth or territorial expansion (expansion of the British Empire), then demand would increase and production grow as a response to that. At the same time, specialisation would increase among the producers. This was a central element in Smith's theory of growth; he argued that specialisation would in itself, for a number of reasons, lead to higher productivity per working hour. A major precondition for this was an increased accumulation of wealth – which had to come from the rich, especially the industrialists and their profits from productive investments. The accumulated funds were required for investment both in more working capital (to ensure employment of additional workers), and in more fixed capital (to increase mechanisation). It followed from this argument that the emerging industrial sector should be considered as the most dynamic one and as the one on which to base aggregate growth. This proposition contrasted with that of the French physiocrats who earlier in the eighteenth century had argued in favour of agriculture as the main engine of growth.

Adam Smith's idea about 'the invisible hand', as well as his hypotheses about accumulation and investment of profits as the most important determinants of economic growth, have played prominent roles in the debates ever since his time. The notion about the 'invisible hand' has been central in the debate about attaining equilibrium and in relation to the state-versus-market controversies (cf. Chapter 18). The theses about sources of growth have similarly had a strong impact upon discussions about causes of long-term growth. Since Smith's original theories were formulated, numerous refinements and qualification have been added, but it is remarkable that some of his basic notions can still be identified as core elements in the debate even after the Second World War.

David Ricardo was one of the first who seriously elaborated on Smith's classical political economy, especially with a land-rent and distribution theory and with the theory of comparative advantages. Regarding the former, it should be mentioned that it has heavily inspired contemporary theories concerning the relationship between agriculture and industry. It enabled Ricardo to identify two other sources of growth in addition to capital, namely technical innovations and international trade.

When Ricardo suggested more sources of growth than did Adam Smith, this was not the result of a more optimistic view. On the contrary, Ricardo was fundamentally pessimistic regarding long-term growth because his analyses led him to conclude that continued population growth and the corresponding increase in demand for food would result in the inclusion of all land for agricultural production – even the so-called marginal land with very low area productivity rates. Utilisation of poorer and poorer land would cause the land rent to go up, mainly due to the farmers' competition for the better, temporarily more profitable, land. This process would result in a redistribution of national income to the benefit of the landed aristocracy, but to the detriment of the industrialists. Simultaneously, the marginal costs in agricultural production would rise with the increased cultivation of marginal land. Food prices would then increase, leading to stronger pressure on wages which would, in turn, eat into the profits of the industrialists from another side. The final result would be a squeezing of the industrial profits to zero, whereby the whole foundation for economic growth would disappear. Only technical innovations and international trade could, according to Ricardo, prevent this sad outcome.

The theory of comparative advantages was elaborated in continuation of the above argument as an attempt to evolve the best possible policy for foreign trade. The basic notion was that each country should concentrate its production in areas where it had comparative advantages in relation to other countries with respect to the productivity of its workers. In accordance with this basic thesis, non-industrialised countries such as Portugal should refrain from trying to build up industries and, instead, continue to concentrate on the production of, for instance, wine. Industrialised countries like England, on the other hand, should produce and exchange industrial products such as textiles and clothing.

With these and many other notions, and the accompanying chains of reasoning, Ricardo came to inspire both Karl Marx and later neo-classical economists. Ricardo is one of the very few theorists who has enjoyed widespread and great respect within both the Marxist and the liberalist traditions.

Thomas Robert Malthus is known primarily for his pessimistic theses on population growth. He believed that the population would grow markedly faster than food production, if it was not constrained, with the poor in particular breeding rapidly. There would be little reason for mentioning Malthus in this context had he not come to function as a reference point in post-war debates on population problems (cf. Chapter 11). Very few researchers in the twentieth century have taken Malthus's exact formulations of the progression in population growth and agricultural output seriously. However, his basic assertion that population will necessarily grow more rapidly than agricultural production has played a central role as a hypothesis that many researchers have taken a position on, either positively confirming or negatively dismissing it.

From a certain point of view, it would be just as appropriate to mention Malthus's contribution to the formulation of an economic crisis theory, which stretched far beyond the thesis of population growth as a prime barrier to economic growth. This contribution could in many ways be seen as a forerunner of Keynes's more elaborate crisis theories of the 1930s.

John Stuart Mill should be briefly mentioned before we leave the classical political economists, not so much because of his new and original contributions to theory construction, but more because he reviewed and commented on the then existing theories in a widely disseminated book, *Principles of Political Economy* (1848).

Common to all the classical political economists was a strong emphasis on generalisation and abstraction. In their analyses, they searched for patterns, causal relationships and laws of motion regarding societal conditions in the short-term perspective, as well as regarding growth and change over the long term. It is these analytic intentions that have been passed down to present-day development research. The handing down has taken place mainly through three main streams of thinking, with Joseph Schumpeter on the sideline.

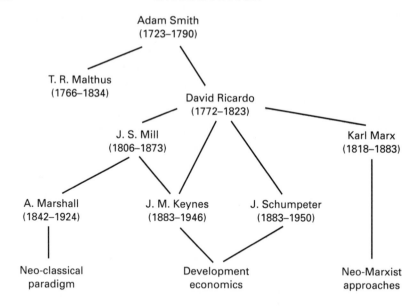

Figure 2.1 Theoretical origins of development economics

With this interpretation, the theoretical family tree can be outlined as shown in Figure 2.1.

Karl Marx (1818–1883) started from the basis of classical political economy, but transformed this body of theory into a far more comprehensive and quite different analytic construction. Only a few features of this will be mentioned here; others will be discussed later in the text in connection with later presentations of the various Marxist approaches within contemporary development studies.

At the outset, it should be stressed that the perspective for Marx's theories was society as a whole and not only the economic processes. Marx was interested in the totality of society and the ways in which this totality changed over long periods of time. His focus was on how and why various forms of society emerged, changed and disappeared to be replaced by new ones. For Marx, the basic driving forces behind societal changes were the social classes which, however, acted within structural limits primarily laid down by the forces of production and the prevailing production relations.

Under capitalism – the most dynamic mode of production in world history according to Marx – the most important sources of economic growth were the valorisation and accumulation compulsions which individual capitalists are subjected to. To achieve a profit, the capitalist must exploit labour by paying the workers less than the equivalent of the value they produce. This was a fundamental element in Marx's labour theory of value, which further assumed that it is the workers and not the capitalists who generate value.

In addition to the valorisation compulsion, the capitalist (the individual factory owner) has continuously to accumulate capital in order to survive in the competition with others, that is expand his capital apparatus through the piling up of surplus value generated by the workers (capital concentration), and through merging with other companies (capital centralisation).

According to Marx, these processes embodied unavoidable tendencies towards increased technical and organic composition of capital, that is the continuous enlargement of technical productive assets in relation to labour and a simultaneous increase of the value of fixed capital in relation to the surplus value produced by the workers. Combined with population growth, this necessarily resulted in marginalisation of large segments of the potential working population and, consequently, the establishment of a large reserve army of unemployed workers. This was, in a sense, the first formulation of the hypothesis concerning jobless growth (cf. Chapter 22). For the capital owners the outlined tendencies meant constant pressure on their rate of profit, because relatively fewer workers were available for surplus production as compared with the more rapidly growing capital assets. This tendency, however, could be neutralised in various ways, including through productivity-enhancing technical innovations, state interventions, and crises which eliminated the least competitive companies.

These basic laws of motion for the political economy under capitalism could not be viewed in isolation from the class struggle, because a large and well-organised working class, according to Marx, had the power to lessen the uncomfortable effects for itself, and in the long run may also be able to overthrow capitalism and introduce first socialism, and later communism. On the other hand, a weak working class confronted with a strong and well-organised bourgeoisie would be forced to put up with miserable conditions.

It is obvious that these summary outlines of Marx's reasoning in no way do justice to his very comprehensive theory; but the same applies to the previous discussion of the classical political economists. It should be borne in mind, therefore, that the intention in the present context is merely to indicate some of the intellectual sources of inspiration for post-war development economics. Readers interested in a more comprehensive introduction are referred to some of Marx's own presentations (Marx, 1972, especially vol. 1, Chs 21–3; Marx, 1857–58: pp. 375–413; Marx, 1969; and Marx, 1965). Regarding the classical political economists the reader is referred to the major works cited above, plus a few summary accounts (Hunt, 1989: Ch. 2; Meier and Seers, 1984).

Joseph Schumpeter (1883–1950) was mentioned above as a theorist on the sidelines of the three main streams of thinking; however, this is not to imply that he has had less influence on development economics. Schumpeter has, in fact, particularly with his main work, *The Theory of Economic Development* (Schumpeter, 1934; German edition 1912), left a considerable legacy in the shape of hypotheses and ideas that continue to be debated. There is special reason to mention his explicit distinction between 'growth' and 'development'.

Growth, according to Schumpeter, was the gradual extension of the capital apparatus and increasing production. Here the classical growth theories were of interest. However, in contrast to these, Schumpeter asserted that development could occur only when technical innovations introduced new production techniques, new products, or new means of organising production – in other words when the production factors were utilised in new ways. In this manner, more fundamental changes would be brought about and new rules of play introduced into economic life.

The innovators, in Schumpeter's conception, were the entrepreneurs, who as a category covered more than the industrialists or capitalists, and who, furthermore, did not themselves need to be capitalists. Schumpeter also broke ranks with the classical conception of capitalist savings and accumulation as being the most important sources of growth. He believed instead that growth was driven by technical innovations, in association with the entrepreneurs' mobilisation of credit in the economic system as a whole (Schumpeter, 1934).

Several changes in the focus of economists preceded Schumpeter's contributions, especially changes away from a primary interest in growth and growth-determining conditions, and towards equilibrium analyses. Around the turn of the twentieth century, long-term growth was taken for granted and consequently attention was shifted to how to achieve the best possible utilisation of given resources – known as allocative effectiveness and efficiency. This implied the arrival of the so-called neo-classical paradigm – and here the Kuhnian term 'paradigm' is more appropriate than in relation to most of the rest of the social sciences, because these neo-classicists really did, and continue to, elaborate a consistent and highly formalised (and mathematically formulated) theory with common assumptions, concepts and rules of validation. It is this neo-classical paradigm that today dominates a very significant proportion of economic research in both the industrialised countries and in many developing countries.

One of the first great theorists within the paradigm was *Alfred Marshall* (1842–1924) whose major work, *Principles of Economics*, first published in 1890, came to replace Mills's *Principles of Political Economy* as the most important standard work within mainstream economics.

We do not delve into the paradigm here. Rather the reader is referred to the discussion of the neo-classical contributions to development research in subsequent chapters (particularly Chapters 5 and 18), in addition to a few major works and text books (Walras, 1954; Samuelson, 1967 or later editions). However, a brief note may be useful at this point: some of the central features of neo-classical economics are certain explicit assumptions about the nature of the economic system and the determinants of economic behaviour. These assumptions include one which stipulates that firms will maximise profits. Another assumption is that consumers will maximise utility.

Combined, these behaviour-determining factors are believed to produce an optimal allocation of production factors and, further, provide the best conditions for economic growth – provided that perfectly competitive markets exist. Price distortions as a consequence of political interference with the market mechanisms will therefore inhibit economic growth.

Before we leave the historical roots of development economics we shall briefly touch on the role that *John Maynard Keynes* (1883–1946) has played. Keynes, who wrote his main contributions during the 1930s, including *The General Theory of Employment, Interest and Money* (1936), was, like the mainstream economists, not particularly interested in long-term growth or in conditions in the colonies. This is why he did not leave behind any elaborate theory of growth and development. On the other hand, he placed the question of the relationship between market and state so firmly on the agenda that he thereby acquired lasting significance for the ensuing development debate (see Toye, 1987: Ch. 2 for an excellent discussion of this).

Probably Keynes's most significant contribution to theory formation and debate concerned the question of the reasons for, and the possible solutions to, the unemployment problem. But he also left behind an important legacy with his analyses and propositions regarding institutional control of international trade and finance, and the associated proposal for establishing what was later to become the International Monetary Fund and the World Bank. Furthermore, Keynes achieved a considerable indirect influence on development strategies through the work of two other economists, Roy Harrod and Evsey Domar, after whom the so-called Harrod–Domar model was named. This model informed the entire way of thinking about economic planning in the Third World during both the 1950s and 1960s (cf. Chapter 16).

After this brief survey of the intellectual roots of development economics, we can turn our attention to the theoretical legacy which has exerted a strong influence on sociological and political development theories.

Theoretical origins of sociological and political development theories

Sociologists normally trace the origins of their discipline back to the French author Auguste Comte (1789–1857), who was also the first to use the term 'sociology'. However, more comprehensive contributions to theory construction appeared later – from Emile Durkheim (1858–1917), Karl Marx and Max Weber (1864–1920). Each of these three theorists can be said to have founded a major school of thought with considerable impact upon different approaches within contemporary development studies.

Emile Durkheim acknowledged explicitly Comte's contribution to establishing sociology as a scientific discipline, but asserted that Comte had not successfully achieved his objective. Durkheim wished to complete the work in accordance with a natural science model, which meant among other things that he would study social phenomena as 'objects' – as if they were as palpable as natural phenomena.

Similar to the classical political economists, Durkheim was concerned with social change processes in the long term. This led him to study the development of the division of labour in society as part of the industrialisation process. Where economists concerned themselves with the impact that the division of labour had upon growth, it was more important for Durkheim to study its social consequences. Durkheim believed that the division of labour would eventually come to replace religion as the most important social force of cohesion, but that the separation and specialisation of labour functions and other swift social changes would also cause widespread *anomie*. By 'anomie', Durkheim meant a feeling of rootlessness and aimlessness which, furthermore, was characterised by a lack of moral guidelines. The breakdown of the traditional orders, which were supported by religion, would result in many people feeling that their lives had lost meaning; they would feel isolated without clear guidelines for normal behaviour.

Durkheim's approach in these areas has clearly influenced post-war modernisation theory (cf. Chapter 12). His reasoning around the concept of anomie is found also in other contemporary approaches like those applied to the study of ethnic and religious revivalism as responses to the breakdown of traditional order (cf. Chapter 23).

Durkheim also engaged himself thoroughly with the causes of suicide. He researched the causes of suicide, not by looking at the individual's motivation but by looking at the external social circumstances in which suicide occurred with a markedly higher frequency. The method of analysing individual behaviour as determined significantly by social circumstances came to influence the further development of sociological methods.

The theoretical heritage from Durkheim was transmitted through at least three main streams. The first one was via the founders of modern social anthropology, including particularly *A. R. Radcliffe-Brown* (1881–1955) and *Bronislaw Malinowski* (1884–1942), who were both pioneers in the evolution of fieldwork methods with well-defined conceptual frameworks. The further development of these methods led to the present functionalist analysis at the micro level, that is analyses based on the view that social conditions and events in the local community are best understood and explained on the basis of their function – with reference to the part that they play for the local community and its maintenance. The second stream went more directly or through lesser known theorists and researchers to functionalism and modernisation theory with a macro perspective. The third stream went via Talcott Parsons (see below).

Karl Marx's contribution to theory formation in relation to the political economy of capitalism has already been briefly mentioned. Here we shall add only a few more observations regarding his role in the context of sociological method and theory. Marx is the only one among the founding fathers of modern social science who has left a strong impact upon both development economics and sociological and political science approaches to the study of Third World development.

Even though in terms of volume Marx wrote much more about the political economy of capitalism, his analytic perspective and method at the same time implied substantial contributions to sociology. As earlier mentioned, Marx's perspective embraced the whole of society. His method implied a systematic tracing of the interactions between the basic economic structures and processes on the one hand, and the political, social and ideological relations and institutions on the other. Marx, in his analyses, assigned to the economic processes a certain precedence over other societal processes, believing that social change was prompted primarily by economic influences.

The dynamism created by technological progress and the development of the forces of production within the framework of a particular mode of production would, in the final instance, also determine the direction and basic patterns of societal changes in the social and political spheres. This was part of the basic idea in his materialist conception of society and history. However, it is important to add that the primacy of economics applied only in the long-time perspective and at the macro level. Further, it is important to note that the class struggle under all circumstances impacted heavily upon actual outcomes and thus mediated, to some extent shaped, impeded, or accentuated economic determination of structural change processes. But underlying all reservations and complicating circumstances, Marx had a clear idea about technological progress and development of the forces of production as constituting the core of the dynamic that changed societies. He also held the view that social and political conflicts which really mattered all had their roots in economic inequality and economic conflicts of interest. This meant, with regard to the methods for the investigation of society, that the researcher should always try to identify the economic–material basis for other social phenomena and further expect, a priori, that the basic structures were far more important to the outcome of social and political processes than people's motivations and wishes.

With respect to both these fundamental notions, *Max Weber* advanced opposing views. He would not, a priori, assign to the economic processes any primacy at all, but on the other hand would not exclude that they could, under certain circumstances, determine the outcome of the social and political processes. In his works, Weber did not explicitly polemicise against Marx, who he apparently had deep respect for as a theorist, but went indirectly against him, for example in his famous book about the Protestant ethic, in which he asserted the critical importance of Calvinism for the breakthrough of capitalism in Western Europe (Weber, 1965). This was like turning Marx on his head, at least as seen from a simple interpretation of Marx. A more thorough comparison of the two theoretical giants within social science research shows, however, that it is somewhat more complicated (Martinussen, 1994).

Regarding the relationship between structure and the individual actor, there is a stronger case for contrasting Marx and Weber. There is no consensus on exactly *how much* of individual behaviour the structures accounted for, according to Marx. However, there is general agreement that Weber in this respect assigned to man as an individual significantly more independence in society. Therefore, Weber also worked much more than Marx with human motivation and rationality as determinants of behaviour as well as outcomes of social conflicts and other processes

Weber has sometimes been taken to task, wrongly, for simple assumptions about rationality as something unequivocal. In reality, Weber worked with many types of rationality, of which the so-called bureaucratic rationality (which actually combined two forms) was only one among several (Bruun, 1972: pp. 221ff.). This was the form of rationality that Weber described as the analytical ideal type in his studies of modern bureaucracy. His approach in this regard did not imply support for bureaucracy and its rationality as an unconditional asset. Weber found bureaucracy unavoidable in a modern capitalist society. He also found this form of organisation and the associated bureaucratic forms of behaviour useful for solving many societal problems. But Weber emphasised strongly that a bureaucratic system which was not subject to democratic control or counterbalanced by charismatic or otherwise popular leaders, was an evil for society.

Where Durkheim focused primarily on the division of labour as an integrated part of industrialisation processes, Weber's main interest was to describe, interpret and explain the emergence of the bureaucratic form of organisation and the related rationality form. These two phenomena Weber viewed not just as dependent variables, but also as independent variables, in the sense that the modes of organisation and rationality, after being engrafted upon modern societies, seemed to act as driving forces for subsequent social change processes. It was in this context that Weber deemed it desirable to have some form of popular influence and control over bureaucracy.

In addition to Weber's substantial contributions to social science theory building, he also laid the foundations for the methodological principle which is now known as *scientific value relativism*. This principle takes as its starting point that there is a logical gap between 'is' and 'ought' – between society, as it exists, and society, as the researcher would like it to be. According to Weber, it was not possible to conduct value-free research. Normative elements would affect all stages in the research process, from choice of themes and methods through collection and interpretation of data to formulation of generalisations and theories. The researcher could, however – and should in the role of researcher – always try to reduce biases, that is the hidden and therefore manipulating influences from his or her own norms and values, by presenting these as explicitly as possible. This would allow other researchers to evaluate and re-test the research undertaken and its results.

Value relativism was brought into development research primarily by

Gunnar Myrdal (cf. Myrdal, 1959; Myrdal, 1968: Ch. 2) and Paul Streeten, but otherwise it has, unfortunately, never achieved recognition as a central methodological principle (cf. Chapter 25).

Other aspects and elements of Weber's method and theory have been passed down through many channels, but often without the same explicit reference to Weber as is found with respect to Marx within the historical-materialist tradition. Some of the explanations for this could be that another dominant, though less sophisticated, theorist of the twentieth century, *Talcott Parsons* (1902–1979), was instrumental in bringing Weber to the English-speaking world. Parsons reduced Weber's complex and open theory to functionalism, into which he also adopted elements from Durkheim. It was a characteristic of Parsons that he found Weber and Marx totally incompatible as theorists, even in the sense that Weber could essentially replace Marx, who had thus become superfluous (Parsons, 1937). This interpretation was adopted by the modernisation theorists in the 1950s and can be found even today among many development researchers, especially in the English-speaking parts of the world.

However, other conceptions of the relationship between Marx and Weber do exist in the literature. Schumpeter, for example, suggested in the 1940s that the two theorists supplemented each other – that there were a number of areas where they were compatible (Schumpeter, 1947). In recent years, this interpretation has gained ground among development researchers who label themselves as Neo-Weberians or Post-Marxists. The latter conceive of themselves as more authentic inheritors of Marxian theory and method than the so-called Neo-Marxists (cf. Vandergeest and Buttel, 1988; Corbridge, 1990).

A simplified overview of the intellectual roots of contemporary socio-logical development research can be summarised as in Figure 2.2. To this should be added that within social anthropology there is a particular structuralist approach, and an approach which is sometimes termed 'symbolic interactionism'. Structuralism traces its roots back primarily to *Ferdinand de Saussure* (1857–1913); symbolic interactionism to *George Herbert Mead* (1863–1931) (for a concise overview, see Giddens, 1989: Ch. 22).

The sociological family tree depicted in Figure 2.2 may also be seen as an overview of the roots of political development theory, although the political science approaches in the post-war period increasingly separated themselves from sociology, developing their own schools of thought. Within the dominant non-Marxist tradition one could identify at least two important approaches: behaviouralism and functionalism, the latter with branches of an institutionalist–structuralist approach.

Behaviouralism focused on individual political behaviour and endeavoured through cross-national studies, which frequently included industrialised countries, to uncover general behavioural patterns and establish general explanations. Here the inspiration from Durkheim was obvious, even though

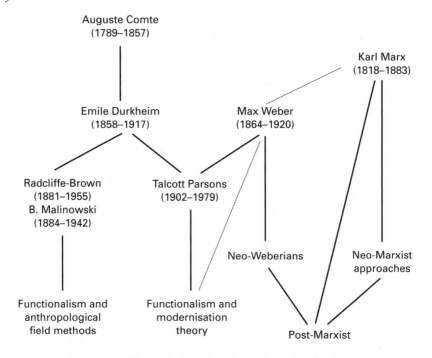

Figure 2.2 Theoretical origins of sociological and political
development theories

the more sophisticated analyses implied considerable refinements in comparison to his (e.g. Lerner, 1958).

Functionalism and the institutionalist–structuralist approach were more preoccupied with political macro-phenomena such as the apparatus of government, political parties, interest organisations, and mass media. The pertinent questions in many of the studies within these schools centred around the functions and structures necessary for the persistence and modernisation of a given political system. In this case, the theoretical origins could be traced back to, on the one hand, sociological functionalism or structural–functionalist analysis and, on the other hand, to the legal disciplines and particularly their studies of the interrelationships between political institutions.

Major controversial issues in development research

Based on the above outlines of the theoretical heritage and by taking into account later theoretical development debates, we can now formulate some of the central and controversial questions that have dominated much of the theoretical discussions. The selection of issues in the present context in no way covers the whole area of development research. Other critical issues will have to be added and considered later in this book. But the questions and the competing answers given to each of them, we believe, do provide a fairly comprehensive introduction to several of the overriding issues discussed throughout the book.

Some of the questions in Table 2.1 relate to perspective and method or are directed at implied or explicitly stated assumptions. Other questions probe into the substance and look at opposing conceptions of, and theories about, what is happening in the Third World and how it can be explained. A final type of questions concerns the choice of development strategy.

Common to all the questions and answers listed in the table is that they are stated in very general and vague terms. More precise formulations can be given only when we have introduced the specific terms used in the various analytic frameworks which are presented later in the book. Further, it should be noted that Table 2.1 as a whole is biased in favour of economic issues. This bias will be corrected gradually as we proceed from economic analyses and theories in the second part of the book to other approaches, reviewed in subsequent parts, which give more attention to political, social, and cultural aspects.

To provide clarity, the presentation is stylised and formally standardised with the issues in the extreme left column, and possible answers in the two other columns. It can be seen immediately that the possible answers in most cases represent extreme positions, with several possible alternatives in between. In a few cases, additional, interrelated answers are given in the same cell. It should be stressed that there is no logical or other compelling correlation between the answers when read vertically.

It should be further added that there is a third, qualitatively different, answer to the strategy question on how to achieve the best possible utilisation of resources, which is to leave it, as far as possible, to the citizens themselves – to civil society and its institutions.

One of the most controversial questions is not included in the table, namely the question concerning what should be understood by development. This question is taken up in the next chapter, which will reveal a multitude of qualitatively different and competing answers.

Table 2.1 Controversial issues in development research

Perspective and method

Which perspective facilitates the best analyses?	A macro perspective – within a macro-theoretical framework of analysis	A micro-analytic perspective – or a mezzo-analytic perspective
Which conception of society provides for the best analyses?	A consensus conception – assuming a genuinely common national interest	A conflict conception – assuming conflicts between opposing interests
Which method will give the best and most robust results?	Formalised mathematical model analyses Hypothetical-deductive method	Qualitative method Historical method Inductive method
Which unit of analysis will provide for the best results?	Individual actors – assuming that their actions are important for determining structures and outcomes	Structures and institutions – assuming that they are important determinants of behaviour

Hypotheses and theory

How does societal development take place?	Through a linear process – as a continuous evolution or in stages	Through a non-linear process
Do Third World countries follow the same path of development as the industrialised countries?	Yes – that is assumed until disproved	No – that is not assumed unless rendered probable
What has been the primary impact of colonialism and imperialism upon the Third World?	Progress and societal development	Underdevelopment or maldevelopment Obstruction of development
Does free trade benefit developing countries?	Yes	No
Do close links with the world market promote development?	Yes	No
Can the state act autonomously?	Yes	No – state actions and interventions are curtailed by prevailing economic structures and the most powerful interests

Table 2.1 Cont.

Hypotheses and theory (cont.)

Does a highly inter-ventionist state promote development?	No	Yes
Which economic sector is the most dynamic?	The industrial sector	The agricultural sector
What is the relationship between technological/economic changes and other aspects of societal transformation?	Technological/economic changes determine other aspects of societal transformation	A dialectic relationship where political and cultural institutions shape technological/economic changes
Which regime form is the most appropriate for Third World development?	Democracy – with a multi-party system and universal adult franchise	Authoritarian regimes which can ensure national co-ordination and long-term planning
What role is played by civil society and its institutions?	Civil society traditions and institutions restrain growth and modernisation	Civil society embodies its own dynamism which provides the basis for survival for many citizens

Strategy

How is the best utilisation of resources achieved?	By leaving the allocation primarily to market mechanisms	By leaving the allocation primarily to the state
Which economic sector should be given the lead role in development?	The industrial sector – and resources should be transferred to this sector from the rest of the economy	The agricultural sector – and resources should be transferred to this sector from the rest of the economy
Which actors would it be best to rely on for promoting socio-economic development?	Private companies and entrepreneurs (Citizens and their community organisations)	The state – central government and/or local authorities
What is the best growth strategy in an international context?	An outward-oriented, export-led growth strategy – with a liberal foreign trade regime	An inward-oriented, import-substituting strategy – with protection of the domestic market

---

CHAPTER 3

Conceptions and Dimensions
of Development

Over the last century, Western conceptions of the world and history have been largely characterised by notions of progress, evolution, and development. Originally the emphasis was on progress and evolution; however, since the Second World War 'development' has become the most widely used term. Regardless of the more specific definition, there is a very widespread tendency to associate something positive, something desirable, with the word 'development'. This applies no matter whether development refers to societies, regions or specified population groups.

During the latter half of the 1940s and the beginning of the 1950s, various conceptions of development appeared, both in connection with the negotiations on the establishment of a new international economic order and in conjunction with the formation of American foreign policy in relation to Europe.

Negotiations on a new economic order took place particularly among the 44 countries who met at Bretton Woods in 1944. The negotiations resulted in the establishment of the International Monetary Fund (IMF) and the International Bank for Reconstruction and Development, now generally known as the World Bank (they started operating in 1947 and 1946, respectively).

The IMF was established to encourage international co-operation in the monetary field and to remove foreign exchange restrictions, to stabilise exchange rates, and to facilitate a multilateral payments system between member countries. The purpose of the World Bank was to encourage capital investment for the reconstruction and development of its member countries. In continuation of this, American policy towards Europe put emphasis on economic reconstruction after the destruction of the war. The best known element in this policy was the so-called Marshall Plan which, through loans and a massive transfer of resources to Europe, attempted to put this part of the world back on its economic feet. The World Bank followed a similar strategy during the same period.

Characteristic of both the official development conceptions and the implementation strategies pursued during the first decade after the Second World War was their focus on the industrialised countries and their economic growth, in a narrow sense of the term.

Since the mid-1950s, the notion of development as something positive and good has been tied particularly to countries and population groups in the Third World. Parallel to the decolonisation of Asia and Africa, the social conditions on these continents increasingly became the object of international attention. In the large industrialised countries as well as in the multilateral organisations, with the World Bank in the vanguard, these conditions were perceived as the result of lack of development or undevelopment. Countries in the Third World – including Latin America – were labelled as being backward in comparison with the countries in Western Europe and North America. At the same time, it was taken for granted that both the 'backward' countries and the highly developed Western societies would benefit from economic growth and modernisation in the Third World. Growth and modernisation in this context were taken to mean a gradual change towards greater and greater similarity with the highly industrialised countries of the North West.

This conception of development, as change processes resulting in greater similarity with the conditions prevailing in the USA and the great industrial countries in Western Europe, was not universally accepted in the 1950s. On the contrary, a consensus has never prevailed – either then or now – on what development is or should be. In a survey from the mid-1980s, 72 different meanings of the term were registered (Riggs, 1984). We shall not try to reproduce this multiplicity. But as the explicit or implicit conceptions of development are very essential components of the theories and strategies discussed later in this book, we shall attempt to summarise the most important basic conceptions and ideas of development.

The order of presentation in the following paragraphs does not reflect any chronological sequence, but should rather be seen as a series of competing conceptions of development. Some of them are still widely used, others have been given up by most researchers and practitioners – or they have been adjusted to incorporate new aspects. Over the last four decades the general tendency in this respect has been to abolish one-dimensional conceptions focusing on economic growth and replace them with multi-dimensional notions incorporating non-economic aspects as well.

More comprehensive descriptions of selected development concepts will appear in connection with the fuller discussion of the various theories. The current chapter can be seen as a kind of overview of the various approaches, in the sense that the conceptions of development, to a large extent, define the special features of the various approaches.

Economic growth

Schumpeter's previously mentioned distinction between growth and development was not generally accepted within mainstream development economics in the 1950s (see Chapter 2). Researchers in this period were often not at all concerned with whether economic growth could at the same time be seen as development. They rather conceived of economic growth as the supreme goal in itself; it was economic growth that the poor countries needed. Thus, economic growth and its determinants and obstacles were natural foci for theory formation.

There was no broad agreement, though, on the exact meaning of the term 'economic growth'. It is a bit of a myth, when critics of the early development economists maintain that they viewed growth as identical to increasing per capita income. None of the major pioneer theorists conceived of the matter in such simple terms. However, it was necessary at that time to be content with a relatively simple *indicator* of growth, because the data and statistics concerning Third World economies did not provide a basis for more sophisticated measurements.

The core of the conceptions of growth among development economists of the 1950s was *increasing production and consumption*, but also increasing employment and improved standards of living. They imagined that progress in these respects would be reflected in the national accounts figures for aggregate incomes. At the same time, they wanted to take into account population growth, because an increase in production and consumption which resulted from this growth or was just proportional to it could not be conceived of as real growth. National income was therefore computed as average per capita income.

The World Bank, which had early on placed itself as the leading international institution in collection, analysis and publication of figures concerning economic conditions and growth in the developing countries, operated with this aggregate measure during the entire period up to the beginning of the 1970s. However, both the World Bank and development economists in general were fully aware that measurements of growth in terms of increased per capita incomes were faulty (reliability problems) and did not in all cases give a correct impression of the conditions and changes (validity problems).

With regard to the former – the question of reliability – the statistics were often of low quality. The poor countries simply did not have the capacity to gather the necessary information. In addition, the entire national accounts were based on measurements of production and consumption in prices which assumed market exchange of all the products. But as large proportions of the production of the developing countries were used in the households themselves, or were exchanged in other ways – through social networks, patron–client relationships, or other kinds of exchange without pricing – considerable sources of inaccuracies for the national accounts were obviously in-built. These conditions have changed in some of the developing countries, but generally the situation is much the same, especially in African countries.

Regarding the validity of national accounts figures, the most serious problem was that they did not reflect the distribution of incomes among the citizens in a society. Therefore, aggregate growth in the per capita income could be a reflection of, say, significant growth for the high-income groups and at the same time a decline or stagnation for the low-income groups.

Precisely this question of distribution became of central concern among development economists from around 1960. This new interest was also prompted by the fact that, at this time, figures began to appear which indicated that growth was frequently very unevenly distributed socially, geographically and between the different economic sectors. The result was a readjustment of the original conceptions in order to take into account the impact upon distribution. At the same time, mainstream conceptions were extended to cover both growth and economic changes in other respects (cf. Chapter 5).

There is still no general agreement on how to define economic growth and development goals; nor on how best to measure socio-economic changes in developing societies. Yet wide approval has currently been gained for a notion which defines economic development as *a process whereby the real per capita income of a country increases over a long period of time while simultaneously poverty is reduced and the inequality in society is generally diminished* – or at least not increased (cf. Meier, 1989: p. 6).

Conceptions of this kind have also been adopted in World Bank analyses. Further, they have informed Bank strategies since the early 1970s. However, considerable fluctuations over time can be observed. Until around 1980, the World Bank was mainly interested in combining growth in per capita income with special assistance to the poor. One of the strategies was described as 'redistribution with growth'; another went under the name 'the basic needs strategy'. In the 1980s, the focus shifted towards aggregate growth in conjunction with restoration of macro-economic balances, structural adjustment, and increased foreign-exchange earnings. Since 1990, the Bank has again emphasised growth for the poor and resource-weak groups – along with aggregate growth – in its overall conception of development (cf. World Bank, 1980; 1990).

Increased welfare and human development

The above definition of economic development embodies a wish, in principle, to improve the living conditions and the welfare of all citizens of a society. However, the indicators for this remained in most of the literature, and the international debate was still limited to income measurements of one kind or the other. As a corollary, it was asserted that growth in real incomes was the main target.

This was disputed by prominent economists such as *Amartya Sen, Paul Streeten, Mahbub ul Haq*, and others who believed that increased incomes should be regarded as a *means* to improve human welfare, not as an end in itself (Sen, 1988; Streeten, 1981; 1994). To these economists, human welfare was the overall objective – the essence of development. Increased incomes and national economic growth were crucial preconditions for improvements in standards of living, but not the only preconditions. This could be easily demonstrated, for example by comparing per capita incomes with indicators of education or health standards. Figures from the mid-1980s thus showed that the average life expectancy in many countries was considerably lower than one would expect from the income figures. Sri Lanka, with an average income of US$360, had an average life expectancy of 70 years, whereas Brazil, with over US$1700, had an average life expectancy of only 64 years (Sen, 1988: p. 12).

With the first *Human Development Report* from 1990, prepared under the leadership of Mahbub ul Haq, the United Nations Development Programme (UNDP) adopted this basic criticism of income measurements and presented a more comprehensive concept of *human development* (UNDP, 1990). The report defined human development as *a process of enlarging people's choices*. At first, attention was concentrated around the choices in three essential areas: the opportunity to lead a long and healthy life; the opportunity to acquire knowledge; and the opportunity to have access to resources needed for a decent standard of living (cf. Chapter 21). To these were later added considerations regarding political freedom and human rights; human development for women as well as for men; environmental and other aspects of sustainability; and themes regarding citizens' participation and opportunities to affect the political decisions in society.

What was originally launched as an alternative goal of development in this way gradually became a new framework for research as well as development co-operation – often referred to by its adherents as the new 'paradigm' for *sustainable human development* (Haq, 1995; Banuri et al., 1995). Some of the aspects and themes included in this new 'paradigm' resemble the conception of development which we shall discuss below as 'development by people'. Other aspects will be discussed later (see Chapter 21).

Modernisation

The basic notions of development mentioned above centre around economic and material conditions, although the concept of human development has recently been extended to include non-economic aspects. However, as was briefly mentioned at the beginning of this chapter, in the 1940s and 1950s there were also widespread conceptions of development as a process of *modernisation*, that is a structural change *process whereby the traditional and backward Third World countries developed towards greater similarity with the Western, or rather, the North-Western world* (Pye, 1966; Apter, 1965).

Among the features of the imitation-worthy modern societies which were especially highlighted were: an extensive division of labour and specialisation, high productivity, self-sustaining economic growth, a well-functioning and active state apparatus, a democratic form of government and equality before the law (cf. Chapter 12). The conception of development as a modernisation process with these characteristics has survived the last 40 years of debates and empirical analysis – particularly outside the research community. The same applies to the idea that economic growth is the core feature of development in the Third World. However, several other development conceptions have emerged as contenders in the debate.

Elimination of dependency

As early as in the 1960s, a number of Neo-Marxist and Marxist development conceptions were elaborated as explicit alternatives to the normative theories about modernisation. Basically, they presented two different types of objectives for the development process. One type had to do with the developing countries' position in the international system; the other with the internal conditions in Third World societies (cf. Chapter 7).

With respect to the developing countries' position in world society, many of the Neo-Marxist theorists held the view that development implied the *gaining of real national independence and self-centred economic progress*. The so-called *dependency theorists*, in particular, were of the opinion that the colonial powers and imperialism had actively underdeveloped the Third World or at least impeded independent development there. The political decolonisation had not changed this in any essential respect – according to these theorists' own analyses. Therefore, there was a need for further de-linking and dissociation from the rich countries (Frank, 1967). The dissociation was not an end in itself, but rather an instrument for gaining the desired national independence. In fact, not all the theorists within this mainstream believed that dissociation from the world market was the best means to achieve independence. On this point the modes of reasoning among researchers were, as we shall see later, very dissimilar.

Regarding the desired internal, self-centred economic progress in Third World societies, the conceptions among the Neo-Marxists and related theorists varied considerably. There was overall agreement that backward countries had to base their efforts on their own particular preconditions, including their own resources. There was also widespread agreement that *the final objective was the introduction of socialism*, because this was the only mode of production that could ensure the economic progress attained was transformed into improvements for the suppressed classes and the many marginalised and extremely resource-weak groups. However, when it came to the formulation of specific development objectives in the short- and medium-term perspective, there was much disagreement. This continues to be the case in the debate among the theorists of this school.

At one extreme one could identify Marxist economists who believed that the best results would be achieved by allowing capitalism, with its strong market forces, to operate freely and penetrate society for a period, claiming that this would bring about the necessary material preconditions for socialism in the shape of highly developed forces of production (Warren, 1973, 1980). Apart from the long-term and final goals being different, there was in this way of thinking a remarkable resemblance to modernisation theory, in the sense that both asserted imitation of the highly industrialised countries as desirable. To the modernisation theorists this was the end goal; to Bill Warren and other Marxists it was a medium-term goal on the road to socialism.

Another extreme position was represented by theorists for whom the decisive factor was the above-mentioned dissociation from the world market and a simultaneous introduction of some form of socialism or at least a state-controlled and centrally planned economy as a first step to reorganising the production structure towards socialism. A special Soviet Marxist version of this line of reasoning emphasised, during the 1960s and early 1970s, the possibility of a non-capitalist path to socialism, that is development of the forces of production under state guidance and without having to rely on the capitalist forces of valorisation, accumulation and market mechanisms (Solodovnikov and Bogoslovsky, 1975).

A third type of Neo-Marxist approaches was more preoccupied than the above with historical and empirical analyses of social classes and the state in the Third World (cf. Chapter 14). They tended to give more emphasis to differentiation and thus formulated a variety of development objectives, with specific reference to the varying conditions prevailing in each of the countries studied. For many theorists within this Neo-Marxist tradition it could still be the long-term goal to bring about socialism, but at the same time they recognised that such a revolutionary transformation was not, in the foreseeable future, on the agenda in the vast majority of developing countries – perhaps in none of them at all.

Therefore, attention was focused on other, more realistic, development scenarios such as democratisation of political life, decentralisation of decision making, formation of co-operatives and general provisions for *a more equal distribution of development benefits*. These theorists remained critical of a powerful central state and a dominant public sector. They envisaged instead a general empowerment of the people through local self-government, collective owner-ship at the community level, and co-operative societies as appropriate goals.

On these – as well as a number of other points – the short- and medium-term development goals resembled some of the goals that had been formu-lated within the liberalist development theories with a focus on non-economic conditions. Here, the general tendency since the 1950s has otherwise been an ever more differentiated and culture-specific definition of development.

Dialectical transformation

This transformation actually started with the so-called *dialectical modernisation theory*, which had asserted itself within anthropology, sociology and political science way back at the beginning of the 1960s. This very complex approach retained, from the classical modernisation theory, the division of social phenomena into two categories: traditional and modern. It further retained the basic idea of development as *a process whereby society adopts more and more modern elements*. But at the same time, the dialectical modernisation theory added a number of nuances and a more dynamic understanding. It underlined that tradition need not be development impeding or in opposition to development at all. Conversely, it was stressed that modern institutions can at times obstruct development and perhaps not even function properly, precisely because they are not compatible with the traditions of the societies concerned. Furthermore, the approach emphasised that traditional societies can in fact be very dynamic, heterogeneous and capable of surviving under a modernisation process. This led to the central idea of the traditional and the modern as social phenomena in *a dialectical relationship where both types of phenomena change in the process, and where the result, of necessity, is a hybrid* (Rudolph and Rudolph, 1967; Gusfield, 1976).

The dialectical modernisation theory conveyed to all notions and theories more respect for the developing countries' unique circumstances and, moreover, tied the conception of development to these. This implied a dismissal of the notion that development is something universal, defined solely by its end goal: the greatest possible similarity to the North-Western industrial countries. Instead an open conception of development was proposed, the contents of which had to be decided in accordance with each individual society's particular circumstances and the preferences of its citizens. Furthermore the dialectical modernisation theory stressed quite strongly the non-economic conditions, both as factors in the economic processes and as important determinants in their own right of societal life and its transformation (cf. Chapters 12 and 17).

Capacity building and development by people

In the more sophisticated development concepts that appeared during the 1960s and the 1970s – also within development economics – the emphasis was shifted away from the simple copying of the industrial countries and from the one-sided focus on economic factors as the determining ones in societal transformation. Instead, numerous definitions of development appeared with a focus on *the capacity to make and implement decisions*. According to these more recent notions of development, a society exhibits development primarily in the form of better abilities and greater capacity to make decisions and implement them effectively. The previously mentioned idea of human development as the main goal can be seen as a variant of the development concept presented here.

The attention given to building autonomous capacity – of political authorities and/or the citizens of Third World countries – can be viewed as an attempt to reduce the ethnocentrism that so strongly characterised most of the earlier definitions. An illustration of this point is that a country's enhanced capacity to reject economic growth – or modernisation – as a goal may be seen as development when these definitions are used.

The capacity-building approach to development – like the dialectic modernisation theory – stresses the different societies' particular circumstances and the priorities of the people and social groups whose welfare and other conditions are the focus of the debate. Accordingly, many of the conceptions of development within this approach refer to people's effective participation in decision making as a necessary part of the whole process. However, there are considerable differences as to the priority assigned to people's participation and how it is understood. Basically, a distinction can be made between two conceptions: one that sees participation as *a means* to promote development goals fixed from above or from outside the community concerned, and another that views people's participation as *an end* in itself.

Both of these conceptions are often associated in the literature with notions about *basic human needs* as the starting point for elaborating development strategies. The normative assumption here is that the satisfying of the basic needs of the many millions of poor people in the Third World must take precedence over all other development efforts. Furthermore, the view is that the poor people do not automatically get a share of the results of growth in times of prosperity and are the first to be hit in times of stagnation and recession. Therefore, special measures have to be introduced to improve the standard of living for the poor. In other words, a special strategy has to be worked out to accommodate these basic needs.

With a notion of people's participation as primarily a means to development there is a tendency that strategies are formulated by central decision makers on behalf of the poor, who are merely drawn into the process afterwards to support the implementation of them. This also implies that the basic needs of the poor are defined by others than themselves.

In contrast to this approach, the development-by-people approach regards *popular participation as a goal in itself*, and as the *process through which other development goals must be defined*. Here the notion of development as increased capacity is shifted from the national level and down to the local level – and from the authorities to the citizens. The economically poor are seen as being also politically weak and, therefore, without decisive influence on the formulation of national development goals. To change this state of affairs and ensure effective participation of the poor in decision making and in defining their own needs, they have to be empowered so that they can *reach up* to the state and the central decision makers. Empowerment, in this context, comprises both conscientisation, in the meaning given to this term by Paolo Freire, and self-organisation of the poor. Further to enhance poor people's access to and influence on decision making, the adherents of the development-by-people approach propose an extensive devolution of powers to local authorities and community organisations (cf. Chapters 15 and 24).

In its more radical form (as in Gran, 1983), the notion of development by people has not gained wide approval in the international debates or in theory construction. But it is noteworthy that UNDP, in its *Human Development Report* from 1993, has placed effective popular participation high on the agenda. The report proposes that the authorities in developing countries – with outside support – should do everything in their power to promote participation of all citizens in both economic and political life, not merely as an instrument to further other development goals, but as a goal in itself – as an important aspect of human development.

Sustainable development

Since the Brundtland Commission's report was made public in 1987 (Brundtland et al., 1987), the international debate on development has been characterised more and more by considerations about the impact of growth and socio-economic change upon the physical environment. Considerably more attention has been given to descriptions and explanations of the cause–effect relationships in this area. At the same time, new environment-related definitions of development have emerged, most often referred to as *sustainable development*. A widely approved notion defines as sustainable development a process that *fulfils present human needs without endangering the opportunities of future generations to fulfil their needs* (cf. Chapter 11).

In the Brundtland Report, the discussion on needs is closely related to problems of poverty, especially in the Third World. It is emphasised that the fulfilling of human needs and aspirations is the most important goal for all development efforts throughout the world. But it is further stressed that the many millions of poor people have a particular justified right to have their basic needs and aspirations for a better quality of life fulfilled, whereas the socially and culturally determined 'needs' of, and wishes for, a life of luxury are rejected as being in contravention of the principle of sustainable development from a global perspective. The report also asserts that sustainable development requires support for values that promote a standard of consumption which lies within the limits of what is ecologically feasible, and which people all over the world can realistically hope to attain.

This strong emphasis on the basic needs of the poor of the world has not gained undivided acceptance either in the theoretical debate or in the practical management of international development aid. But environmental sustainability, as a leading principle, has gained widespread approval over remarkably few years. The conception of sustainability now plays a key role in most discussions about development both in the industrialised countries and in the Third World. This applies to formulation of development objectives as well as in connection with the design of strategies, which increasingly take into account environmental concerns.

Development and security

The vast majority of contemporary development conceptions do not take into account security considerations. Some conflict and peace researchers, however, have attempted to relate their analyses and conceptual frameworks to those of development studies. The normative development concepts proposed in this connection usually stress that poor countries should use their resources on economic and social improvements rather than on armaments and the expansion of their defence and security services. They also emphasise that developing countries with large defence industries should convert their production to civilian use (cf. Chapter 19).

The United Nations system in particular has promulgated conceptions of development such as this. Various reports made at the request of the United Nations' secretary generals, and resolutions from UN general assemblies or special assemblies, have time and time again emphasised the desirability of disarmament-financed development efforts. Central in this context stands the concluding document from a special conference held in 1987 on the relationship between disarmament and development (United Nations, 1987, 1988). In this document it is asserted that security for all nations must be accepted as a top priority, but also that it can and should be achieved at a much lower armament level in order to make more resources available to relieve 'the misery and poverty afflicting more than two-thirds of mankind'. It is further stated that the development process in itself can reduce the non-military threats and thereby make way for disarmament.

In recent years, new dimensions have been added to the concept of security. In its 1994 *Human Development Report*, UNDP suggested a profound transition in thinking – from the security of nation-states to *human security*, the security of people (UNDP, 1994: Ch. 2). The fundamental normative notion here is that human security should be ensured along with other aspects of human development. Human security implies that people can exercise the range of choices available safely and freely and that they have safety from chronic threats like hunger and repression. Development – or progress – in this context means improvements as seen from the individual citizen's point of view; the rights of the individual, personal integrity and well-being are all central. These rights include political freedoms like freedom of speech and the right to organise, but also economic, social and cultural rights.

Often, this focusing on the rights of the individual has been supplemented with particular attention to women's right to equality with men in all respects. Others have added special security considerations as seen from the perspective of ethnic, religious or other minorities. Some researchers and practitioners have paid special attention to the rights of those who have been labelled the people of the Fourth World, that is indigenous people in both the industrialised and the developing worlds who have been squeezed or even banished as a result of the economic and social progress of other, more powerful, social groups. In this case, the focus has not been primarily on the individual person's rights, but rather on those of indigenous people as a group – rights to the land and other resources which they once controlled.

Development as history

The last fundamental conception of development to be briefly discussed here involves a radical break with notions of a common evolution for dissimilar cultures. This conception, which has evolved mainly within modern social anthropology, views development as history, not in a universal sense, but as history of each and every culture of the world.

The normative premise is that all cultures and social forms of life are equal, and that no one is entitled to define the development goals on behalf of others. The researchers – and especially the anthropologists – should concentrate on uncovering and describing each individual culture as precisely as possible, not with a view to changing it but in order to understand it and consequently also to understand their own cultural backgrounds. This does not necessarily mean that adherents to this conception are in favour of freezing or isolating existing cultures – as the Danish anthropologist *Kirsten Hastrup* has expressed it: 'We are not to recommend others to hold on to tradition for the sake of tradition, but we should work as mediators between the West and the Rest, in such a way that the latter group can retain those aspects of their culture which they deem important, and alter or abandon others, which they want to change' (Hastrup, 1990: p. 51). Thus development becomes a culturally grounded process where objectives cannot be formulated by outsiders – where North-Western researchers or decision makers cannot define what is development outside their own cultural sphere. The definition of development has to be left completely and totally to each of the cultural communities, be they national communities with their own state or local communities. Only in this way can the differences in the world be seriously respected and the history of each individual culture recognised as equal to others, including that of the North-Western culture. And only then can development become self-development.

The more precise formulation of this concept is unique to anthropology, a discipline which more than any other has integrated a perspective of difference and a method of reflection in its approaches and theories. However, it should be noted that in the idea of each culture's right to determine its own development objectives and priorities there is a significant overlap with the conception adhered to by the development-by-people approach.

PART II

Economic Development and Underdevelopment

CHAPTER 4

Major Theoretical Currents in Development Economics

In the discussion of the theoretical heritage (Chapter 2) it was necessary to make a distinction between two main traditions of theory building: economic approaches, and sociological and political science approaches. In a similar way it is expedient to separate the discussion of the various theories within development research into theories that focus on *economic* conditions and processes, on the one hand, and theories that focus on *socio-political* conditions and processes, on the other.

This separation is followed in the present part and Part III. In this is reflected the previous and still widespread tendencies to analyse and construct theories within either development economics or the non-economic social science disciplines. The chapters following in Parts IV and V will, as a reflection of more recent priorities in theory building, to a greater extent concern themselves with cross- and multidisciplinary approaches.

In this chapter we shall first look a little closer at how, during the 1940s and 1950s, various major schools emerged within economic development research. This implies a subdivision of the main stream of thought which, in Figure 2.1, was referred to as development economics. In the chapters following, each of these schools will be examined with emphasis on some of the main theorists and their special contributions. It must be stressed from the outset that there are many ways one can divide and categorise the several different approaches; there is no agreement in the literature on how best to do this. Therefore, the chosen procedure should be accepted as only one among several competing attempts.

The idea guiding the present author has been to present and position the selected theories in relation to each other with respect to central characteristics such as their chosen *perspective*, their *development conceptions*, their *methods* and *ideas about the nature of development processes*, together with their *hypotheses concerning the causes of underdevelopment and development*. In connection with this, the various contributions have also been grouped according to the *strategies* that have been derived from the theories (cf. Chapter 1).

The emergence of competing schools of thought

The origin of what can currently be considered development economics may be traced back to research conducted in Latin America in the 1930s and studies undertaken in Western Europe and North America from the mid-1940s onwards. The starting points in both cases were discussions in progress at the time on how specific economic problems should be handled. In Latin America these concerned, above all, foreign exchange problems arising as a result of falling export income for countries such as Argentina and Brazil. In Western Europe and the USA, the discussions centred on how Europe could be put back on its feet economically after the Second World War and, in continuation of this, how Eastern and Southern Europe could be developed. Later, the same question was addressed more and more to the decolonised countries in Asia and Africa (cf. the introduction to Chapter 3).

In order to establish a theoretical foundation for the positions taken in these discussions, the researchers often referred back to the earlier economic theories of Schumpeter, Keynes, Marshall and others (see Chapter 2). It was characteristic of this period that only a few of the development researchers found the neo-classical economic theories particularly relevant. On the contrary, both the Latin American and Western researchers expressly rejected central components of the neo-classical legacy, including the preoccupation with equilibrium analyses and the theory of comparative advantages. Most accepted Schumpeter's basic distinction between economic growth on the one hand, and development as a structural transformation process on the other. Furthermore, most emphasised the importance of an industrialisation process in the developing countries, on the fundamental assumption that the industrialised countries were rich primarily because of their industrial development. The developing countries were conversely primarily poor because they had not attained a high level of industrialisation.

A third common characteristic of the early economic development theories was their stressing of the large productivity differences in the various economic sectors, together with both the open and disguised unemployment in non-industrial sectors. Finally, most theories recommended a high degree of state intervention in economic development processes. The basic understanding was that the state was required as an engine of growth and economic transformation, given the prevailing circumstances – with undeveloped markets and almost no indigenous capitalist entrepreneurs.

However, within a common framework like this there were great differences among individual approaches and theoretical contributions. Diana Hunt, among others, has in her review divided the many theories into two schools: the structuralist theories, and theories of the expanding capitalist core (Hunt, 1989: Ch. 3). The latter may also be referred to as growth and modernisation theories, which is the terminology adopted here.

The structuralist theories were originally advanced by the Argentinean economist *Raúl Prebisch*, the Brazilian economist *Celso Furtado*, and the Chilean *Osvaldo Sunkel*. Their views were essentially adopted by the United Nations Commission for Latin America, ECLA, founded in 1948. Prebisch became the Executive Secretary of ECLA in 1948 and retained the post until 1962. In Europe, the structuralist theories were elaborated partly in parallel to the Latin American ones, but also in some cases with significant inspiration from them. *Hans Singer, Dudley Seers* and *Gunnar Myrdal* may be regarded as exponents of this school, though Myrdal, in particular, represents other approaches as well.

Structuralist economists share a conception of the basic economic structures as a kind of steel frame, which cannot easily be changed just through the accumulation of capital and growth in production and consumption. The neo-classical economist, Ian Little, has polemically characterised the structuralists by saying they consider the world as bounded and flat. In contrast, he has described the neo-classical conception of the world as round 'and full of enterprising people who will organise themselves in a fairly effective manner'. Paul Streeten has responded, just as polemically, that the neo-classicists see the economy as toothpaste or syrup – as an easy flowing substance – whereas, according to the structuralists, it consists of hard, specific pieces of capital goods and individuals trained in specific skills and located in specific areas. Therefore, changes take time and may be extremely expensive (Streeten, 1984). Another common characteristic of the structuralists, especially the Latin Americans and Hans Singer, is their strong focus on external factors as determinants of the development process.

In comparison, the North American and European growth and modernisation theorists have paid more attention to internal factors as sources of, and barriers to, economic growth. Regarding their notion of the basic structure of the economy, they can be said to place themselves in a position between the two extremes represented by the structuralists and the neo-classicists. In their view the economy can develop through sustained accumulation of capital, just as they imagine a certain automatic spreading and trickling down of economic growth in the long run. At the same time, however, they recognise the need for structural reforms and conceive of development as a discontinuous process with different stages. Among the most prominent economists who originally proposed views like these can be mentioned *Arthur Lewis, Ragnar Nurkse, Paul Rosenstein-Rodan, Walt Whitman Rostow, Hal Myint, Albert O. Hirschman*, as well as to some extent Myrdal (whose views, as already noted, were also inspired by structuralist thinking).

Since these pioneers within development economics wrote their classic works, there has been a tendency to differentiation in the theories, but also a contrasting tendency to massive clustering – partly in the area of intersection between the classical structuralists and the classical growth and modernisation theories, partly in extension of the neo-classical tradition. Development economists have generally adopted the structuralists' strong contention that development involves both accumulation and changes in the basic economic structures. Two of the pioneers in this area have been *Hollis Chenery* and *Moshe Syrquin*.

The neo-classical tradition emerged as a strong contender within the international development debate only in the 1980s, but it existed as a competing paradigm parallel to the main streams of development economics from the 1940s onwards; it will be subjected to closer examination in a later chapter (Chapter 18). However, to provide an overview it is useful in the present context to compare the various major approaches, including the neo-classical, at least regarding their chosen perspectives and notions of the fundamental nature of the development process. This is the theme of the next section.

In the succeeding two chapters there is a closer examination of the central concepts and arguments advanced by selected theories that belong to the early growth and modernisation theories (Chapter 5) and the structuralist approaches within non-Marxist economics (Chapter 6). The Neo-Marxist theories are treated separately in Chapter 7, and – together with other Marxist-inspired theory – in Chapter 8. The international division of labour and transnational companies are the themes of Chapter 9. A discussion focused on agricultural development follows in Chapter 10. Finally, environmental issues are raised in Chapter 11, which concludes Part II of the book.

Different perspectives on economic development

It has been stated earlier that, within development research, disagreement prevails as to what extent the methods and theories of the established disciplines have universal validity and thus do not require adjustment to the special circumstances of the developing countries (see Chapter 1). The disagreement is especially pronounced among economists, whose position on the issue plays a part in the defining of the above-mentioned schools.

On closer inspection the differences of opinion can be considered in relation to three interconnected issues. The first has to do with *units of analysis* in research. The second concerns the question of the *scope of validity*, and thereby the fundamental view of the nature of the development process. The third issue relates to the chosen *analytical perspective*.

In neo-classical economics, analyses are focused upon individuals, households and companies, and the markets where these units interact. The perspective is micro-economic from the outset, and it is from here that the neo-classicists work themselves up to the macro-economic level. In this context, they see no reason for making a division between industrial countries and developing countries. On the contrary, they make the same basic assumptions concerning the utility maximisation of consumers, the profit maximisation of producers and the market's central role as the major determinant of economic behaviour. Therefore, a mono-economic approach is applied. At the same time it is taken for granted in neo-classical thinking that economic behaviour, price formation and the other conditions that this school is interested in can all be researched within a separate discipline: economics. In other words, the chosen perspective is in this sense mono-disciplinary.

Development economics, on the other hand, focuses on macro-economic structures and assumes that economic growth is closely interlinked with a structural transformation process. Development economists tend to view the developing economies as qualitatively different from the highly industrialised economies. Research in developing countries, therefore, requires special methods and theoretical frameworks. In other words, economics as a discipline has to operate with a plurality of economic systems, in principle similar to Keynes's distinction between two types of economies: one with full employment and another type with unemployment. With regard to the analytical perspective, development economics stretches from monodisciplinary macro-economic approaches to broadly embracing multidisciplinary approaches, though with a general preference for the former.

Neo-Marxist theorists are to some extent interested in different macro phenomena to the development economists; however, in this introductory overview the similarities are more noticeable. This applies also to the Neo-Marxists' emphasis on the special characteristics of Third World societies, whether they focus on structural heterogeneity in general or specifically on the co-existence of different modes of production. In any case, the peripheral societies are qualitatively different from the capitalist centre formations. As far as the analytical perspective is concerned the Neo-Marxist approaches are, by definition, multidisciplinary. They concern themselves not only with economics, but in fact with the political economy from a holistic, society-embracing perspective.

Using the issues regarding units of analysis, scope of validity and analytical perspective as a framework, the differences and similarities of the three major schools of thought can be summarised as shown in Table 4.1 (with inspiration from Hirschman, 1981; Streeten, 1984; Chenery et al., 1986). It should be emphasised that this overview, by its very nature, ignores the many middle positions that are also present in the literature. To illustrate, some economists apply conventional neo-classical economic theory as the basic framework but allow the particular conditions and circumstances prevailing in developing countries to be reflected in the operationalisation of the abstract concepts (e.g. Laursen, 1987). Other deviating cases would be the approaches referred to as new institutional economics (cf. Chapter 17).

In the following chapters, selected economic theories are reviewed and discussed separately, while others are grouped together in clusters and dealt with as essentially homogeneous or mutually complementing contributions to theory formation. It is worth noting here that most of the main streams of thought concerning economic development and underdevelopment have

Table 4.1 A comparison of different approaches.

Approaches	Unit of analysis		Scope of validity		Analytical perspective	
	Individual actors	Structures	Mono-economic	Plurality of economies	Monodisciplinary	Multidisciplinary
Neo-classical economics	**		**		**	
Development economics	*	**		**	**	*
Neo-Marxist political economy		**		**		**

Note: Two asterisks indicate where the emphasis of the three major approaches lies. In the case of development economics, one asterisk indicates a further area of secondary importance.

gradually changed in largely the same direction, namely away from universal generalisations and towards differentiated conceptions of conditions and patterns of societal transformation. Development and underdevelopment are increasingly conceived as a plurality of processes, each characteristic of groups of societies with particular initial conditions and subject to specific influences. As a corollary, the more recent economic theories tend to emphasise how much the prospects for growth and transformation differ in various categories of developing societies.

The increased attention to Third World variety has made theory construction much more complicated than before but also much more interesting and realistic, in the sense that the empirically grounded theories provide significantly better frameworks for the understanding and explanation of economic stagnation and transformation in developing societies.

CHAPTER 5

Theories of Growth and Modernisation

In the literature, economic growth theories are not often referred to as modernisation theories. When this is done here, it is to stress their similarity to the classical sociological modernisation theories, and thus to demonstrate the very fundamental common conception of the development process as a modernisation process which is embodied in both these – otherwise different – mainstreams of theory formation.

Central to classical modernisation theories is a contrasting of tradition and modernity. This applies to relations between countries, where these theories regard the Western industrial countries as modern and the developing countries as overwhelmingly traditional. It also applies within the individual developing countries, where certain sectors, institutions, practices, values and ways of life are considered as modern, others as traditional. The modernisation theories are concerned primarily with how traditional values, attitudes, practices and social structures break down and are replaced with more modern ones. What conditions promote and impede such a transformation and modernisation process?

With these chosen starting points, it is not surprising that modernisation theories imply a positive assessment of the historical impact of imperialism and colonialism. Through economic dominance and political control, the industrial countries have actively tried to graft their own 'modern' and development-promoting cultures on to the backward societies. The problem in this context has been the backward countries' development-obstructing traditions, institutions, values, and other internal conditions. In line with this retrospective evaluation of the role of imperialism, it is a characteristic of the economic growth and modernisation theories that they claim a favourable net impact for the poor countries in their trade with the industrial countries, as well as for their interrelations with the industrialised world in other respects. It is from this positive relationship with the industrialised North West that the impulses for economic change and progress in the undeveloped societies must come.

The classical development economists – the pioneers in the field who wrote from the late 1940s and up to the beginning of the 1960s – were not agreed on what the most important sources of growth were, or how the process was best set in motion. In what follows we shall look at some of the different views that have characterised the debate up to the present day.

Capital accumulation and balanced growth: Rosenstein-Rodan and Nurkse

One of the earliest contributions to the theory of the nature of backwardness and the conditions for growth came from the Polish-born economist *Paul Rosenstein-Rodan* as early as 1943, in the form of an article on the problems of industrialisation in Eastern and Southern Europe (Rosenstein-Rodan, 1943). In this article and through later works, Rosenstein-Rodan became a prominent spokesman for massive industrial development as the way to growth and progress for the backward areas, both on the European fringe and in the rest of the world. Rosenstein-Rodan expressly distanced himself from neo-classical economics and its static equilibrium analyses, and proposed instead that the growth process must be understood as a series of dissimilar disequilibria.

In a paper from 1957, he expanded this argument further into a theory of the 'big push' as a precondition for growth. The backward areas were characterised by low incomes and, therefore, little buying power. Furthermore, they were characterised by high unemployment and underemployment in agriculture. To break out of this mould, it was necessary to industrialise. However, private companies could not do this on their own, partly because they lacked incentives to invest as long as the markets for their products remained small. The influence of Adam Smith's reasoning was apparent here (cf. Chapter 2), but Rosenstein-Rodan went further with an identification of other growth-impeding conditions, including the companies' difficulties with internalising costs and consequently not being paid for all the goods they produced – for example, the cost of training workers who may then transfer their new skills to other companies.

Rosenstein-Rodan claimed that the barriers to growth could be overcome, but this required active state involvement in education of the workforce and in the planning and organising of large-scale investment programmes. And they had to be large-scale in order to set a self-perpetuating growth process in motion. Rosenstein-Rodan compared the 'big push' with an aeroplane's take-off from the runway. There is a critical ground speed which must be passed before a craft can become airborne. A similar condition applied to the growth process: launching a country into self-sustaining growth required a critical mass of simultaneous investments and other initiatives (cf. also Rosenstein-Rodan, 1984).

Ragnar Nurkse took over and further developed many of Rosenstein-Rodan's major points (Nurkse, 1953). Nurkse asserted that the economically backward countries were caught in two interconnected vicious poverty circles, which can be illustrated as in Figure 5.1.

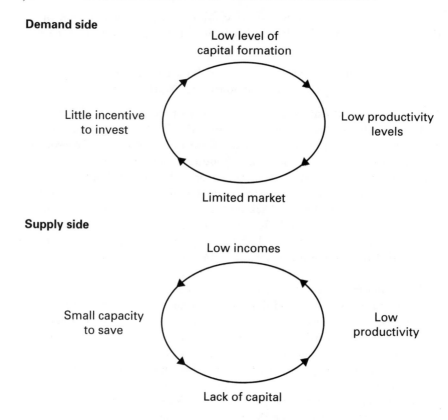

Figure 5.1 The vicious circles of self-replicating poverty

The reasoning behind the circles is that demand in backward countries is low as a consequence of the very low incomes. When demand is low and the market limited, there will not be much incentive to make private investments. Therefore, capital formation and accumulation remain at a very low level. As a consequence, no real productivity improvements occur and incomes, therefore, remain low. On the supply side, the low incomes result in a small capacity to save which, in turn, is reflected in lack of capital and low productivity. The final outcome is reproduction of mass poverty. Nurkse added to this that the whole problem with attaining the necessary savings and capital investments was compounded by rich people's tendency to copy, in their own consumption, the consumption standards and patterns of the industrially advanced countries. This so-called Duesenberry effect implied an increase in the propensity to consume and thus led to a reduction in the actual rate of saving.

The preconditions for breaking out of these poverty circles were, according to Nurkse, the creation of strong incentives to invest along with increased mobilisation of investible funds. This required a significant expansion of the market through simultaneous massive and balanced capital investments in a number of industrial sectors. This depended further on an actively intervening state, which could both plan investment programmes and ensure internal mobilisation of resources. The state was important also to bring about optimal utilisation of foreign aid, which Nurkse brought in as a critical strategy for initiating accumulation of capital on a grand scale.

It is important to note that behind both Rosenstein-Rodan's and Nurkse's modes of reasoning there lay a fundamental assumption that an increased supply of goods – as a consequence of capital accumulation – would create its own increased demand. Both theorists imagined that the market would expand as a consequence of the increased capital investments which, in turn, would continue to grow in response to market incentives.

Unbalanced growth and income distribution: Hirschman and Kuznets

The idea that the growth process could be initiated with balanced capital investments in several sectors at the same time was strongly criticised by, among others, *Albert Hirschman* (Hirschman, 1958). He claimed that, on the contrary, there was a need to maintain and accentuate imbalances and disequilibria in backward economies, because there were other barriers to growth than the limited market and the lack of capital investments. Hirschman emphasised, with inspiration from Schumpeter, that the developing countries' greatest problem was rather the lack of entrepreneurship and management capacity. Hirschman stressed his point by saying that 'if a country were ready to apply the doctrine of balanced growth, then it would not be underdeveloped in the first place' (Hirschman, 1958: p. 54).

Rather than strive for a balanced approach where the resources would be thinly spread over several sectors and managed badly, the developing countries should, according to Hirschman, aim at selected key sectors which had many links backwards and forwards in the economy, and therefore could pull other parts of the economy along with it.

The debate between the followers of the two above-mentioned models of growth continued up through the 1950s and 1960s. Today, however, the focus of attention has shifted from the original dichotomy to considerations concerning the circumstances in which one or the other approach appears to be the more appropriate.

Evaluated retrospectively, it is interesting to note that both models of growth operated with imbalances with regard to income distribution. It was well known as early as the 1950s that the income distribution in the developing countries was generally extremely unequal, but this was not a subject that preoccupied this period's growth theorists. Nurkse was worried that the rich would use their savings mainly on imported luxury goods, but it did not lead him to recommend – as in the case of Myrdal – a redistribution in favour of the poor, because Nurkse did not believe that the poor had the necessary ability or opportunity to save. In this regard he was in line with the predominant conception of this early period that increased savings had to come from the rich in the backward countries. In terms of strategy, therefore, it was deemed legitimate to concentrate on income growth for the rich, who would then increase their savings and thereby create continued growth. After a while this growth, it was implicitly claimed, would trickle down to the poor in such a way that in the end everybody would be better off.

Simon Kuznets was one of the few who stated in more explicit terms his opinion on this subject (Kuznets, 1955). He claimed that economic growth under average circumstances would lead to increased inequality in the beginning, but that this tendency would flatten out and to some extent turn to steadily increasing equality in income distribution. More specifically, Kuznets came to the conclusion that the incomes of the poorest 40 per cent of the population would normally grow more slowly than the average until income per person reached a range of US$700 to US$900. Beyond this range, the incomes of poorer groups would tend to grow faster than the average (cf. Meier, 1989: p. 21).

Several development researchers have tried, since Kuznets stated his provocative hypotheses, either to substantiate it with further data or to reject it. The Indian economists V. M. Dandekar and N. Rath have undertaken particularly thorough studies of the problem (Dandekar and Rath, 1971). They concluded, based on evidence from India, that a higher rate of growth was better than a lower rate of growth for all social groups, rich as well as poor – with the exception of the poorest ten per cent, who did not get any benefit at all from the economic growth in the various states of India. They added to this observation that, seen from the point of view of the poor, a fair distribution of the growth results was of greater importance than a generally higher growth rate, because the poor got considerably less out of a general increase. Dandekar and Rath, therefore, deemed it justifiable to ask how rich the rich should become before the needs of the poor were taken into consideration through political intervention and special initiatives. This question provided one of starting points for the argument that later led to the elaboration of the basic needs strategy (cf. Chapter 21).

Growth poles: Perroux

A third, but less known model of growth was worked out in the 1950s by the Frenchman, *François Perroux* (Oman and Wignaraja, 1991: pp. 23ff.). Perroux divided industry as a whole into two types of subsectors: the dynamic sub-sectors, so-called 'propellant' industries; and the non-dynamic, 'impelled' industrial sectors, which had to be driven forward by the dynamic sectors. This division also had a spatial aspect in that there was a tendency to concentrate the dynamic subsectors in small geographical enclaves, while the others were spread out in backward regions, whose growth and development totally depended on their linkages with the growth poles.

With this emphasis on both the sector-wise and the spatial concentration of growth, Perroux came to act as a kind of forerunner for the many empirical analyses that have since been undertaken of such tendencies. It is today a conventional and widespread conception that the countries in the Third World – with a few exceptions such as Singapore, Hong Kong, South Korea and Taiwan – are all characterised by concentrations of growth in certain sectors and certain geographical enclaves.

In contrast to Perroux's – and Hirschman's – recommendations, the concentration has rarely been optimal as seen from the perspective of the theories of unbalanced growth. The concentrations observed in the Third World do not, generally, reflect strategic imbalances in Hirschman's conception, or development-promoting growth poles in Perroux's terminology. Rather, they represent isolated growth spots which may be interlinked and integrated into global networks but which, at the same time, have not induced growth in non-dynamic sectors or the surrounding backward areas (cf. Chapter 9).

Modernisation and stages of growth: Lewis and Rostow

Each of the above-mentioned theories came to influence subsequent theory formation and the international debates on development problems, but not to the same extent, or with the same intensity, as two additional contributions from the early period: those of *W. Arthur Lewis*, born in the British West Indies, and the American, *W. W. Rostow*. These two economists, in their more elaborate and detailed analyses, differed with respect to conceptual framework and method and they also reached different conclusions. Yet they had so much in common that they came to function as mutually supplementary theoretical frames of reference, particularly in the Western world's development debate from the 1960s onwards. Even in the 1990s, they continue to influence some of the basic notions of economic development.

Lewis and Rostow both focused on rising per capita income as the central measure of growth; they conceived of economic development as a modernisation process; they used as their starting point a model of developing countries with an abundant supply of labour in the traditional sector; they regarded the savings rate as the central determinant for the investment rate and further for the overall growth rate; and finally they viewed the capitalist or entrepreneurial class as an important driving force behind economic growth, essential, in particular, for initiating the process (Hunt, 1989: pp. 62ff.).

More specifically, Lewis took as his starting point a two-sector model of a closed backward economy with an unlimited supply of labour at a sub-sistence wage (Lewis, 1954, 1955); one sector was the capitalist, the other he characterised as the subsistence sector. The capitalist sector employed wage earners, used reproducible capital and paid capitalists for the use of capital. The subsistence sector was characterised by being based primarily on family labour, by not using reproducible capital and by low labour productivity. It was in the subsistence sector that the abundant labour reserves were found, not necessarily in the shape of many unemployed, but rather in the shape of many underemployed. These underemployed workers could be transferred to the capitalist sector without bringing about a decline in the subsistence sector's total production, and at a wage which was determined by the average in the subsistence sector – not by their productivity in the capitalist sector.

Lewis's argument in extension of this was that the most important barrier to economic growth was the lack of accumulation of productive capital – caused, in turn, by the low rate of savings. The central problem in the theory of economic development was therefore to investigate under what circumstances it would be possible to increase the rate of savings and investments in a backward and stagnant economy, where these rates would typically be as low as four to five per cent of national income, up to a level of between 12 and 15 per cent or higher.

Lewis's answer to this central problem was that the poor in the subsistence sector and the workers in the capitalist sector could not produce such increased savings, because they were simply too poor to save a significant proportion of their income. The rich in the subsistence sector could not either, because they were mostly landowners, who used their rents and other income unproductively to buy existing assets rather than to create new ones. Therefore, the capitalists, the other component of the rich in the basic model, had to produce the necessary increase in the savings rate. According to Lewis, they were capable of doing so. On this point, he followed the classical political economics' assumption that the capitalists' profits would be both saved and invested.

Consequently, the central problem was transformed into a question about how the profits could be increased as a proportion of national income. This could be achieved by the capitalist sector's inherent dynamics. Lewis asserted that as soon as a core capitalist sector was established under conditions of unlimited supply of cheap labour, the capitalists would reinvest at least a part of their profits and in this way increase the total amount of capital available. This would attract more workers from the subsistence sector into the capitalist sector, where their productivity would be higher than reflected in their low wages (determined primarily by the subsistence sector). As a result, a relative increase of the profits in relation to total national income would occur and thus bring about an increase in the rates of saving and investment. The final outcome would be sustained economic growth, driven forward by the capitalists. Lewis emphasised that the capitalists did not necessarily have to be private capital owners; the state could play this role, too.

In the presentation of the argument so far we have assumed a closed economy without trade or other transactions with other economies. However, Lewis further extended his model to cover an open economy. This part of his model will not be presented in detail, but it should be noted that one of Lewis's main conclusions was that trade between developing countries and industrialised countries did not promote growth and economic progress in the former. This was explained chiefly with reference to the fact that wages in the poor countries, according to the model, were determined by the supply (subsistence) price of labour, as described above. The increased productivity of labour as a result of transferring to the capitalist sector would therefore be passed on to the consumers in the industrialised countries in the shape of lower product prices. Lewis, with this reasoning, anticipated central elements in Arghiri Emmanuel's theory of unequal exchange (cf. Chapter 7).

Summing up, one can say that Lewis's model gave reasons for optimism regarding the possibilities for sustained growth in the capitalist sector. Lewis regarded this as identical with economic development, but he stressed, at the same time, that the working population in the developing countries – the vast majority – could not count on improvements in their standard of living in the short or medium term if the capitalist growth rate was to be maximised.

Lewis's economic model and his associated theories have been subjected to wide-ranging criticism. However, this should not obscure the fact that his original contribution to economic development theory was both interesting and innovative. Some of the basic elements have since been taken over and amended by some of the more structuralist-oriented development economists who will be presented below (see Chapter 5). Moreover, Lewis's model formed one of the important starting points for Rostow's theory of stages of economic growth and modernisation.

W. W. Rostow formed his basic theory during the 1950s and presented it in its totality in 1960 in the book, *The Stages of Economic Growth* (Rostow, 1960). Variations and extensions have since been published (Rostow, 1978, 1980). Rostow, like Lewis, distinguished between the traditional sector and the modern capitalist sector. Further, he agreed with Lewis that a crucial precondition for lifting an economy out of low income stagnation and into sustained growth was a significant increase in the share of savings and investment in national income. But Rostow was more interested in describing the whole process through which a society develops in different stages. The aim was to identify strategic or critical variables that may be presumed to constitute the necessary and sufficient conditions for change and transition to a qualitatively new stage. Rostow's stage theory was essentially unilinear and universal, and assumed irreversibility.

Rostow divided the development process into the following five stages:

- the traditional society
- the establishment of the preconditions for take off
- the take-off stage
- the drive to maturity
- the époque of high mass consumption.

Each of the stages was thoroughly described in his 1960 book and illustrated with examples from the historical development of selected countries.

One of Rostow's central points was that all societies, sooner or later, will pass through the same sequence of five economic stages. Whether this will happen sooner or later is determined primarily by natural and economic circumstances, but Rostow also assigned some importance to political and cultural conditions.

The conceptualisation of the five stages is not characterised by the same precision in its formulation, or the same internal consistency of reasoning as found in Lewis's theoretical model. Rather, what we find in Rostow are somewhat loosely substantiated generalisations based mainly on experience from a few industrialised countries. This, however, did not prevent Rostow's theory from becoming one of the most popular among decision makers, consultants, and government officials involved in economic planning in the Third World. This applies, in particular, to his propositions concerning take-off into self-sustained growth.

It should be added that Rostow himself, unlike many economic planners and consultants, was quite careful about specifying a long list of preconditions for the take-off. In fact, it is in the discussion of the preconditions for take-off that Rostow has probably delivered his most crucial contribution and on this point even influenced theorists who have not accepted his notion that all economies will pass through an identical series of stages. Therefore, a little more should be said about these preconditions.

Rostow described how, prior to their take-off, the industrialised societies – some of them for an entire century – went through several changes which were all preconditions for breaking out of the traditional structure. To this he added three specific conditions which should all be in place immediately before the take-off. The first was a marked increase in the investment rate; the second was the emergence of particular growth sectors that could function as engines of aggregate economic growth; and the third was the establishment of political, social and institutional frameworks making it possible to utilise the potential in the modern sector and, thereby, pave the way for self-sustaining growth.

Rostow imagined, as noted, that the developing countries would follow the same development pattern as the industrialised countries, despite their being surrounded by a quite different international economic system than were the advanced countries at the time when they took the big leap forward. In this sense, Rostow adhered to a mono-economic approach and thus placed himself, in this respect, outside the mainstream of development economics (cf. Chapter 4). However, in other respects he set the course for this mainstream, not so much in the sense that others adopted his theories – only a few did that – but more by inspiring critical revisions and amendments to the theory's central assumptions and hypotheses.

One of these hypotheses claimed that a markedly increased savings rate would lead to a correspondingly increased investment rate, which further would cause significant industrial growth. A second, related thesis asserted that capital accumulation was the central source of growth in the developing countries. Both these claims were rejected or heavily modified in later theory formation as we shall see in the next section. But prior to that it may be of interest to compare Rostow's basic development thinking – the concept of modernisation through an irreversible process divided into stages – with corresponding conceptions in more mechanistic Marxism including, especially, some of the Soviet Marxist theories.

Rostow launched his theory in 1960 as 'An anti-communist manifesto' (the book's subtitle) – as an alternative to Karl Marx's theory of modern history – and that is what it was in many respects. Among other things, Rostow refuted the Marxist theories of exploitation and suppression of the backward and undeveloped areas. He proposed a number of other interpretations and explanations in opposition to Marxist assertions, and warned against forcing development or turning it in another direction with assistance from the communist countries. That, Rostow declared, could only lead to worse results.

At the same time, however, it is interesting to note that Rostow and many development theorists with a mechanistic interpretation of Marxism have in common the idea that all societies, with almost compelling necessity, must pass sequentially through an identical series of stages or modes of production. The Marxist stage theories emphasise other characteristics, and are often more comprehensive and complex than Rostow's theory. Yet one cannot avoid noticing the striking similarities, especially with regard to the early, more dogmatic Soviet Marxist stage theories (Solodovnikov and Bogoslovsky, 1975). They suggested – in opposition to Rostow – that the underdeveloped countries could escape or completely avoid the capitalist stage by following a special non-capitalist road to development. However, in principle they simply swapped Rostow's model of a capitalist industrial country with the Soviet version of a 'socialist' industrial country. Thus, the Soviet Marxist theory became a special form of modernisation theory. This applied also in the sense that they proposed a positive evaluation of imperialism – only here it was of Soviet imperialism and not the Western industrial countries' imperialism. One of the points to note in this context is that the non-capitalist road to development was only possible with support from the USSR and Eastern Europe.

It has to be added that these remarks on Soviet Marxist theory apply only to the earlier prevailing conceptions. The theoretical debate in the Soviet Union was already, long before the dismantling of the Eastern Bloc, much richer and more nuanced. Many researchers even raised questions about the relevance to Third World countries of the Soviet and East European development model. Furthermore, there was an emerging consensus that the backward countries were too different to follow an identical path of change.

Patterns of development and obstacles to growth: Chenery, Syrquin and Laursen

Among the economists who further developed the theoretical inheritance from Lewis, Rostow, and others, but in the context of more structuralist approaches, *Hollis Chenery* and *Moshe Syrquin* require special attention (Chenery et al., 1986; Syrquin, 1988). In addition, two Danish economists may be mentioned: *Karsten Laursen* and *Martin Paldam* (Laursen, 1987, 1990). We shall look a little closer at selected aspects of their analyses to introduce the contemporary debate on the basic structure of the development process and on the most important sources of – and obstacles to – growth within development economics. In the present section, the focus is on the internal conditions in developing countries. This is followed by a discussion of international perspectives on the growth process in the next section.

In a conventional Keynesian approach, the most important source of economic growth is an increase of aggregate demand for consumer goods and investment goods. From this will follow a corresponding growth in supply and, hence, a new balance (or equilibrium point) at a higher level will be achieved. Growth in aggregate demand can be increased through public investments, but will otherwise come from increased incomes.

Other approaches within development economics emphasise, as was noted in earlier sections, the addition of more factors of production – particularly capital – and technological innovation as the critical sources of growth. Better education of the workforce may, in this context, function as a special source of growth. These approaches essentially assume that increased demand will result from expanded supply. The more structuralist approaches accept these sources of growth, but add reallocation of labour and resources from sectors with low productivity to high-productivity sectors. They also emphasise the interrelations between the different sources of growth, instead of treating each one in isolation. Furthermore, they distinguish between industrialised countries and developing countries regarding the typical composition of growth sources. They view the adding of more factors of production in the economy as a whole – capital, technology, and educated labour – as the most important source in the highly industrialised countries, while in the developing countries a significant proportion of the growth depends on the previously mentioned transfer of labour and resources to high-productivity sectors. Laursen has characterised this transfer as a *process of diffusion* (Laursen, 1987).

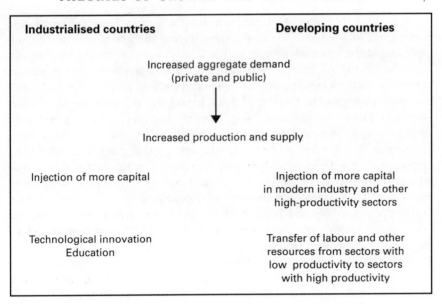

Figure 5.2 Sources of economic growth

Figure 5.2 summarises the various propositions regarding sources of growth.

The basis for the reasoning concerning the diffusion process is a two-sector model similar to Lewis's, with a large rural subsistence sector with disguised unemployment and underemployment. Hence, labour can be transferred to the urban industrial sector without any, or with a very limited, decline in agricultural production. In any case, the utilisation of more labour in industry, due to higher productivity in this sector, will lead to net growth in total production.

In a more elaborate version of the model, the assumption about only two separate and homogeneous sectors is replaced by assumptions about a multitude of sectors with diverse characteristics and different levels of productivity. Urban industry, in particular, is divided into relatively modern, large-scale industry and traditional, small-scale manufacturing and crafts. In the latter sectors, as in agriculture, the existence of disguised unemployment and underemployment along with low labour productivity allows for a replication of the diffusion argument here.

Laursen has observed that there is a tendency for the expansion of the modern large-scale sector to break down the traditional sector too fast, which further implies that industry's job-creating ability is less than the growth in unemployment following from the breakdown. Neither this nor other complicating factors, however, weaken the basic point that it is modern large-scale industry which is the main engine of growth and economic transformation.

A pertinent question then is: what are the factors limiting the haulage capacity of this engine? Here, the more recent theoretical debates do not only emphasise low savings rates and lack of capital for investment, but add to these the lack of foreign exchange. The classical development economists were, like their successors, aware of the need for foreign exchange to finance the necessary imports, but they did not regard this limitation as particularly important, while contemporary development economics tend to give it very high priority as an obstacle to growth, especially in low-income, oil-importing countries. Two further barriers to industrial growth have been identified, namely low growth in agriculture and limited human resources, chiefly with respect to highly qualified labour, business managers and political decision makers, but also regarding human development in a wider sense (Meier, 1989: pp. 64ff.). We will come back to these growth-impeding conditions later and continue here with other aspects of the theories proposed by Chenery, Syrquin and Laursen.

Prompted by an interest in achieving an overview of basic changes in the developing countries' economic structures over a longer period, Chenery and Syrquin, in the early 1970s, abandoned the construction of models. Instead, as some of the pioneers in this respect, they started to carry out a very comprehensive empirical survey of the changing economic structures (Chenery and Syrquin, 1975; Syrquin, 1988: pp. 228ff.). Laursen later carried out a similar investigation, adding new data (cf. Laursen, 1990).

The result of these surveys and investigations was a documentation of tendencies as foreseen in the diffusion model. A clear correlation could be observed between, on the one hand, rising per capita income, and on the other, increasing migration from agriculture and other primary economic sectors into the modern industrial sector. It was also noteworthy that the changes in the pattern of employment were not as marked as the changes in the distribution of investments and in the various sectors' contribution to gross domestic product. The relative growth of modern industry was much more pronounced in these latter respects than when measured in terms of employment. The problems of absorbing the fast-growing workforce in modern industry were reflected in this (cf. Chapter 22). Parallel to the changes mentioned, a further shift towards services, the tertiary sector, could be observed.

It was not the documentation of these patterns that was the most interesting result emerging from the surveys; these patterns were well known from earlier studies. The new and really interesting insight coming from the surveys was that the patterns in most of the developing countries were closely correlated with rising per capita income. The higher the income, the greater the shift away from the primary sector and towards the secondary and tertiary sectors. There were deviating cases, and the statistical significance was not in all cases particularly high, but overall there was a clear correlation. A second interesting result was that distinct stages in the changes of the

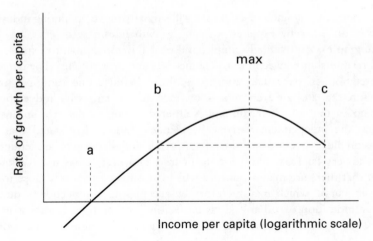

Figure 5.3 Per capita income and growth rates
Source: Laursen, 1987: p. 49

economic structures could not be identified. Rather, the picture revealed was one of gradual changes without leaps.

Another study by Laursen and Paldam from the beginning of the 1980s attempted, with inspiration from Rostow, to demonstrate a causal relationship between income and growth rates (cf. Laursen, 1987: pp. 49ff.). Here also it was difficult to identify distinct stages, but the two development economists arrived at the regression line shown in Figure 5.3. Based on this, Laursen subsequently proposed a division of countries into the following categories:

1. the countries to the right of the curve's maximum, which essentially corresponded to the World Bank's group of high-income, industrialised economies;
2. the countries to the left of the curve's maximum and on to point b, corresponding roughly to the middle-income countries in the World Bank's classification; and
3. the countries to the left of point b, the low-income countries, with those to the right of point a being the poorest with negative growth rates.

Interpreted as a statistical model, Figure 5.3 indicates that middle-income countries with high growth rates are in the process of catching up with the industrialised countries with lower growth rates. At the same time the middle-income countries are in the process of distancing themselves from the low-income countries, particularly from the poorest with negative growth rates.

Viewed as a dynamic model, the figure proposes, among other things, that low-income countries between points a and b, with time, will move into the area of middle-income countries and thereby reach correspondingly higher growth rates. Middle-income countries will similarly move up among industrial countries and thereby experience falling growth rates.

The graph is captivatingly simple, and probably too simple to express any causal relationship between per capita incomes and growth rates. The dynamic interpretation, in particular, appears doubtful because one cannot a priori conjecture that all – or even most – low-income countries will, in due course, move up to the curve's maximum. Neither does the model give an answer to what the independent variable is. Laursen himself has stated that the regression line covers a considerable spread, and that there are countries which lie very far from the theoretical curve. However, it has to be acknow-ledged that there are many countries which are situated relatively close to the parabolic curve, which may therefore be accepted as a reflection – directly or as an indication of other underlying factors – of pertinent patterns in the process of growth experienced so far by a large number of the world's countries.

Global interdependence

This chapter will now conclude with a brief review of a special economic theory that is not really part of the growth and modernisation theories, but which may be interpreted as a supplement to them. It concerns some more recent considerations on the interdependence between developing countries and industrial countries – considerations which to a large degree came to play a role in the Brandt Commission's recommendations (Brandt Com-mission, 1980, 1983).

The *theory of interdependence* has its roots in conventional economic theory. It began to play a role in the development debate during the 1970s, when it became evident how closely the world's economies are interconnected and, in their performance, increasingly dependent upon each other. It provided an occasion for a refining of three forms of interdependence between the developing countries and the industrial countries (Laursen, 1984, 1987: Part IV).

The first form is described as demand dependence. The point here is that demand for a country's production stems partly from domestic consumers and partly from foreign buyers. In the context of interrelations between countries, the point is that the industrial countries have an interest in growth in the developing countries, because such a growth will increase demand for the industrial countries' goods. This, in turn, will promote growth in the industrial countries. The reverse is also postulated to apply, that is the developing countries can sell more of their products in the industrial countries when the economies in these countries grow. In other words, highly developed and less developed countries will function mutually as each other's 'engines of growth' in boom times – and conversely, impede each other's progress in times of recession and economic crisis.

The relationship of interdependence, however, is not a symmetrical one. Using the figures for merchandise trade as a simple indicator clearly reveals that the 23 high-income economies, according to World Bank classifications, are much more important, overall, for world market demand than are the 109 low- and middle-income economies. The former group of countries, in 1992, accounted for more than 78 per cent of the world totals for both exports and imports (World Bank, 1994: pp. 186ff.).

Another way of assessing the extent to which the interdependence is asymmetrical is to look at production figures and data for the average propensity to import and then, based on these figures, calculate the impact of an increase of production in one group of countries upon another group. Calculations like these indicate that a one per cent increase of production in high-income economies will lead to a much higher increase in demand for developing countries' exports than the increase in demand for industrial countries' exports that would follow from a one per cent increase in low-income countries' production (Laursen, 1987).

The second form of interdependence is connected to the supply of goods. The main point here is that the industrial countries are in many areas dependent on products from the developing countries. There are many things which, quite simply, cannot be produced in the industrial countries unless they have access to certain raw materials and other goods from the developing countries. A corresponding dependence on the industrial countries applies to the developing countries.

The third form of interdependence is a little more difficult to describe in a few words. It could be termed welfare dependence. Basically, it has to do with the fact that different countries have different comparative advantages to produce individual products. Tropical fruits can best be grown in countries with a tropical climate, to take one of the more indisputable examples. The important point is, according to the theory, that each country's unique resources must be exploited in the best possible way in deference to other countries' comparative advantages. This way the highest level of welfare will be achieved on a global scale. The assertion need not be tied up with such extreme positions as those contained in the classical theory on comparative advantages, but the mode of reasoning is somewhat similar (cf. Chapter 2).

The strategy emerging from the theory of interdependence is often termed 'global Keynesianism', because it is reminiscent of the measures Keynes suggested at the national level (cf. Chapter 2). The strategy stipulates, among other things, that the industrial countries and the international organisations should transfer vast amounts of resources to the developing countries to initiate economic growth. As a result, demand for the industrial countries' products will increase, thus also leading to growth and progress in that part of the world.

There are a number of problems with this strategy. Based on the theory of asymmetrical interdependence, briefly referred to above, questions have been raised regarding the economic rationality of transferring resources to the developing countries for the purpose of increasing global growth. Transfer of resources may be perfectly rational from other viewpoints, but would not transfers between industrial countries result in greater growth on a global scale? Would it not be better for the industrial countries to aim for growth in Eastern Europe and the former Soviet Union, if the primary objective is to promote global growth?

There is no doubt that the theory of global interdependence, particularly the version stressing the asymmetrical aspects, has focused attention on something central in the relationship between industrial and developing countries. As seen from the poorest countries' perspective, notably in Africa, the theory further raises considerable concern because it can be used to justify the ongoing shifts in global resource flows away from these countries and towards the better-off countries in Eastern Europe, Latin America and Asia.

CHAPTER 6

Structuralist Theories and Industrial Development

The structuralist theories of economic development and underdevelopment were originally launched in parallel in Latin America and Western Europe (cf. Chapter 4). Since then they have been expanded into various more specific versions which cannot entirely be classed with the original approach and propositions. This applies especially to Gunnar Myrdal's influential theory which reaches considerably further and draws in more non-economic phenomena than the structuralists' original approach. Additionally, many of the early structuralist economists have adjusted their theories in the light of both acquired development experiences and significant changes in the global economic system, so that today one can identify various neo-structuralist approaches. Osvaldo Sunkel, one of the early Latin American structuralists, characterises his own recent contributions to theory construction as neo-structuralist (Sunkel, 1993).

Structuralist theories, in addition to representing an alternative body of theory to neo-classical economics, also provided a substantial part of the macro-economic foundation for the theory fragments that appeared during the 1970s concerning the informal sector and basic needs (cf. Chapters 21 and 22). Furthermore, the early structuralists, especially Raúl Prebisch, in certain critical respects can be considered as forerunners to the Neo-Marxist dependency theorists.

This chapter is introduced with an account of the early, notably the Latin American, structuralist theories. After this follows a brief discussion of the special contribution to theory formation made by the neo-structuralists. A third section looks at selected parts of Gunnar Myrdal's theories. Finally, the fourth section contains a brief survey of various strategies for industrial development, including strategies that had their origins in structuralism as well as alternative strategies with roots in competing theoretical frameworks.

Latin American structuralists and Hans Singer

Classical economic structuralism was in many ways affected by Keynes's perspective and method. Among other things, it shared with Keynes a great interest in unemployment. However, in contrast to Keynes's focusing on unemployment as a conjunctural phenomenon, the structuralists perceived unemployment as a consequence of structural conditions, as a phenomenon that reflected economic underdevelopment, and thus as a problem that could be solved only in connection with structural transformation of the Latin American societies with which the structuralists were primarily concerned.

Based on this conception, the structuralists paid particular attention to the barriers that obstructed structural changes. In comparison with the early growth and modernisation theories, which emphasised lack of capital as a major reason for economic stagnation, the structuralists were more interested in the *underlying reasons for the lack of investment*. They were further preoccupied with *the difficulties of financing industrialisation* which they regarded as the principal path of development. One of the major reasons for the lack of investment in Latin American and other underdeveloped economies, according to the structuralists, was the small size of the domestic markets which did not give the required impetus or incentive to the owners of capital. The modern manufacturing sector was typically very small compared to the traditional sector. Because the latter had only a low purchasing power potential while the former had considerable such potential, it was of crucial importance that the modern, industrial sector be expanded.

Celso Furtado and *Oswaldo Sunkel* (cf. Furtado, 1965) argued in this connection for a conception of development whose core was industrial growth and the consequent absorption of the workforce into more productive manufacturing processes. This was essentially in line with the propositions of the growth and modernisation theorists (cf. Chapter 5), but in their further elaboration of the argument the structuralists differed, for example from Lewis, by pointing to the necessity of increasing wages in the modern sector in order to achieve increased purchasing power in the domestic market. Furthermore, the structuralists added a number of new perspectives and propositions by identifying how properties of the basic economic structures posed difficulties for getting an industrialisation process started.

The small domestic markets were part of the problem. These markets could not sustain sufficient demand to support a more extensive industrialisation process. Instead, the strongest incentives to this lay in the international markets. It was here that the demand and the dynamics were greatest, but it was also here that the enterprises of the poor countries were weakest in competition with the companies of the highly industrialised countries. Moreover, the weaknesses of the less developed economies increased when they tried to diversify from export of raw materials and semi-manufactured goods to consumer goods, and further to more capital- and technology-intensive durable consumer goods and capital goods. Therefore, according to the structuralists, it was not possible to base the less developed countries' industrialisation on international demand and exports.

Added to this the poor countries, with their dependency on earnings from export of raw materials, faced great difficulties when they attempted to finance the initiation of an industrialisation process. On this issue *Raúl Prebisch*, in one of his classical analysis from the late 1940s, noted that the prices of raw materials in relation to manufactured goods had decreased steadily from the 1870s and up to the Second World War. This implied that the raw material exporters, that is the less developed countries, had to sell greater and greater quantities of their products just to acquire the same export income. Based on this analysis of the long-term trend of deteriorating terms of trade as seen from the primary exporters' perspective, Prebisch concluded that the economies of the Third World had no option but to industrialise and produce their own manufactured goods (Prebisch, 1950: 1984). Around the same time, the German-born economist *Hans W. Singer* reached a similar conclusion based on different data. Both Singer and others subsequently showed that the trend continued during the following decades, although there were considerable fluctuations for certain primary products like oil after 1973 (see Singer, 1984).

The deteriorating terms of trade for the Latin American and other less developed countries could not, according to Prebisch and Singer, be understood within the framework of the orthodox theory of comparative advantages. This theory claimed that increased productivity, such as that which took place in the highly industrialised countries in the period concerned, would result in decreasing unit prices for their products, and a consequent improvement in the terms of trade for primary exporters.

As this did not happen, and as the prices of manufactured goods on the contrary increased in relation to the prices of primary commodities, it had to be explained with reference to conditions which the theory of comparative advantages simply did not include in its conceptual framework. Prebisch's explanation was that the industrialised countries had been able to absorb all the productivity gains in the form of higher real wages and profits. This was partly due to the power of the labour movements in the industrialised countries, which had enabled workers to secure higher real wages during periods of productivity growth while preventing wages from sliding during periods of stagnation or economic recession. In more general terms, Prebisch argued that both wages and prices in the highly industrialised societies featured a very strong downward rigidity, thus preventing the primary exporting countries from benefiting from productivity growth.

Irrespective of the specific explanation of the deteriorating terms of trade for the less developed countries, the observed trend meant that these countries had to increase their exports very significantly in order to gain sufficiently large foreign exchange earnings to finance the import of continuously more expensive production equipment, if they wished to start an industrialisation process. Prebisch and the other structuralists did not conclude from this that the less developed countries should abstain from industrialising. On the contrary they concluded, as indicated above, that the developing countries should initiate an industrialisation process as soon as possible; it would only become more and more difficult as time went by and the terms of trade further deteriorated. In addition they judged that the poor countries had a right to protect their domestic industries over a long transition period because, as latecomers, they would otherwise be suppressed by the international market mechanisms and the dominance of the large transnational corporations (Prebisch, 1984).

At a more abstract level, the structuralists derived from their empirical investigations a *centre–periphery model*; Prebisch had already begun to use these terms in the 1950s. The centre countries were the rich, industrialised countries, who fully enjoyed the benefits from international trade. The peripheral countries were the poor countries in Latin America, Asia and Africa, who were not capable of deriving any significant benefits from their foreign trade.

It followed from the classical structuralist perspective that the peripheral countries' own capital owners and industrialists could not rise to the challenge of development. Their positions in the initial situation were far too weak. As a consequence, there was a need for catalytic support of different kinds. The structuralist economists in this context emphasised the central role of the state. State interventions and comprehensive investment planning were considered necessary means to accomplish the most rational exploitation of the scarce resources. In order to distinguish the proposed policies and strategies clearly from socialist planning, some of the structuralists referred to the required interventions as 'industrial programming'. This was not seen as a substitute for market mechanisms and private initiative, but rather as a necessary complement.

Another kind of catalytic support could come from foreign investments, international loans on favourable terms, and aid from the rich countries. Transfers of these kinds could all help to reduce the developing countries' balance-of-payments problems and contribute to financing their industrialisation.

Singer, however, was strongly critical of both private investments and commercial borrowing which he believed were mechanisms that tended to hold back the poor countries as dependent partners in the international system. For Singer, massive aid transfers aimed at developing the modern sector were the most adequate and most attractive means. To exaggerate the case a little, Singer almost came to recommend *aid over trade*, because foreign trade under the given international conditions simply could not function as an engine of growth for the less developed countries (Singer, 1984).

These policy recommendations were subjected to steadily stronger criticism during the 1980s. This led to extensive adjustments of the classical structuralist reasoning. But the core of their theory as outlined above has remained intact and continues to play a central role not just among other development researchers, but also in the debate between North and South, especially within UNCTAD, whose agenda even today is strongly influenced by the classical structuralists' ideas and propositions. In a similar way, Prebisch's basic notion of a world divided into a centre and a periphery has been employed, albeit elaborated in many different ways, in much of the later development debate (cf. Chapter 7).

Neo-structuralist theories

Many of the Latin American governments adopted the structuralists' recommendations in the 1960s and 1970s, including import substitution as the major strategy for promoting industrial growth (cf. below). At the same time, most governments took upon themselves the major responsibility for investing in physical infrastructure as well as in education and health systems.

In the beginning, these efforts worked in accordance with the structural economists' expectations, but when import substitution had successfully been accomplished for a variety of consumer goods, and when the demand from the consumers with considerable purchasing power had been satisfied, the strategy ran into problems. It proved far more difficult than expected to carry import substitution beyond consumer goods and on to higher levels, that is durable consumer goods, basic intermediate products and production equipment. Import substitution at these higher levels required considerably more capital, foreign exchange, and know-how – all of which were unavailable in sufficient quantities.

Some of the countries, including Brazil, tried under these circumstances to combine import substitution with an export-oriented industrial development strategy, but soon had to admit that the extensive protection of domestic industry during the first stage had contributed to the growth of many companies that simply could not cope with competition in the international markets. Unfavourable international market conditions in the 1970s accentuated the pressures on the Latin American economies (cf. Bagchi, 1982: Ch. 5).

Thus, contrary to the historical experience of the centre countries, the so-called 'easy phase of import substitution' was not followed by either a broadening of the industrial base or a diversification of manufacturing exports. Instead, industrial growth declined and most of the countries ran into serious balance-of-payments problems and public sector deficits. This reduced the states' abilities to finance physical and social infrastructure development (Kay, 1989: Ch. 2). It was during this period the ground was laid for the massive debt problems which have since so decisively restrained further progress for several Latin American countries (Sunkel, 1993).

Along with this, it became clear to the structuralists that growth in the modern industrial sector had not led to broadly based social progress. Large parts of the population had remained on the sidelines of the growth processes and did not get any sizeable benefits from them. Other population groups had even become further marginalised and experienced the changes as a decline in absolute terms (George, 1988: Chs. 8–9). Furthermore, the structuralists noted that the economic and social transformation processes in

Latin America came to pave the way for military dictatorships instead of promoting the democratisation process they had expected and wanted (Salazar-Xirinachs, 1993).

In the light of the patterns of slow growth and social exclusion exhibited in Latin America – and with inspiration from theories within other areas of development economics and neo-classical economics – the structuralists began, from the beginning of the 1980s, to adjust their approach. They retained Prebisch's original emphasis on endogenous and structural conditions as well as the need to promote domestic industry, but they moved away from the relatively one-sided focusing on the state's role in demand creation and investment planning. They acknowledged that the domestic markets, even in a large country like Brazil, were too small to sustain an extensive industrial-isation process on their own. Instead, they stressed the importance of supporting and promoting the formation of an efficient entrepreneurial class which could cope with competitors in the international markets. The state's role was extended – with considerable inspiration from Schumpeter – to include the supply side, especially regarding the promotion of higher industrial productivity as a basic precondition for improved competitiveness (cf. Salazar-Xirinachs, 1993).

The neo-structuralists have not abandoned their basic proposition that development most come from *within* and that it must be based on a diversified and coherent industrial structure, but they have reduced their expectations with regard to how much can be achieved without a considerable commitment to export. With respect to the conception of the relationship between state and market, and of the state's economic role in general, the neo-structuralists claim that several types of state interventions are still required, but they have de-emphasised the interventions which have to do with control of the transformation process in favour of interventions of a more facilitating kind. This issue will be dealt with in greater detail later (Chapter 18). In the present context we shall move on to a review of Gunnar Myrdal's theory, which in many respects can be seen as an extended and modified version of both the classical and the new structuralist theories.

Myrdal's theory of societal development

The Swedish economist Gunnar Myrdal's extensive authorship cannot, as mentioned earlier, be classed exclusively with the structuralist school of development economics. When Myrdal is considered in the present chapter it is because his basic propositions coincide with those of the classical structuralists, although at the same time they involve a further elaboration within a broader perspective.

Myrdal basically agreed with the structuralists that international trade under the prevailing circumstances in the first decades after the Second World War could not function as an engine of growth for the less developed countries.

To a large extent he also endorsed the structuralists' explanations of this, but he went further with a more general hypothesis on *circular and cumulative causation*. According to this hypothesis, the economic development process was, as a whole, characterised by a dynamic which favoured the already rich and resourceful – whether countries, regions or population groups. Conversely, the dynamic worked to the disadvantage of the resource-weak who, without special efforts, would remain trapped at their low level of development. Applied to international trade, the hypothesis more specifically implied that the terms of trade and the market mechanisms would ensure a 'trickling up' of the benefits to the industrialised countries and prevent the underdeveloped countries from taking advantage of their foreign trade.

Myrdal combined this proposition with the assertion that the rich industrialised countries, especially because of the states' active involvement, had been able to reach a high degree of national integration. As a result, economic growth in these countries tended to spread more effectively to other localities and sectors as well as to other social groups. The integrated economies benefited from both the multiplier and the accelerator effects. Growth in one sector or one region led to derived demand in other sectors and other regions – within the industrial countries' own borders. The result was that the industrial countries came to benefit from a 'virtuous circle' – a cumulative process with self-reinforcing growth (Myrdal, 1956, in Meier, 1989).

The less developed countries were in a very different situation. Here growth was concentrated in small enclaves and a few branches of industry, from where demand for production equipment and other inputs was not directed towards other domestic producers but rather towards suppliers in the industrialised countries. Likewise, the demand from domestic elites with considerable purchasing power was directed towards luxury goods from the rich countries, whose entire consumption pattern they tried to adopt. The combined result was that the less developed and less integrated countries were caught in a 'vicious circle' – a circular constellation of forces that tended to keep them in a state of poverty.

Myrdal also applied his proposition regarding circular and cumulative causation to analyses of income distribution within the poor countries. In his impressive work from 1968, *Asian Drama*, Myrdal elaborated the argument with particular reference to India and other societies in South and South-East Asia (cf. Myrdal, 1968: Appendix 2). In this context, Myrdal explicitly referred to Ragnar Nurkse's poverty circles as an appropriate conceptual framework for analysis (cf. Chapter 5).

Based on very comprehensive studies of the poor Asian societies, Myrdal formulated a much more encompassing theory on economic development and underdevelopment than those proposed under the headings of growth and modernisation theories, and economic structuralism. Myrdal did not confine himself to bringing in other economic sectors such as agriculture, but established a perspective that, systematically, included several non-economic conditions, making his theory a theory of societal stagnation and transformation rather than merely an economic theory. Some of the central features of this theory are considered here, starting with the criticism Myrdal – in collaboration with Paul Streeten – directed against the classical growth model originally proposed by the English economist Roy Harrod and the American economist Evsey Domar: the basic thesis known in the literature as the *Harrod–Domar model*.

In the Harrod–Domar model, the total production in a society was perceived as a result of the investments in the material production apparatus. Output was regarded as a function of capital input. The idea was, stated in simple terms, that a certain investment would lead to a certain increase of total production and hence of national income. The size of the investment needed for a certain increase in the national income depended on the capital–output ratios prevailing within the various sectors. The higher this ratio, the more investment was required. The important point in the present context, however, is the implied assumption that other conditions in society, in principle, could be disregarded, because they were either irrelevant or would change and adapt as a result of economic growth.

For many years after the Second World War this model played a major role in the development debate. Many poor countries even applied the model, albeit in different and often elaborated versions, as a basic framework for their economic planning after independence (cf. Chapter 16). It is still embodied in several planning models. Myrdal and Streeten, however, asserted as early as the 1950s that the model rested on highly unrealistic assumptions which made it of little use either in scientific research or in practical planning work. They argued that the model put far too much emphasis on capital. Somewhat polemically, they claimed that the whole mode of reasoning was like judging a violin concert by the number and quality of violins without regard to the skill of the violinists. To talk of a capital–output ratio implied as much over-simplification as to talk of a violin–melody ratio (Myrdal, 1968: Appendix 3, authored by Streeten).

Instead of the one-factor analysis, Myrdal proposed a more complex conceptual framework which provided for the inclusion of several other societal conditions that affected total production and national income. The framework comprised the following six categories:

1. Output and incomes
2. Conditions of production
3. Levels of living
4. Attitudes toward life and work
5. Institutions
6. Policies.

It is noteworthy that Myrdal here brought in non-economic conditions as central to his analysis. We shall return to these conditions and how they were dealt with in his approach later (cf. Chapter 16). In the present chapter, the focus is on the first three categories which, combined, cover what more traditional economists associate with a society's economic structures and processes.

Myrdal applied the three categories to characterise the situation in the Asian countries that he had selected for investigation in *Asian Drama*, but he argued at the same time that they were applicable, at least in principle, to all other less developed societies.

Through his research Myrdal arrived at a series of fundamental characteristics, not just concerning backward societies (regarded as units of analysis), but also concerning poor population groups within these societies. It is in this connection one finds some of the most thoroughly elaborated analyses of the distorted production structure in South Asia. It is also here one finds excellent descriptions of widespread unemployment and underemployment, of the inappropriate and poor utilisation of natural resources, especially within agriculture, and of the great income inequalities and the nature, extent, and multi-faceted character of mass poverty.

The conditions within the various categories are, according to Myrdal, closely related and there is a tendency for them to change in the same direction. In this connection, it is further underlined that the direction can be both 'forwards' and 'backwards'; Myrdal considered not only the possibilities for development, but also the possibilities for underdevelopment.

Myrdal stressed that the economically backward countries had to pledge considerable resources to set in motion an industrial development process. This was another crucial area where his propositions coincided with those of the structuralists. Myrdal in this connection endorsed the assertion that industrialisation would create more jobs, increase productivity, and significantly contribute to increasing production and incomes in the society. However, with reference to the specific conditions in South Asia's heavily populated countries, by the 1960s Myrdal had already reached the conclusion that even massive industrialisation could not absorb the millions of unemployed or underemployed in agriculture. Consequently, exclusive reliance on industrialisation would be totally inadequate if the goal is socially broad-based growth and a minimum of equity, and not just isolated growth within geographical and social enclaves.

Therefore, Myrdal further argued, the less developing countries must at the same time aim at developing agriculture, which could contribute to increasing employment and thereby the spreading of incomes and assets. The idea was not simply that agriculture should employ more people, but rather that the sector should create a production basis for growth and increased employment in other sectors of the economy. Accordingly, the most important aspect of the strategy was to increase the efficiency and productivity of agriculture. As a vital precondition for this, Myrdal emphasised radical land reforms which could bring about a more equitable distribution of land. Because of the generally higher productivity per area unit among smallholding peasants in comparison to peasants with large land holdings and the landed aristocracy, this would in itself result in a considerable expansion of total production.

The proposal regarding radical land reforms reflected a more basic concern of Myrdal's. He strongly believed that a certain degree of economic and social equality and equity was a precondition for sustained growth. He rejected the widespread conception that there is a contradiction between the objectives of economic growth and those of promoting social equality. Instead, he tried to demonstrate how the existence of poverty and inequality have impeded economic growth. When large segments of the population in backward countries suffer from mal- and undernourishment and other symptoms of extreme poverty, economic growth is obstructed because poverty weakens people and reduces their ability to work – and especially to work hard. Lack of education and understanding of their own potential opportunities further reduces the poor's productivity.

Myrdal suggested many other reasons why the traditional dogma linking inequality with growth was not only morally unacceptable but also factually incorrect as a statement regarding the causal interrelationships. He thus also underlined that even though savings in some poor countries did grow with increasing incomes, it was not at all certain that these greater savings would result in higher growth rates. On the contrary, experience showed that many of the rich squandered their money on ostentatious consumption of luxury goods or transferred the money out of the country.

With his recommendations on equality-promoting reforms and special assistance to the poor, Myrdal came close to formulating what has since come to be termed as the basic needs strategy (see Chapter 21).

Strategies for industrial development

According to structuralist theory, industrialisation is a precondition for aggregate growth and economic development of backward societies. These theories further assert that industrial development under the given international economic conditions has to focus chiefly on import substitution, starting with light consumer goods and thereafter moving on to durable consumer goods, basic intermediates and, finally, production equipment. This sequence was derived from the basic thesis on the size of the market as the most important determinant for investments. The underlying assumption was that in the beginning there would be no market for production equipment. Therefore, it was necessary first to establish an extensive consumer goods industry which, in addition to bringing about import substitution at this level, would create a considerable demand for capital goods and thereby pave the way for the establishment of more capital-intensive industries.

In spite of Myrdal's and other structuralist and neo-structuralist economists' warnings that industry could not be expected to function as an engine of growth under all circumstances, this line of reasoning came strongly to influence many Latin American and Asian societies' development efforts for several decades (cf. Bagchi, 1982: Ch. 5). It is beyond the scope of this book to review in detail the specific elaborations of the industrialisation strategies or the experiences derived from applying them in different settings, but it may be useful to summarise some of the main types of strategies (see Weiss, 1988). These may function as points of reference when reviewing the various theoretical works on particular aspects of industrialisation in the Third World.

The first main type of strategies can be described as *industrialisation via import substitution*. The policies and strategies in this group are characterised by being inward-looking in the sense that they generally aim at replacing industrial imports by domestic production. The above sketched strategy belongs to this main type, but it should be added that it embodies only one of several possible ways of sequencing the import replacements. A particular subgroup of strategies would give priority to heavy industries, often government-owned, and aim at substituting import of basic intermediates and capital goods at a much earlier stage.

Some of the larger developing countries like China, India and Brazil have tried to implement import substitution both for light industry, durable consumer goods and heavy industry, while smaller countries – including most of the African countries – have had to limit themselves to 'the easy phase' of import substitution, that is concerning light consumer goods, and moreover often with emphasis on a small selection of consumer goods. Such limited attempts at industrialisation via import substitution have rarely speeded up industrial growth, among other reasons because this strategy has led to increased imports of machinery and other capital-intensive industrial inputs. Because of the prevailing terms of trade, the prices of the imported capital goods have by far outweighed the earnings in foreign exchange from replacing the import of light industrial products. As a result, the countries concerned have typically ended up with larger – rather than the intended smaller – deficits on their trade with the outside world.

Another main type of industrialisation strategies can be described as *export-oriented* – or as industrialisation via export substitution. The basic idea here is to replace the export of primary products with the export of 'non-traditional products', such as processed primary products, semi-manufactures and manufactured goods of various kinds. This type of strategies also includes several more specific forms depending, among other things, on the kinds of product selected and the sequencing chosen for the diversification strategy. Most developing countries have been able to export only light industrial products which could be produced with limited investments in labour-intensive production processes. Far Eastern high-growth countries such as South Korea and Taiwan are among the comparatively few who have been able to diversify their exports so as to include capital- and technology-intensive products like ships, cars and electronics as well.

We shall get back to a discussion of different industrialisation strategies elsewhere in the book, for example in connection with a model of industrial development and foreign trade (Chapter 8), and in connection with considerations on agricultural development (Chapter 10). In this latter context, a third main type of industrialisation strategies, *agriculture-based industrialisation*, will be introduced.

CHAPTER 7

Neo-Marxist Theories of Underdevelopment and Dependency

Neo-Marxist theories of underdevelopment and development appeared during the 1950s, partly as a reaction against the growth and modernisation theories, partly as the outcome of a long-standing debate concerning the impact of imperialism. The early Neo-Marxist theories were primarily known as *dependency theories*. They were to a large extent influenced by the Latin American structuralists and their analyses of the trade relations between the economically backward countries and the highly industrialised countries.

With respect to the theoretical heritage from the debate on imperialism, it may be of interest to note that Marx had concerned himself with this issue as early as the 1850s. In articles in publications such as the *New York Tribune*, Marx tried to assess what would be the long-term impact of the European colonisation of South Asia. In this context, he arrived at the conclusion that imperialism would probably destroy important elements, including local small-scale manufacturing, and set in motion a significant exploitation of the colonial areas; but, on the other hand, he believed that the European penetration would at the same time remove basic obstacles to the development of capitalism. Furthermore, Marx considered many of the British interventions as directly promoting economic transformation. This applied especially to the building and expansion of material infrastructure, the introduction of the plantation economy, monetisation of commodity exchange, and the initial establishment of modern industry with its concomitant wage labour (cf. Marx and Engels, 1972).

In other words, British rule implied destruction and exploitation in the short-term perspective, but construction and creation of essential material preconditions for the colonial areas' later transformation to capitalism – and thus, according to Marx, genuine societal development. It may be added that Marx later toned down the constructive aspects of British rule in South Asia. He further asserted that the British colonisation of Ireland had only destructive effects.

The interesting point in the present context is to note the wide span in Marx's own conceptions, because this span has paved the way for very different interpretations within the Marxist research tradition. One of the theorists who has championed the view that imperialism has promoted development in the Third World is Bill Warren. We shall look at his main argument later in this chapter. But first we shall deal with the Neo-Marxist mainstream and focus on some of the several theorists who have vehemently rejected this interpretation and instead asserted that imperialism has actively underdeveloped the peripheral societies – or at the very least obstructed their development.

These theorists – most of whom may be regarded as proponents of dependency theory in one form or another – have further claimed that not only imperialism and colonialism of the past, but also contemporary forms of economic imperialism have impeded progress throughout the Third World. They argue that economic domination, as exerted by the highly industrialised countries, is a much more important development-impeding factor than all the internal conditions in the backward countries that feature so prominently in the growth and modernisation theories (for an overview of both theoretical propositions and historical evidence, see Bagchi, 1982).

Causes of underdevelopment: Baran

Before we come to the dependency theories that during the 1970s and after came to dominate large parts of the development debate, it is deemed relevant to look a little closer at the role *Paul Baran* played in establishing the theoretical linkages backwards to classical Marxism.

Baran, who emigrated to the USA from the USSR before the Second World War, wrote his most influential work in 1957. It included both an historical account of the origins of underdevelopment and an analysis of the 'morphology' of contemporary underdevelopment (Baran, 1957). Baran conceptualised underdevelopment in much the same way as his contemporary non-Marxist economists. He emphasised that the backward countries were characterised by dual economies: on the one hand they comprised large agricultural sectors, where productivity was extremely low and the marginal productivity of labour close to zero; on the other, they had small industrial sectors with a high level of productivity. Baran further stressed that the growth and employment potential lay in the industrial sector, but that its expansion was constrained by the small size of the domestic markets as well as by competition from the highly industrialised countries. All these were generally accepted views in the 1950s. The important new feature in Baran's approach and analysis was his attempt to explain this state of affairs, and, in particular, why the backward societies remained underdeveloped. In pursuit of this explanation, Baran introduced a special version of Karl Marx's economic theories with emphasis on class relations and their impact upon the utilisation of the economic surplus.

Where Marx, in his analyses of conventional capitalism, had underlined how the capital owners could expropriate an economic surplus from the working class in the form of the surplus value produced by the workers (who were not paid the full value of their labour), Baran emphasised the extraction of economic surplus in all its forms. In the backward economies, the surplus potentially available for capital formation did not only take the form of surplus value produced by wage labour, but also included the appropriation of surplus from peasants and other direct producers in the form of land rent, interest on credit, and profits from trade. Four main classes each appropriated surplus in one of these forms.

Land rent was extracted by the feudal aristocracy or other big landowners. Interest on credit accrued to the moneylenders, who were sometimes the same people as the landowners. The profit from trade was appropriated by merchants who made a living from buying cheaply and selling dearly. Finally, the surplus value from capitalist production was appropriated by the largely foreign capitalists, but also to a certain extent by the emerging groups of national industrialists.

Baran's crucial point was that none of these four propertied and economically dominant classes had any vital interest in promoting industrialisation and the accompanying transformation of the peripheral economies. The feudal landowners, moneylenders and traders, in fact, opposed this because it would threaten their access to the traditional sources of economic surplus. The foreign and national capital owners were also against it, because a more comprehensive industrialisation process would undermine their monopoly position and force them into competition with new entrepreneurs – which, in turn, could threaten their extraordinarily high profits. In such circumstances capitalism was devitalised and deprived of its growth and development dynamism – the dynamism that, under other circumstances, had created impressive economic progress in the centre formations during an earlier period.

Baran, contrary to the classical structuralists and many later dependency theorists, focused mainly on the internal conditions in the backward societies. It was in these internal conditions, and more specifically in the distribution of power among the classes and control over the economic surplus, that Baran found the primary barriers which had prevented the poor countries from copying the industrialised countries and reaching a similar stage of development. However, Baran also emphasised the international circumstances by underlining that economic development in the backward societies was profoundly inimical to the dominant interests in the advanced capitalist countries. As these countries governed the international economic system, the underdeveloped countries remained trapped in poverty (cf. Palma, 1978, in Meier, 1989).

The only way Baran could see out of the misery was through extensive state interventions to promote nationally-controlled industrialisation. The recommended strategy markedly distinguished itself from those of the structuralists by emphasising the establishment of state-owned heavy industries as a precondition for evolution of the other industrial sectors.

The strategy proposed by Baran, directly or indirectly, achieved some influence on economic planning in countries such as India and China, but did not otherwise come to play any central role in the theory formation within the Neo-Marxist school of thought. On the other hand, Baran's analyses of the causes of underdevelopment became an important source of inspiration for scholars like the American economist, *Andre Gunder Frank*, and other dependency theorists. In addition to Frank, the following section will briefly review the contributions to theory formation from the Egyptian economist, *Samir Amin*, and the Graeco-French economist, *Arghiri Emmanuel*. Frank based his original dependency theory mainly on evidence from Latin America, while Amin drew his conclusions chiefly from empirical analyses of West Africa. Emmanuel drew more widely on the developing countries' trade with the industrialised countries. In terms of analytical perspective he worked only with a few rather limited subject areas – as opposed to Frank and Amin.

After a brief examination of the earlier works on dependency, from the 1960s and the beginning of the 1970s, we shall try to trace the main lines of thought in the debate among the Neo-Marxists during the subsequent decades. This will include, on the one hand, a discussion of what can be conceived of as attempts to further elaborate and refine the original propositions, and, on the other hand, a summary of opposing positions in the debate. In the next chapter we shall follow yet another school of thought with roots going back to Marx and Baran: theories on modes of production and social classes which focus primarily on the internal conditions in peripheral societies.

Metropoles and satellites: Frank

Andre Gunder Frank, like Baran, was interested in identifying the causes of underdevelopment, but unlike his predecessor he did not lay great emphasis on the social classes and their control over the economic surplus (Frank, 1967). Rather, Frank argued that the crucial mechanism for extraction of the surplus was trade and other kinds of exchange of goods and services – not only international trade, but also exchange internally in the peripheral societies.

Frank rejected the dualist conception according to which the underdeveloped countries comprised two separate economies, one modern and capitalist and another traditional and non-capitalist. On the contrary, he claimed that capitalism permeated the whole of the periphery to such an extent that the Latin American and other peripheral societies had become integrated parts of a one-world capitalist system after the first penetration by metropolitan merchant capital. This had established capitalist exchange relations and networks that linked the poorest agricultural labourers in the periphery with the executive directors of the large corporations in the USA.

The exchange relations and the network were described by Frank as a pyramidal structure with metropoles and satellites. The agricultural labourers and the small farmers in the rural regions of the periphery were satellites at the bottom. They were linked, mainly through trade, to the landowners and local centres of capital accumulation, that is local metropoles. These, in turn, were satellites in terms of regional economic elites and centres of surplus extraction. In this way the structure grew – through several links – until it reached the ruling classes and world centres of capitalism in the USA. Throughout this pyramidal structure surplus was appropriated by the centres which, in turn, were subject to the surplus extraction activities of higher-level centres.

According to Frank, empirical evidence showed that the economic surplus generated in Latin America was drained away. Instead of being used for investment in the countries of origin, most of the surplus was transferred to the affluent capitalist countries, especially the USA. Frank's basic point was that the satellites would be developed only to the extent and in the respects which were compatible with the interests of their metropoles. And here experience showed, according to him, that neither the USA nor the other industrialised countries had any interest in genuine development of the Latin American countries. Much indicated in fact that precisely those countries and regions which had the closest links to the industrialised countries were the proportionally least developed. Therefore, the explanation of under-development lay primarily in the metropole–satellite relations, which not only blocked economic progress, but also often actively underdeveloped the backward areas further (this being a process and not a state).

Frank derived from this the much debated conclusion that all countries in Latin America – as well as other Third World countries – would be better off if they disassociated themselves from, or totally broke the links to, the USA and the other industrialised countries. *De-linking from the world market* was the best development strategy. This presupposed the introduction of some form of socialism in the peripheral countries, because the ruling classes, the landowners and the comprador capitalists could not be expected to bring about such a de-linking and thus remove the foundation for their own surplus generation.

Frank's conclusions, according to both contemporary and later critics, were often drawn further than the analyses warranted. However, this did not prevent his fundamental views and conceptions from winning wide dissemination and achieving considerable impact upon the development debate throughout most of the 1970s. Frank's position in this regard came to resemble that of Rostow in the sense that they both, for more than a decade, functioned as major reference points in the debates on dependency and economic growth respectively. Like Rostow, whose position was gradually superseded by more nuanced and empirically better-substantiated theories within his research tradition, Frank eventually was replaced by more complex and differentiated attempts at explaining the reasons for underdevelopment and its dynamics. One of the earliest attempts in this direction came from Samir Amin.

Centre and periphery: Amin

Amin was one of the first economists from the Third World who acquired a prominent international position in the development debates, including the debates in Western Europe and North America. Two of his academic works, in particular, contributed to this prominence: *Accumulation on a World Scale* (Amin, 1974), and *Unequal Development* (Amin, 1976).

While Frank chiefly concerned himself with trade and other exchange relations, Amin was more concerned with the conditions and relations of production. Based on thorough historical analysis of how Europe had under-developed large parts of Africa in the colonial era, Amin worked out two ideal-type societal models with the main emphasis on the structuring of production processes. One model described an autocentric centre economy; the other a dependent peripheral economy.

The model of the *autocentric economy* has features similar to those included in Rostow's description of the industrialised countries in the epoch of high mass consumption (cf. Chapter 5). The autocentric reproduction structure is characterised by the manufacturing of both means of production and goods for mass consumption. Furthermore, the two sectors are interlinked so that they mutually support each other's growth. Similarly, there is a close link between industry and agriculture. The autocentric economy is generally characterised by being self-reliant. This does not imply self-sufficiency. On the contrary, a highly developed capitalist economy typically engages in extensive foreign trade and other international exchange relations. But the economy is autocentric in the sense that the intra-societal linkages between the main sectors predominate and shape the basic reproduction processes. It is the internal production relations that primarily determine the society's development possibilities and dynamics.

It is quite a different matter with the *peripheral economy*. According to Amin, this type of economy is dominated by an 'over-developed' export sector and a sector that produces goods for luxury consumption. There is no capital goods industry, and only a small sector manufacturing goods for mass consumption. There are no development-promoting links between agriculture and industry. The peripheral economy is not self-reliant, but heavily dependent on the world market and the links to production and centres of capital accumulation in the centre countries.

It is further part of the picture of the peripheral economy that it is composed of various modes of production. Capitalism has only penetrated limited parts of the production processes while other parts, and quantitatively greater ones, are structured by non-capitalist modes of production. On this point, Amin's conception is more in line with Baran's mode of reasoning and, hence, in opposition to Frank's definition of capitalism in terms of exchange relations. Amin endorsed the thesis that capitalism dominates the periphery within the sphere of circulation, but he asserted at the same time that pre-capitalist modes of production continue to exist and that they exert considerable influence on the total structure of reproduction.

The distorted production structure in the peripheral countries and their dependence is a result of the dominance of the centre countries. It is the centre countries who, by extracting resources and exploiting cheap labour, have inflicted on the peripheral economies the 'over-developed' export sector. At the same time, the centre countries have prevented the establishment of national capital goods industries and the manufacturing of goods for mass consumption. In these areas the rich countries continue to have a vital interest in selling their goods in the peripheral markets.

If the less developed countries operating under these circumstances are to initiate a development process that can lead them in the direction of an autocentric economy – if they are to achieve growth with at least a minimum of equity in social and spatial terms – then they must break their asymmetrical relationship with the centre countries. In its place they must expand regional co-operation and internally pursue a socialist development strategy.

Amin's basic notion of the differences between the pure autocentric economy and the likewise stylised peripheral economy was taken over by many dependency theorists, but often with the addition of new dimensions and more nuances. Before considering these elaborations we shall briefly overview Emmanuel's – and Geoffrey Kay's – special contributions to the dependency debate.

Theories of unequal exchange: Emmanuel and Kay

Arghiri Emmanuel's theory of unequal exchange, dating from the late 1960s, was in certain respects an extension of Prebisch's and Singer's analyses of the deteriorating terms of trade for the less developed countries, although Emmanuel himself claimed that his mode of reasoning was different (Emmanuel, 1972). Emmanuel tried to explain the deteriorating terms of trade with reference to Karl Marx's labour theory of value. This made his theory somewhat complicated and difficult to review in a few words. The aim here is therefore just to highlight a few main points.

According to Emmanuel, the industrialised countries could buy goods from the peripheral countries at prices below the costs involved in producing the same goods in the industrialised countries – due to the very low wages in the peripheral countries. Emmanuel argued that wages were so low that the workers there were paid the equivalent of only a tiny fraction of the value of the work they performed and the goods they produced. This fraction was considerably smaller than that paid to workers within the same branches of industry in the centre countries. In this sense, a kind of over-exploitation prevailed in the poor and dependent countries. This over-exploitation, according to Emmanuel, was a more important mechanism of surplus extraction than monopoly control over trade (as suggested by Frank). It resulted in a significant transfer of value to the industrialised countries. This transfer of value was at the same time the main explanation of the perpetuation of underdevelopment.

Emmanuel's original theory has since been strongly criticised and reworked in several versions. Doubt has been raised about the theory's general validity. On the other hand, his theory of unequal exchange has sown more seeds of doubt about the blessings of international trade for the underdeveloped countries, thus reinforcing the criticism put forward by the structuralist economists and others. The theory has pointed out some further weaknesses embodied in the neo-classical theory of comparative advantages and its basic thesis that trade under all circumstances will be advantageous for all parties involved.

It may be added here that in the mid-1970s an attempt was made to incorporate a special version of the theory of unequal exchange into *Geoffrey Kay*'s analyses of the causes of underdevelopment (Kay, 1975). Kay argued that unequal exchange was the preferred mechanism for extracting economic surplus of a particular social class, which he termed the *pre-capitalist commercial bourgeoisie*. This bourgeoisie, which also existed in Europe prior to the Industrial Revolution, did not acquire its revenue (as did the industrial and capitalist commercial bourgeoisies) by appropriating the surplus value produced by labour, but on the contrary by exploiting the distortion of prices – a distortion that enabled this class of merchants to buy goods at costs below their real value and sell them at prices above their real value. This was possible because of an exceptional position in the buyers' market, for example as a monopsonist, and a corresponding exceptional position in the sellers' market, for example as a monopolist. The British East India Company and other similar transnational trading companies which operated during the colonial period could be seen as organised representatives of this particular pre-capitalist commercial bourgeoisie.

The emphasis on market position distinguished Kay's theory from Emmanuel's. In certain respects, it resembled instead the mode of reasoning proposed by Frank. The most interesting aspect of Kay's approach, however, is that he took a first decisive step towards a systematic differentiation and, hence, a limitation of the validity of the theory of unequal exchange. It thus followed from his considerations that the establishment of industrial capitalism in the peripheral countries would pave the way for the growth of a 'normal' capitalist commercial bourgeoisie which would not be dependent on price distortions, but would receive its revenue from the surplus value produced by labour in the production processes. As a result, unequal exchange would no longer be necessary.

More specifically, this implied that peripheral societies which experienced considerable industrial development – such as South Korea and Taiwan, but also India, Brazil and Mexico – at the same time would experience a reduction of the value transfers through unequal exchange. Conversely, countries like the small African ones, with very limited industrial production, would continue to be subject to the special mechanisms of surplus extraction referred to as unequal exchange.

Dependent development: Cardoso, Senghass and Menzel

The dependency theories reviewed above had, for some time, had such a great impact in the international development debate that a dichotomy evolved – with these theories on the one hand, and the previously introduced growth and modernisation theories on the other (see Chapter 5). During the 1970s, however, it became clear to most development researchers that none of these schools, in their original forms, was entirely capable of interpreting and explaining the causes and dynamics of development or underdevelopment. As a response, a new series of theoretical contributions appeared. We have dealt with some of them as regards the economic modernisation theories; below we shall look at selected theories that emerged within the Neo-Marxist tradition. But before that it may be useful briefly to refer to the empirical background to the criticisms raised against the original mainstream theories within both traditions.

First, it should be mentioned that the cumulated knowledge about the economic situation in the less developed countries had uncovered such a complex and multifaceted picture that it had become increasingly difficult to use the somewhat simplified conceptual frameworks and analytical models. In particular, it had proved impossible to conceive of the Third World as a large group of countries with uniform economic structures, development conditions and potentials. This applied whether these countries were described as underdeveloped, as dual economies, as satellites, or as peripheral societies.

Next, it should be stressed that actual changes in the less developed countries in general implied greater and greater *differentiation* – accentuation of existing, and emergence of new, differences between the developing countries. To illustrate, they reacted and had to react in very dissimilar ways to the so-called oil crises of 1973 and 1979, just as they reacted very differently to the continued stagnation in the world economy at the beginning of the 1980s. Because of this process of differentiation, it became increasingly inadequate to treat the Third World as a homogeneous group of countries.

One of the few common traits that persisted was that economic progress almost everywhere remained limited to small geographic enclaves, to certain narrowly limited sectors, and to small prosperous social groups. The phenomenon has been characterised as 'Singaporisation' – after the city-state of Singapore, which, although surrounded by backward and poor areas, experienced unusual economic progress as early as the 1960s and 1970s. However, even a common feature like 'Singaporisation' created problems for the classical theories, because it signified general tendencies very different from those envisaged in the theories. 'Singaporisation' corresponded poorly with the expectations of the modernisation theories. It was contrary to these theories that development and modernisation could be encapsulated and distorted to such a degree. Neither did this fit with the experiences garnered from the industrialised countries.

At the same time, the classical dependency theories were unable to explain the extensive industrial development which in fact occurred in many Third World countries. They faced particular problems when trying to understand and explain why, in countries like South Korea and Taiwan, even relatively close links had been forged between agriculture and industry, and between the various industrial sectors. This was in direct contradiction to the main thesis on the obstructing and blocking impact of close association with the world market and the rich countries: South Korea and Taiwan were among those countries most closely linked to the global capitalist structures and the centres of accumulation in the highly industrialised countries.

These and many other factors prompted many development researchers and people who were actively engaged in development work to start looking seriously for other theories and strategies. The relatively closed theories, which at the same time treated the developing countries as a homogeneous group, had had their day.

In their place appeared a number of more open theories which also, in a systematic manner, took into account the differences between the many countries of the Third World. Many of these theories focused on specific aspects of reality, special development problems, and selected factors. One example could be propositions regarding the role of transnational companies in Latin American countries; another could be natural resource management in Western Africa and its impact upon economic performance.

The new wave of theories appeared partly as a criticism of the classical dependency theories; others took their point of departure in the modernisation theories, but elaborated these considerably further. Several of the new theories had little or no intellectual relationship or affinity with either of these two earlier schools of thought.

The Brazilian social scientist, F. H. Cardoso, was one of those who took his starting point in the original Latin American dependency theories (Cardoso, 1974; Cardoso and Faletto, 1979). However, he rejected the notion that peripheral countries could be treated as one group of dependent economies. In addition, he rebutted the idea that the world market and other external factors should be seen as more important than intra-societal conditions and forces, as some of these theories had asserted. Cardoso claimed instead that the external factors would have very different impacts, depending on the dissimilar internal conditions.

So decisive were the internal conditions, according to Cardoso, that he would not rule out the possibility of extensive capitalist development in some dependent economies. Indeed he did observe, in his own thorough analyses of Brazil, that significant capitalist growth had occurred, though without creating autocentric reproduction and followed by marginalisation of large segments of the population. When Cardoso referred to internal conditions, attention was drawn not only to economic structures but also to the social classes, the distribution of power in the society, and the role of the state. His analyses thus reflected systematic attempts at combining economics and political science.

In contrast to Frank, Cardoso regarded the national bourgeoisies of the dependent societies as potentially powerful and capable of shaping development. These classes could be so weak that they functioned merely as an extended arm of imperialism. But the national business community and its leaders could, under other circumstances – as in the case of Brazil – act so autonomously and effectively that national, long-term interests were taken into account and embodied in the strategies pursued by the state.

The kind of development and societal transformation that could be brought about in even the most successful peripheral societies did not correspond to the development pattern in the centre countries. The result was not autocentric reproduction, but rather *development in dependency* (as opposed to Frank's development of dependency). Or as Cardoso himself characterised it: dependent, associated development – that is development dependent on, and linked to, the world market and the centre economies.

In the further characterisation of dependent development, Cardoso used to a large extent concepts and formulations that resembled those of Amin. He thus emphasised the unbalanced and distorted production structure with its greatly over-enlarged sector manufacturing luxury goods exclusively for the benefit of the bourgeoisie and the middle class. Moreover he highlighted the absence of a sector that produced capital goods and the resulting dependency on machinery and equipment imports from the centre countries. But in contrast to Amin, Cardoso was very careful about generalising. He would rather talk specifically about Brazil than about the peripheral countries in general.

In a similar way, Cardoso was reluctant to recommend general strategies for a large number of dependent countries. Regarding Brazil, he pointed to a democratic form of regime as the most important precondition for turning societal development in a direction which would benefit the great majority of the people. Socialism was not on the agenda, and introducing it was in any case not as unproblematic as claimed by Frank and Amin.

Parallel to Cardoso's efforts to adjust the classical dependency theories to the more complex reality of Brazil, a number of German development researchers, under the leadership of *Dieter Senghaas* and *Ulrich Menzel*, carried out a series of extensive historical studies of both centre and peripheral societies. The result was a systematic and elaborate differentiation within both categories of countries (Senghass, 1985; Mjøset, 1993). Their point was that when the centre countries were subjected to closer investigation, it turned out that they too, like the peripheral societies, revealed very different individualised structures and patterns of transformation. There were great differences, for instance, between the Nordic countries and France or Germany.

Based on their historical studies Senghass and Menzel arrived at a dissolution of the dichotomy between centre and periphery. In its place they put a number of patterns of integration into the world economy and the resulting development trajectories. In addition, they reached the conclusion that the international conditions by themselves could not explain why a given society managed, or did not manage, to break out of the dependency trap. Far more important were the internal socio-economic conditions and political institutions in determining whether the economy in a given country could be transformed from a dependent export economy to an autocentric, nationally integrated economy.

From a number of country studies Senghass and Menzel extracted a list of conditions which, in Europe at least, could explain the occurrence of autocentric development (Mjøset, 1993). The important socio-economic variables included a relatively egalitarian distribution of land and incomes; a high level of literacy; and economic policies and institutions that supported industrialisation and industrial interests. The political variables included extensive mobilisation of farmers and workers; effective democratisation to weaken the old elites; and partnership between the bureaucracy, industrial interests and the new social movements.

Senghass and Menzel, when they initiated their ambitious research programme, essentially wanted to find out how much could be learned from the over a century and a half of European experiences that would be of relevance to understanding the basic preconditions for the transformation of dependent, peripheral economies into autocentric economies. There is little doubt that they have produced highly adequate documentation concerning the intrasocietal conditions, but there is also little doubt that their approach can be further enriched by more systematically taking into consideration the basic changes in the world capitalist system which have impacted heavily upon contemporary centre–periphery relationships.

The capitalist world system: Wallerstein

The discussions within the Neo-Marxist research tradition have, since the 1950s, centred around the causes of underdevelopment in the Third World. Some of the theorists have identified these causes primarily within the framework of the individual society, while others have emphasised the external links and dependency relationships. In connection with this problematique, researchers have taken different positions regarding the character and role of capitalism. According to one school of thought, decades ago, capitalism had already penetrated both the world economy and individual peripheral economies to such an extent that this provided a solid basis for understanding the whole problem of underdevelopment. According to another school of thought, the capitalist mode of production has only permeated the centre economies and their international relations with the periphery. The peripheral economies, on the other hand, have been characterised by complex articulations of different modes of production thus creating structural heterogeneity, which in itself has hindered national economic integration and development.

Regardless of their position in this debate, the conceptions presented in the previous sections have used as their point of departure individual societal formations and moved up from there to the international system. The character and the mode of functioning of this system have been seen as determined primarily by the centre formations and the interests of their dominant social classes. In opposition to this view, a competing approach instead starts with the capitalist world system itself, and moves down to analyses of the individual societies and their position within the system. This world system approach has been elaborated, first and foremost, by *Immanuel Wallerstein* (Wallerstein, 1974, 1979, 1980), but has to a large extent been taken over by Frank and Amin in their more recent works during the 1980s and the early 1990s.

Wallerstein's theory did not originate from the classical dependency theories. In the present context, though, it may still be appropriate to compare Wallerstein's considerations with the main propositions of these theories, because this will facilitate an identification of some of his core notions and propositions. Wallerstein operated with a significantly longer historical perspective than the mainstream dependency theories. In addition, he studied not only the structures of the world economy, but also the cyclical fluctuations, the economic recessions, depressions, upswings and booms. One of his points in this connection was that major fluctuations have engrafted upon both the world economy and the international political system some specific characteristics that have been crucial for the individual nations' development possibilities in the period concerned.

Wallerstein consistently used as his starting point the basic features of the global system. The analysis of the individual countries came second, because he assumed that their development prospects depended more on the nature of the global system than on their internal structures. The development prospects are further determined by the individual country's position in the international economic and political system. In this context Wallerstein worked out a detailed ranking of the countries as well as a grouping of them into three main categories: centre, semi-peripheral, and peripheral. The individual country can change its position in the global hierarchy both upwards and downwards. But the framework for such shifts is set by the structures and the prevailing conditions in the world system.

Summarised in these few sentences it is hard to get a proper impression of Wallerstein's quite elaborate theory. Therefore, it should be added that his theory, more thoroughly than the classical dependency theories, reflects the very complicated and constantly changing structures in the international economy. It is also to Wallerstein's credit that he has related the economic analysis to investigations of the international political system and the power relations that permeate it.

Wallerstein has been criticised for focusing exclusively on international conditions and their impact upon the individual countries' development prospects. It is correct that his dominant interest lies here, but the world system theory as such does not preclude careful consideration of internal preconditions and prospects for development. Wallerstein's main point here is rather that the further down in the hierarchy a country is, the narrower are the constraints and barriers to its development established by the world system. Thus, to understand stagnation and underdevelopment in the very poor and dependent countries requires particular emphasis on the global framework and conditions.

It is interesting to note that both Frank and Amin have adjusted their original theories by incorporating some of Wallerstein's propositions, but without accepting the world system as the necessary analytical starting point for all periods in the development of capitalism. On the contrary, Amin has argued that the world system approach has only recently become the most feasible analytical framework, the main reason being that now the economies of the centre countries have become significantly more integrated and dependent on the global economic system. Another reason for paying more attention to this system, according to Amin, is the transformation of the previously centrally planned economies and their increased world market integration (Amin, 1992a, 1992b).

In recently published works, Amin has been particularly preoccupied with what he calls the *new capitalist globalisation* (Amin, 1992b: Ch. 2). This process is characterised by a polarisation and regionalisation of the world economy around three poles: the USA, Japan and the European Union. It is further characterised by a continuous strengthening of the semi-peripheral economies such as South Korea and Taiwan – but as parts of regional networks, not as independent units. Parallel to these trends, many peripheral societies have been subjected to a drastic differentiation process involving relative deprivation. This has prompted Amin to talk about a Fourth World with reference to the African countries, which have fallen further behind in relation to most of the Asian and Latin American countries.

According to Amin, capital accumulation in this new global system has in reality broken down in both the periphery and what was previously known as the Second World, and the capitalist system in its present form will not be able to resolve this accumulation crisis. The main reason is not the dominance of the centre countries and their national bourgeoisies, as claimed by the classical dependency theories. The explanation should rather be looked for in the international financial system and the 'wild orgy of financial speculation', which has undermined the foundations of national production- and growth-oriented policies and strategies – even in relatively strong, centre countries. Amin has sought to capture these prevailing conditions in the title of his latest book, *Empire of Chaos* (1992b).

While Amin may have identified unprecedented new features in the world system, it should also be noted that he has not yet substantiated his recent propositions with empirical studies of the same quality as those he carried out in support of his original dependency theory.

Elimination of dependency: Warren

So far in this chapter we have discussed development researchers whose prime aim has been to adjust, elaborate or supplement the classical depend- ency theories. Other researchers within the Neo-Marxist tradition, however, have rejected the whole body of dependency theories and attempted to replace them with totally different approaches. This applies to, among others, the American social scientist *Bill Warren* (Warren, 1973, 1980).

Warren's main point was: certainly imperialism has led to the creation of a system characterised by inequality and exploitation, but at the same time this imperialism has created the conditions for the spreading of capitalism to the Third World. And not only that. Warren went further by claiming that he was able to prove that capitalism, since the Second World War, had actually developed both in depth and width in the Third World. Although the capitalist mode of production was originally grafted on to the peripheral economies from outside, by the industrialised countries, Warren argued that in the long run it would lead to *elimination of dependency* – or to a development out of dependency. Imperialism has, in other words, laid the foundations of its own dissolution.

Warren saw the situation in the 1960s and 1970s as especially conducive to national capitalist development in the Third World. He referred in this connection to the conflict between East and West, which he believed the dependent countries in general could derive considerable benefits from. He also pointed to the competition between the different industrialised countries, and between the many transnational corporations, and argued that these forms of competition could also be exploited with a view to promoting more independent national development. The difficulties were chiefly the internal conditions in these countries, including a very widespread tendency to pursue totally misconceived agricultural policies, which neither brought about the necessary land reforms nor linked the rural economies to the dynamic capitalist urban economies.

Warren's theory is essentially the classical dependency theory turned on its head. To him imperialism and the world market were in no way obstacles to economic growth and progress, understood as capitalist development. On the contrary, it was from these global systems that the whole process of development would be set in motion. The fact that the result would be capitalism – with its inequality, exploitation, and limited social progress reserved for the few – meant less to Warren; in contrast to Soviet Marxism, he regarded the development of capitalism – for good or evil – as an unavoidable necessity, as a stage all underdeveloped countries had to go through to reach socialism.

Warren must be credited for drawing attention, at an early stage, to the actual growth of industry and other capitalist sectors in the Third World within the framework of Marxist theory. But he did it with such eagerness and intensity that his theory became one-sided and biased, and therefore makes itself most useful as a closing marginal note to the main body of Marxist theory regarding underdevelopment and dependency. On the other hand there is, within this tradition, a pressing need for a better theory which can explain both underdevelopment and development. Attempts to achieve this will be reviewed in the following chapter.

CHAPTER 8

Modes of Production and Social Classes

The Neo-Marxist dependency theories were to some extent formed with reference to Paul Baran's analysis of the causes of underdevelopment, but they shifted the emphasis to aspects and factors which Baran had perceived as being secondary, namely international and external relations. During the 1970s and 1980s a number of other Marxist-inspired theories appeared which, like Baran, underlined the internal modes of production and social classes. They did not disregard the global setting and the relationships of dependence, but merely assigned analytical priority to internal conditions and left it open to empirical investigations to determine the balance between internal and external determinants.

In this chapter, we shall look at some of the contributions within this school of thought, not so much by examining the propositions of individual theories, but rather by providing a thematic description of common concepts and hypotheses. The first section presents a stylised and simplified model of the basic economic structures in a peripheral society. The succeeding section reviews some of the reasons suggested in the literature for assigning a special analytical priority to social classes. The third section gives an overview of how social classes may be related to their economic-structural basis within different modes of production. The fourth section goes more specifically into an analysis of the main industrial sectors under capitalism, and proposes in this connection a categorisation of the peripheral countries on the basis of their industrial and accumulation structure. The presentation in this section may be seen as an attempt to sum up some of the propositions contained both in economic structuralism and Neo-Marxist dependency theories. Throughout this chapter, I present some of my own ideas along with interpretations of existing conceptual frameworks and theories.

The peripheral economy: a simplified model

It is a common feature of many of the previously discussed economic development theories that they assume or postulate some form of *structural heterogeneity* in the less developed countries, in the sense that different production systems or modes of production co-exist. In addition, the Neo-

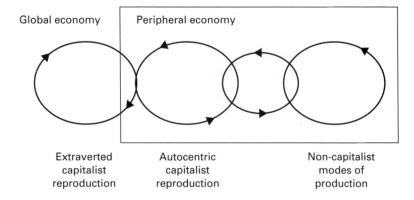

Global economy | Peripheral economy

Extraverted	Autocentric	Non-capitalist
capitalist	capitalist	modes of
reproduction	reproduction	production

Linkages between capitalist
and non-capitalist processes

Figure 8.1 A simplified model of the reproduction processes
in a peripheral economy

Marxist analyses, in particular, argue that the dynamics of underdevelopment
and development are to a large extent determined by external relations.
Production and reproduction processes are, so to speak, *extraverted*. Both
these fundamental notions have been taken over and further elaborated by
the theorists dealt with in this chapter. The two notions may be illustrated
as in Figure 8.1, where the term 'reproduction' refers to the whole and
repeated processes of producing and exchanging goods.

The reasoning behind the model is that the economic processes in a
peripheral economy can be divided into two main categories: the capitalist
and the non-capitalist. There may be several types of non-capitalist processes,
but for the sake of clarity the figure includes only one cycle. The capitalist
processes are further presumed to comprise sub-categories defined by the
nature of the dominant form of capital accumulation, where the most
important distinction is between extraverted and intraverted (or autocentric)
accumulation processes. In addition to the types of reproduction processes
mentioned so far, Figure 8.1 refers to linkages between capitalist and non-
capitalist processes. These linkages may primarily join the non-capitalist types
of production to either externally oriented capital accumulation or autocentric
capitalist processes.

The model cannot, in this very simplified form, be utilised as a conceptual
framework for empirical analyses. It will, for example, often be difficult to
relate specific manufacturing enterprises and their activities unequivocally to
either extraverted or intraverted accumulation. This will require operationalisation of the abstract concepts and elaboration of a set of indicators, which
is far beyond the scope of the present review. The intention here is only to

illustrate with the model how one may proceed with the whole analysis of structural change in peripheral economies from the perspective adopted in the present chapter.

The outlined typology provides, in this context, a framework for distinguishing between three major types of change:

1. Changes in the direction of a higher, or lower, degree of autocentric capitalist production and reproduction.
2. Changes in the interrelationship between capitalist and non-capitalist economic processes implying either a relative expansion of capitalism or a relative expansion of non-capitalist modes of production.
3. Changes in the structuring of the non-capitalist processes, including those such as the introduction of capitalist exchange relations and production relations in certain agricultural sectors or particular rural areas.

To this framework could be added a fourth type of change concerning specific features of the capitalist mode of production, for example the distribution of ownership and control between the state and the private sector, or the degree of monopolisation or oligopolisation in the latter.

This analytical division of change types may further be related to an analysis of social classes, because the extent to which their basic interests are realised fundamentally depends on how the production processes are structured. Changes towards a higher degree of autocentric capital accumulation will thus correspond to the basic interests of the concerned peripheral, national bourgeoisie. Such changes would at the same time go against the interests of foreign bourgeoisies engaged in externally oriented capitalist activities (cf. below). Changes in the interrelations between capitalist and non-capitalist reproduction processes will similarly affect the relative positions of the foreign and national bourgeoisies, on the one hand, and the land-owning classes, on the other.

Again, concrete historical analyses will require extensive elaboration and operationalisation of these abstract propositions (cf. Martinussen, 1980: vols II and III). And again, this is not our concern here. Rather, we shall attempt to outline how, at the same high level of abstraction, the major social classes can be defined in relation to the various modes of production. But prior to that it is necessary to discuss briefly why it may be fruitful to focus on social classes when studying societal change.

Social classes as agents of change

Social classes, in Neo-Marxist analyses, are not actors or agents in the same sense as individuals or organisations, they do not mean to do anything like human actors do. Neither does the class position of individuals determine the behaviour of these individuals; that may be the case for some people, but it is definitely not the case as a general rule. However, social classes may still be appropriate reference points for an analysis of political actions and policies. Objectives and interests can be ascribed to social classes – and actions can be interpreted in relation to class objectives and interests. Outcomes can be analysed in class terms as promoting particular class interests and opposing others, as briefly indicated above. Actions are then given significance in class terms. But – as the Indian scholar *Sudipta Kaviraj* has aptly put it – 'it is men (or women!) who act, and who must act before classes and other abstractions can act through them' (Kaviraj, 1989: p. 168).

The main reason, then, for assigning particular importance to social classes – as compared with other social forces – is that the objectives and interests ascribed to them in Neo-Marxist analyses have to do with their unique bases in the economic structures. Actions promoting the interests of a national bourgeoisie, for instance, at the same time promote particular forms of economic structures, particular modes of production and social relations. Compared to this, the 'interests' of, say, a civil bureaucracy are at a lower level. They may be just as important at a particular conjuncture, in a particular situation. But realising or not realising the 'interests' of a civil bureaucracy will give little or no indication about societal changes at the structural level of aggregation. That is why social classes can be used as mediating concepts linking agency and structures (Burris, 1987).

Further, adherents of Neo-Marxist class analyses believe that social classes reflect and affect patterns of action in the long run: both positively, in the sense that the power of social classes in conjunction with the structural limitations allow certain outcomes and impacts to occur, while others are impeded or prevented; and negatively, in the sense that the absence of powerful and politically organised class representatives may prevent robust patterns from emerging. On this latter point it may be argued that the near absence or extreme weakness of national bourgeoisies in most African countries can be used partly to explain why no coherence has been brought about in state interventions and allocation of resources (cf. Chapter 17). Similarly, the weak position of national bourgeoisies in many Third World societies may be used as a partial explanation of the persistence of non-democratic forms of regime (cf. Chapter 14).

Having noted these reasons for focusing on social classes, it should be added that specific patterns of change in a short-term perspective, and at lower levels of abstraction, cannot be explained with exclusive reference to the interests and relative power positions of classes, as is sometimes claimed by Neo-Marxists. Rather, class analyses should be seen as only an abstract framework, within which there is a need to complement the approach with analyses of human behaviour and its motivation – analyses of what people do and why they do so in terms of the subjective meaning they attach to their actions. Or as *William Liddle* has proposed: social classes and other social forces should be viewed as constraints and opportunities to be weighed by decision makers faced with a problem, rather than as determinants that overwhelm and deny the individuals' capacity for autonomous choice (Liddle, 1992). This is how Post-Marxist, but Marxian, theorists tend to look upon the role of social classes (Martinussen, 1994).

Modes of production and social classes

In the peripheral societies of the real world the various modes of production do not exist as separate entities. Rather, they are interwoven and affect each other to such an extent that numerous economic structures and organisational forms have emerged. Nevertheless, it may be useful to abstract from this multiplicity in order to lay bare some fundamental underlying patterns which one can subsequently use to describe the real economic conditions and their changes over time. We shall do this by focusing on three abstract modes of production: petty commodity production and subsistence agriculture; feudalism; and capitalism.

In its pure form, *petty commodity production* in agriculture is a closed system. The individual peasant household manages the tilling of the land on its own. Both the tools and the land belong to the household. In this way the household is its own employer, though often a simple hierarchy is established with the male head of the family deciding about the utilisation of the other household members' labour. Sometimes there is direct exploitation of women and children, as when the overwhelming share of practical labour is imposed on them while the master of the house and possibly other adult men in the household mostly supervise the work. In any case, any exploitation that occurs remains within the household unit. In pure *subsistence farming*, as this form of production is often labelled, no use is made of outside labour.

To be as self-sufficient as possible every peasant household must grow many different crops and often keep livestock. To a large extent the household also takes care of the manufacture of agricultural tools, clothing and domestic utensils. However, as a rule, a portion of these activities is left to artisans in the village. A number of service functions are, in a similar way, left to specialised groups. The relationship between the land users and these artisans and service providers is generally organised through verbal contract; mostly, payment is in kind, rather than in money.

In its pure form, this type of petty commodity production is no longer found to any great extent in any of the less developed countries. It is unusual to find peasant households who work exclusively for themselves on their own land and never either hire others' labour or work for others. However, for many millions of families in Asia and Africa their situation resembles the one described above in the sense that they *mostly* work for themselves on their own piece of land. As a consequence, they are placed in a special, marginal position – with associated special interests – in relation to the whole process of economic development.

Petty commodity production is not only found in agriculture, but also in urban areas, albeit in a different form. Here, this mode of production is more closely connected to a market and is often integrated into the capitalist production system. Urban small-scale production consists primarily of small family-run craft and repair businesses. A number of them produce or repair finished goods for immediate sale, while others produce inputs for large capitalist enterprises.

The second mode of production, pure *feudalism*, contains two, often interwoven systems. In one – the villeinage and farm labourer system – the producers work for the feudal landowner on his land. The produce goes directly to the landowner. The villeiners often also have a piece of land which forms the foundation for the family's upkeep. Many farm labourers, on the other hand, are totally in the feudal landlord's pay in the sense that they have to work for him in exchange for payment in kind for the family's upkeep.

Under the second system – the sharecropping system – the peasant family work with their own tools on land which they, for a shorter or longer period of time, are given the right to till by the feudal landlord. In return, the peasants must give up a part of the yield to the landlord. The land rent is paid in kind under pure feudalism, but historically there has been an increasing tendency to demand it paid in money. Thus, the sharecroppers have been forced to sell an equivalent portion of their yield to get the money for payment. If this could not be done, or if the harvest failed, they were forced to take a loan from the landlord or from a professional moneylender in the village.

The main classes that can be identified under feudalism are the agricultural labourers, the sharecroppers and the feudal landlords. In addition, a separate class of professional moneylenders might be identifiable. In comparison with the situation under petty commodity production, the feudal mode of production provides the basis for a plurality of classes with differentiated roles in the production process. There is also economic exploitation and genuine class conflict.

Although at an abstract level one may identify these various main classes under feudalism, it is often difficult to distinguish them in reality – even in South Asia where features of feudalism have been predominant over a long period of time. This is due to the fact that feudalism has always co-existed with petty commodity production and, for some time, with capitalism. As a result, various combinations have occurred. For example, many peasant families both own a piece of land themselves and at the same time lease another piece; and the landowners, besides leasing out land, also employ wage labour on some of their property.

Before passing on to a summary description of the main capitalist classes, we should mention another method of determining the classes both in agriculture and in industry. This method was originally inspired by Maoist analysis in China, but is presented here in the form given to it by *John Roemer*.

	Owns land/ capital	Hire labour	Work for others
Landlords/pure rentiers	+	−	−
Rich peasants/entrepreneurs	+	+	−
Middle peasants/small capitalists	+	+	+
Poor peasants/petty bourgeoisie	+	−	+
Agricultural labourers/workers	−	−	+

Figure 8.2 Roemer's matrix of economic classes

In a way it is inappropriate to include Roemer in the present chapter, because he applies methodological individualism and not a structuralist approach, as mainstream Neo-Marxists do. But the way he does it, however, appears to be compatible with the mode of reasoning suggested in the present context. This is mainly because Roemer does introduce structures into his analysis, not as pre-given, as in Neo-Marxist theory, but as created through processes of individual choice and action.

Roemer has worked out a complex theory, formulated in mathematical terms, on exploitation and classes (Roemer, 1982; 1988). It is not this comprehensive theory that is examined here, just the fundamental idea behind the categorisation of the economic agents into various classes. Roemer's *'class exploitation correspondence principle'*, as he terms it, is similar to the principle used above in the characterisation of petty commodity production but now extended to other social classes. The focus is on the degree to which the agents own land or capital and on the degree to which they hire labour and work for others.

Roemer's model can be summarised as shown in Figure 8.2. From this is seen that the method identifies a total of five classes in agriculture as well as in industry. Each of these classes has particular interests that are determined by their economic position. Workers, for instance, have interests in maintaining jobs and achieving the highest wages possible, while those exploiting them have opposite interests.

Figure 8.2 illustrates one method of class identification of relevance also to capitalist modes of production. Another way of identifying classes under capitalism uses as its starting point a structural model of pure *capitalist production*.

In the first stage of a capitalist reproduction process, the capitalist purchases the inputs required for the production process: labour, raw materials, means of production, fuels, intermediate goods, etc. In the second stage, the production process, goods are produced. In the third stage, these goods are sold by the capitalist, who earns a profit because the goods produced under capitalism are worth more than all the inputs that are used in producing them, including labour. The difference – the so-called surplus value – is, according to Marxist theory, due to the fact that the workers add more value to the products than they are paid for. This exploitation takes place as a hidden part of the production process itself and not, as under feudalism, as open extraction of economic surplus. Under capitalism, the finished products are the property of the capitalist, who is free to dispose of them. The exploitation embodied in the work process is the basis for conflicts of interest between capitalism's two main classes, the working class and the capitalist class.

As with other modes of production, in reality the relationships are much more complicated than this very simple model indicates. In the case of capitalism, moreover, the division of labour is so advanced that even the abstract model ought to include several sub-categories for each of the main classes. Concerning capitalism in a peripheral society, a particularly important subdivision is the distinction between a national bourgeoisie and a number of foreign bourgeoisies with economic bases primarily in the highly developed centre formations.

Industrial structure and foreign trade

The previous overview of modes of production and social classes in a stylised peripheral society can be used as a conceptual framework for empirical studies. But it will probably be useful to add to this framework some supplementary concepts that refer to specific features of the industrial structure, because this structure embodies most of the potential dynamism. On this issue, economic development theories generally agree. A central proposition in the following, however, is that the industrial sector does not under all circumstances contain a strong and significant development dynamism. This depends, among other things, on the specific composition of industrial sectors, their interlinkages and the basic patterns of foreign trade.

With reference to a simple two-sector model of the capitalist production and circulation processes in an open society, it is possible to outline the major phases in a possible, but not necessary – or irreversible – economic transformation process in a peripheral country. The model is presented in Figure 8.3. The mode of reasoning behind this model may be summed up as follows. The two major industrial sectors, the capital goods sector and the consumer goods sector, have dissimilar strategic importance for reproduction and development. In general, sector I is of considerably greater importance than sector II, and within sector I, the industries producing means of production, etc. for other sector I industries will usually be of greater importance than those providing machinery, etc. for consumer goods industries. This does not imply that a society with a one-sided reliance on sector I industries will necessarily achieve a higher degree of autocentric

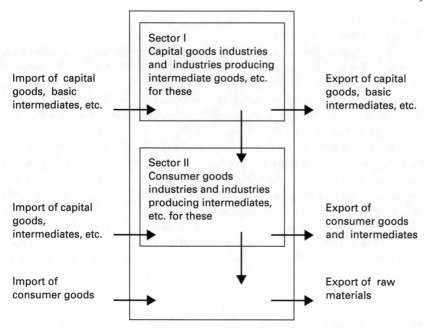

Figure 8.3 A simplified two-sector model of industrial structure and patterns of foreign trade

reproduction, but normally the presence of relatively extensive capital goods industries and other sector I industries will indicate a higher degree of industrial development.

To this, however, must be added one crucial modification: it is of central importance whether existing industries are foreign controlled. To the extent that this is the case, it implies an external orientation of the accumulation processes. In other words, the most essential criteria are not the purely physical aspects of industrial growth, but rather the social aspects and the dynamic they add to investment and other activity patterns. It is a question of the extent to which, and the sectors in which, the domestically controlled industry is developed.

In addition to references to production structures, the model further contains references to associated trade relations with the outside world. The interpretation as regards the import side is that the three main groups of goods noted in Figure 8.3 are assumed to be of unequal strategic significance for reproduction and accumulation. Raw materials have least significance, while the goods for use in sector I are the most important. Furthermore, it is assumed that capital goods for manufacturing of other capital goods are of the greatest importance in the above sense. Consequently, it follows that the degree of dependence of a particular peripheral economy, *ceteris paribus*, will be higher the greater the import share of goods with the greatest strategic importance for reproduction.

In principle, a similar interpretation may be applied to the export side, with the qualification that here the degree of specialisation in the composition of export products – and the degree of concentration with respect to countries of destination – will often play important roles. The more diversified the export – and the larger the number of countries of destination – the better off is the country concerned.

It is evident that all the relationships mentioned will, in practice, be much more complex. Conditions of particular importance include the terms of trade and the rate of substitution for the specific products. But for the present, the model may be used for a general outline of three major levels in a peripheral society's possible industrial development towards a continuously higher degree of autocentric capital accumulation. The same levels can be used for a characterisation of the basic differences between contemporary peripheral countries. For easy reference we may refer to these levels of industrial development as P_1, P_2 and P_3, where P is peripheral societies and the numbers refer to the various levels.

At the first level, P_1, hardly any form of capitalist manufacturing has been established, though there may be extensive petty commodity production. Exports consist almost exclusively of unprocessed raw materials, including agricultural goods. Essentially all industrially produced consumer goods have to be imported.

The situation corresponds to the picture of the less developed countries contained in the theories about the classical international distribution of labour (cf. Chapter 9). It also resembles the descriptions in the early dependency theories, in the sense that it is a backward economy which is totally dominated by foreign interests (cf. Chapter 7). But it should be pointed out that the dominance does not apply to a majority of the direct producers. On the contrary, most of the peasants and petty commodity producers will be very little affected by foreign interests. The decisive feature is that foreign dominance prevails within the dynamic and potentially expanding sectors, and within foreign trade. Mining and plantations are the economic sectors which typically are under foreign control in P_1 societies.

It should be noted that the economic situation outlined has decisive consequences for the state and its mode of functioning. Whether colonial or post-colonial, the P_1 state will be prevented from playing any independent or initiating role in the development processes. According to the class and state theories, this state is likely to be under such strong influence from foreign interests that it can hardly promote any national development that conflicts with these interests. Normally, there will be no intra-societal forces sufficiently powerful to compel the state to support autocentric development (cf. Chapter 17).

The conditions outlined prevail in a large number of less developed countries, especially in Sub-Saharan Africa. But it should be added that the basic limitation of the state's room for manoeuvre often manifests itself in a different form than described. After independence, new political rulers in many of the least industrialised countries have refused to continue close co-operation with the former colonial powers. In some of these cases the influence of foreign interests has in fact been reduced, but this has rarely resulted in economic growth. According to the theories, it is therefore not decisive whether the countries at the lowest level of industrial development can reduce the dependency on international capital *per se*, but whether they can do so in such way that they can, simultaneously, initiate a transformation towards a higher degree of autocentric development. It is exactly in this respect the P1 societies have revealed their great weaknesses and lack of capacity (Olsen, 1994).

Coming now to the second level of industrial development, P2, we move up to the middle in Figure 8.3. At this level, consumer goods industries are established, both foreign controlled and indigenous. A measure of import substitution has taken place as regards consumer goods and non-basic inter-mediates. Some of the goods manufactured may be exported, but typically the emphasis is on producing products that replace imports. Whatever the case, the composition of imports is changed at this level, chiefly due to the increasing need for means of production in the expanding consumer goods industries. Export of raw materials is gradually replaced by export of inter-mediate goods and finished goods from sector II. There is no domestic pro-duction of capital goods or basic intermediates (like steel or basic chemicals).

Class relations are changed in line with the expansion of sector II in-dustries. In many cases the process is started by foreign firms, which has prompted several dependency theorists to claim that the establishment of industrial enterprises in itself does not indicate any important change. The experience is, however, that in this way the foundations for more extensive processes of industrial transformation have been laid. Thus the new industrial-ists, even though of foreign origin, acquire an interest in the expansion of various supporting activities and functions such as a modern banking system, material infrastructure, a communication system and so on. As a result, better conditions are created that benefit the establishment of industry and com-merce under national control.

Therefore, a phase with industrial development under foreign control is often followed by a phase where more and more nationally controlled manufacturing enterprises are built. Hence a national bourgeoisie is gradually created, along with a working class. These classes have a common interest in broad-based industrial development and will thus put pressure on the state to take a more active role than in P1 societies. The state in P2 societies, at the same time, is in a better position to intervene in the economic processes, partly because it has a stronger resource base. It can more easily tax national enterprises than international capital.

This does not mean that states in P2 societies automatically achieve more control over the development process. On the contrary, the whole process of change will often be marked by conflicts and setbacks. International capital will still dominate within several sectors and, through that control, be capable of slowing progress towards a higher degree of self-centredness in capital accumulation. Simultaneously, serious economic problems will often impede industrial growth in the short term. For instance, declining prices in important export goods, in combination with the need to import expensive machinery, can lead to setbacks. But compared to the situation at the first level, it is nevertheless true that the state generally has considerably wider scope for manoeuvre and greater opportunities to influence the direction of development.

A large number of the Latin American and Asian countries have achieved a degree of industrialisation and development in the class structure which corresponds to the second level. The same probably applies to a few African countries such as Zimbabwe.

Some of the developing countries have reached a level further. This is especially true of South Korea, Taiwan, Brazil, Mexico, Chile and India. These P3 countries are characterised by a more coherent and balanced industrial structure with forward and backward linkages. In addition to sector II industries, these countries have some capital goods industries and industries manufacturing basic intermediate goods for the consumer goods industries. To a certain extent, they even have industries which produce machinery, etc., for sector I. But typically, import substitution is confined to machinery, technology, and basic products used in sector II. Consequently, the countries concerned are still dependent on imports from the industrialised countries of more sophisticated machinery and technology. However, they may be in a better position to finance the necessary imports, because they export considerable amounts of industrial products. Export of consumer goods as well as basic intermediate goods, and possibly means of production, is growing.

By the early 1990s, South Korea and Taiwan probably had achieved an industrial structure which, within the framework of the model presented here, placed them in the same category as several of the centre economies in Europe, while India and the other P3 countries mentioned retained too many features of typical peripheral economies to pass beyond this threshold.

Class relations at the third level of industrial transformation are characterised by a considerably stronger national bourgeoisie which has a decisive impact upon the economic policies of the state. International capital may still play an important role, but foreign interests in general have been rendered secondary to those of the national bourgeoisie. In these circumstances the state, in conjunction with national business associations, can take an active part in the development process and in that way contribute strongly to a reinforcement of autocentric industrial development.

As emphasised earlier, a high degree of self-centredness is not equivalent to self-sufficiency. Even a highly autocentric industrial economy, particularly in small- and medium-sized countries, will have a need for considerable imports and exports. The decisive factor is the extent to which the critical investment and other important decisions are taken in accordance with national priorities – that is with a view to promoting a coherent and balanced national industrial structure – and not, for example, in accordance with a global profit and growth maximisation strategy of transnational corporations (cf. Chapter 9).

After this review of the three levels of industrial development and the basic patterns of foreign trade, it may be questioned whether this simply amounts to another stage theory essentially like the one proposed by Rostow (cf. Chapter 5). The answer, however, is no. There is a similarity in the sense that the theory dealt with here makes reference to levels or stages of industrial development. But, first, the theory does not contain any hypothesis to the effect that all less developed countries, sooner or later, will pass through all three stages and become highly industrialised. In fact, it is hard to imagine how a large number of small and very poor countries will ever be capable of reaching any further than the bottom of the second level. Secondly, the mode of reasoning behind the model explicitly states that the process may be reversed as a result of the continuing conflicts of interest and the economic vulnerability and fragility which characterise the developing countries all the way up to the third level. It is only beyond a certain threshold that serious setbacks and actual underdevelopment in the form of de-industrialisation is no longer likely to occur. Thirdly, the present theory does not assume – as does Rostow's – that industrialisation is also bound to lead to broad-based societal development in other sectors. By pointing to India as a country which has reached the third level, it is underlined that comprehensive industrialisation need not lead to either development of the agricultural sector as a whole or to a solution of the very extensive unemployment and poverty problems.

These remarks illustrate, at the same time, the limitations of the model when it comes to explaining patterns of development and stagnation outside the industrial sectors of a peripheral economy. To this could be added that the present theory, as well as many other versions of class and state theories, is particularly weak when it comes to more thorough analyses of P1 societies. To some extent, this limitation is acknowledged in the conceptual framework itself, in the sense that it makes reference primarily to societies where economically based classes have emerged as powerful social forces with a decisive impact upon societal change. To complement the picture, therefore, we shall later take a closer look at alternative theories regarding the state's role in societies belonging to the P1 category (see especially Chapter 17).

CHAPTER 9

The International Division of Labour and Transnational Corporations

Theories of the internationalisation of capital and the tendencies towards a new international division of labour began to emerge in the early 1970s. Like the world system theories (Chapter 7) and the theories of global interdependence (Chapter 5), this group of theories focused on international relations, but they did so in a different manner. Most important, they brought into the perspective the role of private firms in economic development. This chapter will review some of these contributions and discuss the special role of transnational corporations. A particular section will deal with certain important structural changes in the world economy at the end of the 1980s and in the early 1990s.

The internationalisation of capital

Empirical studies carried out in the 1960s and early 1970s indicated that capital was starting to internationalise in new ways. Until then, the dominant feature had been growing commodity trade and internationalisation primarily of commercial capital. The new feature was that so-called productive capital became increasingly internationalised. The change manifested itself in the transfer of industrial production from the industrialised countries to the developing countries, resulting in a gradual emergence of a *new international division of labour*.

The classical division of labour implied that the developing countries almost exclusively exported raw materials to the industrialised countries. In exchange they received the processed goods which were manufactured in the industrialised countries. The first significant changes in this classical division of labour occurred for some developing countries as early as during the period between the world wars. Especially in the larger Latin American countries and in a few Asian countries, a number of industries were established during this period which supplied the home markets. Thus, the countries concerned reduced their import of industrial goods, but all continued to be dependent on the import of machinery and other capital goods from the industrialised countries.

Though companies from the industrialised countries contributed to some extent to the import substitution in Latin America and Asia as early as the

1930s onwards, it was not until the 1960s that they started to establish production in the developing countries to any large degree. They invested mostly in manufacturing products for the home market in the host countries concerned. But a notable new feature was that First World corporations started also to establish production in the Third World with the intention of exporting to the world market. In some cases, this was part of an internal division of labour within the corporations, while in other cases the strategy was to replace production that was previously carried out in the industrialised countries. No matter what the specific motives were, this rapidly expanding relocation and establishment of industry in the periphery implied a considerable change in the international division of labour. Some developing countries began to export industrial goods.

The central question which was asked in the wake of these changes was: why – and why at this particular time? In an attempt to answer this two-pronged question a large number of theories appeared and only a few of them will be mentioned separately in the following sections. The conceptions of some of the other theories are discussed thematically in the fourth and sixth sections of this chapter.

The product life cycle: Hymer

The American economist *Stephen Hymer* was one of the first to deliver a comprehensive analysis of general causes for the internationalisation of productive capital (Hymer, 1976). In his theory, Hymer stressed competition as the driving force that prompted the individual company to spread its productive activities beyond the borders of the home country. However, he also linked competition to a special theory: the product life cycle.

Hymer's central point was that often a single company enters the market alone with a new product or an important improvement on existing products, or possibly just a cheaper method for producing old products. The result in such cases is that the company in question experiences a significant growth in sales, greater earnings, and hence higher profits: altogether, outcomes that provide the company with further advantages in the competition with others.

However, Hymer believed that the advantages would be temporary, because other companies would eventually develop similar products and become capable of producing them just as cheaply. In this situation, the company which was originally the market leader has to look around for new opportunities. It is here that the shifting of production to the developing countries could come in. For Hymer this was just one among several possible strategies, but for others who have tried to apply Hymer's original theory, the transfer of production to the developing countries came to be emphasised as one of the most widely used strategies from the 1960s onwards.

The advantages of changing location to developing countries included the opportunities for reducing labour costs considerably. If the labour cost component in production was large, it could be of interest to the manu-facturing enterprises to produce the products in the labour-abundant poor countries, possibly even for the world market. Further, the shifting of production to these countries would provide opportunities for coming into contact with new markets. By expanding total production along with a carefully planned division of labour within the enterprises, they might more-over benefit from enhanced economies of scale. These and other advantages have been mentioned in many theories. Therefore, we shall look a little more closely at them below.

Hymer's original theory contributed to explaining the internationalisation of capital in general terms but it did not clarify why the changing location of production on a world scale began in the 1960s and continued into the 1970s. To understand the timing, one must turn to some of the subsequent elaborations of his theory, or to other explanatory attempts within develop-ment economics (for example Dunning, 1988). However, it may be just as interesting in this connection to look at a Marxist-inspired theory, worked out by the three German researchers, *Folker Fröbel*, *Jürgen Heinrichs* and *Otto Kreye* – not so much because of any outstanding qualities of their theory but rather because they, at an early stage, pointed to a number of explaining factors that have since been adopted by most schools of thought in this area.

The international division of labour in the 1970s

Fröbel, Heinrichs and Kreye provided a thorough description of the tend-encies towards a new international division of labour as it could be ascertained by the mid-1970s (Fröbel et al., 1980). They emphasised, in this connection, three fundamental changes in global production conditions which, combined, they believed could explain the global shift of production and the new patterns of industrial growth in the Third World.

The first change was the appearance of a steadily increasing reserve army of comparatively *cheap labour* in the Third World. Neither the existing manu-facturing sectors nor any other urban sectors had been able to absorb the rapidly growing labour force. At the same time, the modernisation and increased productivity of agriculture in many countries had further increased the number of unemployed by pushing many farmers, especially the small peasants, out of production. There was, therefore, a considerable amount of available labour. With reference to Lewis and the debate among the early development economists it could be questioned whether this was really a fundamental new feature (cf. Chapter 5). Nevertheless, it is true that the superfluous labour force was particularly visible during the 1970s – at a time when many industrial countries continued to have almost full employment.

The second change was the creation of the *technical possibilities* for splitting up the production processes into many constituent parts, several of which could typically be carried out by an unskilled or quickly trained, semi-skilled workforce. This meant that the companies could use the cheap labour in the developing countries for at least part of their production.

The third crucial change was the development of an inexpensive and worldwide *transport and communications system*. Consequently, geographical distance and location were rendered less significant in economic terms while, relatively speaking, labour costs and technical possibilities for splitting up the production process acquired more importance.

The combined result was that for many companies it became advantageous to reduce total production costs by relocating certain parts of their production to low-income areas in the Third World. The relocation was prompted at this particular time, towards the end of the 1960s, because of the combination of the above-mentioned factors and the existence of full employment in many of the industrial countries. The latter caused wages to increase and thereby inflicted higher costs upon the companies. In order to maintain previous levels of profitability as well as in order to survive in international competition, the companies were therefore obliged to reduce costs. One of the obvious possibilities under the altered conditions was to utilise the cheap labour in the developing countries.

Causes and impact of internationalisation

With their attempt to explain the global shift of production, Fröbel, Heinrichs and Kreye contributed to the intensification of a much broader debate on the causes and impact of internationalisation of capital. Representatives of all the main streams of thought within development economics, whom we have discussed in the foregoing chapters, took part in this debate. It would therefore be too enormous a task to review each of the several theories separately. However, we can draw attention to some of the main propositions. This can be done with reference to four central questions which were given qualitatively different answers in the literature.

First, one may ask what it was that *pushed* the companies in the industrial countries to shift production beyond the borders of their homelands. Some of the suggested answers are mentioned above. Others laid more emphasis on the economic crisis and recession in the industrial countries which bit from the beginning of the 1970s as the major reason for the relocations. Within sectors where the markets were no longer expanding, it was necessary for many companies to look for other market opportunities. A third type of answer referred to the new environmental regulations and other restrictions on company activities that appeared in more and more industrial countries throughout the 1980s and early 1990s.

The second central question in the debate concerned the reasons why companies were *attracted* to invest in the Third World, and why they chose certain countries in preference to others. The cost of labour was one of the most important attractions, as already noted. But it was also stressed by some authors that the workforce should be disciplined and qualified to perform the various functions in the work process. The labour force should preferably be second-generation workers who no longer considered going back to their villages and getting a piece of land. The workers should not be too well organised so that they could effectively press for higher wages. In this context, whether or not the authorities in the host countries pursued a policy that protected the foreign companies against strikes and other workers' actions that could disrupt production played a role.

The legal framework for foreign investment and foreign companies was also influential. Of particular importance were the regulations regarding capital transfers, including repatriation of profits, and tax policies, including exemptions and other advantages offered to the companies by the individual countries. Finally, there were theories that laid great emphasis on infrastructure – to what extent the individual countries had established well-functioning transport systems, communication systems, banking, and other facilities of importance to the running of a company.

A particular approach to studying the relative attractiveness of various less developed countries focused attention on investment transactions from the point of view of financial managers who considered investing in a foreign country. These managers would have to take into account their primary responsibilities: to allocate limited financial resources among competing investment projects, and to choose the least costly methods of financing new and ongoing operations. In a wider perspective, this implies that the company will make the investment only on the condition that the host country concerned offers a certain minimum of advantages and politically determined incentives. In the financial managers' comparatively narrow perspective, this implied minimum is translated into the minimum acceptable rate of return on investment, based on considerations of capital costs and the specific risks inherent in the proposed investment. But not only that. The financial managers also have to consider the proposed investment against alternative uses of the investment funds, that is the opportunity costs. In other words, the minimum required will depend on conditions prevailing in the country considered as compared with conditions prevailing in other countries, where the company could alternatively place its investment.

These conditions may be referred to as the comparative incentive structure, using a term from new institutional economics (cf. Chapter 17). Two major components may be identified: society-generated attractiveness, and politically or state-induced incentives and disincentives. The former would include as conditions the actual and potential market size; the factor and resource endowment of the country; the relative price structure, including the prices and availability of relevantly qualified labour; the basic infrastructure and communications system; basic attitudes to work, etc. The government-induced incentives and disincentives would refer to government policies in general.

The line of demarcation between the two components may be blurred –

partly because the society-generated attractiveness can be influenced in the long run by government interventions, partly because the state-induced incentive structure may be heavily influenced by traditions and institutions in the society. Still, as a simple conceptual framework, the distinction and the various sub-categories may be used to investigate why certain less developed countries appear as more attractive than others to foreign investors, which in turn may contribute to explaining the actual flow of investment mainly to countries in Latin America and the Far East.

The third important question in the debate concerned what could be termed the *global framework conditions* for the internationalisation of capital. Here, the original analysis made by Fröbel, Heinrichs and Kreye stood at the centre of the debate. The fundamental changes which these authors had pointed to were included, in one way or another, in most theories of the international conditions that promoted the relocation of industry to the Third World.

Another source of inspiration for the positions taken in the debate was Wallerstein's world system theory, particularly his underlining of how the international credit institutions and the expansion of an international capital market contributed to creating preconditions for the internationalisation of industrial capital. The World Bank's strong position *vis-à-vis* the developing countries was noted as important for the protection of private foreign companies against undue encroachments from the host-country authorities. Any such encroachment, whether in the form of tight regulations or outright nationalisation of foreign property, would almost automatically lead to the World Bank reducing or suspending credit to the countries in question.

The fourth and last central question concerned the *impact* on Third World countries of the internationalisation of industrial capital and the new international division of labour. The question could be seen as an extension of the classic question regarding the impact of imperialism, though it was now formulated in much more nuanced terms. Attention was directed more to the differences than to the similarities. The emphasis was on dissimilar effects in different developing countries; on differences from branch to branch; and on differences dependent on the specific reasons for internationalisation and the way in which it was carried out. Later in this chapter we look a little closer at a conceptual framework that may be applied for investigating the impact, based on such a more sophisticated approach.

Globalisation and regionalisation of the world economy in the 1990s

The continued theoretical debate on the internationalisation of capital in the 1980s and 1990s has shifted both focus and emphasis as compared with the debates reviewed above, because the processes have once again changed in character. The international division of labour of the 1970s has been supplanted, since the late 1980s, by new trends often referred to as globalisation and regionalisation (Oman, 1994). It is outside the scope of this book to provide a thorough introduction here, but some of the main features should be mentioned along with selected attempts at explaining the basic changes.

Globalisation refers to a process that goes further than either transnationalisation or internationalisation of capital. If one defines the earlier internationalisation of industrial capital as a relocation of certain production processes to other countries, including developing countries, one may characterise globalisation as a much more profound reorganisation of manufacturing, trade and services within a globally encompassing system. The actors are no longer national companies that relocate limited and specialised parts of their production processes under pressure, but globally oriented mega-corporations, transnational corporations (TNCs), who organise their entire production and sales with the aim of being able to operate worldwide. They may continue to have profit centres in their original home country, but they are likely primarily to pursue growth maximisation across national frontiers and with a global perspective.

The rapid growth of global financial markets since the late 1970s, facilitated by national deregulation of financial transactions in OECD countries and by new information technologies, has provided basic preconditions for globalisation in the sense outlined above. Nevertheless, according to the American economist *Charles Oman*, globalisation is more usefully understood as a microeconomic phenomenon – one that is driven by the strategies and behaviour of TNCs, particularly those who have adopted so-called 'flexible' production and inter-firm networking strategies (Oman, 1994).

To understand the behaviour of these corporations, it is not sufficient to consider low labour costs or other factors separately; their strategies are much more complex in the sense that they, at one and the same time, take several factors into consideration. Thus, the most recent theories have also noted that the massive international flows of capital observed since the end of the 1980s have primarily occurred between the three centres of gravity in the world economy, that is between the USA, Japan and the European Union. At the same time, investments in the Third World have been concentrated – not in low-wage areas but, on the contrary – in countries like Singapore, South Korea, Taiwan, Thailand, Mexico and others with a relatively high level of wages in a Third World context.

Access to cheap labour can thus no longer explain much of the movement of productive capital. Two main reasons are given for this in the literature. One is the overall decline in the share of low-skilled labour costs in total production costs in several globally competitive industries. The other is the increased importance of physical proximity both between producers and their customers, and between producers and their suppliers of parts, components and services.

As a result, the trend that we noted occurring in the 1970s, whereby a growing number of companies based in OECD countries shifted some of their production to low-wage areas in Latin America and Asia, has now been replaced by *regional* sourcing and production networks. As noted by Oman, production to serve the North American market that can still benefit from relocating to low-wages sites is more likely to move to low-wages areas within the USA or to Mexico than to South America or Asia, compared to previous periods. Similarly production to serve the European market that moves to low-wage countries is more likely than before to relocate to Southern or Eastern Europe, rather than to Asia or Latin America. Globalisation is thus associated with regionalisation. Oman adds to this the observation that these tendencies have occurred exactly at a time when several poor countries have started pursuing export-oriented industrialisation strategies based on the expectation that they, like the Far Eastern countries during an earlier period, may attract investment from OECD countries.

Other factors, however, may still attract direct foreign investments to developing countries far distant from the home countries of the corporations, such as the search for new markets, as in China and the rest of East Asia; access to a qualified workforce that can handle more complex work processes, as in the case of software production in India; or a wish to enter into partnership with technology-leading companies operating in other regions. But the point is that the explanations must be adjusted to the decisive changes that have occurred in the nature of capitalist production patterns towards more technology-intensive and knowledge-based manufacturing (cf. UNCTC, 1992).

The trend towards regionalisation briefly referred to above has been accentuated in recent years by the breakdown of the centrally planned economies in Eastern Europe and the implosion of the Soviet Union. But the process started much earlier with the decline of US post-war economic hegemony, and the remarkable growth of Japan and the leading European economies, notably Germany. The process has manifested itself chiefly in the form of regional polarisation around the USA, Japan and the European Union, but in such a way that the bearing structures have not primarily been country specific. Rather, they have been based in corporate organisations and integrated networks of TNCs, which have provided the dynamic and determined the direction of development. It is the corporations, through their investments, production, trade and technology transfers, that have created close links between the economies of certain countries and thus brought about a higher degree of *de facto* regional integration.

Some of the recent theories, therefore, emphasise that it no longer makes the same sense as previously to use, as a starting point, the countries as the primary units of analysis. The national economies are often far less integrated than the TNCs' production and distribution systems. Accordingly, it is not so much the countries but to a larger extent the corporations who compete with each other, often in several countries at the same time and in such a

way that their competitiveness in one country interacts with their competitiveness in others.

Michael E. Porter is one of the theorists who has introduced propositions
of this kind, although he has at the same time tried to combine analyses of
the competition among, and the competitive advantages of, the corporations
with analyses of the competitive advantages of nations (Porter, 1990). It is
notable in this connection that in many cases the corporations which have
been able to establish themselves as internationally competitive and dominant
within a particular sector have their home base in the same country, indicating the importance of the home-country environment. One of the
examples studied by Porter is the printing press industry where German
firms have dominated since the nineteenth century. Another example is the
robotics industry where Japanese firms are the industry leaders at the global
level.

It follows from the above observations and propositions that the most
important actors in the new global production system are the TNCs. This
has been emphasised by several theorists even with reference to earlier periods,
before the trends of globalisation and regionalisation were clearly discernible.
These include, within the Neo-Marxist research tradition, theorists like *Paul
Baran* and *P. M. Sweezy* (Baran and Sweezy, 1968). Similarly, *Raymond Vernon*
was one of the pioneers within non-Marxist political economy (Vernon,
1973, 1977).

Since the earliest formulations of theories concerning the TNCs and their
behaviour in the international system, a wealth of both empirical analyses
and attempts at providing theoretical explanations have appeared (for an
overview, see Helleiner, 1989). It falls outside the scope of this book to
review these theories in any great detail, but the following section summarises
some of the main theoretical positions concerning the role of TNCs in
Third World economic development.

The role of transnational corporations in developing countries

There are many good reasons for taking a closer look at the role of TNCs
in economic development. Most important is the fact that the internationalisation and globalisation of capital have taken place overwhelmingly through
these corporations – with them as the chief actors. At the same time, the
TNCs have grown rapidly in size, commanding continuously increasing shares
of world production, trade and services. Hence they have become some of
the most important actors in the world economy today.

There is no agreement on how to define a transnational corporation.
However, it is demanded as a minimum in most of the theories that a
significant proportion of a TNC's activities are located outside the home
country. Some of the theories demand that the foreign activities amount to

50 per cent or more of the corporation's total turnover; others place more emphasis on how the corporation is organised. The definition is not crucial here, but it will be implied in the following that by the term 'TNCs' we refer to relatively large corporations with extensive activities in several countries.

The Centre for Transnational Corporations (UNCTC, now the Division on Transnational Corporations, UNCTAD) of the United Nations has, for a number of years, reviewed the activities of TNCs and their role in the global economy in general, as well as in the developing countries' economic and social development in particular. From the several reports prepared by this institution it may be appreciated, *inter alia*, that international trade between the industrialised countries and the developing countries has increasingly been taken over by TNCs. It is difficult to ascertain the exact proportions, but it is estimated that more than half of the developing countries' exports to the OECD countries are controlled by around 500 large corporations.

Similarly, the TNCs have a strong presence in most of the developing countries. How large a proportion of the total production in these countries they control is not known. Dissimilarities obviously exist between countries, but the foreign-controlled part of industry is probably nowhere less than 10 per cent, the typical percentage lying above 30. Moreover, TNC control is often more prevalent in the most dynamic and expanding sectors and with regard to products of great strategic importance for accumulation, growth and export of manufactured goods.

The corporations exercise a particularly intense form of control over exchange and pricing through so-called *intra-firm trade*, that is transactions between units within the same corporation. Therefore, the market prices need not apply. It is left to the executive management of the parent company, typically located in one of the OECD countries, to decide the rules and the prices according to which intra-firm transactions take place (cf. below). The UNCTC has concluded that, by the end of the 1980s, about one-third of United States exports consisted of intra-firm transactions, while more than two-fifths of total imports from the entire world were transacted in this manner. In the case of Japan and the UK, it was estimated that intra-firm transactions accounted for one-third of the total value of their international trade in the early 1980s (UNCTC, 1992: Ch. VIII).

This information is striking, and particularly interesting at a time when much of the development debate centres around the benefits from leaving more to market mechanisms, not by reducing the control exercised by TNCs but by reducing the role of the state (cf. Chapter 18).

What, then, have been the implications for economic development in the Third World of the significant roles played by TNCs? This is the overriding question the theories have tried to answer. They have done so in very different ways, and the answers vary from very positive to very negative assessments. Neo-classical economists have generally come to the conclusion that the corporations have had favourable net effects on the economies of the developing countries. The analyses and theories of development economists have remained more open about the question and their assessments vary from one extreme to the other, covering the whole spectrum, while Marxist researchers have overwhelmingly focused on the negative impact of TNCs upon the economic and social development of peripheral societies.

Instead of reviewing the individual theories, we shall try in the following to extract some of the pertinent observations and propositions from both the theoretical discussions and the extensive literature on empirical findings. To facilitate a systematic presentation it will be useful to start by outlining a simplified model of resource circulation within a TNC that has established a branch or subsidiary in a developing country. This model, shown in Figure 9.1, may serve as a frame of reference for our exposition (Martinussen, 1988; 1992).

The model can be interpreted as a number of sequences or successive phases in the circulation and utilisation of resources. In the first phase, a certain amount of money is transferred from a parent company in an industrial country to a branch or subsidiary in a developing country. The capital transferred may amount to a substantial share of the total investment required, but it may also, depending on the circumstances, constitute merely a fraction. A TNC always has the option of raising capital within the host country – from public financial institutions or from local investors.

The second stage of the process involves the buying of the inputs required for the production process: labour, raw materials, means of production, fuels, intermediate goods, know-how, etc. These inputs may be acquired locally but they may, alternatively, be imported from the parent company. If they are imported, the TNC may apply *over-pricing* in order to ensure a transfer of resources from the subsidiary to the parent company. Over-pricing – which is one form of transfer pricing – implies that the parent company charges prices above those prevailing in the world market.

After the production process, which constitutes the third stage, the resource circulation process enters the fourth stage where the products are sold in the domestic or foreign markets. If the subsidiary sells commodities or services to the parent company, this provides the corporation with yet another opportunity for the transferring of resources. The commodities and services may be sold at prices significantly below those prevailing in the world market. Even if this *under-pricing* in intra-firm trade does not take place, the TNC is still left with opportunities for transferring resources in the form of profit remittances or divestments.

One of the points emerging from this model is that it cannot be determined a priori whether any transfer of resources from the subsidiary to the parent company will actually take place. That depends on several factors; the most influential of these, according to some of the theories, relate to the conditions of capital accumulation and long-term profit maximisation in a

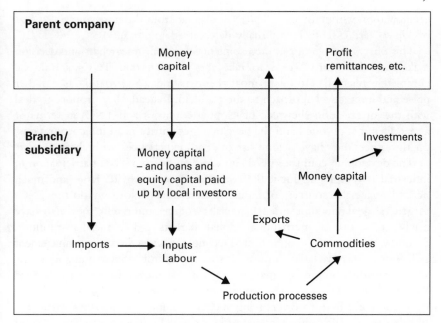

Figure 9.1 A simplified model of resource circulation within
a transnational corporation

national as well as a global perspective. The same factors partly determine
the extent to which a TNC will apply its global distribution and marketing
network to increase exports from the host countries where it is operating.
Other theories emphasise the long-term market potential of the host country
and assert that TNCs will gear their strategies more to these than to short-
term profit calculations.

Irrespective of the more specific explanatory propositions, it is interesting
to note some of the more general features of the theories as regards their
conceptions of the decision-making structure within TNCs and concerning
the basic factors that determine TNC behaviour. On these points, it is a
widely held view in the literature that profitability considerations and other
behaviour-determining interests of a TNC are located in the parent company – not in any of its subsidiaries. Further, the parent can wield effective
control over affiliates, if it wants to. The implication is that the whole question
of how and where resources are allocated and utilised within a TNC is
decided on the basis of the parent company's interests – not on the basis of
the interests of any particular branch or subsidiary. The methods and the
specific ranking of interests and priorities may vary according to the organisational set-up of the corporation and its corporate strategies with regard to
control, decision making and expansion – but the basic proposition remains
valid (Tsurumi, 1984). In other words, the resource allocation and capital

accumulation within a typical TNC – looked at from the host country's point of view – are essentially externally determined.

This observation has prompted some development researchers and decision makers in the Third World to take the position that TNCs should be completely rejected. However, most theorists today regard this as a rather naive and impractical approach to the problem. Instead, they propose to deal with the interrelations between developing countries and TNCs in terms of a real dilemma: on one hand the developing countries need the corporations; on the other, they have a long list of 'bad' experiences with them.

The developing countries need and can benefit from TNC participation in industrial development. First, the corporations can provide large and much needed financial resources for industrial investment. Not only do the TNCs in general generate substantial financial resources internally; they also have privileged access to international capital markets and financial institutions. Secondly, they can offer sophisticated technology, know-how and management skills not readily available from other sources. Thirdly, they command access to superior distribution and marketing networks suitable for increasing Third World exports. Fourthly, TNC operations can create employment. Finally, they may contribute to diversifying and 'deepening' the industrial structure. In other words, TNCs may indeed offer sizeable net benefits to Third World host countries.

Many corporations have, over the years, supported and promoted some developing countries' industrial growth in these respects. But – and this is the other side of the dilemma – many corporations have at the same time, in many other countries, structured their activities in such a way that the net impact has been modest or even negative for the host countries (Lall and Streeten, 1977; Martinussen, 1988; 1992).

Without claiming any general validity, it may be of interest to review some of the conclusions drawn from empirical investigations in a number of host countries. This can be done by comparing the above-mentioned potential advantages of the TNCs with actually observed consequences of their operations.

Regarding the provision of *capital* for investment, the TNCs have often – despite their command over very considerable financial resources and easy access to borrowing in the international market – transferred to most host countries only little capital. Instead of financing new activities themselves, the corporations have often preferred to raise most of the investment capital in the host countries' capital markets which, moreover, has sometimes crowded out national industrialists by pre-empting scarce local capital resources. In addition, most TNCs have repatriated large profits to their parent companies, either openly by means of dividend remittances and technical payments or more covertly by means of transfer pricing. As implied, not all TNCs have used these methods. Their modes of operation vary greatly from country to country, from branch to branch, and over time.

However, the point is, as noted in relation to the model above, that the TNCs themselves are in position to decide whether to make a net transfer of capital into or out of a host country. There is not much individual developing countries can do in terms of controlling the capital flows within TNCs; all these host countries can do is merely to compete with each other to attract investment from the foreign corporations by offering them the best opportunities and conditions.

Regarding the *transfer of technology*, it should first be recognised that TNCs have supplied many developing countries with needed technology. The problems encountered relate to the rather high prices they have had to pay for this technology. Often they have had to pay for the same generic technology several times, because it has been imported by a number of companies under different brand names. In addition, the transferred technologies have rarely been adapted to the specific conditions and the factor endowment of the host countries, with the result that the utilisation of foreign technologies has often resulted in increasing import needs – because of this failure to design them to exploit local resources. Finally, it is generally held that imported technologies have rarely stimulated national research and technology development. TNCs have typically surrounded their transfer of technologies with a number of restrictions which have prevented the host country companies from further developing them, or from using them to increase exports.

With respect to the impact of TNC operations upon the *export performance* of host countries in the Third World, closer examinations reveal that very few countries have benefited significantly from the potential access to international markets through the corporations' global distribution and marketing systems. TNCs have frequently shown little interest in producing for export and, instead, have preferred to sell to the domestic markets in the host countries. When they have established production to serve markets in the industrial countries, they have tended to apply the transfer pricing mechanism and other mechanisms in such a way that only a small proportion of the earnings have ended up in the respective host countries. Therefore, export increases through the TNCs have not had the same favourable effects on a country's balance of payments and economic growth as would have been the case if national companies had been responsible for the exports.

Neither these nor other 'bad' experiences with TNCs, however, warrant a conclusion to the effect that developing countries should break off all collaboration with these companies. Such a simplified conclusion would correspond to the mistakes in the classical dependency theory; it would ignore the first side of the dilemma. In addition, it would ignore the considerable differences that can be observed from country to country, from branch to branch, and from corporation to corporation.

As noted in the previous section of this chapter, there are strong indications that the significance of TNCs has become greater in recent years, both globally and especially in relation to the developing countries. These large corporations have increased their control over world investments, production, trade, and technology transfers. This increase is an extension of trends that have been discernible since the 1960s, but apparently a further accentuation has taken place since the collapse of the centrally planned economies and the accompanying strengthening of global market forces and the spreading of the idea that much more should be left to these forces. More than 60 countries have in recent years carried out substantial liberalisations in their foreign trade policies and, as a corollary to this, in their policies concerning foreign investments. A similar number of countries have in different ways taken steps towards deregulation of the private sector in general. Together with large-scale privatisation of state-owned companies and the opening up of large investment areas for private, including foreign, companies, these policy changes have given far greater latitude for TNC activities in the Third World. The corporations have used this latitude to increase their investments and other forms of engagement very considerably, not only in manufacturing but also to an increasing extent in infrastructure, utilities, and the service sector in the widest sense (UNCTC, 1992: especially Chs I–VI; UNCTAD, 1994).

Despite the problems encountered by many developing countries as a consequence of the activities of TNCs, there is not much point in looking for solutions that try to keep the large corporations out. On the contrary, such a strategy, according to many researchers, would result in further marginalisation. On the other hand, most researchers currently agree that host countries must enact regulations to try to control TNC activities, with a view to minimising detrimental effects and maximising the positive consequences. This may contribute to turning the TNCs into more effective engines of growth, as seen from a host country perspective. Because of the serious difficulties that host country authorities face when trying to interfere with corporation priorities and activities, however, they may have to accept the possibility that, even with a well-designed regulatory framework, the TNCs might transfer a substantial part of the economic surplus generated by growth to other countries.

CHAPTER 10

Focus on Agricultural Development

The presentation of the theories of economic growth and development has so far mostly stressed the role of the industrial and other urban sectors. In the present chapter, we turn our attention towards some of the several theories which have, instead, put special emphasis on agriculture – either as a sector that should be developed in order to remove the barriers to further industrialisation, or as a sector whose development is seen as an end in itself.

Taking a long-term view of these theories, there was at first a tendency to tone down the strong worries expressed by classical political economists, especially David Ricardo, that agriculture would become a barrier to growth. Thus, development research in the 1950s was mainly concerned with agriculture as a source of the economic surplus, labour and raw materials required for industrial development. Later, an increasing number of development researchers came to the conclusion that, unless the sector itself was developed, agriculture would sooner or later become a serious obstacle to both industrial and aggregate growth. Moreover, many theorists who acknowledged the limited potential of the urban sectors for absorbing the expanding labour force began to perceive growth and development of agriculture as primary targets. Increased production in agriculture came to be viewed as a necessary prerequisite for creating better living conditions for the millions of people in the rural areas.

The following sections take a closer look at the various conceptions. The first section briefly discusses the contribution that agriculture can make to overall growth; in particular, the sector's role as a source of economic surplus is examined. The following section deals with some of the distinctive characteristics of agriculture that have to be taken into account in economic theory. The third section touches on the issue of peasant rationality. A review of theories about urban bias follows, a bias which many researchers have identified in the mode of functioning of the market mechanisms as well as in the policies pursued by a large number of Third World governments, notably in Africa. The two remaining sections focus on the internal development of the agricultural sector. Here, institutional reforms and technological innovations have been selected for closer scrutiny from the list of determining factors.

Agriculture's contribution to aggregate growth

For development economists like Arthur Lewis and Rostow, agriculture was characterised by extensive underemployment and very low labour productivity, the marginal productivity of labour approaching zero. Thus, it would be possible to transfer a substantial labour force from agriculture to industry and other more productive sectors without bringing about a decline in the agricultural sector's total production. For the same reasons, such a transfer was necessary to create growth (cf. Chapter 5). Within the framework of this reasoning in its pure form, agriculture was thus reduced to a reservoir of labour. This mode of reasoning was subsequently nuanced and modified by Lewis and Rostow themselves, but it was other development researchers, including *Simon Kuznets* (Kuznets, 1966), who came to be known for their more comprehensive theories concerning the position and role of agriculture in economic development.

Kuznets distinguished between three forms of contribution made by agriculture to aggregate growth. The first form he called *the market contribution*. His main point here was that agriculture makes a contribution to growth by purchasing products from other sectors, at home or abroad, and by selling products to other sectors. The second form Kuznets termed *the factor contribution* which referred to the transfer of resources from agriculture to other sectors, where they were utilised more productively. Finally, Kuznets characterised the third form as *the product contribution*, by which he meant growth within the agricultural sector itself.

If, for the present, we ignore the product contribution, Kuznets's propositions can be incorporated in a simplified model as shown in Figure 10.1. The model refers to four different types of interrelation between the agricultural and the industrial sectors.

In the first interrelation, the two sectors are linked through the domestic market. Agricultural products are sold as consumer goods to the populations in the urban areas. In addition, agriculture provides raw materials for various branches of manufacturing. Conversely, the industrial sector sells consumer goods to the rural population along with intermediate products, like fertilisers, and machinery of various kinds for use in agricultural production.

In the second type of interrelation, the two sectors enter into exchange relationships indirectly via the international markets: goods from both sectors are exported for which foreign currency is received. These earnings, in turn, make possible the import of consumer goods, raw materials, intermediates and capital goods to the two sectors.

The third type of interrelation establishes a connection between agriculture and industry via the credit system. In the simplified model, the savings from each of the two sectors are used to finance loans and investments in agriculture and industry, respectively, either in proportion to the savings or in a different manner.

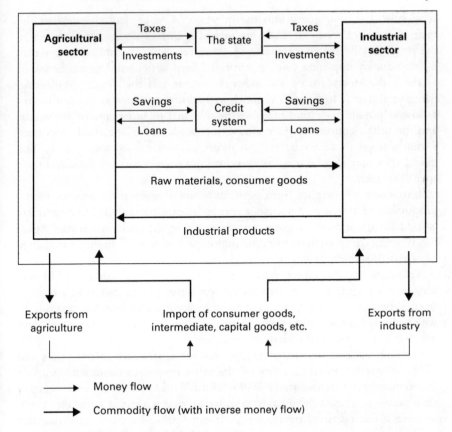

Figure 10.1 A simplified model of the interrelations between agricultural and industrial sectors

Finally, the fourth type of interrelation refers to the financial flows that are established through the state's collection of taxes, duties, etc., on the one hand, and public investments, subsidies, etc., on the other.

Based on this model, we can briefly describe the variety of roles that the agricultural sector may play in the aggregate growth and development processes. First, we shall look at how economic surplus can be extracted from agriculture and transferred to industry and other urban sectors. This can be done with reference to the model's four interrelationships.

Extraction via the domestic market can take the form of unequal exchange of industrial and agricultural goods, where the industrial goods are sold at 'artificially' high prices and the agricultural goods at 'artificially' low prices. Marxist economists would interpret this to imply a transfer of value, because industrial products are then sold at prices above their 'real' value, while agricultural products are exchanged at prices below their 'real' value. Other economists, without going into the question of value, would note that the relative prices or terms of trade are turned against agriculture and therefore the process will involve a transfer of resources. The state may possibly play a role here by imposing price controls to keep agricultural prices down.

From the viewpoint of the industrial sector and the urban populations, the crucial aim is to acquire as much agricultural produce at prices that are as low as possible – within limits set by the total requirements of the sector and the urban consumers. In contrast, the producers in the rural areas have a vital interest in achieving as high prices as possible for their goods. The model thus may also be used to introduce the main actors involved and their special interests.

Extraction of surplus from agriculture via foreign trade implies that a proportion of the foreign exchange earned by exporting agricultural products is used for the import of goods that are used in the industrial sector. Again the state may play an active role by imposing a system of multiple exchange rates that discriminate against agriculture.

Transfers via the credit system can be achieved by using part of the savings from agriculture to finance industrial development. Similarly, a transfer from agriculture to other sectors may be brought about through taxation, in which the burden on agriculture is greater than the public investments and government services provided to agriculture.

Looking back at the debate on the role of agriculture in the 1950s and 1960s, it may be noted that one of the most frequent recommendations of this period was that the states in the Third World should do everything in their power to extract the greatest possible economic surplus from agriculture and use it for industrial development. It can further be ascertained that this was exactly the way most states in Asia and Africa acted (cf. below). Thus, they contributed to the transformation processes which the economists of the time summarised as: a reduction of the workforce in agriculture, and a relative reduction of agriculture's contribution to gross national product as a consequence of the rapid expansion of manufacturing and other urban sectors.

Without rejecting these basic conceptions of the expected – and necessary – transformation processes, some development economists, as early as the beginning of the 1960s, strongly warned against this concerted squeezing of agriculture. Among these were B. F. Johnston and John Mellor, who in a classic article from 1961 argued that agriculture should not only provide resources for industrialisation, but should also be developed with the aim of increasing the supplies of foodstuffs and raw materials for industry (Johnston and Mellor, 1961). If this did not happen concurrently with industrialisation and urbanisation, agriculture would, as a stagnant sector, bring the whole process of national development to a halt. Johnston and Mellor went even further by proposing that the two main sectors, in principle, should be developed in parallel – although they did admit that the capacities of most developing countries, and especially the capacities of the states, were insufficient for handling both at the same time.

In a number of empirical studies undertaken since the beginning of the 1960s, other development economists have demonstrated a high degree of correlation between the two main sectors' growth, in the sense that essentially all developing countries with substantial industrial growth over longer periods have also had considerable growth in agriculture. This applies, notably, to the newly industrialised countries in the Far East. Often, growth in agriculture has even preceded sustained growth in industry in the few countries with a very good performance record. In contrast, the majority of the developing countries, especially in Africa, have experienced stagnation in both the main sectors (cf. Timmer, 1988).

Evidently, these patterns and correlations may be explained by other factors, but there is currently general consensus that massive resource transfers from a stagnant agricultural sector cannot provide the basis for sustained aggregate growth.

Agriculture's distinctive features

As economic development research became increasingly interested in the agricultural sector, it also moved towards a more systematic description of the distinctive features of the sector. At the general, abstract level this led to the underlining of the specific conditions of production in agriculture, including the importance of the soil and the climate; seasonal variation in employment, income, nutrition, etc.; decision making by a large number of households; and household use of a significant part of the production (Timmer, 1988; Gill, 1991).

Soil is the most crucial production factor in agriculture. From this follows, among other things, that production has to be extended over a large geographical area. As a consequence, agricultural production presupposes extensive transport systems and storage facilities. These conditions are typically integrated as central elements in economic theories of agriculture. New institutional economics in this context highlights the great significance of the transaction costs involved.

With respect to *climate*, most development efforts in relation to agriculture have been aimed at reducing the possible detrimental impact on production, but none the less it is generally recognised that agricultural production depends on fluctuating climatic conditions to a considerable extent. Delays in the monsoon rains in South Asia, or periods of drought in Africa, continue to have a significant impact upon agricultural output – which, in turn, affects aggregate growth and societal development in a broader sense.

The importance of climatic variations and the interdependence of agriculture and other sectors can be illustrated with reference to the effects of a failing monsoon in South Asia. The first thing that happens is that agricultural production drops. This starts a chain reaction, as the associated reduction of farmers' incomes leads to decreased demand for fertilisers and other inputs for agricultural production. Simultaneously, the decline of incomes leads to less demand for industrial products in the rural areas, especially manufactured consumer goods. Parallel to these developments, a failing monsoon normally is followed by greater shortages of electricity, because part of the supply relies on hydro-electric power. Together with the decreasing demand, the drop in electricity supply often precipitates perceptible reductions in industrial production as a whole. In this way, the effects of a failing monsoon spread to the whole economy.

In many African countries, where the linkages between agriculture and industry are not as close, the effects of fluctuating rainfall may be different. A likely outcome here is that farmers withhold even the modest part of their production which they previously marketed, because they need it for their households. Thus, food shortages are created in the cities. A possible further outcome is a drop in export earnings, precisely when there is a particular need for such earnings to finance the compensating importation of food. Longer periods of drought in Africa also frequently lead to large migrations away from the hardest hit areas. As a result, the overloading of vulnerable ecological systems is often moved to areas which were not initially affected by the drought (see also the next chapter).

Seasonal variation in agricultural production was not incorporated in the early theories of macro-economic development. Arthur Lewis's original model, for example, assumed that the agricultural sector was burdened with so many underemployed and unemployed workers that the marginal productivity of labour was zero. This assumption has been criticised for disregarding the seasonality problem. Thus *Gerard J. Gill* has argued that, while at certain times of the year the employment of additional labour would contribute nothing to production, at other seasons labour has a high marginal product and would therefore add to total production (Gill, 1991: Ch. 1).

Gill has further argued that seasonal variation in agriculture has an important social dimension in that it causes problems primarily for the poor. Rich peasants, who can finance their consumption from current income as well as from past income (savings) and future income (borrowing), can generally avoid the negative impact of seasonal variation. They are much better off than the poor peasants and agricultural labourers, who are able to use only their current income for consumption. The poor typically have no or very few savings, and rarely have access to credit on favourable terms. As a consequence, they may starve during the 'hungry season' – the period before harvest. Because of their vulnerable position they often become both economically and socially subordinate to rich peasants on whom they depend for assistance during the 'hungry season'.

The conditions of production in agriculture vary considerably from one area to another, but it is a common characteristic that the natural environment and the climatic conditions constitute rigid outer limits. It is also – in practically all developing countries – a common feature that production decisions are made by a very large number of actors. In contrast to organised industry, where it is often a few company owners and corporate managers who take the important decisions concerning investments, production and sales, agriculture is characterised by thousands or millions of households, each reacting individually to the given natural conditions, climatic variations and market signals. This raises the issue of peasant rationality.

Peasant rationality: Schultz

For many years there was a tendency among development economists and Western researchers in general to see the farmers in the Third World as irrational, because they apparently did not recognise and exploit the opportunities available to them for increasing their production and incomes. The subsistence farmers, in particular, were regarded as irrational, because they continued to produce only for their own households – even though they could, with modest investments, increase productivity and production and thereby enjoy the benefits of selling to the market.

Notions of this kind still thrive among many decision makers in both the developing countries and international organisations. However, the views among researchers are today far more sophisticated and rooted in empirical analyses of peasant household decision making. These analyses have revealed other forms of rationality which guide the peasants' mode of taking decisions. The analyses have shown that risk avoidance and risk-minimising behaviour are both necessary and more sensible than profit maximisation that involves considerable risk-taking. The vast majority of peasant households quite simply cannot afford to run any great risks such as taking loans for investments or restructuring their production with new seeds or different crops. Even if they could, the poorest do not have access to borrow money for such purposes since future crops are rarely accepted as collateral and they cannot take the risk of placing their small holdings at the mercy of moneylenders. In cases where they do have access to credit, they normally have to pay exorbitant interest rates.

The less prejudiced analyses of the peasants' behaviour have thus indicated that these producers generally act rationally in terms of their own situation and in terms of the way they perceive the options available to them. It is also important to remember that each individual peasant household is not only a production unit, but also a consumption unit. An analytic distinction is possible, but hardly appropriate if the intention is to understand the many decisions these households take, based on considerations of both consumer needs and production possibilities.

T. W. Schultz (Schultz, 1964) was one of the first scholars who more systematically dispelled the traditional conceptions of peasants. Schultz totally dismissed what he saw as the traditional perception of peasants as essentially lazy producers, who only wanted to produce what was necessary for the household, and who otherwise preferred to waste a lot of resources on ceremonial events like weddings and funerals. Instead, Schultz argued that the peasants were 'poor, but efficient'. Using a trial-and-error strategy they had over generations tried to discover how they could most appropriately allocate their scarce resources and achieve the highest possible efficiency under the given technological conditions. In continuation of this argument, Schultz asserted that neither market signals, in the form of higher prices, nor policy-induced incentives for peasants could bring about production increases or productivity improvements. To achieve these goals it was instead necessary to introduce new technologies and at the same time ensure that the peasants, or at least a proportion of them, could actually access such new technologies. Schultz further claimed that the peasants, because they were rational actors, would react to changes of this kind and apply the new technologies, if they had the opportunity to do so.

It follows from these propositions that it is necessary to consider very carefully the kinds of strategy most likely to promote growth-oriented behaviour among peasants and thus contribute to agricultural development. Some of the reasons for aiming at increasing agricultural productivity and production have already been mentioned above, particularly as regards the need for such development as a basic precondition for sustained aggregate growth. To this may be added arguments that refer to agricultural development as an end in itself, and as a means to relieve rural poverty and contribute to improving the living conditions of the many millions of small peasants and landless who, with the current distribution of land and other assets, are cut off from participating fully in the 'conventional' types of development processes.

The British economist *Michael Lipton* is one of those who, with particular force, has argued for support to agricultural development along these lines. The next section will review his now classic criticism of the imbalances in favour of the cities – referred to by Lipton as 'the urban bias' – and briefly mention some of his core recommendations on strategy, some of which resemble those put forward by Robert Bates (cf. Chapter 17).

Urban bias: Lipton

The most important class-conflict or clash of interests in the Third World, according to Lipton, is not between labour and capital; nor is it between national and foreign interests. It is between the rural classes and the urban classes – between city and countryside (Lipton, 1977). In this conflict, it is generally the urban classes which dominate. And they do so because political power is concentrated in the cities.

Average rural incomes are typically around one-third of urban incomes.

At the same time, public and private services are much more extensive in the cities and towns than in the rural areas. In addition, both the state and the market mechanisms generally function in favour of the cities by extracting surplus from agriculture in the ways which we have noted earlier. Lipton finds these imbalances unreasonable, both from a normative perspective of equity and from a commitment to relieve poverty where it is greatest and where most people suffer from it. But Lipton goes further than that by arguing that concentration on urban development and neglect of agriculture have pushed resources away from activities where they could help growth *and* at the same time benefit the poor, and towards activities where they do either of these, if at all, at the expense of the other. From a societal development perspective, therefore, the only sensible and rational strategy is to concentrate far more resources in agriculture.

One of the reasons why Lipton has such strong reservations about a commitment to urban growth, especially organised industry, is that manufacturing and other urban sectors have proved incapable of absorbing all but a fraction of the fast-growing labour force. But he refers to other reasons as well, like the scarcity of capital which characterises most developing countries. In societies with very little capital available it is particularly important that it is used in the best possible way. That, according to Lipton, implies a concentration of capital in agriculture and with the small peasants and their families, who are much more effective than the industrialists in terms of producing more output per additional unit of capital input. In other words, poor countries with large agricultural sectors and a large rural population should allocate more resources to agriculture. Lipton does not suggest that developing countries should focus exclusively on agriculture, but he recommends that the biases be corrected and especially that the extensive transfer of resources from rural to urban areas be terminated. Manufacturing and other urban sectors should not be subsidised with massive resource transfers; rather, they should grow as a result of an agriculture-driven growth process.

Lipton's original formulation of the theory of urban bias has given rise to a comprehensive debate. Many researchers have tried to refute the basic propositions. A number of them have done so with reference to empirical evidence from selected countries where they claim that, in reality, no transfer of resources or other biases have occurred. Other researchers have attacked the perspective and the conceptual framework in Lipton's analyses (cf. Varshney, 1993). The criticism has prompted Lipton himself to adjust and expand the original theory, but not to abandon the most central theses. He has accepted that the theory does not apply to all developing countries; South Korea and Taiwan constitute exceptions, as do some of the Latin American countries. But, on the other hand, an urban bias has been maintained in the majority of African countries with catastrophic consequences (cf. Lipton, 1993).

Instead of looking closer at the many nuances and differentiations in this debate on the relationship between rural and urban sectors in various societies and at various stages of transformation, attention will be shifted in the next two sections to the major strategies which have been proposed to increase agricultural production. A distinction may here be useful between institutional reforms and technological innovations.

Institutional reforms in agriculture

Michael Lipton's recommendations for reforms and new strategies can largely be considered as institutional, in the sense that they address themselves to an altering of the policy-induced incentive structures and the institutional framework for agricultural production. This applies to his basic idea of allocating more resources to the highly productive small farmers through political intervention, including land reforms. In the following paragraphs, we shall briefly review land reform issues as well as some other principal types of institutional reform.

The case for reform is often introduced in the literature with the assertion that productive forces in agriculture can only be further developed under certain economic, social and political conditions which rarely obtain in Third World agriculture. From a growth perspective it is generally a question of removing institutional barriers to growth, while from a distribution perspective it is emphasised as a goal in itself to remove inequality of access to, and control over, land and other means of production.

The case for land reforms that involve a redistribution of land to small farmers can be argued from both these perspectives. The distribution aspect is here self-evident. Less obvious but equally important is that, even from the point of view of growth, a transfer of land may be economically justified. The reasoning is that the large and wealthy landowners – unless they have become capitalist producers and therefore subject to the imperatives of accumulation – do not have strong incentives to increase productivity or production. They do not need to do so in order to generate the necessary income, and may even have reason to suspect that a marked increase in production will result in lower agricultural prices – so much lower that the total net return becomes modest or possibly negative.

The implications of this incentive structure have been observed in the form of low area productivity on large holdings, particularly in Latin America and Asia. Several researchers have, on the basis of empirical studies, concluded that there is an inverse relationship between holding size and output per area unit (Berry and Cline, 1979). The smaller holdings are in this sense the most productive. Others, however, have contested this thesis in its simple version and, instead, argued that the correlation is not linear but U-shaped, meaning that productivity will first increase with expanded holding size and subsequently decline with further expansion beyond a certain threshold (Myrdal, 1970; Roy, 1981).

To the extent that it can be substantiated that small or medium-sized holdings are more productive than large holdings, a redistribution of land in favour of the former can be convincingly argued. In practice, the whole matter has proved to be more complicated, however. The land reforms enacted in South Korea, Taiwan, Egypt and a few other countries are often cited as successful, because they have clearly had a positive impact upon growth as well as redistribution and the promotion of equity. But in the majority of the documented cases it has been hard to discern any visible effects on productivity and overall agricultural growth. This may in part be attributed to the fact that the land laws enacted have provided the large landowners with considerable scope for evading the rules. In most cases, moreover, the legal stipulations have permitted the large landowners to surrender poor-quality marginal land, which the small farmers have had difficulty getting any return from. In a few cases, the actual implementation of the reforms has led to a decline in total production, and in some of the countries studied, notably Mexico, the new small farms apparently were less productive than big private farms (Oman and Wignaraja, 1991: pp. 44ff.).

These are some of the reasons why land reforms cannot succeed alone, but have to be supplemented with more direct support to small farmers in the shape of agricultural extension services, expansion of the credit system, and generally better access to services and inputs. When it comes to share-croppers and tenant farmers, for example in South Asia, additional measures are required to provide these producers with security of tenure, without which they will lack sufficient incentives for increasing productivity. Other efforts aimed at enhancing the productivity of smaller landholdings include the formation of co-operative societies for production, trade and credit, and extension of the material infrastructure – not only in the form of feeder roads, etc., but also in the form of public storage facilities and adequate arrangements for transportation. An overall aim should be to prevent the small farmers' produce from being wasted during storage or transport.

In practice, efforts along these lines have often been pursued only half-heartedly by Third World governments. Small farmers have not constituted a powerful lobby that could effectively pressure the governments. Moreover, to the extent that infrastructure and services have been developed in the rural areas, the better-off and resource-strong groups have often been able to capture for themselves the greatest advantages.

Despite the difficulties, the institutional reforms continue to be seen as essential, if not vital, in development strategies for agriculture. This, however, applies less to redistributive land reforms than to other institutional changes. Since the early 1980s, land reforms have increasingly been viewed with reservations among researchers and policy makers, partly as a reflection of political resistance from those who would lose from reform, partly because of the mixed and ambiguous empirical experience. Over the same period, interest has increased in productivity-improving measures through techno-logical innovations.

Technological innovations and
'the green revolution'

The arguments in favour of focusing on technological innovations can be traced back to Schultz's classical analysis from 1964 and similar considerations of technological changes as the most important sources of growth for agriculture. Some researchers, like Hayami and Ruttan, believed that technological changes would have the greatest impact if they were based on decentralised research – close to the producers and with their involvement (Hayami and Ruttan, 1985). In the real world, meanwhile, it became a few large international centres, transnational corporations and international organisations who came to decide the direction and content of much of the agriculture-related research and development efforts. It was these types of global actor that came to control the shaping of the technologies of the so-called *green revolution*.

The term 'green revolution' refers to many different combinations of agricultural techniques. The constituting central element is the introduction of new high-yielding varieties of basic crops. Such varieties were developed in large research centres set up with substantial funding from donor agencies and private foundations, like Rockefeller and Ford. Two of the most important centres were established in Mexico and the Philippines, from where new varieties of wheat and rice were disseminated to a number of countries in Latin America and Asia, as well as to some countries in Africa.

The special feature of these new varieties is that they, under the right conditions, can increase the yield per area unit significantly and thereby expand the output from agriculture considerably. It should be noted, however, that the right conditions are not always easily obtained, because they include access to a carefully controlled water supply and fertilisers, to be used in exactly measured amounts and at the right time during the period of growth. In addition, the new varieties are generally more vulnerable than the traditional ones to plant diseases and insect-attacks. Therefore, they have to be sprayed or in other ways treated with pesticides and insecticides.

The proponents of the technology of the green revolution – like Johnston, Mellor and Ruttan – have argued for it in both economic and social terms. From a purely economic perspective, they have claimed that the green revolution as an agricultural strategy is distinguished by the absorption of more labour; by utilising effectively scarce fertile land; by being scale-neutral and thereby equally suitable for small and large landholdings; and finally by utilising capital efficiently. The considerable growth in production, especially among crops like wheat and rice, has furthermore resulted in several developing countries becoming self-sufficient in food crops. Some of them have even been able to increase their agricultural exports and thereby their foreign-exchange earnings so that they become better equipped to finance industrial development.

From a social perspective, the scale-neutral aspect of the green revolution has been emphasised as a source not only of growth but also of social distribution and equity in favour of resource-weak groups in agriculture. The proponents have claimed that the new technologies can be exploited by all groups of farmers and, because of the associated increased demand for labour, even the landless will benefit. In this sense the green revolution has, in the eyes of its adherents, come to replace land reform as the central strategy for promoting agricultural development with equity.

Other development economists, like Lipton and *Keith Griffin* (Griffin, 1979) have acknowledged the scale-neutrality of the green revolution. But they have also argued very strongly that the new technologies are definitely not resource-neutral. Because the new varieties are only high yielding when combined with irrigation, extensive use of fertilisers, plant protection, etc., this form of cultivation assumes that the farmers either have resources to buy these necessary inputs or have access to credit. None of these conditions obtains for a very considerable proportion of the small-scale farmers in Asia (or Africa). Therefore, the green revolution has benefited these farmers appreciably less than the large-scale farmers.

It may be added that the large-scale farmers' switching to the cultivation forms of the green revolution in both Latin America and Asia, according to the critics, has been followed by a considerable degree of mechanisation. This has reduced the absorption of labour and, in some cases, may have even brought about a net decline in employment in agriculture. Observations of this kind have led to continued emphasis on the need for land reforms and expansion of agriculture-related services, notably credit, as essential preconditions for growth with equity.

Another type of criticism which has been directed at the green revolution has emphasised the ecological effects of the new cultivation methods. The increased use of pesticides, herbicides and chemical fertilisers has, it is claimed, resulted in contamination of the soil. The use of pesticides, moreover, has encouraged the development of stronger pests which, in turn, has called for even more powerful chemicals. Some of the critics have pointed out that, particularly in parts of Asia, the rate of increase in food production has recently gone down because of ecological problems resulting from the green revolution – in the form of soil depletion, salinisation, etc. (Shiva, 1991).

The criticism of the green revolution has not to any notable extent restrained the switching over to the new forms of cultivation in several countries in Latin America and Asia. On the other hand, continuous adjustments of the agricultural strategies have occurred, when governments and international organisations have tried to extend the green revolution to new regions and countries, or to new groups of producers. In this connection, greater emphasis has often been given to disease- and drought-resistant varieties in an attempt to introduce the green revolution in larger land areas with poorer soil quality. To a certain degree this has implied a shift in favour of farmers with poorer soil and fewer resources. At the same time, this shift has made it possible to extend the green revolution to larger areas of Africa, where soil quality in general and recurring periods of drought in particular are the central problems.

In their enthusiasm over the results obtained with the green revolution in several countries, some of the proponents, including *John Mellor* (Mellor, 1986), have argued that many developing countries could benefit from turning agriculture into the leading sector, and by betting on an agriculture-based and labour-intensive development strategy. Now that it has been demonstrated that technological innovations in agriculture can lead to considerable productivity increases and growth even during periods of stagnation in industry, it has also, according to Mellor, been demonstrated that agriculture can increase economic surplus on its own. Thus, agriculture has proved capable, under changed technological circumstances, of creating a greater supply of food and other agricultural products, while at the same time creating an increased demand in the agricultural sector for products from the urban sectors. In this sense, agriculture has been able to function as an engine of growth – even to the extent that it can promote and sustain industrial growth.

An overall conclusion concerning the role of agriculture and the most appropriate strategies to develop this sector is not warranted at this stage. The empirical evidence is too mixed and too open to conflicting interpretations, probably as reflections of the several different factors that influence agricultural performance under the very diversified conditions obtaining in Third World countries. The views and propositions briefly reviewed above should, therefore, be taken as selected contributions to a still-continuing debate. Further contributions to this debate will be considered in the following chapter and later in Parts IV and V of this book.

CHAPTER 11

Development with Limited Natural Resources

The main streams of thought within development economics have until recently paid little attention to environmental problems. Instead, they have taken for granted that the depletion of natural resources, increasing pollution and other environmental problems are of a temporary and surmountable nature. The basic assumption was that human innovativeness and techno-logical development would provide solutions in the long term.

This development optimism has been subjected to continuing criticism from other disciplines, partly from biologists and demographers who have pointed to the explosive population growth as a source of exhaustion of the earth's resources, partly from natural scientists generally who have argued that many natural resource and pollution flows have already grown beyond their sustainable limits, and many more are likely to do so within a few decades. Their combined assumption is that even with resource-saving and pollution-reducing technologies, continued population growth and global growth in material consumption will result in an uncontrolled decline in production, because the required natural resources will no longer be available or be made unusable by degeneration (Meadows et al., 1992).

There continues to be much disagreement on the significance of popu-lation growth and natural resource constraints. However, development researchers as well as social scientists in general have, during the 1980s and 1990s, shown considerably greater interest in these issues. This has not – yet – brought about a comprehensive and systematic integration of demographic and environmental matters into conventional development theories. Rather, population growth and environmental problems have been dealt with either as marginal additions to existing bodies of theory or as separate fields of empirical investigations.

This chapter first looks at some of the principal positions that confront each other in the debate on the 'population problem'. Then follows a brief discussion of the interrelationships between environment and development. The chapter's final section deals with theories concerning management of natural resources.

It should be noted that the following brief account is not a general introduction to demographic theories or environmental issues in the Third

World. What is attempted is merely to indicate where and how these topics can be related to the theories reviewed and discussed in other chapters of the present book. Moreover, whereas population and environment issues encompass major natural science elements, the account in the following will be confined to social science perspectives and analyses.

Population growth – resource or problem?

The debate on population growth and its significance for the development process can be traced back to Malthus's hypothesis from the nineteenth century that population, if not constrained, would grow significantly faster than food production (cf. Chapter 2).

This pessimistic view was adopted and further elaborated in the 1960s by the American biologist *Paul Ehrlich*. In his book, *The Population Bomb* (Ehrlich, 1968), Ehrlich described how the seriousness of the population problem dawned on him 'one stinking, hot night in Delhi', where in a taxi he attempted to make his way through the human masses in 'a crowded slum area'. That was when Ehrlich, in his own words, got to know 'the feel of over-population'. The Indian-born social science researcher *Mahmood Mamdani* a few years later criticised Ehrlich's description in strong terms by noting that a hot summer night on Broadway in New York or Piccadilly Circus in London would have put Ehrlich in the midst of a far larger crowd. Based on this observation, Mamdani argued that apparently Ehrlich was disturbed not by the number of people, but by their 'quality', that is their poverty (Mamdani, 1972).

The contrasting of the views of these two authors does not reveal their theoretical understanding of the implications of population growth, but it reflects appropriately the often strongly emotional forms of reasoning which have characterised much of the international debate on population issues. Disregarding this aspect of the debate, at least four basic conceptions of the significance of population growth may be identified. Three of these conceptions provide frameworks for specific strategies aimed at solving what is seen as the core of the 'problem'.

The reason strategies have been elaborated only in relation to three of the four conceptions is that population growth is simply not regarded as a problem in the remaining one – which we will discuss first. The Danish social scientist *Ester Boserup* is one of the researchers who, in support of this conception, has argued that population growth and increased pressure on natural resources, notably land, are decisive preconditions for technological innovation and hence for productivity improvements in agriculture. On the basis of historical studies in both developing countries and Europe, Boserup reached the general conclusion that population growth and increased population density acted as dynamic and development-promoting factors. Increased population pressure on land, according to her, prompted farmers to adopt progressively more intensive systems of land utilisation – to move from land-using technologies to land-saving cropping systems (Boserup, 1965, 1981). Where population pressure did not occur, as in parts of Africa, productivity remained low. A similar conception has been championed by *Julian Simon* who, based on extensive empirical studies, has identified a positive correlation between population growth and productivity increase. And not only that. Simon reached the conclusion that, in general, the rate of growth in productivity has been higher than the population growth rate (Simon, 1981).

Confronting this expressly optimistic view of development is Ehrlich's conception of population growth as the paramount problem confronting humanity. In his 1968 book, Ehrlich asserted that the limit had already been reached for the number of people that could live on the earth. He therefore foresaw that the 1970s would be characterised by famine, with hundreds of millions of people starving to death.

In a more recent work from 1990, written together with Anne Ehrlich, the fundamental views are repeated and it is emphasised that at least 200 million people, mainly children, have died of hunger and hunger-related illness in the intervening period (Ehrlich and Ehrlich, 1990). Although the overwhelming majority of these deaths occurred in the Third World, this recent contribution to the debate places considerable emphasis on over-population in the rich countries such as the USA. This follows from a change of perspective, with the view now focusing more on resource consumption and less on the number of people, the underlying notion being that each inhabitant of the rich countries on average exploits much more of the natural resource base than an inhabitant of the poor countries. The basic thesis remains unaltered, however: over-population and the continued growth in the world's total population, presently at a rate of more than 95 million people per year, is by far the greatest problem facing humanity.

The Ehrlichs further assert that the problem must be solved by population control – not just family planning – on a very large scale. Failing this one civilisation after another will disappear, due to such immense eroding and depletion of resources that even the life support systems will break down (Ehrlich and Ehrlich, 1990). A contribution to the solution of the problem can be made by decreasing the consumption of resources per capita and by introducing more environment-friendly technologies, but these strategies can only bring about a precarious balance between population and resources if the total number of people is also reduced.

In recent social science analyses there has been a widespread tendency to recognise population growth as a problem, though without accepting the doomsday prophecies from biologists and other researchers within the natural sciences. This, the third major conception of the population problem, uses as its starting point a differentiating approach that tries to distinguish between short-term difficulties and fundamental, long-term problems. In accordance with this approach, the overall research strategy has been to find out more about the circumstances under which population growth and high population density create serious obstacles to continued economic growth, as opposed to the circumstances in which these obstacles are overcome through technological development.

Neither the growth of population nor its composition and geographic distribution are seen here as independent variables, but rather as intervening or even dependent variables. High fertility rates among the women of the developing countries are not viewed in isolation, but as a result of the social conditions under which these women and their husbands live. Poverty, high infant mortality and the absence of any social security systems for the old combine to stimulate the demand for more children. In poor households, children are not only ends in themselves; they are also means by which the parents can add to the labour force in the short term and, at the same time, provide for future support during their old age. Children are seen as a human resource and as producers – not primarily as consumers of scarce natural resources (Mamdani, 1972; Lappé and Collins, 1979).

A particular variant of this approach has been proposed by the Australian demographer *John Caldwell*. He has attempted to explain fertility changes by investigating what he calls the *wealth flow* between parents and children (Caldwell, 1982). In societies where there is a net flow of wealth from children to parents, as when the former produce more than they consume, there is no economic gain from restricting the number of children, as seen from the perspective of the household – or, more precisely, from the perspective of the dominant decision maker within the household, usually the male head.

There may be other, non-economic reasons for restricting the number of children, but Caldwell's point here is that only when the wealth flow is reversed, and the children have become a net economic burden to the households, will overall fertility rates really start to decline. This is not likely to happen in poor households which depend primarily on subsistence agriculture. It is likely to happen, on the other hand, in households that depend on wage labour and other types of income from 'modern' economic sectors. In order for a fertility transition to take place, according to Caldwell, other conditions need to change as well, including the introduction of mass education, exposure to 'Western' norms and values, and appropriate supplies of family planning facilities and devices. It is, however, the demand side of the equation, not the supply side, which is the basic determinant.

On the basis of such conceptions, the population problem cannot be solved in isolation by means of family planning and population control but only in association with economic and social development which removes the incentives to have many children. There need not be a simple correlation between socio-economic progress and fertility decline, particularly not in the short term, but the basic contention is that such a correlation occurs in the long run.

Frances Moore Lappé and *Rachel Schurman* have added further perspectives to the debate. Their approach, the fourth type in the listing here, is characterised by a focus on power structures (Lappé and Schurman, 1989). Essentially what they have attempted to do is to find reasons for the persistence of the poverty and insecurity that keep the fertility rates at a high level, even in societies that have experienced considerable socio-economic changes. They argue in this context that the major explanatory factor is the distribution of power within households as well as between poor households and the rest of society. One of their main points is that to poor people, who live in insecurity and without access to even the most basic resources, the bringing of several children into the world can be seen as a defence mechanism against a repressive power structure. Therefore, aggregate socio-economic growth, modernisation and urbanisation are not by themselves sufficient to bring about fertility decline among the poor. Any strategy aimed at bringing down the birth rates must also aim at empowering the poor and giving them greater control over their own lives. Women especially must be empowered to choose other survival strategies than those based on large families. This, in turn, requires that they be given better access to earning opportunities, primary health care service and old age care; it requires that they are better educated; and it requires that they have access to safe and acceptable forms of contraception.

Lappé and Schurman have reached the general conclusion, based on their comparative studies of selected developing countries, that all the countries which have succeeded in bringing down their birth rates have also, during the same period, experienced radical social changes – changes which have given women new earning opportunities and other security- and status-enhancing alternatives to that of bearing and raising children.

Lappé, Collins, Schurman and other social scientists have undoubtedly contributed to making the debate on the population question more sophisticated and nuanced. This should not, however, conceal the fact that so many people have already been born in many countries and areas of the Third World that the non-renewable natural resources have come under such pressure that the foundations of life, both for their own and future generations, are threatened.

The discussion of environmental issues in the following sections makes only a few direct references to population growth, but it should be borne in mind that this growth – along with economic growth and increased or changed technological exploitation of natural resources – provides the basic dynamics and further compounds the environmental problems.

Environment and development

The views on the interrelationship between environmental protection and economic development vary greatly in the literature. At one extreme, one finds the position that environmental concerns are unimportant because technical solutions will be found in the long run; at the other, that the carrying capacity of the earth has been reached, or will be reached in the near future, and that further exploitation of the resource base should therefore be avoided. Somewhere in between these extremes the desirability of continued economic development is recognised, but, because of a rising concern about whether environmental constraints will limit development and whether development will cause serious environmental damage, it is accepted that future economic activities have to be shaped differently than in the past in order to avoid potentially devastating outcomes.

This and the following section will look at some of the main positions in the international debate and attempt to relate these to economic development theories. Global environmental problems such as carbon dioxide emissions, deterioration of the ozone layer and the greenhouse effect, although extremely important and potentially life-threatening, are not dealt with in the present context. Rather the focus is on the problems which have been deemed, by various authors, the most important for poor countries and poor people in the Third World. A few observations regarding the global depletion of resources are included, though, mainly because this is how many adherents to the most 'pessimistic' views approach the matter.

The most immediate environmental problems as seen from the perspective of the poor differ from those most important for affluent and highly industrialised countries. Thus, *scarcity and depletion* of resources – land, forests, water, biodiversity, etc. – are generally more important than *pollution* of air and water. To most poor people, probably more than one billion of them, the most serious and immediately life-threatening problems relate to unsafe water, inadequate sanitation and soil erosion. However, pollution problems do affect many people in poor countries, notably in mega-cities like Calcutta and Mexico City. The World Bank in a recent report has added to these dangers the health hazards associated with indoor smoke from cooking fires and outdoor smoke from coal burning (World Bank, 1992). In a similar vein, one could point to the occupational health and safety problems faced by millions of workers on plantations and in manufacturing enterprises.

Even though the pressures on natural resources per capita in the large majority of Third World countries are far less than in the highly industrialised countries, the pressures on non-renewable resources are often critical. This has to do with eco-systems' greater vulnerability in many developing countries, but is also caused by widespread poverty and poor people's efforts to improve their living conditions. Environmental problems in the Third World are often manifested far more intensely and more immediately than in the highly industrialised part of the world because survival margins there are very small; even minor decreases in yield and productivity (for example, as a result of land erosion) in an already low-yielding agriculture may have disastrous socio-economic effects.

The linking of environmental and development problems is not new; it goes back several decades. But it began to affect development research in earnest only from the 1970s onwards. Among the studies which prompted researchers to pay more attention to environmental issues was the report, *Limits to Growth*, published by the Club of Rome (Meadows et al., 1972). The authors of this report raised a number of critical questions concerning the then prevailing growth philosophy, especially the assumption that growth on earth could continue for ever. They came to a very different conclusion: if the then prevailing growth trends in world population, industrialisation, pollution, food production and resource depletion continued unchanged, the limits to growth on earth would be reached within 100 years. The authors also argued, however, that it was possible to avoid this outcome – but only if production techniques were fundamentally altered to take into account environmental concerns. At the same time material consumption had to be reduced, especially in the rich countries, to achieve a global equilibrium.

The publication of *Limits to Growth* gave rise to an extensive international debate, but generally the report's tones of disaster and the expectation of the approaching breakdown of the ecological systems were dismissed as scientifically unsubstantiated. Critics pointed in particular to the report's underestimating of the ability of technological innovation to increase productivity with progressively lower and more efficient utilisation of resources.

Three of the original four authors of the Club of Rome report have reacted strongly against the development optimists. On the basis of analyses of developments in the intervening period, published in 1992, they came to the conclusion that resource depletion and degradation have happened even faster than envisaged in the previous study, and therefore the earth is getting closer to its limits faster than originally assumed. Many essential resources, by 1990, had already surpassed rates of exploitation that were physically sustainable, and in many areas the environment had degraded so far that regeneration was no longer possible (Meadows et al., 1992).

We will not here look closer at either these or other gloomy predictions, but instead briefly review some of the main positions in the international debate on environment and development. This will also reveal how the environmental concerns have gradually 'climbed' higher and higher up the international development agenda since the 1970s.

In addition to the Club of Rome report, another important event in the early 1970s that triggered increased interest in the linkages between environment and development was the UN conference on human environment held in Stockholm. Among the outcomes of the Stockholm conference was the establishment of the United Nations Environmental Programme (UNEP). Apart from UNEP, it was to a large extent a number of international non-governmental organisations (NGOs) and research institutes which were at the forefront and setting the trends in the formulating of reports and strategies regarding environment and development during the 1970s. These included the World Resources Institute, International Institute for Environment and Development, and the International Union for the Conservation of Nature (now the World Conservation Union). Later the World Wildlife Fund (WWF, now the Worldwide Fund for Nature) also came into the picture. During the 1970s, these institutions and organisations prepared or commissioned several studies and strategy papers. The latter included guidelines for environmental impact evaluations of development projects with emphasis on the long-term perspective. Other papers dealt with broader environmental impact evaluations that encompassed whole eco-systems instead of looking only at isolated activities and their effects. Some of these papers related issues of poverty and survival strategies closely to the environmental problems faced by developing countries. As part of the exercises, notions of environmental sustainability were introduced and discussed extensively.

Later, in the Brundtland Commission's report published in 1987, the core term was changed from 'environmental sustainability' to 'sustainable development'. This was defined as 'meeting the needs of the present generation without compromising the needs of future generations' (Brundtland et al., 1987; cf. Chapter 3).

During the 1980s, environmental concerns were increasingly taken into account in official development co-operation as well as in the international fora within the UN system. With reports from a commission under the leadership of Willy Brandt, published in the wake of the oil crises, issues of global economic interdependence had been brought to the attention of decision makers throughout the world (Brandt Commission, 1980, 1983). With the report from the Brundtland Commission a few years later, global common interests and interdependencies in the area of the environment were placed centre stage. The latter report convincingly argued that the environmental problems had now reached proportions that required the global community to formulate a joint strategy for a 'common future' – for sustainable growth and development. The report further asserted that there are no conflicts between the goals of poverty eradication, socio-economic development and environmental protection.

The concept of sustainability – or at least the term – and the implied principle of aiming at both global and national ecological balances have been adopted by essentially all the organisations within the United Nations system, as well as by most other international and national agencies involved in co-operation with Third World countries. However, among development researchers the concept has been heavily criticised. The next section summarises this criticism and adds a brief discussion of the prospects, in abstract terms, of achieving sustainable development in a Third World context.

Sustainable development: trade-offs and win–win situations

The concept of sustainable development proposed by the Brundtland Commission has been criticised by development researchers for being too normative, too imprecise and impossible to operationalise. The way it was formulated by the Brundtland Commission further implies a danger that too much emphasis is given to preserving all natural resources, while it is evident that successful development will require depletion of some forms of natural capital and transformation of other forms into different types of physical and human capital. Following this line of reasoning, the overall goal should rather be to preserve natural resources in some aggregate sense, with losses in some areas replenished or compensated for in other areas.

The Brundtland Commission has also – despite the many strengths in its analyses – been criticised for having limited its strategy recommendations mainly to moral requests which, furthermore, are not addressed to anyone in particular. The Commission has pleaded urgently for changed and more environment-friendly attitudes and practices. On the other hand, it only sporadically discusses the fundamental conditions, under which private companies and other development actors operate. Similarly, very little is said about the conditions established by market prices and competition for the production and survival strategies of companies. In the case of some resources such as metals and minerals, scarcity and what economists call 'social value' – that is the value to society as a whole – are to some extent reflected in their market price. Here the dynamics of substitution, technological innovation and structural change are strong and may hence contribute to preserving the said resources.

In many other cases, however, such as water, forests and biodiversity, there is no correlation between social values and market prices, and therefore no economic incentives to avoid depletion or damage. In these cases it may be profitable, as seen from the perspective of individual companies and individual users, to exploit and produce without considering the environmental impact. Or formulated another way: it does not pay off to produce in an environment-friendly manner, because this often increases production costs for the individual companies and thereby restricts their profitability, or it reduces the incomes of land and forest users.

In the debates among development researchers, situations like these are often referred to in order to illustrate the incompatibility of goals of environmental protection and goals of economic development, as seen from the producers' perspective. Economists describe them as *trade-off* situations. These are not confined to situations where discrepancies occur between social values and market incentives. The literature also provides many examples of trade-offs where development efforts by producers in one area, for instance the cutting down of forests by users or exporters of timber, lead to environmental degradation and reduced income opportunities for other producers in other areas, for example lower yields on adjacent agricultural holdings due to land erosion caused by the deforestation.

With the World Bank's *World Development Report* for 1992, which dealt with the environment and development debate as a prelude to the UNCED conference in Rio de Janeiro the same year, the trade-off discussions were supplemented with the identification of so-called *win–win* situations. These are scenarios where increased production both improves the environment and enhances the capacity for long-term development. This applies, for example, where the construction of dikes or water tanks creates increased productivity in agriculture by making better use of rain water. A three-fold example would be the planting of trees around fields, protecting food production against wind and land erosion; at the same time, the planted trees can produce useful products such as berries, nuts, fuelwood, etc. and also contribute to the improvement of the soil quality by being nitrogen-fixing, etc.

Another type of win–win situation has been identified by researchers primarily concerned with poverty alleviation that is at the same time environmentally sustainable. A major point in this context is that there is often scope for substituting employment for environment depletion or pollution, that is utilising more labour while at the same time saving or preserving natural resources. *Michael Lipton* has mentioned as an example the direct application of fertilisers, especially nitrogenous fertilisers, to the root zone (Lipton, 1991). This would offer an opportunity to obtain a given level of agricultural output per area unit with more labour and less fertiliser than before. According to Lipton, there are many other ways in which human labour might be substituted for environmental depletion or pollution, fighting poverty and increasing sustainability in the same operation.

With examples and considerations like these, the World Bank and others have tried to show the complementarity between environment and development which the Brundtland Commission took as its starting point, but without arguing further for it in its analysis. The Bank's advisers have summed up their position by asserting that economic development and improved management of natural resources are complementary activities. Without protection of the environment, the capacity for long-term economic and social development will be undermined; without economic development, it will not be possible to protect the environment, chiefly because the many millions of poor people in the developing countries will then be forced to drain the natural resources further in their immediate vicinity.

The considerations regarding complementarity can be related more directly to the situation of small farmers: when they attempt to increase production without any concern for the environmental consequences, this is not because they are unaware of the negative effects, but because the poverty squeeze they are in does not give them any other choice. If the environmental problems in the poor countries are to be handled properly, the starting point has to be a poverty eradication strategy that aims at improving the livelihoods and production conditions of the poor. Only through elimination of the causes of poverty (or by breaking the negative poverty circle), and through the creation of a surplus from production, can environment-damaging forms of production be turned into a 'virtuous circle', where increased production and protection of the natural resources are linked.

For the World Bank, the outlined complementarities have been used as a basis for a series of policy recommendations of a neo-classical kind, where the market – guided by the state – is given a key role. According to the Bank, there is considerable scope for pursuing policies that simultaneously promote income growth, poverty alleviation and environmental improvement. Such policies include removing subsidies which encourage excessive use of fossil fuels, irrigation water and chemical inputs. State intervention is required to change the incentive structures provided by the market, but rather than replacing the price signals with a complex system of political controls, the state should confine its actions to influencing market prices and building on the positive links between increased efficiency and reduced resource exploitation. Further, the state should clarify the rights to manage and own land, forests and fisheries, because by doing so incentives will be created that encourage the peasants and other users to take better care of their natural resources and exploit them in a more sustainable manner. In general, the Bank recommends that natural resources be given economic 'values', and that the costs of depletion and pollution should be taken into account. Thus, user charges should be considered where appropriate, as in the case of both water and forests, in order to bring about environmental consciousness.

The World Bank has undoubtedly pointed to some of the central issues in its analysis and policy recommendations. The problems arise, according to the critics, when the recommendations – often in association with structural adjustment programmes – are implemented with a rigidity that overlooks local variation and the specific socio-economic conditions obtaining in the greatly dissimilar developing countries. This is the case, for example, where elimination of subsidies on fertilisers increases prices to a level where only the wealthier peasants can afford to buy them and thus maintain production at target levels. Although poor peasants may compensate to some extent for reduced input of fertilisers by applying more labour-intensive techniques, as mentioned above, the general experience is that a considerable increase in the price of fertilisers will often result in a worsening of their conditions – and possibly their eviction from the land. The final outcome of the withdrawal of subsidies under such circumstances could imply a transfer of resources from poor to rich, not the intended win–win situation.

As alternatives to the World Bank's environmental strategies, attention is directed to attempts at formulating integrated strategies under terms such as *ecodevelopment*. The basic idea here is to elaborate specific development strategies for each ecological region, and to formulate them in such a way that individualised solutions are found for each region that take into account both the ecological and the socio-cultural conditions obtaining. The aim, moreover, is to meet both the short- and long-term needs of the population concerned. Accordingly, ecodevelopment strategies operate with criteria of progress that are related to each particular case, and adaptation to the environment plays an important role. The goal of development here has no universal meaning. The poor and 'backward' countries should not look for the images of their own future in the 'advanced', industrialised countries. Rather each of them should look for such images in their own ecology and culture.

Conceptions of this kind can be traced back to *Ignacy Sachs* (Sachs, 1974), but a similar approach has been proposed by development researchers such as Michael Redclift and Björn Hettne (Redclift, 1987; Hettne, 1990). In these parts of the environmental discussion, emphasis is given to a re-formulation of concepts like self-reliance, democratisation and people's participation in a context of adapting development efforts to the existing environment. In a sense, these parts of the debate belong to the schools of thought treated in this book under headings like 'alternative development' (cf. Part V).

The international debate on environmental problems reached a climax with the UNCED conference in Rio in June 1992. This conference was preceded by the preparation of numerous reports, including country strategy notes for the improvement of the environment in most of the participating countries. The extensive preparations suggested that a breakthrough in international environmental co-operation was perhaps close, but the results of the UNCED conference were generally disappointing. Few binding (and later ratified) agreements were arrived at, and the expectations of the developing countries about additional aid transfers to preserve and protect the environment were certainly favourably received, but did not meet with commitments proportionate to these expectations. Nor were they proportionate to the extent of the problems.

Environment as a theoretical development problem

Environment as a development problem inserts itself at the intersection between nature and society. On the one hand, environmental problems are mainly problems which have to do with the surrounding nature; on the other, it is evident that environmental problems have considerable social, political and economic consequences, as well as causes. The analysis of environmental problems must therefore of necessity combine analytic approaches from both the natural sciences and social sciences, that is cross the traditional disciplinary barriers and establish a holistic view of environmental problems and natural resource management.

Environmental problems, as products of processes in nature and as products of human actions, thus complicate the matter in at least two ways. First, it is by tradition difficult for representatives of natural sciences and social sciences to communicate and understand each other, because their perspectives, approaches, concepts and 'discourses' are so dissimilar. It is even more difficult for them to establish multidisciplinary collaboration which cuts across the conventional disciplinary boundaries – and limitations. Second, there are considerable obstacles to establishing theoretical propositions regarding the nature–society relationships which go beyond rigidly defined disciplinary boundaries. At the same time, appropriate solutions cannot be achieved by natural scientists expanding their discipline's subject area to include the political-economic aspects; nor can solutions be found by social scientists who try to act as experts in areas like soil science or climatic changes. The environment as a theoretical problem thus involves an as yet unredeemed challenge: to establish a new theoretical framework for scientifically investigating the interrelations between nature and society (Dickens, 1992).

It is beyond the scope of the present review to delve further into this problem. Instead we shall confine ourselves, in the following paragraphs, to mentioning briefly the different perspectives on environmental problems that can be identified within social science research on development. Two main positions can be highlighted which continue to characterise much of the literature.

The first position, essentially in line with classical dependency theories, claims that most global environmental problems are the outcome of the unrestrained development of capitalism. Environmental problems faced by Third World countries, according to this position, are further aggravated because of global processes of economic exploitation. Transnational corporations, particularly the large agro-business firms, are the major actors in these processes. They operate under conditions where there are no economic incentives to make them act in an environment-friendly manner. On the contrary, many resource-depleting and polluting firms are attracted to the poor countries as a result of the more lenient policies and regulations pertaining to their activities in poor, peripheral as opposed to affluent, centre countries. In the latter group of countries, environmental protection legislation has increased steadily over the last decade, while most poor countries have not dared to introduce similar restrictive policies for fear of scaring away foreign investors.

The second position, broadly in line with neo-classical economics, does not regard capitalist development as the problem. Rather, capitalism and production under market conditions are seen as part of the solution to many environmental problems. When the market economy advances, and when the previously free goods – water, land, forests, etc. – are assigned economic values, unrestrained exploitation will be significantly limited. The reasoning behind this assertion is that environmental deterioration to a large extent is the consequence of pervasive externalities in the extraction, processing, transport, consumption and disposal of goods and services. Externalities are costs (and benefits) not borne by agents engaged in economic activity. By 'correcting' the distortions in the price/market system arising from such externalities – that is by assigning costs to environmental damage and forcing these costs upon the relevant actors – governments can assist in improving resource management without hindering continued capitalist development.

At a lower level of aggregation and abstraction there has, since the early 1980s, been a pronounced tendency among development researchers to focus more and more on the specific conditions under which the direct producers in developing countries produce and manage their natural environment. Researchers are increasingly interested in how producers decide what to produce and how to produce it. They look at the factors which are taken into account and, based on their observations, they try to understand the reasons for adopting specific production strategies. Often this kind of research is associated with a recognition of the direct producers' specialist knowledge of how sustainable production may be achieved, if they were not so restricted by the scarcity of resources and the squeeze of poverty.

On the basis of this recognition, various theoretical propositions have been formulated regarding natural resource management, especially in agriculture. The next section will briefly review some of these propositions.

Natural resource management: Blaikie, Hardins, Ostrom and Wade

Peasants in the world's many poor and densely populated countries are often forced to overuse and exhaust the land, because this is their only survival strategy in the short term. Where possible, peasants are further prompted to bring more and more land under cultivation. This is often the only economically rational choice in a situation where poverty and increasing population pressures force them into short-term efforts to increase production.

The intensification of land use often results in soil erosion. The incorporation of more land leaves less public land (for example for communal grazing) which then tends to become overused, or it results in the extension of agriculture on to soils that are not suitable for cultivation. The cultivation of the marginal, and in the ecological sense vulnerable, land can perhaps during the first seasons provide the intended increase in production, but subsequently there is a high risk of degradation and erosion which, in turn, leads to a decline in production.

From the debate about environmental deterioration and natural resource management, two approaches appear to warrant particular attention. One of these applies a broad political-economic perspective and pays special attention to the interests of the various actors involved. This approach further focuses on the structural barriers which, while promoting the interests of certain actors, at the same time prevent others from pursuing their interests. The second approach is inspired by new institutional economics, game theory and rational choice theories. Here, the attributes of the resources as economic goods, and the incentive structures that govern the behaviour of the actors, are central elements (cf. Chapter 17).

The British geographer *Piers Blaikie* can be seen as a prominent representative of the political-economic approach (Blaikie, 1985; Blaikie and Brookfield, 1987). In his analysis of the political economy of soil erosion in developing countries, Blaikie attempts to combine a 'place-based' concern with where more specifically soil erosion occurs, with a 'non-place-based' concern for political-economic relations between people who use land, and between them and others. He further applies a bottom-up approach, beginning with the smallest unit of decision making (the household or a logging company), and moving up through local political organisations like the village council to the government and the international system. Which decision-making units should be included in a specific study, according to Blaikie, should be left to the analyst to determine. The important thing is to take into consideration all the actors which, in a given area, affect land use and thus potentially have an impact upon soil erosion.

Blaikie comes to the conclusion that the occurrence of soil erosion can often be explained with reference to an altered use of the land. This, in turn, is the result of rational decisions taken by the land users. To illustrate: if there is a shortage of labour, some parts of the cultivation will be done with less care; rehabilitation of terraces and micro-terraces is frequently among the first tasks to be neglected.

While the traditional farming-systems approach limits itself to analysing the activities on the individual agricultural holding and seeks the explanations for soil degradation at the micro-level, Blaikie and other adherents of the political-economic approach look at the household as part of a much larger system (cf. Belshaw, Blaikie and Stocking, 1991). They argue in this context that although agriculture is the main activity for rural households, it is not the only activity. Peasants have other income opportunities as well. Therefore, they have to decide on their allocation of time and resources to different types of activities. As a result of the households' dissimilar control over resources and their access to income opportunities, they will pursue very different resource management strategies. Similarly, at a higher level of aggregation, different social classes have varying interests in relation to land management. The point is that all these aspects of the soil-erosion problematique have to be studied in order to arrive at substantiated explanations. The same applies to other types of resource degradation.

With respect to soil erosion, Blaikie claims that, generally speaking, only households above a certain level of income and with control over a certain amount of assets can afford to manage land utilisation with a long-term perspective. At the same time, ruling classes in many less developed countries are frequently not very concerned about soil erosion and its impact, because it will not directly affect them. Hence, the policies pursued by Third World governments are often unconcerned with the problem – and a large number of poor peasants are unable to tackle it on their own.

According to Blaikie and other adherents of the political-economic approach the problems of soil erosion – and other types of resource degradation in rural areas – are aggravated by the integration of peasant economies into the world economic system. Moreover, several structural adjustment programmes have further added to the difficulties by altering the conditions for agriculture and the use of resources in many developing countries (Winpenny, 1991). Redclift, among others, has pointed to the importance of the international distribution of labour in agricultural production and to the trade policies of the industrialised countries (especially the European Community) as factors which fundamentally reduce the poor countries' competitiveness and thus the profitability of agricultural production. As a consequence, the affected peasants' opportunities for pursuing long-term sustainable resource-use strategies are severely restricted (Redclift, 1987).

The political-economic approach has contributed to incorporating ecological systems and issues into the perspective of social science research by emphasising the interrelations between physical nature and societal structures and processes. The approach makes it possible to consider and analyse resource degradation, depletion and pollution within a wider perspective, encompassing socio-economic conditions such as market mechanisms, forms of ownership and security of tenure, etc. However, neither Blaikie nor any other exponent of this approach can be said to have elaborated a coherent theory with general explanatory power. Rather, what they have contributed is a conceptual framework which can be used to structure empirical analyses.

The second approach to studies of resource management focuses on the importance of social institutions for economic activities and processes. The basic thesis is that degradation – or conservation – of natural resources can be understood and explained by looking at the users' incentives to exploit the concerned resources as opposed to the incentives for not over-exploiting them. It is further argued that several different institutional arrangements and sets of rules can be appropriate for sustainable exploitation of natural resources, but that it depends to a large extent on the character of these resources and the role they play for the various actors involved. By this is meant, for example, whether one actor's consumption of a given resource affects other actors' opportunities for using it. Another important aspect is whether one person or group of users can exclude other users.

One category of resources – the *common-pool resources* – has attracted particular attention in the theoretical debate in recent years. The common-pool resources are interesting because these are resources that are both scarce and at the same time of such a nature that the costs of over-exploitation do not reveal themselves immediately; moreover, those guilty of the over-exploitation cannot be forced to pay. Common-pool resources typically include common grazing areas, common forests, common fishing waters, and the like. They have often been overlooked both in connection with the formulation of economic policies and in the context of international development co-operation. Agricultural policies have mainly focused on privately owned agricultural land. The common-pool resources, however, are often very important reserves for the rural population, notably the poorest.

Garrett Hardin's celebrated article, *The Tragedy of the Commons* (1968), was one of the first analyses to uncover the very complex interaction of different factors involved in a long-term rational use of these types of resources. Hardin's aim was to show how degradation of the environment can be expected whenever many individuals use a scarce resource in common. He illustrated the logic of the argument with a pasture open to a large number of herders. His core point was that a rational herder would add more and more animals because he receives immediate benefits from his own animals – and only much later bears a small share of the costs resulting from over-grazing. Hardin concluded that here lay the tragedy of the commons: 'Each man is locked into a system that compels him to increase his herd without limit – in a world that is limited' (Hardin, 1968). What Hardin's model showed, in other words, was that in relation to common resources the optimum strategy for the individual is not the optimum strategy as seen from the point of view of the local community or society in a broader sense.

Local customary rules in the past often prevented over-exploitation of common resources, but, with increasing population pressure and spatial expansion of agricultural production, these systems have tended to break down. They have been replaced either by increased state control or privatisation of the commons. Both these strategies, however, have serious shortcomings: state control over grazing areas, forests or fishing waters is very expensive – particularly in comparison with the economic surpluses extracted from these commons. Moreover, it is a general experience from the Sahel countries in Africa that state control has not prevented the over-exploitation and depletion of the resources (Lawry, 1989).

Neither has privatisation of the natural resources always proved to be a good solution. First, some resources such as fishing waters can only with great difficulty be allotted to different users. Secondly, the very strength of the pastoralist production systems is their mobility. Allotting particular tracts of land to them would prevent the herders from taking their animals to areas where the grazing is particularly good at a given time. Thirdly, and most importantly, privatisation in most cases will not benefit the poorest who will continue to depend on the commons – for grazing, fuelwood, etc. When common resources are privatised these poor people are left with even fewer resources to exploit which, in turn, is likely to result in overuse and long-term degradation, followed by declining living standards for those dependent upon the remaining common resources.

Hardin's analysis has prompted extensive literature that has sought to nuance his views (for example Bromley, 1989; Ostrom, 1990; Wade, 1988). Some of the critics have pointed to the paradox that if Hardin's analysis were correct, why then are not all common-pool resources tragically depleted? In addition, they have put emphasis on finding the types of institutions and collective arrangements which will provide the individual with stronger in-centives to follow a strategy in harmony with the optimal strategy for the community. *Elinor Ostrom* and *Robert Wade* should be singled out here for their attempt at mapping and systematising the conditions for long-term sustainable use of common resources. These conditions are several, and they concern the physical character of the resources, the number of users involved, the social rules governing their behaviour, and the role of the state.

Elinor Ostrom's 1990 study may be used to illustrate the mode of reason-ing applied (Ostrom, 1990). Based on extensive analyses of cases where appropriators have successfully managed their common-pool resources she, on the one hand, shows that imposition of private property rights or central-ised regulation are not the only ways to solve the problem outlined in Hardin's model. On the other hand, she tries to identify the institutional arrangements supplied by appropriators that are most effective in ensuring sustainable resource use. She tries to find out why some appropriators can supply themselves with adequate rules, compliance with those rules and collective monitoring of conformity to the rules, whereas others cannot. Ostrom confines herself mainly to small-scale common-pool resources.

A detailed review of Ostrom's conclusions will not be attempted here. Rather, we shall limit the presentation to pointing out some of the 'design principles' proposed by her for elaborating appropriate rules. The first prin-ciple is to define clearly the appropriators who are authorised to use a particular common-pool resource. The second is to relate the rules to the specific attributes of the common-pool resource and the community of users. The third is to have the rules designed, at least in part, by local appropriators themselves. The fourth is to work out rules for monitoring by individuals accountable to the local appropriators. The fifth and last principle is to design rules concerning graduated punishments for those not conforming. When resource users are faced with rules meeting these criteria, Ostrom argues, safe and credible commitments can be made, provided the overall (expected) net benefits are greater that what could be achieved by following short-term, egoistic strategies. Ostrom suggests a rather complex framework for analysing this latter issue, which we will not go into further.

Although Ostrom's and other scholars' criticism of Hardin was to a large extent motivated by a wish to challenge his 'tragedy perspective', their analyses have not really removed the gloomy expectations associated with the common-pool resources. The institutional arrangements that, based on experience, have proved the most adequate and effective for sustainability – self-organ-isation and self-management of the resources – are mainly based on a complicated combination of preconditions which cannot simply be created or reconstructed as per directive. Collective self-management is a socially and culturally embedded institutional arrangement which, if it does not exist, will take a long time to bring about – and success is likely to be achieved only under specific conditions.

In the present context, we have concerned ourselves mainly with common-pool resources, but the approaches and methods applied in Ostrom's and others' institutional analyses can, in principle, be extended to other types of natural resources. In addition, they can, as we shall see later, be used to deal with economic issues more generally (cf. Chapter 17).

PART III

Third World Politics and the State

CHAPTER 12

Political Development and State Building

In the chapter on the theoretical heritage (Chapter 2) we saw how social scientists had a tendency to divide themselves along subject traditions and separate schools of thought. This division also characterised most of the mainstream development research all the way up to the 1970s, and even today continues to play an important role. In a similar way as within development economics, there has been within sociology and political science a widespread preference for constructing comparatively narrow mono-disciplinary theories, even to the extent that the political science approaches have distinguished themselves from the sociological and social-anthropological discourses.

The Marxist-inspired approaches have, in principle, aimed at establishing multidisciplinary perspectives, but even within this mainstream of theory construction the political and economic aspects of the political economy have been given very different emphases. Thus, Neo-Marxist dependency theories have been preoccupied mainly with economic processes and have paid much less attention to politics and the state. In contrast, there has emerged from the class and state theoretical approaches a tradition of primarily focusing on non-economic conditions, although these have also been studied in relation to the economic-structural foundations.

The following chapters will take a closer look at some of the most widespread and influential theories of politics and political change in the Third World. The emphasis is on political macro-phenomena, including state building and forms of government. This presentation and discussion can be seen as a parallel to the review of the theories of economic development and underdevelopment. Later – in Part IV – we shall see how many development researchers over the last two decades have attempted to combine the economic and political perspectives within more comprehensive and multidisciplinary theoretical frameworks. However, no simple chronological sequence can be observed in the sense that multidisciplinarity has replaced monodisciplinary approaches. Rather, the latter continue to exist alongside the former.

The theories concerning politics and state in the Third World are rather extensive and multifarious. In comparison with the economic theories they have, in addition, often been formulated as separate attempts to interpret and explain particular phenomena in a specific context – and not as answers to common fundamental questions concerning continental or global issues. As a corollary, the political science debates have not become integral parts of one comprehensive international debate, as has been the tendency within development economics, but rather have retained their character as a number of separate debates. This makes it more difficult to create a general overview and at the same time penetrate deeper into the pertinent features of the individual attempts at interpreting and explaining. We shall, however, try to strike a balance through a discussion of certain basic conceptions and central theses proposed by a number of selected theories. Particular attention will be given to their *conceptions of the role of politics in society*; *the interaction between the political processes and the social order*; and *decisive factors affecting state building, forms of regime and political change.*

As part of the presentation, we shall focus upon normative elements in theory formation. This requires no further justification, if scientific value relativism is acknowledged as a basic methodological principle (cf. Chapter 2). None the less, it is worth emphasising here that theories of political change, in particular, invoke critical evaluations of whether the normative elements cause distortions and biases, because these theories often apply ethnocentric conceptions of development. The dangers of distortion and bias are furthermore not only present in such explicitly normative theories, they are also found where the desirable is replaced by experience-based expectations because these, in a similar way to normative premises, can place reality perceptions in a sort of conceptual straitjacket. Critical alertness is thus required in connection with both liberalist modernisation theory and Marxist periodisations of political history on the basis of modes of production and class rule.

Before reviewing a selection of the most influential political science theories, it may be useful briefly to consider why political macro-phenomena in the developing countries were given much greater attention during the 1950s and continued to attract considerable attention in the following decades. It is noteworthy that the upswing took place primarily in the USA, and only later and to a less pronounced extent in the former European colonial powers. This was probably due to American foreign policy in this period being significantly more globally oriented than that of the other Western industrialised countries. Concurrently with political decolonisation in an increasing number of developing countries, and under the influence of the distinctive bi-polarisation in the international political system, this led to larger parts of the Third World becoming of interest to American policy makers.

Under these circumstances, the conditions were favourable for greatly increased funding of American political science research on the developing countries. At the same time, the influential American Social Science Research Council adapted itself to the new circumstances by appointing a committee to initiate and co-ordinate comparative political studies. It was this committee and its two first chairmen, *Gabriel Almond* and *Lucien Pye*, who gave strong impetus to both theory construction and empirical studies of political conditions and political development in Latin America, Asia, the Middle East and Africa (cf. Riggs, 1981; Randall and Theobald, 1985: pp. 21–33).

By the end of the 1960s, this section of American political science continued to hold a prominent, if no longer dominant position in the construction of theories on political conditions and processes of change in the developing countries. Seen in retrospect, it appears appropriate to term the product of this school of thought the *classical political modernisation theory*. The use of the word 'classical' – as will become apparent – does not signify an uncritical recognition of the theory, rather an observation that this school functioned in important respects as a reference point for the subsequent elaboration of several other political science theories.

Classical political modernisation theory: Almond and Coleman

Almond, Pye and other representatives of this school rarely, after 1960, used the term 'modernisation theory' themselves. Instead they referred to their approach as a *political development approach*. The similarities with the sociological and economic modernisation theories of the time are, however, so striking that stressing these seems warranted.

Among the common features is the basic dualism: the contrasting of the traditional and undeveloped on the one hand, with the modern and developed, on the other. Like the economic growth and modernisation theories (cf. Chapter 5), the political development theories were characterised by optimistic conceptions of modernisation as mutually reinforcing sequences of economic growth, social and political stability, national integration and democratisation. The developing countries were backward, but they were on their way into a modernisation process, chiefly thanks to the strong Western influence during both colonial rule and after independence.

It was difficult to find empirical justification for this optimism – even in the 1960s. Therefore, almost from the start, the classical theory was criticised for containing a strong element of wishful thinking combined with a value-loaded, positive attitude towards the political systems of the USA and other highly industrialised North-Western societies. These systems were seen as modern, developed and complex. They were seen as being characterised by an extensive differentiation and specialisation in political life; a democratic form of government; citizen equality; well-functioning, universalistic and impartial public administration; and considerable capacity for managing societal development and the distribution of goods and benefits not allocated by the market mechanisms (Pye, 1966; Coleman, 1976).

On all these dimensions, according to classical modernisation theory, the political systems in Latin America, Asia and Africa were undeveloped and bound by traditions. It was recognised, though, that considerable differences existed among the developing countries, but these variations were not assigned central importance in theory construction because all systems were expected to undergo a common process of change, where the different traditions would be destroyed and replaced by institutions and structures similar to those found in the modern and highly industrialised societies. A precondition for this transformation was, however, a massive and continuous transfer and engrafting upon these societies of Western-type institutions such as modern, Weberian bureaucracy; popularly elected bodies; political parties; interest organisations; and Western education and legal systems.

It was an important point in the classical modernisation theories that the developing countries were in a *state* of underdevelopment, which preceded their modernisation. Underdevelopment was not conceived of as a dynamic process and definitely not seen as a result of either colonisation or other influences from the industrialised countries.

Implicit in the notions of promoting political development through transfer of Western institutions and strategies for the entire state-building process there were several assumptions. One of the most central was the assumption of the autonomy of the political system *vis-à-vis* the rest of society. Political development and forms of regime were overwhelmingly determined by political conditions; other societal factors appeared in the classical theory only as part of 'the environment' – as an unspecified number of factors whose relative importance was, moreover, not specified.

Certain adjustments of the classical theory occurred during the 1960s and at the beginning of the 1970s. The several empirical studies undertaken within the conceptual framework proposed by the political development theorists led in fact to many reinterpretations and revisions of both concepts and hypotheses. Many of the American researchers delivered, despite the theoretical straitjacket, concrete insights of lasting importance. In the overall theory construction, the revisions were most clearly expressed towards the end of the 1960s, when the focus was shifted from the underdevelopment syndrome and the evolutionary change process to the *crises in political development* (see Binder et al., 1968).

The revisions were, however, far from sufficient to secure a leading position for the classical theory into the 1970s. It was, in particular, the dynamic and normative elements in the theories on political development which slipped into the background during this period. Many of the central concepts, on the other hand, have survived and are still used in much of political development research. We shall therefore dwell for a moment upon these concepts and the conceptions of the political system and its processes contained within them.

To acquire a general overview of the terminology in the classical political modernisation theory, it will be useful to go one step backwards to the theoretical framework originally proposed by the American political scientist,

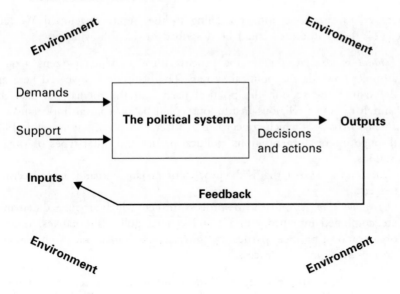

Figure 12.1 Easton's model of a political system

David Easton. It was his systems analysis of political life that provided much of the basis for Almond's conceptual framework in the 1960s.

Easton worked out a systems theory which he assumed could be applied, in principle, to all types of society (Easton, 1953, 1965). In a simplified form, Easton's model of a political system can be represented as shown in Figure 12.1. The model refers to all the actions and all the types of behaviour which affect the authoritative allocation of values for a society. The system is open to the environment, from where it receives inputs in two forms, partly as demands, partly as support for the persistence of the system. Within the political system itself, the inputs received are processed and transformed into outputs – that is decisions and actions – which further impact upon the environment and, through a feedback-loop, upon the conditions under which the political system exists.

Using this simplified model as his point of departure, Easton worked out an extensive and coherent abstract theory of the political system. His main interest was to uncover the conditions under which political systems persist, not only in an unchanged form, but also in changed forms. We shall not look closer at Easton's own theory, but some of the concepts which Almond, based on Easton's systems theory, elaborated further with special reference to the developing societies will be noted (Almond and Coleman, 1960).

Almond was interested in establishing categories of processes whose more exact contents and character could then subsequently be described in empirical analyses of political conditions in the underdeveloped countries. Almond operated in this connection with four different types of processes. With reference to the conditions prevailing in the highly developed Western societies, these processes could be described in the following way:

1. *Political socialisation*, that is the process through which citizens acquire attitudes towards the political system. The institutions involved here are the family, the school, the political party and the media, but also the church or other religious institutions could be of central importance.
2. *Political recruitment* which concerns the citizens' involvement in political life through interest organisations, political parties and other types of organisations.
3. *Articulation of interests*, that is the process of making demands upon decision makers.
4. *Aggregation of interests*, that is the process through which articulated demands are combined into programmes and general policy alternatives. Interest organisations, political parties and government bureaucracies all play important roles in this process.

With the help of these categories, the conditions in different developing countries could be described with particular emphasis on the deviations from the conditions in the industrialised countries. Almond and other researchers who used this approach found, for example, that political socialisation often took place through several parallel processes, and often in such a way that it was hard to get widespread support for the existing political system. Similarly, interest aggregation in many developing societies turned out to be inefficient, and therefore the political system was overloaded and threatened with breakdown.

Almond also tried to categorise the political system's output. Here he operated with three categories, which largely resembled the traditional trisecting between legislative, executive and judicial authorities. He simply labelled them a little differently, namely as three functions: rule-making; rule-implementation; and rule-adjudication.

In the further elaboration of the concepts up through the 1960s and the 1970s, Almond and the other political development researchers gradually put more emphasis on a political system's *capacity* in different respects. They turned their attention away from the input categories and directed it instead towards the political system's capacity to respond and adapt – and thus in general secure its own survival. A total of five functions and capacities were emphasised as being decisive:

1. *The extractive capacity* The system's ability to extract physical and human resources from society and mobilise them for particular purposes.
2. *The regulative capacity* Its ability to regulate and control the behaviour of individuals and groups.
3. *The distributive capacity* The system's ability to allocate goods, services, status and other kinds of opportunity in society, and at the same time secure the

necessary support from sufficiently large proportions of the politically active population.

4. *The symbolic capacity* The extent to which the system commands symbolic means of creating support for the national political entity and its government.

5. *The responsive capability* The ability to react adequately to inputs. This could imply repression of certain demands and the transformation of others into outputs in the form of decisions and actions.

The overall point of studying the political systems of the developing countries was to determine whether these systems were sufficiently well-equipped and strong enough to cope with the pressures from the environment. A further question was whether they were capable of promoting economic and social development along with political development. The four general problems that the classical political modernisation theorists were preoccupied with in their quite extensive empirical studies can be summarised as:

1. The problem of state-building, that is creating bureaucratic and other structures that can penetrate and integrate society and ensure the required support needed for the political system to persist.
2. The problem of nation-building, that is creating a political community and promoting the citizens' transfer of loyalty from smaller groups, like tribes and local communities, to the larger political system.
3. The problem of participation and getting the citizens to participate actively and positively in political life.
4. The problem of distributing and redistributing goods to secure the well-being of the citizens, both as a goal in itself and as a means to bringing about the support for the state-nation, the form of regime, and the government in office.

Even though the classical modernists' approach in its entirety retreated into the shadow of several competing approaches and schools from the beginning of the 1970s onwards, these four major problems have remained central issues for much of political science research. And many of Almond's concepts can still be identified, albeit mostly in modified versions, in this research (cf. also Chapter 19). In the present context, however, we shall leave this school of thought and turn our attention towards some of the alternative approaches and their understanding of the political conditions and political development in the Third World.

The first alternative approach, dealt with in the next section, may be referred to as dialectical modernisation theory. There then follows a brief review of selected theories and strategies regarding state building. The dependency theories and their understanding of the political processes are taken up subsequently. A brief discussion of a special variation of the modernisation theories – David Apter's attempt to progress further in the theory construction with emphasis on consequences of the modernisation process – then follows. The chapter is concluded with a section on Jean-François Bayart's theory of historical trajectories which tries to understand how states and political systems are individually created as complex products of long-term evolution.

It should be noted that there is no chronological order in this sequence of presentations. The whole period since the end of the 1960s has been characterised by parallel elaborations of competing, and to a certain extent mutually exclusive, theories.

Dialectical modernisation theory: Gusfield and the Rudolphs

The methodical approaches and theories categorised here under the term *dialectical modernisation theory* do not have the same unitary characteristics as political development theory. On the contrary, there is great multiplicity in many respects. The main reason for grouping them together in spite of that is that they do share some fundamental common conceptions regarding the interaction between political processes and the social order, as well as with respect to notions about the most important factors affecting state building, the form of regime and political change.

The dialectical modernisation theories retain from classical theory the distinction between tradition and modernity, but add nuances and dynamics to it. Thus, they emphasise that tradition need not impede development. Some traditional institutions may even promote political development by ensuring a smooth transition from old practices to new ones. Modern institutions, on the other hand, when implanted in a traditional setting may sometimes restrain political development or perhaps come to function in unexpected ways. The theories further emphasise that traditional societies are not necessarily stagnant, but may be very dynamic, heterogeneous and vigorous. Traditional institutions and practices may even be revitalised when confronted with attempts to modernise society (cf. Gusfield, 1976).

These views lead to the central conception of tradition and modernity as social phenomena that interact in a dialectical manner, where both phenomena are altered in the process, and where the result is not simply modernisation but numerous different processes of change. Instead of following the same pattern of change, as envisaged in the classical modernisation theory, the developing societies will follow different trajectories determined to a large extent by their traditional institutions and practices.

The politicisation of the Indian caste system – and conversely the castes' critical importance for the formal political processes – is often cited in the literature as an example of a so-called dialectical interaction. As a traditional institution, the caste system has changed markedly during the twentieth century, but at the same time certain aspects of the system have been revitalised and today exert a strong influence upon modern political institutions, for example political parties, and make them function quite differently in India than in other societies where a similar social structure is not found (Rudolph and Rudolph, 1967).

On the basis of conceptions such as these, the traditional or tradition-bound institutions and practices in the developing countries cannot be ignored. On the contrary, they have to be researched carefully, because they impact heavily upon how a modernisation and development process will be shaped. In keeping with this view, much research within this school has concerned itself with penetrating analyses of indigenous social, political and cultural structures, institutions, practices and norms. In particular, social networks (including patron–client relations), ethnicity and religion have been focused on. Assessed retrospectively, there is no doubt that the dialectical modernisation theories have contributed significantly in these areas to our understanding of the complex dynamics involved in the so-called modernisation processes.

Originally, dialectical modernisation theories were based chiefly on studies in India and other societies in Asia. Furthermore, most of the studies in the 1960s and 1970s focused on the micro-level. In both these respects decisive changes have occurred since then. During the 1980s, in particular, empirical studies of African societies contributed most to theory construction. At the same time, the perspective has generally been scaled up and extended to cover societies in their entirety (Sandbrook, 1985; Hydén, 1983, 1986).

Several of the more recent theories of political and social order in Africa deserve special attention, both because of their contribution to theory construction, and because they shed new light on African societies, especially on the forms of regime and the decision-making processes. We shall later raise these again for discussion in connection with different attempts to interpret and explain the forms of regime in the Third World (Chapter 13).

Dialectical modernisation theories, as is implicitly stated in the above, are not narrowly focused on the political processes alone. Basically they are concerned with the much broader interactions between society and state. The present account should therefore be seen as only a partial introduction. Other aspects of the problematique and the issues dealt with by dialectical modernisation theories are further discussed as part of the review of the political economy of development (Chapter 17), and also in Part V of the book where the attention is on civil society.

Political order and state-building strategies: Huntington and Clapham

The third group of theories to be reviewed here is characterised by a strong focus on political institutionalisation and the capacity of government. Moreover, the individual theories are characterised by close linkages between hypotheses and recommendations – between findings concerning causal relationships and proposed strategies for state building. The theorists lumped together in the following paragraphs disagree on the specific hypotheses and recommendations, but they share a preoccupation with the need for institutionalisation and strengthening of government agencies in order to establish order and consolidate the state-nations in the Third World.

One of the first and most consistent theories on state building was formulated by *Samuel P. Huntington* towards the end of the 1960s (Huntington, 1968). Huntington shared with the classical political modernisation theory several of its basic assumptions, including the expectation that political development in backward societies would be brought about by introducing institutions according to the Western model. But Huntington was not optimistic, and he clearly stated that the classical theories' conception of the modernisation and development process as mutually reinforcing sequences of change was erroneous. Instead he referred to the several cases of political breakdown and setbacks which could be observed during the 1960s, notably in Africa.

In his interpretation of the events, Huntington concluded that the nature of the transformation process in the developing countries – especially in the early phases – was such that it would lead to political instability or even chaos if steps were not taken as part of the state-building process to neutralise these effects. One of his theses was that the initiation of an economic development process led to expectations which far exceeded what could be redeemed. The result would be increasingly widespread and intensified frustrations among the citizens which, in turn, would prompt uprisings and rebellions. If popular participation were encouraged in such circumstances, through the introduction of democracy and civil rights, there would be imminent danger of a political breakdown.

Huntington therefore asserted that things had to happen in a different order. Generally, the state apparatus had to be extended and the political processes thoroughly *institutionalised* prior to the initiation of the economic and social development processes. This was an important precondition for political stability and consequently for sustainable progress. More specifically, it was the components of the civil administration with responsibility for law and order, as well as the military, which had to be strengthened in the initial phases. This, according to Huntington, was a realistic strategy because these state bodies were already the strongest components of the post-colonial states.

Huntington's theory and state-building strategy has never enjoyed any widespread respect among development researchers. For many years, the criticism from this quarter has been scathing. Not least, Huntington's conceptions of the military as a monolithic actor with considerable capacity for co-ordination and promotion of economic development has been opposed vehemently and with indisputable empirical support (cf., for example, Randall and Theobald, 1985: pp. 77–98). In addition, his attempt to justify military regimes has been met with strong opposition.

Despite these and other criticisms against Huntington, his conceptions and basic strategy have had considerable influence – mainly on political decision makers – in both developing and industrialised countries. Huntington's perspective and focus has moreover left permanent marks among the development theorists. Only few have accepted his specific version of the state-building strategy with its clear preference for the controlling and ruling components, but many have adopted the more basic ideas of strengthening the political institutions before, or at least in step with, economic and social changes. In that sense, Huntington can be seen as one of the first exponents of the many later theories and strategies concerning *reaching-down* state building.

What these theories and strategies basically have in common is the notion of the state, and above all the bureaucracy, as the central and most important political institution in the development process. Consequently, it is of vital importance that the state and its various agencies are strengthened considerably so that they can 'reach down and out' to the citizens, and thereby lead or pressurise the citizens into behaviour which is appropriate for promoting economic development.

We shall not, in this context, look closer at the various theories and strategies for strengthening the public administration's capacity and efficiency. But it should be briefly mentioned that the international debate on this topic, during the 1970s and 1980s, became steadily more nuanced and differentiated. Opinions expressed moved towards an increasing understanding: (a) that Western institutions and the state-building strategies pursued by the industrialised countries cannot simply be transplanted to the developing countries; (b) that the developing countries are so different that different strategies must be applied; and (c) that the public administration must accept 'the people' as *partners* in the development process – not just as clients or a passive target group of intended beneficiaries.

Parallel to these tendencies it has been pointed out that although the law and order components in most developing countries probably concentrate and exercise more power than other state apparatuses, and although they are probably crucial to political stability, a development-promoting state-building strategy could still never be based exclusively on these components. With a typology from *Christopher Clapham*, one could say that attention in institution-strengthening strategies has gradually moved away from the repressive components, via the government bodies responsible for tax collection and extraction of other financial resources from society, to bodies with responsibility for genuine development functions (Clapham, 1985).

Considerations of this sort lead naturally to more open questions about how the entire political system can be organised, so that the partnership between the public administration and 'the people' becomes a genuine one.

According to Clapham, very few Third World governments in practice address the issues in this open manner. Rather, they tend to pursue strategies for socio-economic development which are aimed primarily at consolidating political power (cf. Chapter 17). In the academic debate, however, it is in this context that theories and strategies concerning decentralisation and popular participation come in and try to supplement or even replace the more top-down state-building approaches and strategies. In a way, it is also here that theories of people-managed development and *reaching-up* strategies for empowerment of popular organisations take their point of departure (cf. Chapter 24). The same applies in a slightly different sense to the theoretical conceptions of the administrative process as a learning process, where it is – and this is an important point – the citizens and reality who are the 'teachers' and the government officials the receiving party, the pupils (cf. Korten, 1980; Chambers, 1983: pp. 201–17). However, both these schools break so radically with traditional state-building strategies that they would better be discussed in the context of the civil society (in Part V).

Instead, attention will now be turned towards Marxist-inspired approaches to the study of political phenomena in the Third World. The next section briefly assesses the contributions made by some of the dependency theories. Other and more substantive contributions, as seen from a political science perspective, are discussed later in the book (Chapter 13).

The political dimension in dependency theories

From our review of Samir Amin's and Andre Gunder Frank's contribution to the dependency theory debate (Chapter 7) it is evident that they did not primarily focus on political circumstances or political development. Their primary concern was to identify the reasons for, and the nature of, economic underdevelopment in peripheral societies. However, as part of their analyses they did propose certain generalisations regarding politics, an important one being that political institutions and practices were subordinate to external economic linkages and the dependency embodied in these relations. This dependency was further perceived as being so strong and all-embracing in its effects on the underdeveloped society that autonomous, national political development was out of the question. At the same time they refuted that 'modernisation' of the political institutions or special state-building strategies could break the fundamental dependency on the metropoles (Frank), or the centre formations (Amin).

Against this background, it appears somewhat paradoxical that both Frank and Amin nevertheless imagined that peripheral societies could achieve a de-linking from the world market through the introduction of socialism, since such a fundamental change had to be based on intra-societal forces that were otherwise not seen as important determinants for state formation and societal development. In this respect, the early dependency theories contained notions that were parallel to those embodied in classical modernisation theory regarding evolutionary, irreversible changes towards greater similarity with the industrialised countries. The end-goal was different in the sense that industrial capitalism was replaced by a socialist model, and the transformation process was described as a revolutionary change brought about by the working class alone or in association with other classes and social forces, yet the very basic idea that backward societies had to transform themselves according to non-Third World models was the same.

Teodor Shanin was one of the few theorists who pointed out these similarities. In addition, he criticised not only the early dependency theories but also much other Marxist-inspired theory for relying too heavily upon ethnocentric conceptions that were based on experience from Western Europe in a particular historical period, the characteristic features of which could not be found in the Third World either before or after political de-colonisation (Shanin, 1982). Assessed in a broader perspective, it appears warranted to conclude that the early dependency theories provided only a modest contribution to theory construction on political macro-phenomena in the Third World. They had a tendency to reduce the state to an instrument of international capital; as a consequence, they paid very little attention to studies of the political processes and the different class structures and power relations in peripheral societies.

On the other hand, it should be noted that Frank and Amin represented more than just a clash with the economic modernisation theories. They also left behind relevant arguments against the political development theories' probably exaggerated ideas about the backward countries' national independence and the autonomy of their governments. Frank and Amin undoubtedly went too far in their reasoning, but in doing so they idiosyncratically paved the way for a more balanced consideration of the external and internal determinants of the state's mode of functioning and political development in the Third World.

One of the earliest attempts at a more balanced approach came as early as the beginning of the 1970s from Cardoso. Amin and Frank themselves subsequently modified their theories in the same direction (cf. Chapter 7; Frank, 1981). Other attempts at a more balanced approach, featuring an even stronger emphasis on the significance of the internal socio-political conditions, were formulated as class and state theories within the Neo-Marxist tradition. The following two chapters will look more closely at these contributions, in connection with a thematic discussion that focuses on the pertinent characteristics of the political structures and forms of regime in the developing countries. Before that, we shall briefly look at one theory that tries to incorporate the consequences of modernisation (Apter), and another which in a more radical way attempts to break with the traditional political development approaches (Bayart).

Modernisation, marginalisation and violence: Apter

The American political scientist, *David Apter*, delivered his first contribution to the theories of political development as early as the mid-1960s (Apter, 1965), but it is his more recent reflections from the latter half of the 1980s that are under discussion here (Apter, 1987).

In his book, *Rethinking Development*, Apter directs criticism towards both the classical modernisation theories and the dependency theories from the same period. Modernisation theories are described as much too optimistic and characterised by wishful thinking. This was the case, in particular, when these theories argued that there was a positive correlation between economic development and democratisation. In addition, Apter sees these theories as far too preoccupied with the political system in a narrow sense. The theories are concerned with the attainment of equilibrium and the system's capacities for maintaining such an equilibrium, even while basic changes take place. In the same way as state-building theories, modernisation theories therefore focus too much on how to establish institutions and new political functions aimed at keeping society in check.

The dependency theories are criticised by Apter for breaking with Marx, whose analyses were much more securely anchored in the underlying structures and long-term historical perspectives. The dependency theories, moreover, are all too optimistic with regard to the potential for introducing socialism, and with regard to development under socialism.

In an attempt to correct and partly replace modernisation and dependency theories, Apter elaborates a new conceptual framework centred around notions of development, innovation, marginalisation and violence. He shifts primary attention away from the state and the formal political system and, instead, focuses on the impact of modernisation processes in a civil society context. What he finds to be the overriding impact here is violence – not sporadic violence but a very widespread 'disposition to violence' and the actual occurrence of organised violence.

The *disposition to violence*, according to Apter, results from the tension between innovation and marginalisation. Innovation is a process essential to industrialisation. By its very nature, however, innovation produces both winners and losers, the latter being the excluded and marginalised. The point now is that the increasing numbers of people who, throughout the Third World, are being marginalised tend to react with violence against the state. So widespread and pronounced is this tendency that Apter – with a parallel to the debate on environmental constraints – talks about the 'social limits of growth'.

The marginalised groups react with what they perceive as legitimate violence. In other words, they do not recognise the state's monopoly on the legitimate use of violence, but rather establish a parallel political discourse and process outside the framework of the state. In contrast to the classical modernisation theories, Apter progresses to hypotheses on disorder in the development process, and indicates how the protest against the state creates its own dynamic – its own political life which is characterised by an alternative 'mytho-logic' and the appearance of entirely different frames of reference for the understanding and interpretation of events and experiences. Violent protest movements have their own way of interpreting their goals and justifying their actions. They tend to turn violence into a form of symbolic capital, as opposed to economic capital, and they exploit this symbolic capital to present their cause as one of good versus evil, unrestrained by the norms and codes of conduct embodied in the formal political system.

Because of the increasing importance of violence as a 'post-modern' phenomenon as a result of economic development in the poor countries, Apter argues that the whole framework for development studies must be radically revised so that it can encompass the disorder and destruction resulting from large-scale violence. This is what Apter has attempted to do in *Rethinking Development*, both at an abstract conceptual level and with reference to a number of illustrating cases. We shall not go into further detail here but, albeit from different perspectives, return to the issues of marginalisation and socio-political reactions to 'modernisation' in Part V (especially Chapters 22 and 23).

Historical trajectories: Bayart

Like Shanin and Apter, the French political scientist *Jean-François Bayart* has criticised both modernisation and dependency theories, but from a different perspective (Bayart, 1991, 1993). His main point is that both these opposing schools of thought have paid far too much attention to external factors as the major determinants of political change in Africa, Latin America and Asia. As a consequence, the similarities of the economic and political problems faced by societies on these three continents have been exaggerated, giving rise to the invention of what Bayart calls 'the fantasy of the Third World' and, in particular, to the postulate that the states in former colonial areas are simple products of colonial rule and Western dominance. An associated point in Bayart's criticism is that the two schools of thought, as well as social science studies in general, have applied 'ahistorical comparativism', by which he refers to their neglect of the historical roots of contemporary phenomena.

Bayart proposes to replace these faulty, ethnocentric and ahistorical analyses with an approach characterised by acknowledgement of the historical irreducibility and the great political diversity of the 'Third World'. He uses the term 'Third World' descriptively only, not as a concept for theory construction. Instead, Bayart emphasises that many political systems existed prior to colonialisation, and that these systems had considerable impact upon the modern states, each of which should therefore be considered and understood as a complex product of societal development over long periods of time. The modern states in Africa and Asia need to be analysed in light of what Fernand Braudel has called the '*longue durée*'. Bayart further suggests the application of Perry Anderson's concept of the *historical trajectory*, which insists upon the distinct historicity of the many ways in which states develop (Anderson, 1979).

The recourse to history in a long-term perspective does not lead Bayart to disregard the very significant changes during the colonial period and the decades after political independence. On the contrary, he notes the serious disruption caused by Western colonisation of Africa and Asia, including the intensification of political and social control made possible by the establishment of bureaucratic institutions, both administrative and military, and the introduction of modern transport and communication systems. Similarly, the insistence upon the distinctive histories of individual states and political systems – the historical trajectories – does not lead Bayart to give up comparative analysis in a contemporary perspective. In his main work, *The State in Africa* (Bayart, 1993), he actually combines the reconstruction of the historicity of the modern state with several comparative studies aimed at also identifying common trajectories and characteristics shared by many of the African states. He proposes three ways of analysing the modern state in Africa and asserts that, in principle, the same methodologies may be applied throughout the 'Third World'.

The first method consists of analysing the state in the context of the evolution of 'civilisations'. Here Bayart identifies some common features of African societies, like limited development of productive forces, extensive agriculture, animal husbandry without private land ownership, and weak social polarisation.

The second method of apprehending the historicity of the modern state focuses on the systems of inequality and domination. In Africa, according to Bayart, these systems are very different from the class relations known in the Western capitalist societies. Therefore, other concepts have to be elaborated in order to grasp African realities.

The third method suggested by Bayart shifts attention to the cultural construction of politics, particularly the role of religion. Hinduism and Islam are mentioned in this context as extremely important for the shaping of politics in India and the Arab World, respectively.

Combining the three methods leads Bayart to identify several historical trajectories which give form to politics and the state. Examples are the British system of government, the Soviet model, Islamic conceptions of the state and indigenous categories of royal or lineage power. Bayart also refers to these trajectories as 'discursive genres', by which he stresses that each of them is associated with a particular 'language use' (cf. Chapter 22).

Bayart is one of the political scientists who most consistently has integrated the long-term historical perspective while simultaneously stressing how states and political systems are individually created. In both respects, however, Bayart may also be seen as representing a contemporary trend among development researchers, particularly among Indian and other Asian researchers (cf. Manor, 1991; Kaviraj, 1991).

Their concern with the long-term historical perspective and the specific patterns of political development is generally commendable and a called-for correction of mainstream approaches that are often insensitive to unique characteristics of Third World political institutions and practices. Their chief weakness, at least in the way these new approaches have developed so far, is the vagueness of the concepts elaborated. This vagueness, combined with the grounding of the concepts and theories in specific and separate historical trajectories, makes comparisons and general theory construction difficult. It is often not clear whether the validity of the interpretations and explanations is confined to one particular society or extends to groups or types of societies, like Sub-Saharan Africa or South-East Asia.

The next chapter, while acknowledging the diversity and specific historical trajectories, will present attempts at interpreting and explaining the emergence of different forms of regime, not in the individual countries but in different categories of countries. An underlying assumption is that under certain conditions one form of regime will be established, while in different circumstances other types of regime will emerge.

CHAPTER 13

The Political Heritage and Forms of Regime

Classical modernisation theories within political science considered the political systems and the predominant forms of regime in Third World countries as undeveloped, but did not attempt to give any elaborate explanation of the prevailing conditions. They were more preoccupied with producing recommendations on how these countries could set in motion a political development process. Their most important contribution to theory formation, therefore, concerned identification of adequate strategies to bring about the various forms of political modernisation which they deemed to be universally attractive to less developed societies. Something similar applied to Huntington's state-building strategies (cf. Chapter 12).

In comparison, this chapter reviews a number of attempts at understanding and explaining similarities and dissimilarities in the political structures of Third World societies. Previously, the starting point for such attempts was often the pertinent question: *why have democratic forms of regime prevailed in so few countries in Asia, Africa and Latin America?* This will be the central theme for the first part of this chapter, while in the second part we shall address the issues from the perspective of contemporary debates on *the prospects for democratisation.* In a sense, this implies turning the original research question on its head by asking why parliamentary democracy is becoming more prevalent, and under what circumstances this regime form is likely to be introduced and consolidated.

Throughout the chapter, reference will be made to other themes which may contribute to illuminating the political situation in a wider perspective. The issues will be examined further in the next chapter, where the significance of class relations for the form of regime is the focus for discussion.

The colonial legacy: Alavi

Development researchers and political scientists with an interest in the Third World have often studied governments and politics within a relatively recent time frame. This, basically, is a reflection of the low priority they have assigned to original and indigenous institutions and traditions. It is characteristic, though, of most of the attempts at explaining the prevailing forms of regime that they go back to the colonial era, and thus take as a starting point the fact that the overwhelming majority of the developing countries, for long periods of time, have been subjected to European political dominance. Foreign rule has left a political legacy which for many years after independence has affected the government and politics of these societies.

The Pakistani social scientist *Hamza Alavi* was one of the first systematically to draw attention to the political legacy which the colonial rulers left behind in the shape of a special form of state and regime (Alavi, 1972). Alavi summed up his main point of view in a theory published in the early 1970s, arguing that the colonial state was *overdeveloped* in relation to the societal structures in the colonial area. The governmental apparatuses were created by the colonial powers to suit their interests. They were characterised by highly developed civil and military bureaucracies and Western-style legal systems. These features were inherited by the post-colonial states which, according to Alavi, exhibited similar forms of overdevelopment as did the colonial states since other intra-societal conditions had changed very little in the intervening period.

The claim of political overdevelopment could be seen as a provocative counter argument to the theories of political underdevelopment; but closer inspection of the arguments makes it clear that the disagreement was more apparent than real. What Alavi claimed, really, was that colonial and post-colonial political systems were characterised by lack of symmetry and uneven and discordant development.

The central idea in Alavi's conception was, namely, that states engrafted on the colonial areas comprised only the executive and judicial components of a complete state, whereas the legislative components – elected representative assemblies – were either absent or played very marginal roles (Alavi, 1982). There were, to be sure, examples of the colonial power allowing the establishment of local elected assemblies, and, in exceptional cases towards the end of the colonial era, national assemblies as well (as in the case of Ceylon, now Sri Lanka). But this did not change the general picture: the European governments kept to themselves the powers to direct the colonial governments rather than allowing these governments to respond to general guidelines and policies decided by elected parliaments representing the population of the colonial areas.

In comparison with the democratic governments in several of the colonial powers, such as Britain, the states in the colonies could therefore be characterised as amputees. They lacked, so to speak, one of the three major 'limbs' of the state – from the perspective of the citizens, the most important one in that only the representative legislative assemblies provide channels for popular participation in political decision making. Expressed a little differently, the colonial (and post-colonial) states could be characterised as being overdeveloped with respect to their civil and military bureaucracies, but at the same time *underdeveloped* with respect to their democratic components – the elected assemblies and the party systems. Formulated in this way, the seemingly strong disagreement between Alavi and political modernisation theory recedes.

With political independence, the post-colonial societies took over the 'amputated' states of the colonial era. The result was that they were left with overdeveloped civil and military bureaucracies and underdeveloped parliaments and party systems. There were large differences from country to country, but the trend occurred almost everywhere in the areas which were decolonised in the twentieth century. The same was the case, moreover, when the Latin American countries achieved their political independence in the previous century. But here one could say that it was less conspicuous, because the colonial powers themselves during that period did not have any democratic institutions.

The further consequences of this political legacy from the colonial era were manifold, but we shall confine ourselves in the following paragraphs to a closer examination of how the non-democratic forms of rule were further underpinned by other factors in the post-colonial period.

Non-democratic forms of government

The theories about post-colonial regimes – Alavi's as well as those proposed by others (for example Saul, 1979; Clapham, 1985) – were elaborated within a broader perspective and often with a view to describing and explaining political systems and political life in general. However, it is deemed justifiable to focus here primarily on their attempts to explain the forms of regime occurring in post-colonial societies, partly because of the importance of this issue in real situations, partly because of the central place it occupied in several of the theories themselves. As indicated earlier, we shall begin by discussing why so many post-colonial states retained the autocratic and non-democratic character inherited from the colonial period.

It would not be appropriate to present the contribution of each individual theory; this would give rise to too much repetition. Therefore, the presentation will be structured under headings that refer to the most important explanatory variables.

The military and civil bureaucracies and their interests   Practically all the theories of the forms of regime in developing countries put special emphasis on the relatively independent roles of the military and the civil bureaucracies. Where the theories differ from each other is in their further analysis and assessment of these roles.

The modernisation theories have a tendency, as implied earlier, to perceive the military officers and public officials as modernisation agents who, to the benefit of societal transformation, act rather independently of other social and political groups. Opposing this conception, various Neo-Marxist theories, although recognising the great significance of the military and civil bureaucracies, view this as a major problem for Third World societies and regard the bureaucracies as agents acting mainly on behalf of foreign capital and other foreign interests. A third category of theories emphasises the role of the military as a vanguard organisation acting in the interest of a not yet fully established bourgeoisie – or in the interest of a still weakly organised socialist alliance of peasants and workers.

Despite these and other differences, there is nevertheless widespread agreement that the military and civil bureaucracies in most developing countries are the strongest and best-organised interest groups. There is, furthermore, agreement that both these groups, as a rule, have a common interest in a form of regime which concentrates the greatest possible powers within the executive branches of the state.

To this can be added, as emphasised by Alavi and others, that many military officers and government officials perceive themselves as 'custodians' of some kind, guarding national unity and state security and above the politicians' special interests and bickering. These self-perceptions can be traced back to the officers' and civil servants' roles in the colonial era where they were responsible for maintaining law and order. This often brought them into conflict with the politicians of the day, who with their demands for reforms and political independence were seen as insurrectionists and trouble-makers – a perception which many officers and officials had difficulty divorcing themselves from after independence, when the politicians formally took over government. Under the circumstances prevailing immediately after independence, it was an obvious and attractive option for the officers and top echelons of the civil bureaucracies to take over power in many countries. Only in a few countries was there a sufficiently developed party system and interest organisations strong enough to counteract this tendency.

This situation has not changed significantly in many countries. But it is important to note that in the countries where decisive changes have taken place, these changes have gone in the direction of strengthening the independent organisations of the citizens, whether in the form of political parties or in the form of interest organisations representing economic groups like the business community or labour. This is the case in many of the Latin American countries as well as in East and South-East Asia. Therefore, the prospects for democratisation in these societies have been enhanced throughout the 1980s and 1990s (see the section on opportunities for democratisation later in this chapter). Contrary to these tendencies, however, other, mainly poorer countries in Africa and South Asia have continued to experience a very strong presence of the military and civil bureaucracies in political life. In some cases, this continued presence may be explained with reference to a strengthening of popular movements in the form of communally or ethnically based parties or organisations which have been seen as a threat to national unity or the security of the state.

National and ethnic conflicts   Many national and ethnic conflicts have their roots in distant history but have undoubtedly often been further exacerbated in the colonial era, chiefly because the boundaries of the colonies were drawn without considering national or ethnic lines of division in the population. As a result, population groups with different languages and other national characteristics were in many cases forced into what they regarded as an artificial political community, first under European rule and since under a post-colonial regime.

Despite the fact that many post-colonial states were created in this manner, without a homogeneous national basis, some of them have very successfully managed to build up a common national identity in their populations along with widespread loyalty to the political authorities. However, in a number of other cases the national differences have provided fertile soil for violent conflicts. We shall look a little closer at this issue of identity formation along national and ethnic lines later (in Chapter 23). In the present context, attention is drawn only to its effects on the form of regime.

Linguistic multiplicity, in particular, has provided fertile ground for ethnic problems and political unrest – not by itself, but in combination with economic and political conflicts of interest. Language-based communities have rarely fought each other unless they have, at the same time, confronted each other in tough competition for economic or political benefits and privileges. In order to promote their own interests, under such circumstances the competing social groups have tried to give their mother tongue a position above the other languages. As part of this endeavour, various elite groups have often tried to mobilise support from larger population segments by referring to a common language and a common identity based on this language. In this way, many people have been mobilised against other linguistic communities which before were not perceived as adversaries.

Language is just one among several categories of characteristics which may facilitate identity formation and political mobilisation; others include religion and tribal affiliations.

The main point to note here in relation to such conflicts is that when ethnic, national or religious identities have been formed, and confrontations have manifested themselves in extensive violence, experience shows that the conflicts are extremely difficult to solve through democratic processes. The theories in this area emphasise, among other things, that when the conflicts have reached a certain level, there is a general tendency for the extremists to take over leadership of the various communities and movements.

Under such circumstances it is often seen as an attractive or easy option to send in the military, in an attempt to find a military solution to what originally was, and essentially continues to be, a social conflict. The result is rarely successful. At the same time it further weakens the opportunities for democratic development.

Rural–urban contradictions   Other frequently occurring confrontations which impede democratic development in Third World countries are based on conflicts of interests between rural and urban population groups. These conflicts are most clearly articulated in Africa, but occur also in a number of Asian societies and a few weakly industrialised countries in Latin America.

The theories dealing with the importance of these interest conflicts for the political systems and the form of regime can, for the sake of clarity, be summarised in a simple line of reasoning.

Let us assume that a democratic form of regime with universal suffrage has been introduced. Let us further assume – as is typically the case in the societies referred to – that 70–80 per cent of the voters live in rural areas. Under these circumstances it is highly likely that agricultural interests will gradually gain more and more ground, as the rural voters become mobilised and better organised into political parties. Over the longer term there is not much the representatives of the urban population and urban sectors can do to counteract this trend. Even in the short term, an intensified conflict regarding development strategy can arise. Notwithstanding that agriculture and industry, in the long run, have to be developed in parallel in order mutually to support each other – as emphasised in most of the economic development theories – there are bound to arise questions about the short-term allocation of investments, the relative pricing of agricultural and industrial goods, and so on (cf. Chapter 10). With a strong parliament dominated by agricultural interests, industry and other urban sectors may therefore suffer.

According to the theories, the conflict of interests will – when it has reached this point – result in a change of regime form. This will typically happen by the cities 'rebelling'; for example by the urban population demonstrating vehemently against higher prices of bread or rice. It is precisely these types of demonstration that have occurred very frequently in the last 30 years. Regardless of whether the rebellion assumes this or other forms, the result will often be a political upheaval which removes power from the parliament and instead strengthens the executive branches of the state. It should be noted in this context that government officials and military officers have interests that are closely aligned with those of the rest of the urban population. Thus, these state-employed groups will be urged by political unrest and upheavals to take action to restore law and order – essentially in accordance with their own perceived economic interests.

This reasoning adds a political dimension to Michael Lipton's view that power in most developing countries is concentrated in the cities and that their interests will consequently prevail (cf. Chapter 10). The combined outcome under the assumptions outlined above is a general tendency towards a further weakening of the democratic institutions and processes.

International conflicts   International conflicts are yet another type of circumstances which may impede democratisation in the Third World.

In the international politics literature, the East–West conflict was often highlighted as a significant factor in Third World democratisation, up until the dismantling of the Communist regimes in Eastern Europe and the break-up of the Soviet Union. It was emphasised that both super-powers often supported military regimes and other autocratic regimes out of a fear that the countries concerned would otherwise slip into an alliance-free position, or possibly even join the opposite 'camp'. As part of their foreign policies both the USA and USSR provided extensive military assistance to a number of developing countries whose international support they deemed of special importance. Further, the super-powers have on several occasions actively supported or directly intervened in local conflicts between developing countries. The result of such forms of super-power interference was invariably a strengthening of the already predominant militaristic tendencies in several Third World countries.

These militaristic tendencies could be further strengthened by conflicts which originated internally in the developing countries. These could include conflicts regarding the demarcation of the border between two countries – conflicts which moreover often had their roots in the colonial powers' division of areas of interest without consideration of local conditions. Or they could be conflicts conjured up by weak governments, trying to put a lid on internal opposition by diverting attention to an outside enemy.

The changes in the international system, from a more or less distinct bi-polarity to a situation where the USA assumes a position of unique strategic military importance, has as yet only had modest manifestations in theory formation within the discipline of international politics (Viotti and Kauppi, 1993: p. vii; Holm and Sørensen, 1995). In relation to the issue discussed here, however, there is hardly any doubt that the global changes have removed some of the reasons for the super-powers' support of non-democratic regimes. Russia does not have the same economic resources for this as had the Soviet Union; and the USA no longer has the same incentive. On the contrary, within its newly expanded room for manoeuvring, the American government can more effectively demand that governments in the Third World introduce elections and multi-party systems – along with a strengthening of their market economies (cf. Chapter 19).

Parallel to this expectation, it should be noted, though, that the dissolution of the bi-polar political and military world order has probably given greater leeway for regional and local armed conflicts which will generally work against the democratisation processes and, instead, promote military control and other authoritarian forms of regime. This applies not only to the peripheral areas of the former Soviet Union and Yugoslavia, but also to countries in Asia and Africa.

Non-democratic institutions and traditions   Several other factors can be mentioned which stand in the way of democratic development. In several societies the obstacles also include strong traditions and institutions inherited from a distant past, and which are today difficult to reconcile with democratic regime forms and public participation in the political processes.

The Canadian political scientist *Richard Sandbrook* has, with reference to Africa, emphasised that only in very few countries does there exist what he calls a legitimising ideology (Sandbrook, 1985). By this is meant a set of generally accepted principles, according to which government power can be exercised. Such generally accepted principles are not found in many African societies. Not even the basic democratic principle of respecting majority decisions is widely accepted. This may to some extent be explained by the continued existence of separate identities that make citizens view themselves as belonging primarily to ethnic, religious or other socio-cultural groups within the political community. Under these conditions if a majority consists of people mainly from groups other than one's own, there are no strong reasons to accept its decisions as binding.

Other political scientists have characterised African politics as personalised and 'not yet' governed by regulations that effectively prevent the unsanctioned use of coercion and violence (Jackson and Rosberg, 1982b). African politics are most often a personal or factional struggle to achieve control over the governmental apparatus and public resources. In circumstances like these, governments in many African countries – as well as in a number of the other developing countries – have had to justify their exercise of power with reference to ideologies and principles very different from those providing a foundation for democracy.

The following sections will briefly deal with some of the most important legitimising principles, and the mixed forms in which they occur in various developing countries. In certain respects this presentation is an elaboration of the attempts at explaining the frequent occurrence of autocratic forms of regime. But in other respects it contains an expansion of the perspective and a more penetrating analysis of the interaction between Western influence and the former colonies' own inherited traditions and political structures.

Invented traditions   When looking closer at this interaction, it should be noted that the more sophisticated theories do not operate with a simple dichotomy between Western influence and indigenous traditions, institutions and ways of living. Instead, these theories see the interaction as a process which has now been going on for many generations, with the result that the societies concerned today exhibit several hybrid forms. The basic conception corresponds, in other words, to that of the dialectical modernisation theories.

Researchers like *Eric Hobsbawm* and *Terence Ranger* (Hobsbawm and Ranger, 1983) have asserted that the British rulers in the colonial areas, at an early stage and quite deliberately, supported and more or less 'froze' certain traditional institutions. Others, on the other hand, they sought to suppress and dismantle.

The interventions were part of the divide-and-rule principle in British colonial politics. They were also connected to indirect rule, which the British established in many areas by relying on selected traditional leaders whose position was, in return, consolidated by the colonial power. Finally, the interventions were seen as manifestations of a general principle of letting different groups of 'natives' develop in line with their own traditions, which again were different from the white settlers' traditions and values.

One of the conspicuous results of this colonial policy, according to the above-mentioned theorists, was an accentuation or even an invention of traditions, and more specifically a cementing of the tribal identities and institutions in many areas of Africa. Without the British involvement, the tribes and tribal conflicts would not have had the significance they have today.

We shall not go further into a discussion of these or other related theories, but will emphasise that they are useful corrections to widespread and simplified conceptions of the so-called traditional institutions as expressions of reaction and conservatism. Though they may often seem this way, when studied more carefully the reactionary and conservative features may frequently turn out to have been grafted on to the traditional set-up by Western rulers.

In some cases, however, traditions and institutions have been resurrected or invented as a reaction against Western influence. This has happened extensively in societies where Islam has occupied a strong position. Of particular importance for the forms of regime emerging in many of these countries is the fact that their rulers have openly rejected Western conceptions of democracy and popular sovereignty and, instead, have adhered to original Islamic ideas of divine sovereignty. The next section will briefly review these ideas as a first example of elaborate alternatives to democratic forms of legitimacy. The section following this will discuss in greater detail the theories of personal rule, primarily in an African context.

Islamic conceptions of the state

The literature on the Islamic conceptions of the state does not amount to theory in the ordinary, causal sense of the term. Normally a theory would primarily attempt to grasp and explain reality and how different phenomena in reality interact with each other. A causal theory would also invariably contain value-loaded statements and explicit or implicit ideas about how the world ought to be. However, in Western development theories – both mainstream and 'alternative' – attempts have been made to tone down these normative elements. This is not the case with the Islamic theory of the state which is almost exclusively a normative theory.

The most central point in this normative theory is that all exercise of power ultimately has to be justified with reference to the will and precepts of Allah (cf. Rosenthal, 1965; Ferdinand and Mozaffari, 1988). This basic principle of divine sovereignty is interpreted and adapted in many different ways in the Islamic world. In its most extreme, so-called fundamentalist interpretation, the principle implies that all rules and precepts for both religious and social life are given in the Koran and in the narratives of the actions and words of the Prophet Muhammad. All that is left to contemporary rulers is to interpret the so-given rules and precepts. This interpretation must be undertaken by an autocratic ruler with assistance and guidance from the religious scholars, the *ulama*.

According to the less fundamentalist conceptions, only the basic rules are given beforehand. They therefore need to be further elaborated and adapted to new circumstances. But not even in these less dogmatic normative theories is there any prominent place for elected representatives. It remains the responsibility of the religious scholars to ensure that the modern laws and political decisions are in agreement with Islam.

The fundamentalist version of the Islamic state theory has had only very limited impact in practice, although it should be noted that it has influenced to a significant extent the forms of regime adopted in Iran and Saudi Arabia. The less fundamentalist conceptions have, on the other hand, achieved a very great dissemination in the sense that they exert considerable influence on political life in many countries with Muslim majorities. This applies, in particular, to the Arab world, but the influence is also found beyond this area in countries such as Pakistan and Malaysia. The result is not everywhere an undemocratic form of regime; other forces have in some cases, like Egypt, ensured widespread support for popular sovereignty and democratic principles. The main point to note here, however, is that in countries dominated by Islam a general pressure, mainly from orthodox Muslims, is mounted against Western-type democracy. In particular, they often oppose women's participation in public life, and refuse to accept members of religious minorities as equal citizens.

Outside the Islamic regions of the world, ideas of divine sovereignty are of much lesser significance. In most African countries it is difficult even to identify any generally accepted legitimising ideology, as indicated earlier. Sandbrook and other researchers have tried to capture some of the characteristics of the African societies by focusing on personalised rule and patron–client relationships. Their interpretations and explanations are discussed in the following section.

Personal rule and patron–client relationships

The more recent theories of African politics reflect the general trend in development research in the 1980s and 1990s towards greater emphasis of the specific conditions in individual societies. Therefore, they are also to a large extent based on thorough empirical studies in selected countries.

The basic theoretical framework varies. Some of the new approaches are related to dialectic modernisation theories, while others may be regarded as variants of political economy approaches. Some of them are inspired mainly by the liberalist tradition, particularly Max Weber and Neo-Weberian scholars, while others are closer to the Marxist and Neo-Marxist streams of thought. An interesting point, however, is the impact the empirical studies have been allowed to have upon theory formation in general. As a result, the original theoretical formulations have been considerably revised and a genuine debate between different schools of thought has emerged.

As an illustration, it can be noted that many of the new, Marxist-inspired theories actually discard the conception that one or more social classes dominate the mode of functioning of the African states. The main assertion is that social classes in African societies are not yet sufficiently developed and organised to play any independent and decisive role. This reformulation of the original class theories has paved the way for more context-sensitive analyses of African politics within the Marxist tradition. We shall return to this issue in the next chapter, while in the following paragraphs we shall focus attention on the non-Marxist contributions.

Among these, the studies made by *Robert Jackson* and *Carl Rosberg* deserve a special mention (Jackson and Rosberg, 1982a). Other important contributions have been made by *Richard Sandbrook* (Sandbrook, 1985), and *Göran Hydén* (Hydén, 1983, 1986).

A very central point in the theory proposed by Jackson and Rosberg is that politics in most African states is characterised by non-institutionalised government, where the person takes precedence over rules. Irrespective of the formal institutional arrangements, African states are essentially governed by personal rulers, paramount leaders who rule more in their personal capacity than in their capacity as office-holders within the formal governmental set-up. The paramount leaders rule and control, not by virtue of popular sovereignty or other legitimising ideologies, but rather by the virtue of their command over important public resources and goods which they can share with others to ensure political support. The personal rulers, furthermore, prevail to a certain extent by virtue of their control over the military and civil bureaucracies, that is over the most important apparatuses of coercion. With inspiration from Max Weber's sociology of leadership and authority, this exploitation of the offices of state to procure advantages and power for oneself and one's allies has been described as *patrimonialism* (Roth, 1968).

It is important to note that by emphasising that African politics is less institutionalised and more personalised than contemporary European politics, Jackson and Rosberg do not claim these to be unique features confined to the African continent. They rather regard personal rule as a distinctive type of political system which may be found in most societies in a transitional period prior to the establishment of impersonal, constitutional government. Even in most European states, modern political institutions took hold only after powerful personal rulers had first established effective governments and associated their personal authority with the new institutions. Thus, personal rule in Africa must be regarded in a similar manner, as possibly the only adequate system of governance under the conditions prevailing – but also as a system that, in the longer term, has to be replaced.

The styles of the personal rulers vary greatly. Jackson and Rosberg distinguish between four major types of governance: 'princely rule', where the paramount leader has sufficient power and authority to preside over the political game and keep it orderly without having to resort to coercion and physical repression; 'autocratic rule' based on the personal ruler's control over public administration; 'prophetic rule' where the top leader possesses sufficient charisma to convert other politicians into missionaries and 'charm' the masses into becoming supporters; and 'tyrannical rule' characterised by open use of force. Just after independence, princely rule was the most common, while later autocratic rule become more widespread after the first-generation national leaders died.

Common to all the systems of personal rule is that they link the rulers with the citizens not directly but through patrons who, in turn, are linked with clients, possibly through other patrons at lower levels. A political system of personal rule does not, like the system envisaged by David Easton, respond to public demands and support by means of public policies and actions (cf. Chapter 12). Rather, it is a system of patronage through which rewards in the form of public resources and privileges are distributed downwards from the paramount ruler and his close associates who, in return, receive support.

The system is closely tied to the informal, more traditional forms of organisation in the societies, including the patron–client relationships. Richard Sandbrook speaks in this connection of political clans. These can be cross-sectional groupings with many different characteristics, for example shared educational background. The important point is that the clans function as political interest groups, normally under the leadership of autocratic clan leaders.

The system of patronage, according to the theories, works by the personal ruler doling out generously from the public resources and benefits he controls. This patronage is extended to his own clan members and also to a selection of clan leaders whose political support is deemed necessary. The clan leaders can then, at their level within the power hierarchy, use some of their resources in a similar manner to ensure political backing from certain lower-placed clan leaders – and so on, until crumbs from the tables of the mighty eventually fall on the small-scale farmers and other poor people.

It should be added that in essentially all the African countries there are too few resources available to benefit more than a diminutive minority of the population through patronage. Therefore, the system is built to a large extent upon expectations and illusions of some day getting rewards from the men of power. In addition, the system is built on selective suppression of clans and other population groups who are not satisfied with the benefits they are offered.

It is a central point in the theories that the political top leaders, in order to maintain power, need to enter into a close alliance with the civil bureaucracy. It is through this alliance the personal rulers achieve control over significant public resources, and it is through this they gain access to a distribution system. The result of the close alliance is that African administrative apparatuses – which were originally introduced by the colonial powers as autonomous and rational Weberian bureaucracies – in reality were turned into instruments of political power. They became, so to speak, *invaded from above* by the paramount leaders who pressurised the administrative bodies into functioning primarily as major components in the patronage system.

Seen from a development perspective, this displacement in the operations of the state administration implies allocation of public resources and benefits which are neither authorised nor legitimate according to traditional Western thinking. Therefore, this patronage system is also frequently described using terms such as corruption, nepotism and favouritism. These strongly value-loaded expressions, however, are generally rejected in the theories of personal rule which, instead, emphasise that patronage is one of the few systems which, in a foreseeable future, is sufficiently effective to hold together many of the African countries and ensure the maintenance of national political leadership.

Theories of personal rule and patronage have been worked out not only with reference to Africa. Similar theories exist with reference to Asian societies. Particularly within social anthropology, theories have been propounded concerning patron–client relationships and political rule by patronage. But it should be added that on closer inspection the theories appear to be very different.

Furthermore, it should be noted that neither the social anthropological theories, nor the new theories of personal rule in Africa, give a full picture of the political processes. The latter, as explicitly stated by Jackson and Rosberg, deal with only one dimension of African political life. Yet, they can be used as a supplement to the more traditional political development and Neo-Marxist theories. Especially in relation to class theories, as already indicated, the new approaches can be seen as valuable corrections when it comes to societies with weakly articulated social classes – that is the type of societies which, in Chapter 8, were characterised as P1 societies.

Prospects for democratisation

In the previous sections, attention was drawn to the conditions which have obstructed the emergence and consolidation of democratic forms of regime in the Third World. In this connection, we presented selected theories about government and political rule in African and other least-industrialised countries. To this should now be added considerations on the prospects and preconditions for democratisation, especially considering that, in the last 15 years, more than 30 developing countries have introduced some form of democratic rule with multi-party systems.

The next chapter will discuss theories that relate the explanations of the form of government in a given country to the prevailing class structure and the distribution of political power based on that structure. This will lead to identification of certain basic preconditions for democratisation. The present section will focus on attempts at explaining the prospects for democratisation mainly with reference to political culture and problems of legitimacy, that is with a perspective and an approach similar to those adopted by the theories dealt with in this chapter.

Before reviewing the various hypotheses proposed it is necessary briefly to discuss the meaning of democracy. When dealing with reasons for the absence of democracy, it may be justifiable to apply a vague definition, but this does not suffice when focusing on the prospects for democratisation.

According to standard Western textbooks, *democracy* is a way of organising government and citizens' participation in it. The democratic way of organising government involves:

- *competition* for government positions;
- citizen *participation* in the selection of political leaders; and
- a number of civil and political *liberties* – or human rights in the narrow sense.

The more specific definitions vary considerably. One of the attempts at defining more precisely the meaning of democracy *as a political system* stands out, however, because it has been widely accepted in the Western academic discourse, namely the definition proposed by *Robert A. Dahl*. According to his definition, the *core characteristics of democracy* are (Dahl, 1971):

- meaningful and extensive competition among individuals and organised groups for the major positions of government power;
- a highly inclusive level of political participation in the selection of leaders and policies, at least through regular and fair elections, such that no major adult social group is excluded; and
- a level of civil and political liberties – freedom of expression, freedom of the press, freedom to form and join organisations – sufficient to ensure the integrity of political competition and participation.

This definition may be taken as a starting point from where we can continue by adding a few more aspects to the concept of democracy.

When dealing with questions of democracy and regime forms in general in the context of poor countries, it is common to link questions concerning government and popular participation with social and economic development. It is often stated in this context that there is a close link between respect for human rights and democracy, on the one hand, and the ability to sustain economic and social development, on the other. This is further utilised as a justification for supporting development of democratic institutions and norms in the developing countries.

The argument, however, is weak. Very few comparative and cross-national studies indicate a causal relationship between democracy and sustained economic and social development – almost irrespective of the specific definitions adopted. A major comparative study conducted in the 1980s even concluded that democracy is not incompatible with a low level of development (Diamond et al., 1988). It could be added that a causal relationship between such complex and composite structures as democracy and economic development would also be highly surprising from a theoretical point of view.

Rather than try to attach legitimacy to democracy-strengthening activities with reference to their expected economic and social impact (that is the traditional way of thinking about development), it is suggested here that the political objectives of democratisation be given a priority of their own. This would be in line with contemporary thinking about societal and human development as consisting of equally important economic, social, political and cultural aspects (cf. Chapter 3).

This essentially normative argument in favour of democracy can be further strengthened by an assumption and a hypothesis. The *assumption* is that the objectives of development cannot be determined in any universal manner but have to be decided by the population and the citizens concerned. The *hypothesis* is that democratic procedures and protection of human rights are important preconditions for setting development objectives, because they ensure broad participation and legitimacy.

Whether democratic regime forms are also the best frameworks for promoting overall economic growth and aggregate social development of a country is then a secondary question. Or perhaps even a question at a lower level of priority, if looked at from the point of view of the individual citizen for whom societal development may be important but less so than his or her own well-being.

A similar mode of reasoning may be applied to citizens' participation in political decision making. The main argument here is that a certain degree of economic and social equality is a necessary prerequisite for ensuring political equality. There is a certain threshold below which poverty and hunger prevent people from effectively exercising their democratic rights.

We shall return to this argument later in the book (Chapter 24). The main focus is currently on the aggregate level. Further, to clarify the context within which the recent discussion on the prospects for democratisation has been situated, it may be appropriate to make a distinction between at least three different aspects of democracy:

1. Democracy as a *political system* – or more specifically as a form of regime.

2. Democracy as a prevailing *norm* for decision making in political organisations and associational life.
3. Democratic *attitudes*, tolerance, fair treatment of minorities, and respect for all citizens' basic rights at the individual level.

It is clearly the first aspect which preoccupies the central position in the debate that we shall review here. This is also the aspect of democracy which, in the several countries experiencing democratisation, has prevailed over the others, although the other two dimensions of democracy have recently attracted more and more attention in academic debates as well as in political discussions in Third World countries.

The overriding question is why a democratisation process in the narrow sense, in the form of establishing constitutional democracy as the prevailing regime form, has recently been initiated in so many countries. Numerous answers have been given to this question, partly referring to general conditions identified in the, mainly Western, social science literature as conducive to democracy, partly referring to political changes in the Third World which have increasingly brought about these conditions.

According to one type of analysis, democratisation processes have been initiated because the autocratic rulers and military regimes have turned out to be very vulnerable when they have not been capable of meeting demands for rewards and economic progress from considerable segments of their populations, especially the business community and other well-organised groups of citizens. It is precisely in periods of economic decline – which many countries in Latin America and Africa have experienced since the beginning of the 1980s – that it has become increasingly difficult for many autocratic regimes to satisfy a sufficiently large number of the influential groups. Consequently, the economic crises in these countries have resulted in a *de-legitimisation* of the governments in office (Sørensen, 1993: Ch. 2). In some cases, this has merely led to a change of the ruling group without changes in the form of government, but in several other cases the outcome has been an incipient democratisation process.

Some of the autocratic regimes have themselves initiated the process in an attempt to involve a wider group of decision makers as being co-responsible for the economic and social difficulties and adversities; others have been forced to step down by an increasingly strengthening opposition. Especially in some of the Latin American countries such as Argentina, Peru, Brazil and Chile, the democratisation processes have been carried forward by relatively well-organised political opposition movements. In Africa, the picture has in this respect been more blurred, and the introduction of democratic forms of government here should often be considered as marginal adjustments aimed at securing the continued rule of the present incumbents (for example in Kenya). The changes in a number of the Asian societies should probably be interpreted in an entirely different way, especially regarding the democratisation in high-growth countries such as South Korea, Taiwan and Thailand, where the business communities and the new middle classes have played significant roles.

Regardless of the specific forms of the democratisation processes, it is apparent that in the Third World as a whole there have been, over the last decade, movements away from autocratic forms of government and towards formal democracy with multi-party systems. It will take us too far to attempt to go into the many different explanations for these changes that are given in the literature, particularly because these explanations are frequently tied specifically to the individual countries and their unique circumstances. However, some types of causes suggested may be worth mentioning.

The de-legitimisation of autocratic regimes referred to earlier is one such type of cause. Apart from being compounded by economic crises, some of the recent works on the subject have also emphasised the significance of the dismantling of the Eastern military bloc and the introduction of democratic systems in Eastern Europe (Sørensen, 1993: Ch. 2). These fundamental changes have, at the level of ideology, undermined both the autocratic regimes and the one-party systems and provided inspiration for the popular movements already active in African countries. Moreover, they have – as noted earlier – removed some of the causes for super-power support for non-democratic regimes.

Another type of factor which has similarly promoted the democratisation processes in many developing countries is undoubtedly the pressure which has increasingly been exerted by bilateral and multilateral aid organisations. It is noteworthy that such pressure was largely not to be found just a decade ago. At that time the donor organisations showed a widespread reticence about discussing internal political matters in the recipient countries. This was viewed as undue interference in the internal affairs of sovereign states, even though it was difficult to see, even then, why demands on these states regarding their political systems should be more improper than the demands regarding their economic and social systems. The basic attitude has changed significantly since the end of the 1980s, with more and more aid organisations starting to make demands on the recipient states concerning the non-violation of human rights, especially civil rights such as freedom of speech and freedom for the citizens to organise. Gradually, these demands were extended to include demands for democratisation in the shape of multi-party systems and the holding of free and fair elections.

In addition to such specific and narrowly time-bound reasons for democratisation, the process has been explained with reference also to more profound changes in the affected societies. An example of this is the spread of primary and secondary education to continuously larger segments of the population. With the resulting greater insight and understanding of society and politics, these newly educated citizens have articulated demands for popular participation in the affairs of the state. Another example refers to urbanisation, which in a number of countries has brought together so many people in the cities that they can press through their interests in the democratic decision-making processes – unlike previously, when introduction of universal adult franchise tended to favour the majority populations in the rural areas. A third example – of special significance for the countries which have experienced considerable economic progress – refers to Seymour Lipset's classic assertion that economic prosperity beyond a certain point is highly likely to promote democratisation (Lipset, 1959).

Even though the literature thus exhibits several attempts at explanation, we probably have to recognise that neither regarding the frequent existence of autocratic forms of government, nor the recent democratisation trends, do we have robust, general theories which can be widely applied to explain the forms of government in the Third World. The question is whether the class theories, reviewed in the next chapter, are any more capable of providing such a general theoretical framework. Before taking up this issue for discussion, however, we shall conclude the present chapter with two brief notes: one on democracy and governability, the other on democracy and human rights.

Democracy and governability

Introducing democracy may imply a number of positive consequences, as seen from the perspective of ordinary citizens. But a democratic form of regime is not necessarily associated with political stability and may, under certain circumstances, result in a serious crisis of governability, as shown by the Indian scholar *Atul Kohli* (Kohli, 1991).

Kohli, in a highly acclaimed study of discontent and political development in India, has argued that an interventionist democratic state typically encourages considerable politically oriented activism. The pervasiveness and intensity of such activism tend to be even higher in low-income societies, because alternative outlets for competitive energies here tend to be limited. However, following to some extent the argument presented by Samuel Huntington (cf. Chapter 12), Kohli claims that it is the disjuncture between, on the one hand, institutionalisation and institutional adaptation and, on the other hand, the degree and nature of political mobilisation which primarily determines the outcome.

India's political system remained stable for several years, primarily because of the dominance of a single party, the Indian National Congress. But towards the end of the 1960s this single-party dominance was increasingly replaced by multi-party competition. At the same time, the Congress party was internally weakened due to factional conflicts. As an overall result, the state's capacity to govern – that is the capacity simultaneously to promote development and to accommodate diverse interests – has declined. Along with this decline, order and authority have been eroding, as is often manifested in widespread activism outside the established political channels.

In the empirical part of the study, Kohli convincingly demonstrates how, at the district level, discontent and political power struggles have increased. The previous alliance between the Congress Party and local 'bosses' has broken down in many areas. At the same time, traditional authority patterns have been undermined by the emergence of competing elites willing to utilise any sets of appealing symbols and available means – including violent means – for political mobilisation aimed at improving their electoral chances.

Based on observations like these, Kohli concludes that India's political periphery has become increasingly difficult to govern. There are exceptions to this trend, like West Bengal where strong leaders and disciplined ruling parties have moderated the impact of corrosion of authority. But the general picture has been one of weakened political parties and government institutions and increased personalisation of power, not only at the lower levels but at state and national levels as well.

With some hesitation Kohli concludes that the democratic form of regime may itself have contributed to 'over-politicisation' of the Indian polity. This does not lead him to suggest that democracy should be curtailed. Instead, he argues for a strengthening of party organisations and for bringing the state's capacities for governing in line with its very comprehensive commitments.

Kohli wrote his analysis prior to the economic reforms introduced in India in 1991 and, thus, at a time when the Indian state was among the most interventionist in the Third World. It would be interesting to follow up on his study by investigating the implications of the ongoing reductions in the role of the state. Within his own conceptual framework, this might amount to bringing the commitments in line with the state's capacities rather than the other way around. Anyhow, the argument presented by Kohli on the possible implications of democracy – in a complex society with numerous cleavages and conflicts of interest, and under conditions of deteriorating political institutions – is definitely worth taking into account.

Democracy and human rights

The previously reviewed theories of the forms of regime have mainly focused on political processes at the macro-level. But as indicated in the preceding two sections, the question of democracy may be posed at a disaggregate level as well, either with a focus on the governability of the political periphery, as done by Kohli, or from the perspective of the citizens. In the latter case, protection of citizens' rights occupies a particularly central position when the form of regime is assessed.

Protection of human rights, experience shows, does not always follow automatically from a democratic form of regime. Democratic societies – with India as a prominent example – may, on the contrary, be characterised by a considerable discrepancy between the formal rules and their actual implementation, especially as seen from the point of view of resource-weak citizens. Even though a democratic form of government does not in itself guarantee the protection of the rights of the citizens, it should, on the other hand, be added that military regimes and other autocratic forms of regime normally imply that such a protection of rights is not even encouraged by the authorities.

It is evident that one has to be extremely careful when trying to generalise about the protection of citizens' rights in the Third World, both because the countries exhibit great variation and conditions change very rapidly. None the less, it may be useful to point out some of the most frequently occurring deviations from a kind of ideal-type situation. Such a benchmark may be described as follows:

1. The decision-making processes are open and transparent.
2. The rules, according to which the government acts, are general and universal.
3. The scope for bureaucratic discretion is relatively moderate.
4. Enforcement is generally effective.
5. The citizens are encouraged to organise themselves autonomously in associations, interest organisations, parties, etc.
6. The legal system aims at protecting the citizens against the authorities.
7. The citizens have many channels of access to the state apparatus, and there are possibilities of appeal.

Even though the Scandinavian states probably come relatively close to this benchmark, it is important to emphasise that the above ideal-type description is not a generally valid assessment of the actual conditions in the highly industrialised countries. Therefore, no simple contrasting of highly industrialised and less developed countries is proposed in the following account of some of the most frequently observed deviations from the ideal type in the latter category of countries. These deviations – which occur to widely differing extents – can be summarised as below:

1. The decision-making processes are relatively closed and non-transparent.
2. The rules according to which the government bureaucracy acts may be general and universal, but often they are contradictory and frequently unknown to those concerned.
3. The discretionary element is very prominent, permitting the bureaucrats to implement policies in a selective manner and in accordance with their own particular obligations and preferences.
4. Enforcement is generally ineffective and selective.
5. The citizens are not encouraged to organise themselves autonomously, though sometimes they may be mobilised in state-controlled interest organisations, parties, etc.
6. The legal system formally aims at protecting the citizens from the authorities, but rarely has the necessary capacity for this.

7. The citizens in general have very little opportunity to access the state apparatus and the decision makers, and there are only few effective opportunities for appeal.

The results of this state of affairs with respect to the protection of citizens' rights are to some extent self-evident. Two particular features, however, should be noted. First, the protection and rights of citizens in their capacity as citizens is very limited. Instead, their protection and rights are mainly determined by other factors such as social status, social and political affiliations, and economic and political resources. Consequently, the second feature is very extensive distortions biased against resource-weak citizens and groups in the society. The large majority of the citizens, who do not have either the economic or political resources to demand their rights, are badly off in relation to the political and administrative authorities. They often have no real opportunities for securing their rights – and others rarely do it for them.

Based on this mode of reasoning, a strategy for promoting democracy in a wider sense than just introducing formal rules and procedures must focus on human development for the resource-poor and politically weak sections of society (UNDP, 1993, 1994). Within this perspective, it may be argued that political empowerment of poor people, of women in general, and of minorities, are all more important matters than the further strengthening of elite-dominated democratic institutions. Empowerment of the poor is a precondition for their actual participation in political decision making and for giving them real opportunities for influencing their own future as well as for exercising their constitutional rights.

Later in the book (Part V) we shall deal more extensively with the implications of social and political inequality and the strategies proposed to ameliorate the situation, as seen from the point of view of those excluded from effective political participation in both democratic and non-democratic systems. Presently, we leave the topic with the above summary description as an indication of just how much may be involved in securing good political and administrative practices and protection of the rights of all citizens in a developing country.

CHAPTER 14

Social Forces and Forms
of Regime

Political development theories refer in various ways to the conditions in the 'environment', which are presumed to influence the political system and its transformation. The theories of forms of government in the Third World reviewed in Chapter 13 take the analysis a step further by more systematically taking into account societal conditions as explanatory variables – as factors promoting or impeding the emergence and continued existence of various regime types. The theories to be reviewed in this chapter may be seen as further elaborations of the analyses of societal preconditions, while at the same time they try to build up a common framework for more specific theories concerning different types of developing societies. The central concept in these theories is the notion of class, not in the narrow sense but as seen in connection with other social forces which, in contrast to classes, do not have a direct basis in the economic processes. The central thesis is that forms of state and regime to a large extent are determined by the interests of the social forces and their relative power positions.

The basis for the following considerations are more abstract notions and theories which were originally proposed by Marxist-inspired theorists such as *Nicos Poulantzas* (Poulantzas, 1973, 1978) and *Erik Olin Wright* (Wright, 1978, 1985). In the present context, however, their contributions are interpreted so as to make room for combinations with aspects of class theories elaborated within the Weberian tradition (cf. Chapter 8 and Val Burris, 1987).

Social forces as regime form determinants

Class and state theories share a basic conception of the political processes as being in themselves important and relatively autonomous. Adherents of this theoretical approach have often been inclined to lay the main emphasis in their analyses on intra-societal conditions and power relations. As a consequence they may have underestimated the importance of external influences. It is worth noting, though, that the approach itself remains open to the question of whether it is the internal or external conditions that play the dominant role in the determination of the form and mode of functioning of the peripheral and post-colonial state.

Class and state theories view the form of regime and the entire organ-isation of political life primarily as a product of the conflicts and struggles between economically based classes, including classes based outside the societal formation in question – like the national bourgeoisies based in the highly industrialised countries. It should be further noted that the theories also recognise that other types of social groupings can impact upon govern-ment and politics. These include the military and the civil bureaucracies.

One of the central propositions, however, is that the social classes hold a position of primacy. It is the classes and their relative power positions that determine whether, and to some degree how, other social forces can affect the form of state and regime. If the social classes are weakly developed and weakly organised – and no class or coalition of classes is therefore in a position to push through its interests – there is a possibility that social forces without a basis in the economic processes can gain decisive influence. This, on the other hand, is less likely to happen where social classes have con-stituted themselves as both economic and political forces.

The theories further assume that the individual classes and other social forces will seek to influence the form of regime in such a way as to gain optimal influence on the formulation of policies and their implementation. In particular, they will seek to optimise their influence by bringing about a concentration of the exercise of political power in precisely those organs of the state where they have the best possibilities of affecting decision making and/or implementation.

Based on assumptions like these, the class and state theories have stimu-lated more concrete analyses of the conditions prevailing in individual Third World societies. The studies undertaken have revealed a complex picture with great variations. With reference to Africa, some researchers have found a kind of symbiosis between international capital and the national bourgeoisie as being the main determinant of regime form (Langdon and Godfrey, 1976). Others have identified the petty bourgeoisie as the ruling class, or at least as the most important social force to support the government (Meillassoux, 1970; Shivji, 1976; Saul, 1974, 1979). A third group of scholars have come to the conclusion that social classes have only a limited and sporadic influence on the state (Hydén, 1983). Going beyond the cases from Africa, the picture becomes even more complex when adding the interactions between social structures and regime forms identified in Latin America, Asia and the Middle East (Martinussen, 1980; Olsen, 1994).

Rather than try to review these differences we shall attempt to illustrate the mode of reasoning in some of these analyses by looking a little closer at social forces and forms of regime in post-colonial India and Pakistan. The conclusions from this analysis will subsequently be generalised into a set of hypotheses regarding the importance of social classes and other social forces for determining regime forms in the Third World. The observations and propositions presented in the following sections are based mainly on previous studies undertaken by the present author (Martinussen, 1980, 1991c).

Social forces and forms of regime in India and Pakistan

The central question that we shall address here is: why is it that, since political independence, India has had a democratic form of regime, while the attempts to establish a stable democratic system in Pakistan have failed? By examining the interests of the most important social classes and other groupings and their relative power positions, at least a partial explanation for this can be given.

After independence, the civil and military bureaucracies in both societies were interested in power being concentrated in the executive organs of state. This would give these groups the greatest possible direct influence on decision making and policy implementation. Conversely, the working class, the land-owners and the peasants in both countries were most interested in a democratic form of regime, where power was concentrated in popularly elected parliaments. The bourgeoisies of the industrialised countries did not have well-defined interests in this respect, so for the sake of simplifying the argument we may ignore them here.

As for the national bourgeoisies, our analyses revealed that they had clearly articulated – but quite different – interests. The Pakistani bourgeoisie favoured a regime form that concentrated as much power and decision making as possible in the executive branches of the state, the main reason being that this class was weak in political terms for at least three decades after independence. Although powerful in economic terms, Pakistan's business community had almost no autonomous organisations to promote its interests, and its relations with the political parties were weak. The Pakistani bourgeoisie, therefore, had to rely heavily on the civil and military bureaucracies – and continue to do so even in the 1990s.

The Indian bourgeoisie, on the other hand, had already developed close relations with the ruling party, the Indian National Congress, before independence. Its interests would vary according to the location of the principal contradiction in relation to other major social classes. After independence, when the major problem was to achieve control over the state apparatuses inherited from the colonial power, the national bourgeoisie was prompted to favour a democratic form of regime. Conflicts between national and foreign capital over economic strategies and policies also pushed them in this direction. Later, when major conflicts emerged between the national bourgeoisie and the landed aristocracy, the former supported a gradually increasing concentration of policy making in the bureaucratic set-up in order to reduce the influence of the very strong landed interests in parliament. This process culminated with the declaration of the emergency in 1975 which – over a

	Executive branches	Legislative branches (elected assemblies)
Civil bureaucracies	X	
Military bureaucracies	X	
The Pakistani bourgeoisie	X	
The Indian bourgeoisie	X	X
Workers and salaried classes		x
Landed aristocracies		X
Peasants, agricultural workers, etc.		x

Figure 14.1 Social forces and their primary access points within the state apparatuses in India and Pakistan

crucial period of just 18 months – suspended the political influence of the landed aristocracy and thus paved the way for far-reaching land reforms that facilitated the 'green revolution' and the re-institutionalisation of 'normal' parliamentary-democratic procedures.

The comparative analysis of India and Pakistan adumbrated above can be summarised as in Figure 14.1, which illustrates where the major social forces have had the best possibilities of exerting influence. A large cross indicates that the class or grouping in question has had good access and influence possibilities; a small cross or none indicates correspondingly modest or difficult access. It is noted that the significant difference between India and Pakistan concerns the political position of the two national bourgeoisies. As regards the other social forces, identical marks are used – even though the reality was and is, naturally, more complex.

To indications of the primary access points given in Figure 14.1 should now be added investigations of how much power the different social forces could mobilise and utilise to promote their respective interests concerning the form of regime. There is no doubt that the social forces favouring an autocratic form of regime in Pakistan were more powerful for a long period than those favouring some form of democracy. The decisive power was presumably the national bourgeoisie, but it should be noted also that the working class in Pakistan was in an unusually weak position to promote democracy. The same applied to the landowners and – to an even higher degree – to the peasants, who totally lacked national political organisations. When further to this Islam's importance as a legitimising ideology and the *ulama*'s general opposition to democracy is added, it becomes understandable why the form of regime in Pakistan became so distinctly autocratic during the 1950s and remained so until the end of the 1980s, even though formal parliamentary democracy was introduced for brief periods.

In India, on the other hand, the social forces favouring democracy were presumably the most powerful throughout almost the whole period since independence. Again the decisive social force appears to be the national bourgeoisie.

With caution we may generalise from these conclusions to a general hypothesis, which asserts that the form of regime in a peripheral society is primarily determined by the national bourgeoisie's economic and political position and power. A similar thesis was proposed as early as the 1960s by *Barrington Moore*, who concluded his studies, including studies of a number of industrialised societies, with a general assertion to the effect that the emergence and consolidation of a democratic form of regime depended on the presence of a strong bourgeoisie. Without a strong bourgeoisie there could be no democracy (Moore, 1966).

The national bourgeoisie as the critical factor

In more specific terms, the hypothesis derived from the comparative studies of India and Pakistan claims that, *provided* the national, industrial bourgeoisie assumes a position as the leading economic class, and *provided* the bourgeoisie at the same time is politically well-organised and has good opportunities to affect the decisions in the representative and democratic institutions of the state, *then* the form of regime is likely to be or become predominantly democratic.

Conversely, if the national bourgeoisie is weak economically, and at the same time has little opportunity to achieve an impact through the democratic institutions and processes, then there is a greater probability that the form of regime will be or become autocratic and characterised by the civil and military bureaucracies' dominance within the state apparatus. In this situation, the national bourgeoisie is only a critical factor on account of its weak position. Therefore, the positively formulated explanation in this case must, to a large extent, refer to other social forces – for example as in the theories on the form of regime in the least-industrialised societies (cf. Chapter 13).

The third element of the hypothesis is therefore probably the most interesting. This element implies an assertion that if the national bourgeoisie is strong in economic terms but weak in relation to the democratic decision-making processes, then the form of government is most likely to be auto-cratic. In this situation, the bourgeoisie has the requisite strength to push through its interests in the narrowly defined economic processes, but can only complement the promotion of these interests through the state provided that power is concentrated in the executive branches – and not if it is concentrated in the representative-legislative branches, where agricultural interests will then typically dominate the decision-making processes.

P1 societies without a national bourgeoisie	Autocratic form of regime	
	The political organisation of the national bourgeoisie:	
	Primarily in relation to the executive branches	Comparatively well in relation to legislative branches
P2 societies with a non-hegemonic national bourgeoisie	Autocratic form of regime	Parliamentary-democratic form of regime
P3 societies with a hegemonic national bourgeoisie	Autocratic form of regime	Parliamentary-democratic form of regime

Figure 14.2 The national bourgeoisie and the form of regime

The whole theory is in reality somewhat more complicated, but we can illustrate the basic propositions as shown in Figure 14.2. Here the bourgeoisie's position is related to the three main levels of industrial development (P1, P2 and P3) as described earlier in this book (cf. Chapter 8).

'Hegemony' in Figure 14.2 is defined as a position of relative power which ensures the realisation of the essential interests of the class or class fraction in question. The realisation of these interests will not depend on the use of oppression and coercion. Rather, the interests of the hegemonic class have been elevated to the position of 'national interests' which are recognised as such by other major social forces.

It may be inferred from Figure 14.2 that the hypothesis proposed places more emphasis on the bourgeoisie's political organisation than on the level of industrial development, as it states that a shift from P2 to P3 does not automatically lead to the introduction of parliamentary democracy. This only happens if the bourgeoisie at the same time is well organised in relation to the representative organs and thus in relation to the democratic decision-making structures.

So far we have been interested in how the social forces, their relative power positions and their mutual relationships determine the form of regime. However, it is also part of the reasoning in class and state theory that a particular form of regime embodies systematic biases favouring certain social forces and disfavouring others. The numerically strong but economically weak classes like peasants, workers and rural labourers thus have little opportunity of gaining influence under an autocratic form of regime. They perhaps also have few opportunities under a democratic form of regime, but *ceteris paribus* they will have better possibilities of exerting influence on policy formulation in a system with recurring elections and greater openness surrounding the political decision-making processes.

The class theories concern themselves not only with the interaction between classes and the form of regime, but also with the wider role of social classes in the whole development of a society. Therefore, the brief presentation here should be seen in connection with both the theories about modes of production and social classes reviewed earlier (Chapter 8), and with the state theories discussed later (Chapter 16).

It follows from the class theory perspective that the forms of regime are determined to a higher degree by the social forces in society than the other way round. But it does not necessarily follow from this that the form of regime is determined exclusively in this way. It does not follow either that the state thereby becomes reduced to an instrument for realisation of the special interests of certain social classes. On the contrary, the class theory discussion has for many years been strongly preoccupied with the question of the state's autonomy of action – or relative autonomy – within the limits set by economic structures and societal forces. This issue will be discussed later (in Chapter 16).

Concluding the discussion of the class theories' view on the form of regime it should be emphasised that they have their explanatory strengths at the higher levels of aggregation and abstraction. When it comes to the more detailed analyses of political life, it is necessary to turn to other conceptual frameworks and theories. In many cases, in this connection, a better understanding of the least-industrialised societies can be particularly successfully achieved by combining the theories reviewed in Chapter 13 with the overall hypotheses proposed in the present chapter. With respect to the more industrialised developing countries, a combination with theories on democratisation and other political development theories would probably be appropriate.

CHAPTER 15

Decentralisation and Local-level Politics

The theories reviewed so far concerning politics and state in the Third World have focused overwhelmingly on macro-phenomena – on countrywide or national political structures and processes. In this is reflected the widespread conception among researchers and decision makers that the central state is the most important, or at least one of the most important actors in the development process. However, as was emphasised in the discussion of the state-building strategies, this conception has to an increasing extent been combined with a recognition of the need to expand the state institutions downwards with a further view to entering into a genuine development-promoting partnership with the citizens and their organisations (cf. Chapter 12). In addition, several political science theorists have argued in favour of various forms of political and administrative decentralisation as part of the democratisation efforts. In the present chapter, we shall look a little closer at arguments of this kind, along with considerations and theories that concern themselves with local-level political institutions.

Different forms of decentralisation

The term 'decentralisation' has been used to encompass a variety of alternative institutional and financial arrangements for sharing power and allocating resources. Four major types are often differentiated: deconcentration, delegation, devolution and privatisation. These types refer mainly to the formal set-up, while two additional types of arrangements – top-down principal agency and bottom-up principal agency – identify aspects of substance in the formal set-up (Cheema and Rondinelli, 1983; Silverman, 1992).

Deconcentration refers to the handing over of administrative or managerial responsibility to sub-national units within line ministries or other sector-specific national agencies. This relationship is established, for instance, between many national departments of education, health and police, on the one hand, and deconcentrated branch offices of these central departments on the other. Deconcentration normally implies that the field units and field staff are given some discretion to adjust national plans and directives to local conditions. But the room for manoeuvre varies greatly from one country to another and from One sector to another. In pure deconcentrated systems, local governments do not exist as discrete entities, and there is no mechanism at the local level for mandatory horizontal co-ordination and integration. Involvement of the local population in this case will normally be limited to participation in the implementation of centrally determined policies.

Delegation is the form decentralisation takes when public enterprises and other semi-autonomous government agencies are assigned responsibility for implementing sector investments or for operating public utilities and services. Delegation occurs primarily in sectors like energy, communications, ports, water and transport. Delegation may or may not entail deconcentration, depending on whether the agencies concerned establish a branch office system for their operations.

The concept of *devolution* is based on the idea that political power and legitimacy originally and naturally belonged to the central state. Consequently, all decentralisation below that level requires special justification. Devolution, then, is the transfer of authority and responsibility to regional or local governments with their own discretionary authority.

In devolved systems, responsibility for a range of operations encompassing several sectors is assigned to local authorities, which are established as corporate bodies in the legal sense with powers to raise revenue and incur expenditures. Their *de facto* administrative and financial autonomy may be circumscribed by inadequate institutional, manpower, and other resources and capacities but, in principle, devolved systems are characterised by the parallel existence of discretionary authority at sub-national levels. The overseeing role of central government is here limited to ensuring that local authorities operate within broad national guidelines with respect to those functions for which the local bodies have been given the authority to exercise discretion. In highly developed devolved systems, project-implementing agencies are often responsible to regional or local governments, rather than to sector ministries.

Local self-government can be both democratic with popularly elected assemblies, or non-democratic where the local political leadership is typically selected by regional powers, or possibly directly by the central authorities.

Privatisation, as a type of decentralisation, refers narrowly to government agencies divesting themselves of responsibility for project implementation or for providing infrastructure and services. The divestment may transfer the tasks to private sector enterprises or to non-commercial organisations. The latter are referred to here as non-government organisations (NGOs).

As regards the two types of agency introduced above, the *top-down model* indicates that local authorities exercise responsibility primarily on behalf of central government agencies. They may do this with respect to all their functions or to just some of them, while retaining autonomy and discretionary powers regarding the residual functions. When acting as principal agents on behalf of central governments, local authorities do so under direction and close supervision. Normally, the costs involved are fully covered by the central agencies concerned. The *bottom-up model*, on the other hand, implies that local authorities perform certain functions on behalf of lower levels of government, or even on behalf of user groups or other citizen organisations.

Applying these concepts to the situation as it appears in most developing countries, it is characteristic that decentralisation chiefly appears in the form of deconcentration and delegation. It is only in a minority of countries in the Third World that we find comprehensive devolution and thus strong, local self-government (Martinussen, 1995: Chs 1 and 5). Correspondingly, the central state in most cases has handed over only very limited powers and duties to private enterprises and NGOs. This is gradually changing in the 1990s, particularly in favour of commercial enterprises, as will be seen later in this book (see especially Chapter 18).

The fact that local self-government has been strictly limited has had important implications for the manner in which development work has been undertaken. Most important, perhaps, is the tendency to plan and implement development projects within vertically integrated processes without any notable horizontal co-ordination or integration at the local level. It is primarily the sector or line ministries that have been responsible for the planning and execution of development projects, including investments in infrastructure and service delivery. Local authorities, to the extent that they have been established at all in practice, have rarely had the opportunity to become effectively involved in the decision making and prioritisation ongoing in the line ministries and their branch offices.

Foreign aid agencies have in general either co-operated with the line ministries or established their own project organisations outside the administrative apparatuses of the state altogether. The latter strategy has prevailed in most African countries as well as in poor South Asian countries like Bangladesh and Nepal, while in other developing countries close collaboration with line ministries has been the normal procedure. In both sets of cases, local authorities have typically been excluded from both the planning and the management of development projects.

These arrangements have frequently been criticised by both researchers and advisers, who have claimed that greater involvement of local authorities in many cases would give better results than the centrally controlled procedures. We shall look more closely at the arguments in favour of decentralisation in the form of devolution, first by briefly discussing the development objectives which correspond to a strengthening of local authorities and, subsequently, by outlining possible overall strategies for decentralisation.

Decentralisation and development objectives

Within the discipline of public administration, alternative decentralisation arrangements are often discussed as ends in themselves or as means to achieve improved administrative performance. Development studies most often relate the issue of decentralisation to achieving economic and other objectives beyond administrative matters. We propose to combine the two perspectives. Administrative performance is important because the capacities and capabilities of government agencies are extremely low and yet critical in most Third World countries. But at the same time, administrative effectiveness and efficiency have to be viewed in relation to broader societal objectives.

Decentralisation in the form of devolution may be promoted to serve particular political interests, as when ethnic or other communities demand some form of local self-government. Transfer of powers to local institutions may also be prompted by a central leadership's interest in sharing the blame with others for poor economic performance or for not being able to deliver basic services to the citizens. But most often the objective of devolution at the political level is the positive one of increasing constructive popular participation in decision making, plan formulation and development work.

In economic terms, the objectives often stated for devolution focus on increasing local resource mobilisation as part of overall resource generation for development; provision of better services and local infrastructure; more efficient utilisation of resources; and more generally increasing total government capacity to facilitate and promote economic, social and human development.

At a more narrow administrative level, objectives often refer to increased effectiveness and efficiency in general and financial management; increased transparency and accountability; and a better adaptation of government activities to local conditions and locally perceived needs and priorities.

It should be emphasised here that the potential trade-offs among the multiple objectives may be both positive and negative. Thus, achieving a high degree of devolution may or may not be conducive to improving efficiency in resource utilisation. That would depend, among several other things, on the institutional and manpower capacities available at the local level. Likewise, increased involvement of citizens in decision making may or may not result in enhancing local resource mobilisation. A majority of the citizens may simply oppose further attempts at generating revenues for the public authorities.

Despite these complicating circumstances, it is worth looking at the arguments made in support of decentralisation and local autonomy in many developing countries. This will also imply brief considerations about the degree and character of decentralisation that are deemed the most appropriate under specific circumstances.

Strategies for decentralisation

The considerations in much of the literature about decentralisation take as their starting point the efforts to strengthen the mobilisation of resources and secure a better utilisation of these towards improving service delivery and socio-economic development.

Initially disregarding any addition of new resources and concentrating on improved utilisation of the resources available, a central question becomes how the responsibilities and tasks can best be allocated between the different public bodies, and between these and the private enterprises and organisations.

There is considerable debate over which specific criteria should be used in determining the most appropriate allocation of responsibilities and functions. It is commonly agreed, however, that at least the following two criteria should be applied:

- *effectiveness*, that is the degree to which a stated objective or condition is achieved or maintained; and
- *efficiency* which refers to the quantity of resources expended in the effort to achieve a stated objective or condition. This criterion basically implies cost minimisation for attaining specific degrees of goal achievement.

Based on these criteria, the overall guiding principle would be to assign individual responsibilities and functions to the institution or organisation capable of discharging them most effectively, and at the lowest cost. This would imply the best possible utilisation of resources, provided there is no conflict between the objectives, and provided these are stated clearly and unambiguously.

Since this is rarely the case, and since striving only for administrative effectiveness and efficiency will often result in a purely technical optimisation of resource utilisation, development researchers frequently add other criteria. One such criterion may be *responsiveness* – in terms of the degree to which an institution or an organisation responds to citizen needs and demands and adapts to changing conditions. Responsiveness often implies a degree of accountability which, in turn, requires transparency and access to decision making as seen from the citizens' point of view. This conception is found both in theories of democracy and in the literature on good governance published by the World Bank and other international organisations (cf. Moore, 1993).

Formulated as a criterion in relation to decentralisation strategies, it becomes a question of which bodies are best suited to respond to the citizens' needs and demands, and most capable of organising themselves and their work according to these needs and demands.

Based on these three criteria (effectiveness, efficiency and responsiveness), two prominent decentralisation theorists, *Shabbir Cheema* and *Dennis Rondinelli*, have proposed two interrelated hypotheses. In a slightly elaborated form, the first hypothesis asserts that the knowledge of local needs and the responsiveness to changing local conditions are, generally speaking, better at local government level than at regional or national level. Further, democratically elected local authorities are in a better position than non-democratic local government institutions to respond to citizen demands. It follows from this hypothesis that as many development and service functions as possible should be turned over to local authorities, particularly where these are democratically elected.

According to the second hypothesis, which is also elaborated a little further here, there may be other reasons for limiting devolution. For example, economies of scale can be lost by transferring tasks to local authorities. In addition, these authorities may lack sufficient financial, technical, and managerial resources and skills to perform the functions. Finally, there may be tasks which by their very nature are regional or national, such as the exploitation of mineral deposits or the solving of large-scale environmental problems. For these reasons there will be a number of tasks which are most appropriately left to regional or national authorities (Cheema and Rondinelli, 1983; cf. also Rondinelli et al., 1989).

In other words, a balance must be aimed at. Rather than uncritical devolution, the goal should be an allocation of responsibilities and tasks which takes into account the above-mentioned factors. This applies at least in the short term. But in the longer-term perspective, decentralisation theories often recommend a strengthening of the local authorities, so that they gradually become able to take over more and more tasks (Martinussen, 1995: Ch. 9). In official statements, this is also what governments in many Asian and Latin American countries, as well as in some African countries, claim is their policy.

Sometimes, long-term policies for devolution are guided by what may be referred to as the *subsidiarity principle*. This implies that if a function can be carried out at a lower level in the governmental system, then it should be carried out at this lower level, mainly because the citizens' participation and influence would thereby be increased. In a more radical form, the subsidiarity principle states that all necessary functions in a society or community should be carried out as close as possible to the citizens – and preferably by the citizens themselves or their own organisations.

The subsidiarity principle can be applied exclusively to formal government. Then it would lead to strategies for long-term strengthening of local authorities. However, in its more radical form, the principle can also be applied beyond the formal governmental set-up, in which case it would lead to delegation and privatisation – to the handing over of more and more responsibility to commercial enterprises or NGOs.

Pluralism, competition and choice

It is evident from the extensive empirical literature on local self-government in different Third World countries that the whole issue is much more complicated than the previous sections indicate. In reality, the questions concerning realisation of objectives and the promotion of socio-economic and human development cannot be discussed solely with reference to the allocation of responsibilities and tasks, not even if considerations of the private sector are included.

That a locally elected body and the associated local-level administration, in principle, are best at solving a given task, does not mean that these institutions in practice will do so. This will largely depend on the local power structure and the kinds of interest that are reflected in the actual mode of functioning of the local authorities. On this point, it is a general observation that local elites often – also in democratic systems – have been able to invade and take over local authorities and force on them a mode of functioning which is in their own narrow interests.

There are instances of devolution and introduction of democratic procedures at the local level leading to clear improvements in terms of increased public participation and influence, as well as in terms of more accountable and development-oriented planning and development work (Webster, 1990). But there are also many examples of such improvements failing to appear, or of the transfer of more authority to local bodies even strengthening the local community elites and giving them more legitimacy – and thus greater opportunity for pursuing their special interests (Bienen et al., 1990; Alam et al., 1994).

Observations of this kind have given rise to cautiousness in strategy recommendations and prompted researchers to formulate more complex decentralisation strategies. Of particular interest in this connection are notions about pluralism, competition and choice in the whole set-up for service provision and development work. The basic idea is to let line ministries, local authorities, foreign aid agencies, private companies, trade unions and NGOs work side by side, instead of organising them all within the framework of a single hierarchy. Citizens should have a multitude of channels through which they can access resources and seek support and favours. They should have a choice. As a corollary, providers of public services and local infrastructure would have to compete with each other. This will undoubtedly lead to many overlaps and duplication of efforts, resulting in a waste of resources as seen from a purely academic point of view. However, the main point in the present context is that pluralism and competition are likely to improve the situation for many, particularly poor and less powerful people.

The reasoning behind this assertion is quite simple: if the local council is totally dominated by a community elite, other groups can approach one or more of the other institutions or organisations providing services or infrastructure. If the NGOs within the health and water sector primarily try to create political support for a local 'big man' or politician, the non-benefited citizens may approach the line ministries' deconcentrated offices and possibly persuade them to meet demands for health care or water. There is no guarantee, of course, but the plurality and a certain amount of competition will probably put the weakest groups in a better position than the one they would be in were all resources within a given area controlled by a single authority.

PART IV

The State and Socio-economic Development

CHAPTER 16

The State and the Development
Process

The majority of the theories presented so far in this book are predominantly concerned with *either* economic *or* political conditions and changes. In many of the theories, this disciplinary limitation and focusing is deliberate. This is not the case with the Marxist-inspired theories, which none the less in a corresponding way are often characterised by a partial perspective with particular emphasis on either economics or politics and state.

Limiting the perspective is obviously necessary if one wants to penetrate deeper with an analysis. The implied criticism here is therefore not aimed at limitations *per se*, but rather at limitations which are dictated by the traditional division into subject disciplines – not by the subject matter or theme. This is directed not just at the broader disciplines such as economics and political science, but also at more narrowly defined areas such as foreign trade, business economics, international politics and comparative politics – to mention just a few of the sub-disciplines that through their demarcations of their subject matter have affected theory construction in development studies. The point is that none of these disciplines or sub-disciplines has been created or demarcated by a primary interest in understanding the development problematique in the Third World. Therefore, it is unavoidable that the disciplinary divisions sometimes constitute obstacles for understanding this problematique, simply because development problems and processes have been demonstrated to affect all aspects of society.

Accordingly, we will in the following look closer at interdisciplinary and multidisciplinary approaches. This does not imply, however, that we propose to scrap the monodisciplinary approaches and their extensive theory building. On the contrary, they must be recognised for their penetrating insight into selected aspects of societal development. What we shall to do try is to bring the monodisciplinary theories into a more comprehensive framework for understanding broader societal conditions and transformations in the Third World. This may be done by drawing attention to theories that attempt to integrate economic, social, political and cultural perspectives.

To avoid unacceptable superficiality as a consequence of a very wide perspective, it is necessary to focus attention on a series of narrowly defined but interrelated themes and problems. The important point is that each of them will be dealt with, not from the perspective of a particular discipline, but from a multidisciplinary perspective.

The first issue to be addressed concerns the interaction between the state and socio-economic development processes. In the present chapter, we shall first introduce various conceptions of society and state, and then move on to discussing state-managed development and economic planning. The next chapter (Chapter 17) draws attention to approaches and theories concerned with the political economy of development. Themes addressed here include state autonomy and capacity, and social conditions under which the states operate in different Third World societies. Chapter 17 also includes a section on new institutional economics. Chapter 18 then reviews the recent debates on whether the state or the market can and should play the leading role in economic development. Part IV concludes with considerations on the security problems of the developing countries and the importance these have for the states' way of acting and for development processes (Chapter 19).

Seen in a broader perspective, the main theme of the theories and discussions reviewed in these chapters is the state and the economic processes. In Part V, we will leave this perspective and instead take as a starting point the civil society – that is all the complex and multifarious structures and institutions which lie outside the state and the corporate economy but which, at the same time, have both a determining influence on them and independent importance for societal development and the everyday life of citizens. Some of the approaches presented in Chapter 17, particularly those concerned with peasant economies, social networks, and the state as seen in these contexts, introduce important issues relating to the civil-society perspective. They are dealt with in the present part of the book, however, because in the international debates they have been discussed primarily in relation to the state-economy – or political-economy – perspective.

Society and state: a classification of basic conceptions

In much of the social science literature about the developing countries, the state is mentioned as an institution of quite special importance for the development process.

In conventional economic theory, the state is often referred to as an important initiator and catalyst of growth and development. Sometimes it is stated in very specific terms what the state should do to bring about certain changes. Many of the development strategies reviewed in Part II of this book can be seen as appropriate examples. But it is rare in these theories and strategies to find an accurate indication of what should be understood by the term 'state'. Nor is it common to find thorough considerations concerning the possibilities for carrying out one or another type of development strategy. There is a tendency to conceive of the state as an independent institution that functions in accordance with the decisions of rational decision makers.

In the dependency theory literature, the role of the state also is highlighted. But in contrast to economic theory there is here a tendency to deprive the state and its decision makers of any form of independence – until socialism has been introduced. Especially in the classical dependency theories, the actions of the state are seen as being largely determined by the interests of international capital. Therefore, from the perspective of these theories there is no compelling reason to investigate more closely the institutional set-up and mode of functioning of the state in peripheral societies.

None of the opposing conceptions offered by these schools of thought is suitable, if the objective is to reach a deeper understanding of the role and possibilities of the state in relation to the economic and social problems of developing countries. In that case one must turn to other theories.

An interesting contribution in this connection is Gunnar Myrdal's theory of the 'soft state'. Other relevant theories are constructed with a basis in various general theories about social classes and state power, mainly within the Neo-Marxist tradition. Finally, it is worth noting that during the last decade there have also appeared some splendid and thought-provoking analyses of the state, in extension of both economic development theory and non-Marxist political economics. We shall look at selected examples from these different theoretical schools of thought. Prior to that, however, it will be useful to produce an overview of the different basic conceptions of the relationship between the state and society.

At the abstract level, these basic conceptions are not worked out with particular reference to the conditions in the Third World. Most of the theory construction pertaining to the state and its role in society has rather been elaborated in – and with reference to – the Western industrialised societies. This in itself should give reason for caution when trying to apply the different central concepts and hypotheses in a Third World context. But with this warning in mind one may, from the elaborate and conceptually rich theoretical debate on the state in highly industrialised societies, obtain an overview and a comprehensive frame of analysis that can – with modifications and due attention to the prevailing circumstances in various types of Third World countries – undoubtedly strengthen the analyses of state–society relationships in these contexts.

The state – as other institutions – can be described with the help of four analytic dimensions. A particular state conception may correspond to one of these dimensions, or to a combination of two or more of them. The four dimensions are the state as:

1. a *product* of conflicting interests and power struggles, possibly also as a reflection of a many-sided dominance which makes it an agenda- and discourse-setting institution;
2. a *manifestation of structures* which lay down the framework for its mode of

functioning and impose a certain order on both the state and the rest of society, and thus to some extent determine the behaviour of the citizens;

3. an *arena* for interaction and conflict between contending social forces; and

4. an *actor* in its own right, which by its form of organisation and mode of functioning exerts a relatively autonomous influence on outcomes of conflicts and other processes in society.

The two first-mentioned analytical dimensions resemble each other in that they both focus on the state as a product of the surrounding society. When a distinction is proposed between the two it is to highlight that the first dimension puts great emphasis on the role of social and political actors, whereas the other pays more attention to the economic structures' direct determination of the form and mode of functioning of the state.

We shall use these four dimensions to describe and compare different state conceptions in connection with a fundamental distinction between, on the one hand, society-centred approaches, and on the other, state-centred approaches.

A *society-centred* approach a priori assigns primacy to societal structures and social forces – economic structures, social classes or interest groups, depending on the type of conceptualisation of society. A society-centred approach rests on the assumption that societal structures and social forces have a greater impact upon the state than the state upon society, although some kind of interplay or dialectic relationship is implied. Using Nicos Poulantzas's distinction between state power, state apparatus and state functions, the society-centred approach concerns itself with clarifying how and to what extent state power – which is located in society – determines the form and mode of functioning of the state apparatus (Poulantzas, 1978).

A *state-centred* approach, on the other hand, is a mode of inquiry that focuses on the actual behaviour of the state apparatus and the autonomy exercised by that apparatus and its personnel. The approach need not imply an assumption about the state as having a greater impact upon society than society upon the state. Without minimising the importance of societal actors and variables, the proposition implied is merely that the state can advantageously be accorded analytical priority (Clark and Dear, 1984). Although some of the state-centred approaches investigate the relations between society or economy and politics without assuming a very high degree of state autonomy, it remains a general feature of the whole approach to look for autonomy and autonomy-enhancing actions – rather than for state-external factors and their modes of determining state form and state interventions. The state is regarded as an independent actor, rather than as a product of conflicting interests and power struggles.

We can now summarise the four dimensions and the two approaches as shown in Figure 16.1. In this are furthermore added examples of state conceptions which in various ways combine these dimension and approaches.

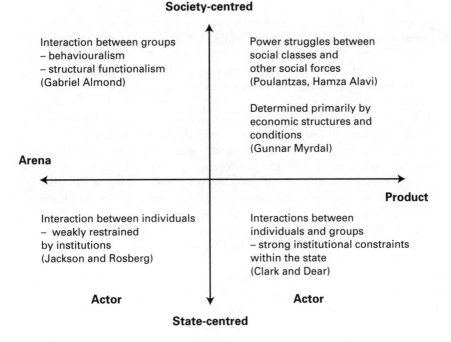

Figure 16.1 A classification of state concepts

The dimension referred to as manifestation of structures is in the figure subsumed under the conception of the state as predominantly a product. It must therefore be noted that the quadrant that combines a society-centred approach with a conception of the state primarily as a product contains at least two main conceptions: the state as predominantly determined by the economic processes and their structures, and the state as predominantly a product of interest conflicts and power struggles between classes and other social forces.

Other dimensions may be relevant for a more detailed account of the different state concepts, like the relative importance of intra-societal and extra-societal structures and forces – or the importance attached to historical legacies. These aspects are taken up only where they are deemed particularly relevant in the following.

We have already reviewed and discussed some of the conceptions mentioned in Figure 16.1, including Gabriel Almond's analyses of the political system as an arena for the processing of demands and support from different social groups (in Chapter 12). The state is not a central concept in Almond's analysis, yet it is worth noting that to the extent that he or other representatives of contemporary mainstream political science approaches deal with the state or its constituent parts they do so primarily from a society-centred perspective. Further, they tend to attribute to the decision makers within the political system a high degree of autonomy as actors. Another conception noted earlier is the one proposed by Hamza Alavi (in Chapter 13). The same applies to Jackson and Rosberg whose view of the state basically corresponds to the conception found in the theories of autocratic or personal rule in Africa (also in Chapter 13).

The other theories and their adherents referred to in Figure 16.1 are briefly reviewed below. In addition, it should be noted that Figure 16.1 – besides categorising various conceptions – may also be used to characterise the existing states in different developing countries. It could thus be considered whether there is a basic and inversely proportional relation between the degree of industrial development and the degree of state autonomy, in the sense that the state leaders and the bureaucrats can play more independent roles in the weakly industrialised societies, and less independent roles in societies where industrial development has simultaneously led to the creation of strong economic interest groups (Martinussen, 1991c).

It is interesting to look at the state-centred approaches from this perspective. One of the representatives of these approaches, *Eric Nordlinger*, has summarised the core of the statist perspective as featuring: (a) public officials' forming of their own policy preferences; and (b) the state acting on these preferences despite their (likely) divergence from those of the most powerful private actors (Nordlinger, 1988).

Other representatives of the state-centred approaches, particularly those informed by aspects of historical materialism, will not go this far. *Gordon Clark* and *Michael Dear*, for example, have tried to strike a balance between what in their view is a society-oriented reductionist approach and the approach which assumes complete state autonomy. Clark and Dear characterise the state as both capitalist and autonomous. It is capitalist in the sense that it is embedded in the social relations of capitalism, but it is simultaneously an institution of power and an actor and authority in its own right. In other words, the state is a lot more than an entity that concentrates and exercises class power located outside its apparatuses, as propounded in Poulantzas's analysis and the structuralist tradition.

Clark and Dear recognise that the specific economic and political structures under capitalism give capitalists a great deal of unilateral power, but they stress that it is the state that ensures the maintenance of the capitalists' exploitative hold over the means of production, and sources of wealth and economic power in general. They criticise the structuralist conception for assuming that the economic relations exist logically prior to the state so that, in effect, the state is dependent upon the play of class antagonisms. Instead, they argue that capitalism is not merely an economic system but also a political system – that legal entitlements and liabilities do as much to define the social relations of capitalism as the market system of commodity exchange. In this sense, the state is part of and just as important as the non-state societal structures (Clark and Dear, 1984).

An interesting thing about the state-centred approaches when applied in a Third World context is that they assign central importance to the civil and military bureaucrats' independent roles. In this respect, they resemble the basic assertions in the theory about the overdeveloped post-colonial state (cf. Chapter 13). The state-centred approaches appear, paradoxically, more relevant here than in relation to the highly industrialised countries where they were originally elaborated.

It is further worth noting that after the breakdown of the state apparatus in the former centrally planned economies of the Eastern Bloc, the state-centred approaches appear inappropriate for explaining this breakdown, which must rather be seen as the outcome of changes and actions outside the state. On the other hand, the state-centred theories had something to offer in the analyses of the exercise of political power as long as the Communist parties were strongly entrenched within the state apparatus in these countries.

In contrast to Clark and Dear, Gunnar Myrdal has in his analyses of the state, especially with regard to the conditions in South Asia, taken as his starting point the significant societal determination of the state and its mode of functioning.

The 'soft' state: Myrdal

Myrdal's whole approach aimed at combining economic analyses with the analyses of non-economic societal phenomena. The economic aspects of his theory are already mentioned in the section on Myrdal in Chapter 6, where it is also noted that he categorised the non-economic conditions under three headings: attitudes towards life and work; institutions; and policies (Myrdal, 1968: pp. 1862ff.).

By attitudes towards life and work, Myrdal referred primarily to attitudes which in one way or another have obstructed economic growth and development. He included in this category, among others, low levels of work discipline, punctuality and orderliness; superstitious beliefs and irrational outlook; lack of alertness, adaptability, ambition and readiness for change; contempt for manual work; submissiveness to authority and exploitation; and submissiveness to a divine ruler determining destinies of individuals to such an extent that working for a better standard of living was rendered pointless.

'Institutions' unfavourable to development, according to Myrdal, included land tenure systems like sharecropping; undeveloped institutions for private enterprise, employment, trade and credit; and a weak infrastructure of voluntary organisations. He emphasised, in particular, how sharecropping arrangements in South Asia had impeded agricultural growth. With these arrangements, where the sharecropper had to 'rent' land against a payment of, say, 50 per cent of the produce, there were no incentives to invest in productivity improvements. Nor did the sharecroppers have any strong incentives to work harder than necessary to sustain themselves and their families at the same level.

Other types of institutions which, according to Myrdal, were detrimental to development were the political-administrative agencies. He described public administration in the Third World as inefficient and unsuitable to manage the development process. In this context, Myrdal, like the Neo-Marxist state theorists, drew attention to the political legacy from the colonial era. The state in these countries was not created to promote and manage development, but rather to secure the interests of the colonial powers in terms of law and order and the collection of taxes. Therefore, sweeping administrative and political reforms were required before the state in post-colonial societies could come to function efficiently in relation to the development processes.

Myrdal further noted that the laws in developing countries were, as a rule, formulated in such weak and imprecise terms that a considerable degree of discretionary power was left with the government officials. This instigated corruption. When the officials have to make a ruling, for example in connection with an application for import licences, it might be natural for the applicant to offer some sort of commission or bribe to achieve a favourable result. The officials, on their side, might not have any strong hesitations about receiving such a gratuity.

These are just a few among many symptoms of what Myrdal called 'the soft state' (Myrdal, 1968: Ch. 18, 1970). At a high level of abstraction, the term refers to an unwillingness among rulers to impose obligations on the governed, and a corresponding unwillingness on their part to obey rules laid down even by democratic procedures. The soft state is not capable of implementing policies that go against the interests of the bureaucracies or powerful groups in society. Government officials frequently co-operate closely with exactly those powerful individuals and groups they are supposed to supervise and control. The officials often simply refuse to follow orders or implement decisions when these go against their own interests, or get in the way of further co-operation with the external interest groups to which the officials are connected.

Myrdal claimed that most of the states in the backward countries are 'soft' in this sense. Therefore, they can be exploited by powerful individuals and groups.

There are interesting similarities between the soft state concept and the conception of the state contained in the theories of African autocracy and patronage (cf. Chapter 13). But Myrdal related his state analysis more directly to the theory of economic development. This was achieved chiefly through his sixth category: policies. This category comprises political interventions and politically induced changes applied to conditions in the other categories. Co-ordination of policies aimed at speeding up development and creating the necessary preconditions for self-sustaining growth was treated by Myrdal under the heading of 'planning'. We shall turn to this topic in the section below.

With the notion of the soft state, Myrdal laid the groundwork for a fruitful analysis of interactions between the state and economic development processes. The main problems probably lay in a too-superficial analysis of the structures and powerful social forces which limit the room for manoeuvre of the state in relation to the socio-economic processes. In addition, in the actual theory construction there is too little consideration of the differences between the developing countries. On both these dimensions supplementary analyses can be found in the Marxist-inspired class and state theories, as well as in the theories of the political economy of development (cf. Chapters 8 and 14, and Chapter 17, respectively).

State-managed development and economic planning

Myrdal's theories are complex and sophisticated, but with respect to his conception of the state it appears warranted to conclude that they rely heavily upon an assumption about the state being the most important engine of growth and structural transformation. The 'state' in this context is not the state existing in most underdeveloped countries, but the state that could be created with the help of political determination and comprehensive administrative reforms. In this sense, Myrdal's theories and strategies belong to the large group of theories that have adhered to conceptions of state-led or state-managed development, and in this context emphasised the importance of economic planning. We are not talking here about imperative planning as in the former Soviet Union or China in the past, but about indicative planning in mixed economies. Theories concerning the latter assign to the state important initiating and co-ordinating functions in relation to the private sector, while the former adds to this an extensive, centralised control and replacement of the market mechanisms.

The theoretical debate from the beginning of the 1980s onwards has questioned the ability of the state to direct and manage development, claiming that the institution *per se* is inappropriate for the purpose and should therefore be 'rolled back' to give way to markets and the private sector (cf. Chapter 18). However, attempts at state control and planning have played, and continue to play, a central role in several Third World countries. Consequently, there is reason to dwell a little on the theories and conceptions which have provided the impetus for state-managed development. In this connection, we have to distinguish between, on the one hand, the economic theories with relatively narrow perspectives and the theories which have attempted to include both social and political institutional conditions on the other.

Many of the theories reviewed in Part II of the present book contain elements that may be seen as economic planning theories with a narrow perspective. They envisage that the development process can be initiated and accelerated with the help of different forms of state intervention. The state is not made the object of any independent analysis but is, so to speak, assumed to be capable of performing the necessary functions. In contrast to these conceptions, we have noted, *inter alia*, Myrdal's assertion that the states, as they exist in most developing countries, are not capable of performing these tasks and, in addition, that the tasks are in reality far more complex.

We shall look a little closer at this criticism of narrowly defined economic planning in this section. In the next section we shall follow up on the criticism by discussing some of the considerations concerning increased people-participation as a means to making planning and implementation more effective and efficient. In both these sections we shall limit the discussion to approaches which basically assume that the state should and can function as an engine of development, albeit there are many nuances implied here – ranging from central planning of the command type to broader attempts at activating the citizens in plan preparation as well as in implementation. The scope of variation corresponds essentially to the differences between the state-building strategies, which pay attention only to central government agencies, and the state extension strategies concerned also with decentralisation and attempts at reaching down and out to the citizens (Chapters 12 and 15, respectively).

Broadly formulated, *development planning* is an effort to identify the most appropriate means and measures for achieving specific development objectives. Economic planning may further be described as conscious efforts on the part of government to influence, direct and, in some cases, even control changes in the principal economic variables (consumption, savings, investment, exports, imports, etc.) in order to achieve a predetermined set of objectives concerning growth and the sectoral and regional distribution of growth (Todaro, 1971: Ch. 23).

The supporters of economic planning have argued in several different ways for the necessity of extensive state intervention. *Rosenstein-Rodan* stated as early as in the mid-1950s a now classic argument based on a distinction between allocation of consumer goods, allocation of production and allocation of investment (cf. Meier, 1989: pp. 513ff.). Rosenstein-Rodan recognised that the market mechanisms would often function tolerably well and bring about equilibria with regard to allocation of consumer goods and production, but he emphasised at the same time that the market could not secure an optimum and growth-promoting allocation of investments. He referred to the conventional assumption that the individual investors, under free market conditions, would maximise their private net marginal product. This behaviour would not automatically lead to a similar maximisation from the point of view of the society. In addition, the lifetime of equipment is long so that the investors' foresight is likely to be imperfect, and their capability for acting rationally more limited than that of a buyer and seller or of a producer. Rosenstein-Rodan further emphasised that capital markets, more as a rule than as an exception, were notoriously imperfect, governed not only by prices but also by institutions and traditions.

Other theorists had emphasised that market mechanisms are simply not present in relation to considerable parts of the production and exchange in backward societies. Moreover, even in highly developed market economies there will always be market failures. The economic literature describes at least five situations where the market mechanisms cannot be relied upon to provide the most efficient and appropriate allocation of goods and services: where natural monopolies exist; where increased production is associated with decreasing unit costs (for example electricity, gas and water supply); where substantial externalities exist and are not reflected in the accounts of private suppliers (for example pollution and environmental damage); where it is difficult to charge for a service or to exclude those who do not pay; and where merit goods are involved (Roth, 1987: pp. 7ff.).

In more general terms, the arguments for economic planning have been based on three major claims:

1. Individual preferences and decisions regarding investments do not necessarily lead to an optimum allocation and development-promoting utilisation of the scarce resources of the society.
2. The market mechanisms do not function properly in the less developed countries.
3. Even where the market mechanisms function well, they do not lead to changes and development, but may simply reproduce an equilibrium at the low level of development prevailing.

On the basis of notions like these, the planning theorists have worked out different propositions regarding policies and state interventions which could remedy the shortcomings. In this context, at least three main forms of planning can be distinguished, each taking as a starting point certain macro- or sector-economic models (Todaro, 1971, 1982: Ch. 23).

The first model, the *aggregate growth* model, deals with the entire economy in terms of such macro-economic variables as savings, investment, consumption and production. Its simplest and most widely used version is the Harrod-Domar model, according to which the capital/output ratio determines how large an investment is required to generate a predetermined increase of the total income of a society. The model assumes that capital is the major constraint on aggregate economic growth. In many countries where inadequate foreign exchange reserves have acted as the principal bottleneck, planning models have often concentrated on foreign trade and the transfer of financial resources from abroad through aid and international private investments.

The second model, the *sectoral growth* model, divides the economy into two or more main sectors, and plans are worked out for each of them, or possibly for a combination of sectors. The most important analytical tool for appraising alternative sectoral investment projects here is the so-called benefit–cost analysis, by means of which one tries to indicate the total value of probable benefits and weigh this against the total costs. The higher the ratio, the more attractive the investment concerned.

The third model goes one step further than the sector model, as it specifies the linkages between the different sectors or industries. All sectors are viewed both as producers of outputs and utilisers of inputs from other sectors. Direct and indirect repercussions of changes in any one sector are calculated for all the other sectors. Such models are often described as *input–output* models. Planning based on these models aims at indicating the investments and the specific composition of production factors (capital, land and labour) required to make all the sectors grow concurrently and without blocking each other's growth with either insufficient demand or insufficient production.

It has been a characteristic of most developing countries since their independence that they have to a varying, but generally considerable extent applied economic planning in their efforts to achieve a better utilisation of scarce resources, with a further view to promoting specific forms of economic change – particularly growth in the industrial sector.

During the 1950s and 1960s, nearly all the countries in the Third World initiated one form or another of economic planning, mainly with five-year planning horizons. Some of the countries, like Cuba, introduced central planning of the command type where the exercise came to cover practically all investments and furthermore was imperative, that is directly controlling most material and financial resource allocations according to a specific set of growth targets. In the overwhelming majority of developing countries, however, planning became less of the controlling type and was often limited to public investments.

In relation to the private sector, including both modern capitalist production and the subsistence economy, planning remained indicative, with projections and recommendations on policies that could promote overall targets. India and a few other countries tried, in the period up to the beginning of the 1990s, to influence resource allocation and investment priorities in the private, industrial sector more directly through extensive regulation and licensing, but otherwise it was typical for most state authorities to limit themselves to the planning of public investments. Sub-Saharan African governments generally had to confine themselves to initiating very limited planning within particular sectors, and even that proved ineffective in several cases.

Development planning in the Third World has been aimed predominantly at economic conditions in a rather narrow sense. As Myrdal has expressed it, planning has been limited to production, incomes and standard of living, whereas the preconditions for production and growth in the wider sense have been excluded. Neither prevailing attitudes towards life and work nor questions concerning political and cultural institutions have been taken into consideration (Myrdal, 1968: Appendices 3 and 4).

For these reasons, there has been a tendency for development planning to be detached from the socio-political setting. It has become an academic pursuit, with sophisticated but highly unrealistic models. The problems of Third World planning were further compounded in the 1970s and 1980s as it gradually became clear that many of the theories on which it was based were faulty and insufficient. This led to widespread frustration among planners, and many even talked about a crisis in economic planning.

The crisis did not immediately lead to radical changes, which could be attributed to the fact that planning is not exclusively a rational economic activity but also has important political functions. In the literature, it is often noted that development plans are to some degree worked out to protect public authorities and their officials from becoming overburdened with demands from different interest groups. Thus, plans can be used to reject demands and wishes which do not correspond with the priorities in the officially agreed planning documents. Other authors have emphasised that development plans are prepared to give foreign aid agencies and development banks the impression that requested grants and loans will be used in accordance with precisely interconnected priorities in the economic policies of the country concerned.

In addition to such shallow premeditations, it is a further part of the picture that no obvious alternatives to the models used in economic planning have been forthcoming. Nor has there been the necessary knowledge and expertise to improve on the planning models and procedures.

Even though the crisis in planning did not immediately lead to decisive changes in practices, it did prompt in many developing countries a fruitful, critical debate on planning and its functions. In this debate, it has been stressed that planning is a complex and multifaceted social process, in which the actual preparation of the five-year plans is reduced to a single stage among many. It is emphasised in this connection that the planning process has to start with the identification of needs, wishes and development possibilities. And this identification has to take place at a decentralised level, out in the local communities and with the involvement of as large a part of the population as possible. The reason stated in the theories for this is that it is the population of the local communities who best know both their problems and the development possibilities available (cf. Chapter 15). Furthermore, it is assumed that the local population will later be more motivated to take part in development work if they, at an earlier stage, have been involved in the decision-making processes. Thus, the debate came to point towards the possible benefits of increased public participation, benefits which we will consider briefly in the next section.

The critical debate about development planning did not confine itself to the preparation of plans and other dimensions of the input-side. It addressed the output-side, too, that is the implementation of the plans, both in the shape of general economic policies and concrete projects. It is in this connection that different development researchers have come to expose the many barriers obstructing or delaying the implementation of development plans in accordance with the stated intentions. The barriers could be economic, political, institutional, or of a socio-cultural nature; in practice, they often turned out to be a combination.

The comprehensive theory formation in this area will not be further discussed here, because it is largely contained in theories reviewed elsewhere in this book. It shall be briefly indicated, though, how these theories may also be viewed as propositions regarding the problems of transforming development plans into specific development initiatives.

The problems can, *inter alia*, be ineffectiveness, inefficiency, and lack of capacity in the state agencies. Or they can be related to politicisation and corruption of the cadres of officials who are responsible for the implementation of development policies. The problems can furthermore lie outside the state administration and rather concern the power relationships in the surrounding society, such as for example when transnational corporations or powerful landowners are, in practice, capable of eluding political regulations and control, even in situations where politicians and officials do their best.

These and many other problems encountered during the implementation of development plans and policies have been dealt with earlier in this book (particularly in Chapters 9, 12 and 14). Other related aspects are taken up for discussion in the two following chapters. People's participation in the planning process, however, is not a central issue in any of these contexts. We shall therefore end the present chapter with a short discussion of this theme.

Participatory planning

There are several, partly contradictory theories about people's participation. Classical modernisation theories from the 1950s and the 1960s saw widespread and active people's participation as a problem. In some of the theories, participation and democracy were actually viewed as incompatible with rapid economic growth. Too much involvement of the masses in decision making would impede growth, because ordinary citizens lacked the foresight and imagination required to plan for the future.

Other modernisation theories acknowledged that broad public participation in political life could probably be reconciled with economic growth and modernisation, provided the participation was carefully organised and controlled. According to Samuel Huntington, the important point was to prevent the degree of public participation from exceeding the degree of institutionalisation, that is the extent to which the participation could be channelled through established institutions functioning in agreement with the government's overall policies. If political participation exceeded the degree of institutionalisation in this sense, this would lead to political breakdown and pave the way for military take-overs (cf. Chapter 12). Huntington has since modified this categorical interpretation and agreed that increased public participation should itself be seen as worth striving for. He further accepted that it could, under less restricting preconditions, be reconciled with economic progress (Huntington and Nelson, 1976).

For many years, the only real alternatives to these theories of participation were the Marxist-inspired class and state theories. They did not necessarily disagree with the modernisation theories on the point regarding the relationship between mass participation and economic growth, rather they phrased the problems in a different way. Instead of contrasting democracy and economic growth, they raised questions concerning the specific forms of economic development that would emerge, depending on the pattern and extent of public participation. Class and state theories put particular emphasis on the asymmetric participation of the various social classes, along with their very different opportunities for accessing and influencing decision-making centres within the state machinery. The general point was that economic policies and their impact upon development patterns would be shaped primarily by the most powerful classes, those with a strong organisational infrastructure and easy access to the state. Other classes would be losers in the struggle for benefits and privileges (cf. Chapter 14).

Class and state theories further stressed that the social classes best organised vis-à-vis the state were typically also the most powerful economically, dominating both production and the market. In contrast, the peasants, rural labourers, workers and other economically suppressed classes held weak positions on the political scene. They were poorly organised; often they were divided according to geographical, ethnic and religious affiliations. In most societies, there was a decisive division between men and women. And finally, should there be tendencies towards a mobilisation and organisation across these and other lines then, the Neo-Marxist theories claimed, experience showed that the political authorities would in such cases intervene with suppressive measures.

As a corollary, the state in these theories was not regarded as a neutral entity that could be overburdened because of extensive public participation in political life. The state was certainly the scene of the battles which were fought between classes, but it was at the same time a reflection and manifestation of class dominance. In a very fundamental manner the state organised and facilitated the ruling classes' political participation. Conversely, the state disorganised the other social classes.

The class and state theories were formulated with particular attention to the predominantly capitalist countries, where the dominant classes were international capital, the national bourgeoisie and, possibly, a feudal aristocracy. However, in principle the theories could be applied also to less industrialised societies of the P1 type (cf. Chapter 8) or to socialist-oriented regimes, where the state's organising functions would then benefit other classes.

Around the mid-1970s, a third type of theories of people's participation emerged (Uphoff et al., 1979). They did not constitute a coherent group of theories elaborated within the same conceptual framework but, in comparison with the two above-mentioned schools of thought, the new approaches introduced different perspectives and propositions. Unlike the modernisation theories, they asserted that people's participation was useful for promoting economic development. Further, they expressly adhered to the value premise that the poor ought to receive a fair share of economic growth. In comparison with the class and state theories they differed, *inter alia*, by assuming that it would be possible to mobilise and organise the poor segments of the population with active support from the state.

There might be strong opposition from vested interests and considerable changes in the power structure might be required; nevertheless, the new theories of people's participation claimed that a considerable increase in poor people's participation, in both economic and political life, could be attained and that this would benefit national development. They rejected the basic notion of antagonism and mutually exclusive interests of contending social classes. In a sense, one could say that they replaced the assumption about a zero-sum game contained in Marxist analyses with an idea about a plus-sum game where everybody stood to gain from increased people's participation.

A number of the new theories originated in the debate about the basic needs strategy (cf. Chapter 21). The International Labour Organisation of the UN (ILO) has played an important role in their formulation. The World Bank and several of the United Nations' specialised agencies have also contributed to formulating theories and strategies focusing on people's partici-pation and its potentially positive impact upon development (ILO, 1976, 1978; FAO, 1981; UNRISD, 1981–83).

In the strategies proposed by official aid agencies there has been a tendency to see participation as a *means* – not as an end in itself. They have often taken their starting point in Nurkse's poverty circles or similar conceptions of the nature of poverty replication (cf. Chapter 5). Based on these, the aid organisa-tions have then noted the several problems encountered when trying to reach resource-poor target groups with assistance programmes and projects. It is in this context that they often pointed to insufficient involvement of the target groups in project preparation and execution as major obstacles to success.

To overcome these obstacles, some of the organisations – notably ILO, UNICEF and FAO – came forward with proposals regarding more extensive involvement of intended beneficiaries. The overall aim was to accelerate the development process in accordance with the priorities and emphases estab-lished by the authorities of the individual developing countries. Some official aid organisations went a step further by proposing more people's participation as a means to learn more about the wishes and priorities of local communities but, generally speaking, this bottom-up approach was left to the non-government development organisations.

Promoting participation was seen by the aid agencies as creating, directing and maintaining, with popular support, organisations designed to satisfy the requirements of the poor (Jazairy et al., 1992: Ch. 12). Common to the poverty-oriented strategies proposed was, moreover, a particular interest in four issue areas: (a) *who* should participate; (b) *how* the concerned groups should participate; (c) *what* the scope of the participation should be, that is the questions to be decided upon with the involvement of the intended beneficiaries; and (d) *how much weight* should be given to the wishes and demands expressed by the 'people' as compared with the priorities arrived at by the official authorities.

The specific strategies of the official aid agencies differed with respect to these four issue areas. However, there was a widespread tendency to restrict the proposals to limited and controlled popular participation within the frameworks established by the authorities and the existing official institutions. This to some extent reflected Huntington's original worry about too much public participation exceeding the capacity of the official institutions and threatening political stability. In some cases, as another reference to this worry, the strategies for increased participation were combined with efforts aimed at strengthening local government institutions. Some agencies, though, went a step further in this respect by suggesting institutional rearrangements, not to retain control, but rather to adapt to increased popular participation. The idea here was that to the extent local authorities wished to pursue a strategy of poverty alleviation, they had to be restructured so they could allocate resources in response to popular demand.

Another approach to the problems has also taken as its starting point the poverty circles and the planning process, but in combination with conceptions of mass economic poverty as closely interrelated with political poverty (Streeten et al., 1982; Lisk, 1985). The poor who live under such bad conditions that their basic economic needs are not satisfied are, at the same time, unable to influence the political decisions affecting their lives. Thus, they are in a double sense cut off from effectively impacting upon the basic mechanisms which keep them in poverty.

Development projects where the poor are involved in the implementation may be beneficial in some respects, but this strategy is insufficient. As long as participation is controlled and limited to being a support activity for state development planning and state-centred institution building, the poor will remain without any real influence on the development process and priorities in the broader sense. Only by involving the poor in prioritisation and other aspects of political decision making can there be a move away from the narrowly defined interests of the powerful and richer segments of their societies.

The Swedish development researcher *Göran Hydén* has expressed a similar opinion by saying that instead of the state's attempt to *reach down* to people, they should be enabled, on their own terms, to *reach up* to the state. Non-government organisations, international as well as indigenous, may play important roles in this context, according to Hydén. These organisations, if they are genuine NGOs, are much closer than government to the poorer sections of society. Their staff members are normally highly motivated and altruistic in their behaviour and show a much greater cost-consciousness and financial discipline than government officials. They are often flexible and more capable than government agencies to adjust and adapt to specific local circumstances. A final major potential advantage is the independence of NGOs *vis-à-vis* the interests organised in the state apparatuses. In the long term, the NGOs may thus contribute to real empowerment of the poor (Hydén, 1986: Chs 5 and 6). We shall come back to the theories and strategies which in this way shift the focus from state building to mobilisation and self-organisation of the citizens in Chapter 24.

Many of the new theories of participation rarely refer to any conflicts of interest between different segments of the 'people'. Some of them do recognise, however, that expressions like 'the local population' and 'the poor' in reality cover groups with conflicting interests, and which are therefore difficult to unite in a common association. The gender dimension is often emphasised as particularly important here (Moser, 1991). Poor women have interests that differ considerably from those of poor men. Thus, they need to have their own organisational framework to promote these interests. Otherwise they may not benefit from economic improvements, even when the poor men experience such improvements (cf. Chapter 21). Other theories pay special attention to the dissimilar interests that peasants and rural labourers have, and the consequent necessity of organising these groups separately.

What these different theories have in common, and what is important, is a recognition of the solidly substantiated fact that the development process does not automatically distribute the benefits according to need, merit or effort. The distribution is determined rather by economic and political power. Consequently, each population group has to organise itself according to common interests. This is one of the preconditions for achieving a share of the benefits accruing from any economic progress.

CHAPTER 17

The Political Economy of Development

Chapter 16 dealt with the interaction between the state and the development process at a relatively high level of abstraction, and without distinguishing between different basic patterns in the socio-economic foundations of the states. It is such distinctions that will be introduced in the present chapter, where we shall look closer at a group of theories concerning the political economy of development. These theories operate with limited areas of validity, as they refer to certain societies over specified periods of time. The validity area is not always explicitly defined, but it is an underlying effort in these political economy approaches to generalise about, and explain, the dissimilarities between different types of developing countries. They often refer to certain regions in the Third World or even to named countries.

In comparison with the mainly monodisciplinary approaches, it is characteristic of theories about the political economy of development that they try to uncover the patterns and trends of change in the relations between state and society within a broad perspective comprising interest groups, social conditions and cultural factors. Some of them are state centred, while others are more society or economy centred. Some of them give priority to understanding and explaining the role of the state in the development process, where others are more preoccupied with the role of the citizens as economic actors. Related to this, some of the theories emphasise institutions as units of analysis and view these as important determinants of individual behaviour, while others apply methodological individualism and rely on assumptions regarding individual motivation and, based on these, work out hypotheses about events and outcomes at the macro-level.

As a result of these basic differences in the methods applied, theories of the political economy of development cannot be viewed as parts of a single approach, but should rather be viewed as a number of dissimilar contributions to the understanding of economic dynamics and the state in a societal context.

Finally, it should be noted that the Marxist and Neo-Marxist theories discussed earlier in this book can be seen as a particular brand of theories about the political economy of development. They have been dealt with in other chapters chiefly because they have been elaborated either as predominantly economic or as predominantly socio-political theories. In the present chapter, we shall consider Marxist theories only as regards their contribution to understanding the relative autonomy of the state under varying societal conditions. Apart from this proviso, the interest is concentrated around non-Marxist theories.

Strong and weak states: Evans, Johnson and Sandbrook

The state-centred theories, which started to appear in the mid-1980s, emphasise that Third World states are very different with respect to their societal basis, their institutional form and their mode of functioning. Or to quote Peter Evans: 'States are not standardized commodities. They come in a wide array of sizes, shapes, and styles' (Evans, 1989).

Where Myrdal generalised about the states of the developing countries by describing them as 'soft' and in their existing form unable to function as engines of growth and development, these new state theories have paid more attention to the differences, especially between the Far Eastern and the African states. In the light of the experience from the Far Eastern high-growth countries, these theories have emphasised that apparently not all the states in the Third World have been unable to promote growth and economic transformation.

Peter Evans is one of the theorists who, on the basis of empirical studies, has tried to work out a typology of different states. He distinguishes between three main forms: predatory, intermediate and developmental (Evans, 1989).

The *predatory state* is characterised by an incoherent and inefficient state administration, which has very little capacity to promote economic and social development. The predatory state is, moreover, controlled by a small political power elite, possibly an autocratic ruler who uses the state and its resources to promote his own narrow interests. Evans takes Zaire as a prototype of this form of state.

At the other end of the scale Evans places what he calls the *developmental state*, a state characterised by a well-developed coherent bureaucracy, resembling Max Weber's ideal-type bureaucracy. Empowered by strong internal networks and a homogenous administrative culture this state has considerable capacity to perform all the functions assigned to it, ranging from security policies to economic policies. The developmental state further has a considerable degree of autonomy *vis-à-vis* both the political power elite and the economic interest groups in the society. This does not mean that the state is insulated completely from these groups and the rest of society. On the contrary, the developmental state features many and close connections with the most important private interest groups, especially big business corporations, but there is a clear division of labour. The political power elite dominate long-term strategic decision making, but leave implementation to the state bureaucracy which may formulate more specific guidelines for

economic activities, but without interfering directly in the day-to-day operations of the private corporations. South Korea is referred to as a prototype
of a developmental state.

Between these two extreme forms, Evans places – with Brazil as an
example – the many *intermediate* developing country states which have built
up a certain administrative capacity. These administrations have occasionally
and in certain respects achieved positions independent of the political power
elite and the economic interest groups. The internal structures of these states
remain fragmented, divided and unstable but they perform significantly better
than the predatory states.

Chalmers Johnson has studied the Japanese state with a view to identifying
the structures and institutional prerequisites that have contributed to ensuring
the country's economic 'miracle' (Johnson, 1982). The basic features are
summed up in his concept of the *capitalist developmental state*, which Johnson
believes can serve as a role model for other states.

The basic features resemble Evans's developmental state, but they are
specified in greater detail in Johnson's work. The capitalist developmental
state has four fundamental characteristics. The first is political stability and
a system that insulates its bureaucrats from direct political influence so that
they can function technocratically. The second characteristic is an elaborate
division of labour between the state and the private sector under the overall
guidance of a planning authority which establishes the long-term goals but
otherwise does not interfere with private sector activities. The third characteristic is the state's extensive and continuing investment in education, combined
with policies to ensure the equitable distribution of opportunities and wealth.
The fourth characteristic is the state's preference for policies and interventions
based on the price mechanisms. The capitalist developmental state pursues
market-conforming interventions, rather than market-repressing or replacing
interventions. In this sense, according to Johnson, Japan and the other high-
performing East Asian countries have combined capitalist entrepreneurship
with social goal setting in a unique and effective manner.

Johnson's overall recommendation to other states and their political leaders
is that they should copy these features of the Japanese state. If they do so,
it will be appropriate to increase the involvement of the state in economic
processes. In this respect, Johnson represents a neo-conservative and
mercantilist approach that emphasises the autonomy and strength of the
state as preconditions for accelerating social development. This point of
view resembles Huntington's recommendations regarding comprehensive
extension of the state apparatus (cf. Chapter 12). But whereas Huntington
was mainly concerned with the security of the state and the maintenance of
social order, Johnson pays more attention to the development function of
the state and views a successful accomplishment of this as the best insurance
for the survival of the state.

Richard Sandbrook, in connection with his analyses of Africa, has also referred to the East Asian states as developmental and interventionist (Sand-brook, 1986). Sandbrook emphasises other aspects of state interventions as the most important for the promotion of successful capitalist growth, such as a legal framework that ensures security of property, public services that directly facilitate production, and regulation of foreign economic relations to maximise national benefits. However, his more important contribution is contained in his analyses of just how differently the vast majority of states in Africa have functioned as compared with what he terms successful late developers such as Japan, South Korea, Taiwan and Brazil.

The features highlighted by Sandbrook are essentially those noted earlier in the discussion of African autocractic regimes (Chapter 13), but he specifically links these features to the role of the African states in the economic processes. Sandbrook proposes that a major problem is that many African states lack the capacity to establish the crucial conditions for capital accumulation. Another problem is that they act in economically irrational ways. To survive as political leaders in the context of the legitimacy crisis in most African societies they have to exploit public funds and utilise them to promote their own narrow political interests.

The problem is not primarily the size of the public sector and the amount of means and resources which are drawn away from the productive economic processes, it is more the whole social 'climate' which is fostered by a power elite and a bureaucracy that are more interested in short-term political benefits than in long-term economic progress for the whole of society. Therefore, the waste of public resources is combined with an atmosphere in which productive investments are discouraged in favour of easy profits through political manipulation. The combined effect has been economic stagnation in most African countries (cf. also Sandbrook, 1985).

Many other development researchers have looked into the role of African states from similar perspectives. One of them, *Christopher Clapham*, goes as far as to claim that economic development policies – not just in Africa, but in the majority of the poor Third World countries – are state development policies (Clapham, 1985: Ch. 5). The rulers' real goal is not to contribute to economic and social progress but to strengthen the state and the groups who control it. To the extent that the state intervenes in the economic processes, it does so primarily with a view to reallocating resources towards those who have political power.

The strong emphasis on the state's and the political rulers' inability and unwillingness to support societal development may function as an important correction in relation to the conceptions of narrow economic theories concerning a rational state which, under the right guidance from the econom-ists, can and will opt for effective development-promoting policies. But the question is whether the balance has been pushed too far in the other direction by the contemporary state theories' very cynical view of, in particular, the African leaders and their bureaucracies. Policies pursued by most African governments – and by governments in other poor countries – may not have been the most appropriate from a purely economic point of view, but they may have been the most feasible from the point of view of the political power elite, for whom security considerations and socio-political stability have had to take precedence over aggregate economic growth (cf. Chapter 19).

It should further be remembered that other conditions beyond the control of the power elites have contributed greatly to making the economic tasks extremely difficult, notably for the governments of Sub-Saharan Africa. Thus, through most of the period since their political independence, the countries of this region have had to wrestle with falling world market prices on their export products and increasing relative prices on their imports. In the wake of this deterioration in the terms of trade followed the debt problem. A large number of African countries, in the 1980s and early 1990s, had to pay more in debt service charges than they received in the form of official aid and foreign investments. World Bank economists have tried to prove that the terms-of-trade decline has not acted as a major factor in Africa's poor growth, which they attribute mainly to poor policies (World Bank, 1994: Ch. 1). Yet, even they acknowledge that external factors as a whole, although surmountable, have made the task of developing Africa more difficult.

We shall look further into these matters both in the present chapter and later in the book. But first we shall briefly discuss in more general terms the extent to which Third World states can act independently. Some of the Neo-Marxist class theories have dealt with this problem in ways that may supplement the above notions of strong and weak states.

State autonomy and state capacity

There is little doubt that the state-centred theories can contribute to an appropriate understanding of the organisational form of Third World governments, and of the impact the varying forms of institutionalisation have upon their mode of functioning in relation to macro-economic processes. However, it will probably complement the overall picture if these theories are combined with Neo-Marxist class theories and their propositions regarding the limited room for manoeuvre allowed by the basic economic structures and power relations prevailing in different types of Third World societies.

We have discussed some of these propositions earlier, in connection with modes of production and social classes (Chapter 8), and in connection with issues concerning classes and forms of regime (Chapter 14). We have seen how the structure of production and the pattern of industrial development, mediated through the social classes, limit the options open for state interventions. We have also noted the particular significance of the existence or non-existence of a well-established national bourgeoisie. States in the so-called P1 societies without a national bourgeoisie would, according to the theoretical propositions, be cut off from playing a decisive role in promoting national capitalist and self-centred development. They would be heavily influenced by the interests of the centre bourgeoisies and thus the demand to subordinate their national interests to global capitalism. In contrast, it was asserted that states in P3 societies, with a basis in an established national bourgeoisie and other important internal social forces, would be far better equipped to promote intraverted capitalist development.

The principal hypothesis that can be derived from these considerations contains two central elements. First the abstract one: that a peripheral state's opportunities for effectively promoting self-centred capitalist development are determined and limited basically by the economic structures and class relations. Second the differentiating element: that the more consolidated and diversified the industrial base, and the more powerful the national bourgeoisie, the better are the possibilities for the state to push further in the direction of self-centred capitalist development.

This two-pronged hypothesis does not imply a claim to the effect that economic structures and power relations alone decide the variations in the form and impact of state interventions. The basic structures and power relations merely establish certain, sometimes wide, limits within which the form and impact of economic policies are more specifically determined by the form of regime, the capacity and the efficiency of the state bureaucracy, the chosen development strategy, and the other conditions that the state-centred analyses have emphasised so much.

We shall not discuss further these very general notions but instead focus briefly on propositions regarding the societal determination of the state's mode of functioning in P1 societies. Here the Danish development researcher, *Gorm Rye Olsen*, among others, has sought to limit the area of validity for the hypothesis regarding the national bourgeoisie's decisive role (Olsen, 1994). Based on comparative studies of Egypt, Iraq and Saudi Arabia, Olsen has reached the conclusion that it is not the bourgeoisie or for that matter any of the other social classes which dominate and shape state interventions in P1 societies. Rather, it is the civil bureaucracy and armed forces that are the most important social forces determining not only state interventions, but the whole development trajectory in the least industrialised, peripheral societies. Especially in Iraq, the two bureaucracies have turned out to be the most dynamic and decisive forces.

The proposition is interesting because it contributes to a positive formulation of the hypothesis concerning the role of the national bourgeoisie in societies where this social class is largely absent. Olsen originally assumed that his conclusions contradicted the principal hypothesis. That need not be the case, however. Looked at more carefully, his proposition may be taken as a reference either to outcomes that imply basic changes or to outcomes that essentially reproduce existing societal conditions. Interpreted in this way Olsen's proposition becomes compatible with the principal hypothesis, because this states that in P1 societies, where the national bourgeoisie and other capitalist classes are weak, the civil and military bureaucracies may fill the power vacuum and achieve significant influence over the policies of the state. In this sense, these groups, their particular interests and their power struggles, may be claimed to act as decisive factors. However, with reference to Olsen's own analysis of Iraq, which concludes that the bureaucracies have not been able decisively to contribute to capitalist development, the conception has to be reformulated. What they have been capable of doing is merely to govern structural un-change and economic non-transformation. The Egyptian bourgeoisie, on the other hand, has been able to force upon the country's state agencies a number of functions which have successfully promoted internally directed capitalist development.

With reference to the theories about the state in Africa noted above, one could generalise these observations and summarise them in the form of an additional principal hypothesis stating that in societies without well-established capitalist classes, and especially without a national bourgeoisie, the state is unlikely to be capable of promoting structural transformation. The particular interests of the civil and military bureaucracies, and the narrow interests of the political power elite, may be realised in the short-term perspective, but this will rarely imply any structural changes or any intense efforts aimed at promoting economic growth (Martinussen, 1991c). Formulated in this manner, the additional principal hypothesis can provide an alternative or supplementary framework to the one embodied in World Bank notions of inappropriate economic policies as the major reason for stagnation in African and other poor countries.

The following sections will examine other approaches and theories which, in different ways, have tried to capture the special features of the interaction between state and society in countries with a weak industrial base.

State, market and peasants: Popkin and Bates

There are a number of different theories concerning the role of the state in the development process in countries where the industrial sector is undeveloped. These theories often focus on the interaction between the state and peasants.

One of the theorists who is centrally placed in this connection is the American scholar *Robert Bates* (Bates, 1988). He represents a 'new political economy' which has not originated from the Marxist tradition but from development economics. Bates's approach, perspective and method can be found in their basic form among many development researchers, including *Samuel L. Popkin* (Popkin, 1988). In contrast to Bates, Popkin has primarily concerned himself with the conditions in Asian agriculture.

Common to the two researchers is their attempt to use methodological individualism to try to understand and explain what is happening in agriculture outside the reach of the market mechanisms. They are concerned with the peasants' mode of choosing as rationally acting individuals, but at the same time judge their choices against what would be rational as seen from the interests of the village or society.

Popkin has contributed to an increased insight into the causes of the often large discrepancy between, on the one hand, what is rational for the individual peasant and, on the other hand, what would be the best choices for the village or for the peasants as a social group. For example, Popkin has shown that the individual peasant behaves quite rationally when he wishes to maintain a fragmentation of his land into a large number of small plots, even though this makes cultivation difficult. His major point is that the peasant thereby achieves a spreading of the risks due to, for example, the weather, plant diseases and other conditions. Yet, the fragmentation undoubtedly implies an overall loss in productivity and in the amount produced for the village as a whole. This example illustrates a central feature of Popkin's approach: always to seek to understand social outcomes on the basis of individual rationality and individual preferences. Furthermore, the analysis should be extended to the organisations and institutions through which the individual choices are aggregated into societal choices. Here, the market is only one among many important institutions. The peasants' way of organising themselves and the forms of management in the local communities are other important institutions.

Bates essentially adopts a similar approach but he has further extended the politico-economic analysis – which Bates himself calls a *rational choice approach* – to the decision makers at the national level. Both the peasants and these decision makers are assumed to act rationally. The pertinent research problem is to uncover the character of this rationality and understand its implications for the choices that are made.

In one of his now classic works, Bates takes as his starting point the established fact that a significant increase in agricultural production is a precondition for national growth and development in the overwhelming majority of African countries (Bates, 1981). Then he asks what the causes are for the stagnation, and even decline, that has been observed in many areas of the African continent. In considering the question, Bates asserts that to neither the physical nor the biological conditions can be attributed any decisive influence. The economic and social conditions under which the peasants produce are much more important. If these conditions embody sufficiently strong incentives for the peasants, nearly all obstacles can be overcome, according to Bates, but this can only happen within certain institutional frameworks.

The next step in his reasoning is a general claim that the free-market forces provide the peasants with the best and strongest incentives to increase production. In contrast, market mechanisms which are manipulated to favour the cities, work badly – as is evident in most African societies. On the basis of comprehensive investigations in a large number of countries, Bates concludes that states with varying forms of political interventions constantly seek to extract resources from agriculture and transfer them to other sectors (cf. Chapter 10). He claims that African governments in general have intervened in markets in ways that have harmed the interests of most farmers. On the one hand, by protecting domestic industries from competition, they have increased the prices that farmers must pay for goods from the urban sectors. On the other hand, through the use of political power they have lowered the prices that farmers have received for their products.

Against this background, Bates asks the following provoking question: what makes rational decision makers pursue an agricultural policy which is detrimental to both agriculture and national development? In answering the question, Bates invokes theoretical considerations regarding the role of agriculture in economic development and the modernisation process in general. More interesting, however, are his propositions regarding the purely political functions of agricultural policy. Here he reiterates some of the views mentioned in the discussion of forms of regime in Africa (Chapter 13). But the explanations offered by Bates, in important respects, penetrate deeper into the problematique. Let us illustrate this with one of his many thought-provoking points.

Bates states that positive pricing policies for the peasants would undoubtedly prompt them to increase production, especially if at the same time they were given the opportunity to buy goods from the urban sectors at the same or lower prices than before. But these policies are not attractive for the political elites. They would be met with strong opposition from the urban population, who benefit substantially from the low prices of agricultural goods. Consequently, a price increase in itself would be a risk in countries where urban interest groups are important for the survival of the political rulers. Further, a universal price increase for agricultural goods would not distinguish between supporters and dissidents, but only between agricultural producers and others. Thus, positive pricing policies would imply high political costs in terms of loss of support in the urban areas; and their political benefits would be low in terms of their ability to secure support from the countryside. For these reasons, African leaders have preferred different types of policies (Bates, 1981: Ch. 7).

The preferred package of measures implies agricultural policies, including price policies, which have disfavoured peasants in general. But, at the same time, some peasants have been offered, on a selective basis, various development and public works projects and services which, for those concerned, have compensated for the negative impact of agricultural price policies. In other words, the African leaders have exploited the political advantage of apportioning the benefits. They have used public resources to support selected groups of peasants, who in return have supported the political rulers.

In more general terms, African rulers – and also, we might add, many governments in Asia and other parts of the Third World – have preferred projects with a limited geographical coverage and specified target groups to universal policies. This is because such targeted interventions can be used as rewards for friends and supporters – or to buy goodwill from powerful opposition groups whose support the leaders are dependent upon.

The implied submission of economic development considerations under political power considerations has in recent years been emphasised by several development researchers. *Göran Hydén* deserves special attention in this connection, because he has tried to integrate this fundamental observation into a more comprehensive theory concerning the interaction between politics and economics and between state and society in the least industrialised countries.

Before turning to Hydén, it should be briefly mentioned that other scholars have criticised Bates for, *inter alia*, assuming the lust for power as an overriding attribute of political leaders rather than investigating more closely the motives of these leaders (Liddle, 1992). Others have noted that African governments, in particular, have been under strong external pressure, from the World Bank and other international agencies, to increase savings and transfer resources from agriculture to industrial development (Berry, 1993). This pressure may have been just as important in explaining the agricultural policies pursued as the conditions indicated by Bates.

However, neither these nor other critical objections have really disputed that Bates's approach has come to some interesting conclusions that are probably worth investigating further in relation to both African and other poor developing countries.

The state and the economy of affection: Hydén

Göran Hydén's most important work appeared as early as 1983 with the incisive title *No Shortcuts to Progress* (Hydén, 1983). The book contains an extensive study of development experiences from Africa, especially East Africa, and a number of interesting propositions regarding what the African societies need if they are to climb out of their economic crises and stagnation. Although written more than 10 years ago, the book continues to provide inspiration for much of the international debate on development.

A central starting point for Hydén, in both this book and later works (Hydén, 1986; Hydén and Bratton, 1992), is that most African countries still contain a significant pre-capitalist element in the form of a peasant mode of production. In this he agrees with many other social scientists who have studied Africa. Similar conceptions are moreover found in theories about Asian agriculture, particularly that of South Asia.

The peasant mode of production is characterised by primitive technology, small production units, virtually no product specialisation and very little exchange between the various units of production. The individual units mostly produce for themselves and not to any large extent for a market. Each household has a high degree of autonomy but very limited scope for producing a surplus. Production is often cleverly adjusted to local conditions, but they live in a kind of symbiosis with nature. They are not able to manipulate nature because of their rudimentary technology (cf. Chapter 8).

Under the peasant mode of production, there may certainly be close co-operation between households, but this co-operation is not a part of the production system itself but rather a reflection of social networks existing outside the production processes. Similarly, the state is not a necessary part of the system. It is therefore often looked upon by the individual peasant households as an unnecessary and sometimes parasitic foreign element.

Hydén does not confine himself, however, to observing this separation of the state from the peasants, but ventures into an analysis of the whole social structure which none the less binds the two elements together in African societies. It is in this connection that Hydén elaborates his most central concept: the *economy of affection.*

The term denotes a network of support, communication and interaction among structurally defined groups connected by blood, kin, community or other affinities, including religion. The economy of affection links together in a systematic fashion a variety of discrete economic and social units which in other respects are autonomous. Hydén asserts that such networks manifest themselves strongly in most of Africa – not just in the rural areas but also in the cities. The fact that many families are divided into two segments, one rural, the other urban, adds new dimensions to the economic decision making of each unit. A major point is that economic decisions in general are embedded in social and other non-economic conditions, essentially as proposed by Karl Polanyi earlier (Polanyi, 1957). Like economic decision making, the interrelations between the households and families are governed primarily by non-economic factors. The mutual obligations do not have any direct connection to the production processes. Rather, they are being regulated by tradition, social status and other socio-cultural factors.

The good thing about this economy of affection, according to Hydén, is that it forms a social safety net of tremendous importance. As such, it secures the survival of many people. Further, the network of obligations provides help to many sick and distressed, and to innumerable invisible refugees, who are resettled with relatives, friends or tribal relations after natural disasters, wars or personal bankruptcy. The economy of affection may even serve a developmental role in a local context by diverting surpluses generated by the formal economy to people who are unable to produce a surplus and who do not have access to formal lending.

The problem with the economy of affection is that it tends to hold back national development by delaying changes in behavioural and institutional patterns capable of sustaining aggregate economic growth. Another drawback is that it functions together with social inequality. This implies that the numerous poor, in order to obtain a minimum of social security, have to throw themselves into the arms of the rich clan leaders, especially the ones who have control over large public resources.

The economy of affection tends to perpetuate a narrow outlook, both geographically and socially. Problems and options are not considered in a wider context, but only in the context of the village or the small social groups to which the households belong through the network of obligations. As a result of this, Africans often use their resources in ways that are unfavourable to economic growth. As the economy of affection is more or less invisible from the point of view of the state, it is very difficult to implement development policies and at the same time avoid the trickling away of public resources. Precisely because most people feel a stronger obligation towards their family, relatives or clan than to the state, public resources are used mainly in accordance with social and political objectives – not economic ones. 'Nepotism' and 'tribalism' prevail in bureaucratic decision making as well as in recruitment practices.

Hydén emphasises that the scope for misappropriating public funds is considerable under the present political conditions. The African states are not at all geared to initiate and manage economic development. In this respect they resemble Myrdal's soft states in South Asia (see Chapter 16). In addition, the African states are not firmly rooted in the production system. They sit 'suspended in mid-air over society' (Hydén, 1983: p. 7).

The states are generally over-developed in terms of size, and with respect to the tasks they try to accomplish. But they are certainly not overdeveloped with respect to the capacity and ability to formulate and implement a coherent development policy. In these vital respects, they are extremely ineffective and lack the power to penetrate and manage socio-economic processes. In this connection, it does not help that the African states often have control over considerable physical means of coercion, because such means are quite unsuited to improving and controlling economic development – especially in the rural districts.

Against this background, Hydén finds it very unfortunate that the political leaders in Africa have so clearly preferred the state and the bureaucracy to the market as the most important mechanism for allocating resources, investments and incomes. The choice is understandable when it is remembered that the political leaders after independence had control over the state, while the market was controlled mainly by foreign capital and a few domestic entrepreneurs. But the choice was fatal, because it has led to an incredible waste of resources. Instead of productive and development-promoting investments, resources have to a large extent been channelled through the economy of affection and the patronage system. Public funds have been used for building political support and to pay off accumulated 'social and political debts' – rather than for promoting growth or bringing about economic transformation.

Under prevailing conditions, the state agencies function very differently from those in the highly industrialised countries. Certainly the formal bureaucratic institutions and procedures grafted on to the African states by the colonial powers were the same, but here they came to function in a societal context and a political culture with no particular respect for the bureaucratic norms. The state agencies are not seen as neutral tools for implementation of national policies, but rather – and rightly, says Hydén – as tools of the political rulers. Their mode of functioning is basically a reflection of the politicisation and the invasion of the state administration from above (cf. Chapter 13). To this should now be added the invasion from the side, through the economy of affection. This horizontal invasion occurs because the networks of mutual obligations also include the government officials.

Even though it is characteristic of many of the top and middle-level government officials that they have received training and gone through socialisation processes which have separated them radically from the surrounding society, most of them have retained a feeling of loyalty to specific groups (including relatives and others) who have contributed, directly or indirectly, to their careers. Thus, the gaining of a position in the state administration has put the officials in positions of social debt to others, both within and outside the state apparatus.

The friends outside expect a particularly favourable treatment from the officials they have earlier helped or with whom they share affinities. Conversely, others cannot expect a similarly favourable treatment, unless they provide something in return, possibly in the form of gratuities. Western researchers and aid workers have often called this corruption, but assessed in the African context it is little more than a new version of the exchange of favours and services in accordance with deep-rooted traditions.

It is also a part of the picture of the balloon-state and the economy of affection that there exists a large parallel, or black, market. Ineffective states which, for example, try to lower agricultural prices for the sake of the towns will, almost out of necessity, be confronted with a black market where prices are regulated by supply and demand. This is the situation in most African countries.

Hydén, in his analyses, concludes that the most important obstacle to a solution of Africa's economic crisis is the combination of the economy of affection and the maldeveloped, ineffective states. Therefore, a sustainable development strategy must attack exactly this combination.

Hydén's propositions, when they first appeared, added a breath of fresh air to an otherwise enclosed and stale debate. Neo-classical economists and institutions such as the World Bank and the International Monetary Fund (IMF) had at that time been claiming for many years that the best development strategy was to rely on free-market forces (cf. Chapter 18). However, their point was often stated in a less than convincing way. It was mainly derived from abstract theories and experiences from selected industrial countries, rather than emerging as a result of open-minded studies of African or other developing countries.

In contrast to the neo-classical position, a very broad section of development researchers had emphasised the necessity of comprehensive state regulation, as noted earlier in this chapter. And many had directly recommended a sort of pseudo-socialist development strategy with the main emphasis on the state sector. On the basis of other considerations, several African leaders (as noted) had come to similar conclusions. Evidently, both approaches, like the neo-classical ones, were strongly influenced by ideology as well as the narrow interests of the various groups of actors.

In this setting, Hydén's recommendations concerning development strategy stood out as interesting and thought-provoking, not so much because they introduced anything new, but because they were advanced within a different theoretical framework and with new arguments. Hydén's point was, briefly stated, that what the African countries need most is more capitalism. This applies to both production, where the peasant mode of production must be dismantled, and the market. According to Hydén, reliance on capitalism and free-market forces will, more effectively than any political measures, contribute to breaking down the unfortunate aspects of the economy of affection and the system of patronage. A well-functioning market economy, by providing positive incentives, could persuade the peasants to produce more and thus make a contribution to national development, while at the same time earning more money for themselves.

Another reason why more capitalism is the key to development in Africa is that it can bring into existence a national bourgeoisie strong enough to compete with international capital. On this point, the African governments have not been able to present any remarkable results.

Finally, it should be mentioned that the socialist alternative is to some extent worth considering, according to Hydén, but he views it as being totally unrealistic under the prevailing conditions in Africa. In addition, socialism assumes great economic rationality among the decision makers at all levels. Neither this rationality, nor the necessary development-promoting institutions can be introduced by decree, but must emerge and be consolidated along with radical changes in the whole production system and social structure.

Hydén's theories have been developed with particular reference to African societal conditions. Therefore they cannot, without modifications, be applied to other Third World countries. However, there is little doubt that the Swedish development researcher, with his concepts of the economy of affection and the balloon-state, has touched on basic structures and conditions that exist in one form or another in many of the least-industrialised countries with weakly organised parties, interest organisations and popular political movements. On the other hand, it should be noted that Hydén has strongly emphasised certain, selected characteristics of the society–state interrelationships, while disregarding others.

Therefore, the recommended strategy may have a limited applicability beyond addressing the specific problems discussed by Hydén. Moreover, the 'more capitalism' strategy should definitely be seen and evaluated in relation to a number of different objectives. More capitalism may increase aggregate growth but is not likely to improve the living conditions of the poor and resource-weak segments of the population, at least not in the short term. In recognition of this, Hydén's more detailed proposals do contain various ideas on how to empower representatives of the poor through decentralisation and strengthening of NGOs. He also suggests various measures to curb the negative social impact of free market forces.

Both Hydén's analyses and his strategy proposals have given impetus to an extensive debate. *Nelson Kasfir*, among others, has raised the fundamental question of whether Hydén has given a correct description of the peasant mode of production, and especially whether he is correct in assuming the African peasants' high degree of autonomy (Kasfir, 1986; Cliffe, 1987). Others have contested the validity of Hydén's predominantly negative evaluation of the significance of the social networks for economic progress and pointed out several instances where these networks have promoted growth, although mainly for selected groups.

New institutional economics

Representatives of the more rigorous versions of new institutional economics hardly consider themselves a part of the cluster of theories of the political economy with which the present chapter is concerned. They rather conceive of their theoretical contributions as extensions of the domain of economic theory, with adjustments of the basic assumptions regarding individual be-haviour. They see it as supplementing the neo-classical equilibrium analyses with more process- and change-oriented studies. Finally, they conceive of their focusing on other institutional arrangements than just the market as another expansion of the area covered by economic theory.

When new institutional economics are nevertheless reviewed in connection with the political economy approaches, it is because they share an interest in studying economic phenomena within a wider societal context. All the theories discussed in this chapter apply perspectives that reach beyond the economic production processes and beyond the market mechanisms. They bring in not just other economic institutions, but also social and political institutions. It is the specific methods of inquiry and the conceptual frameworks which primarily distinguish them.

New institutional economics in fact comprises several approaches, each with its own special emphasis. One school thus puts special emphasis on transaction costs and proposes that the institutions which evolve to minimise these costs are the key to understanding the performance of economies. This school can be traced back to *Ronald Coase* (Coase, 1937, 1960). His pioneering contribution was to show that general economic equilibrium theory had no explanation for the existence of firms. Yet, firms clearly exist and even constitute the dominant form of organisation in any capitalist economy. Coase related the failure to explain the existence of firms to the assumption of costless and timeless exchange contained in equilibrium theory. He tried to explain the existence of firms exactly by pointing out that every transaction involved costs – the costs of discovering what the relevant prices are, the costs of negotiating and concluding contracts, and the costs of monitoring and enforcing the contracts. The corporate organisation, the firm, would make possible a reduction of these transaction costs. This was, in a few sentences, Coase's major point.

His analyses of why firms have emerged as both economic actors and administrative organisations have since been elaborated by, among others, *Oliver Williamson* (for example Williamson, 1986). Transaction cost theory has been applied to other institutions by *Douglass C. North* (North, 1990), and applied to sharecropping systems and other socio-economic institutions in developing countries by *Pranab Bardhan* (Bardhan, 1984, 1989).

Another prominent school within new institutional economics concerns itself primarily with the effects of economic actors being incompletely informed. This has important consequences for the mode of operation of the market mechanisms. *Joseph Stiglitz* is one of the researchers who has undertaken comparisons of the markets in industrialised and developing countries (for example Stiglitz, 1989). These comparisons have led him to emphasise how important it is to study forms of exchange other than the market and, in association with this, the institutions and organisations that take part in these other forms of exchange. Stiglitz has highlighted that the political authorities have a great need to understand both the real functioning of the market and the parallel forms of exchange, before they decide to intervene with planning measures and control. In this connection, it is not a good idea, according to Stiglitz, if the state simply interferes where the market is not functioning properly. It should be investigated first what kind of processes are at work and how they can most appropriately be altered or manipulated in order to promote certain development goals. The following chapter will look more closely into this problematique concerning the market and the state.

The different schools of thought within new institutional economics are not discussed further in the present section. Rather, the aim is now to summarise some of the more fundamental characteristics of new institutional economics as a whole. An appropriate way of doing this is to compare these approaches with neo-classical economic theory, as *Harvey Liebenstein* has done (Liebenstein, 1989). In neo-classical economics institutions other than the market play no major role. Using investments as an illustration, Liebenstein has noted that neo-classical economics consider these as a function of specific economic variables such as income and interest rate. The consequences of investments are analysed as being determined primarily by the marginal capital/output ratio. Liebenstein then poses a number of questions not asked by neo-classical economics which may be important in order to understand the investment process as a whole. Some of these questions include the following: How are banks organised? Are they good at assessing who should and who should not get loans? In what firms will the investments be made? How are these firms organised? How does the nature of the organisation of a firm determine the consequences of the investments? These are some of the important questions that new institutional economics add to the perspective of neo-classical economics.

To emphasise the basic distinctions further, the following simplified presentation may be useful:

In neo-classical economics three assumptions apply:

- Households maximise utility.
- The market shapes economic behaviour.
- Firms maximise profits or a utility function comprising both profit and growth.

In new institutional economics, the following correcting conceptions are emphasised:

- The market is not the only institution which shapes economic behaviour. The market is merely one among several aspects of the total incentive structure in a society.
- The market – the invisible hand – has little or no influence on the economic behaviour inside the firms. Intra-firm behaviour is shaped by a completely different governance structure – the visible hierarchy and a vertically integrated system of transactions organised by the management. Not the market and its competitive price system, but the firm's own organisational set-up and procedures are the most important determinants.

With respect to intra-household behaviour, this is shaped by yet another governance structure – or several other types of incentive structures. The same applies to behaviour within the state apparatus.

It should be added here that the key term in new institutional economics, 'institution', is defined in several different ways by the many authors. Basically, the term refers to both formal and informal rules, procedures, and norms of behaviour. An institution is a set of constraints which governs the behavioural relations among individuals and groups (cf. Nabli and Nugent, 1989). In this sense both the market and formalised state agencies, as well as labour unions and other organisations, can be seen as institutions.

Continuing the comparison of new institutional economics with neo-classical economics, the perspective proposed by the former can be summarised in the three main components shown in Figure 17.1.

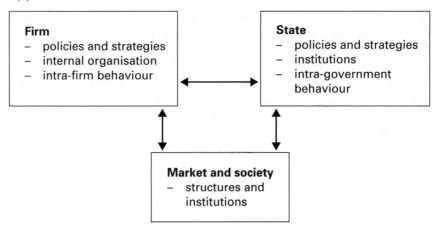

Figure 17.1 The incentive structure in new institutional economics

Applying a wider perspective, like the one indicated in Figure 17.1, to the structures and institutions which influence the economic behaviour of individuals and groups would, no doubt, provide a good framework for a multifaceted analysis of, say, the total incentive structure governing investments in a developing country (cf. Martinussen, 1993). Rather than just looking at the traditional economic variables and their effects on investment decisions, such an approach would stipulate additional analyses of the firms' internal organisation and corporate strategies as determining factors. It would draw attention to the impact of state regulatory systems and, moreover, introduce investigations of the formally applicable rules as well as the actually prevailing patterns of implementation and enforcement, including the norms that apply to evasion of rules in the country concerned.

Douglass North has used a similar perspective in a study of the most important institutional prerequisites for successful industrial development (North, 1990). He has in this connection emphasised the following conditions as essential: (a) security of property rights; (b) an effective and impartial judicial system; (c) a transparent regulatory framework; and (d) an institutional framework that promotes and permits complex impersonal exchange and interaction. The fourth category of prerequisites includes the establishment and enforcement of contracts; the establishment of limited liability corporations; and entry and exit regulations for private firms.

In his more detailed analyses North has added some further preconditions like a fiscal system in which expenditures are tied to tax revenue; a private capital market; patent laws and other instruments to promote the growth of innovative activity; etc. He has also emphasised that the incentive structure as a whole should reduce rent-seeking behaviour. All these preconditions were, according to North, present when industrialisation took place in Britain;

that was not the case, however, in Spain in the sixteenth and seventeenth centuries. The point here is that North's description of Spain during that period may be used as a valid characterisation of the majority of the countries in the Third World in the post-war period. In particular, it should be emphasised how personalistic relationships continued to play vital roles and how rent-seeking behaviour was promoted, rather than impeded, by the incentive structure as a whole.

In this way, North's theory of institutions, institutional change and economic performance may provide an interesting framework for trying to explain, with reference to non-economic factors, why so many Third World countries have not been successful in their attempts at industrialising. Public investment, foreign aid, planning, and other measures aimed at promoting industrial growth have not been sufficient, because prevailing institutional conditions have distorted their impact.

The macro-analytical perspective, which so far has been applied in the discussion of new institutional economics, actually characterises only a lesser part of the theory construction within this research tradition. Several important contributions concern, instead, very detailed studies of forms of contract, such as for example the sharecropping system, property rights systems and institutional arrangements for the enforcement of contracts; or they focus on other phenomena at the micro- or mezzo-levels (cf. *World Development*, 1989). However, it is beyond the scope of this introduction to go further into these theories. What can be done, as an illustration, is briefly to review how a new institutional economics approach can grasp the unique rationality behind the sharecropping system and thereby contribute to an explanation of its continued existence in, for example, India and Bangladesh (Bardhan, 1984).

The sharecropping system in its most extreme form implies not just a forced surrendering of harvest yield from the producers to the landowners, but also a surrender which is totally out of proportion with the land rent and the landowner's contribution to the arrangement as a whole (cf. Chapter 8). Or, to be more correct, this is how it appears. Neo-classical economists have therefore dubbed sharecropping as irrational and inefficient, and neo-Marxist researchers have characterised it as exploitative. New institutional economists, however, have proposed that sharecropping need not necessarily be inefficient. It may even have features favourable to the sharecropper, compared with a simple rental contract. Specifically, its risk-spreading character is attractive to the poor peasant who produces in a high-risk environment and who, exactly because of poverty, is highly risk-averse. The sharecropping arrangement may be the only option for the poor peasant who has no access to other forms of credit or insurance and no access to an open market.

One of the general propositions of new institutional economics, implicit in the above illustration, is that one should always study the origin of a particular institution and its actual mode of functioning, as seen from the perspective of the various parties involved. Only then may it be determined whether the concerned institution is useful and necessary, or superfluous.

The critics of the neo-institutional approaches have, to a large extent, based their criticism on precisely this search for the utility of the institutions, which is claimed to have obscured the importance of the power structure. Thus, with respect to the analysis of sharecropping the critics have asserted that this institution continues to exist mainly because the landowners have the power to maintain it.

Concluding this section, it should be noted that the new institutional economists have greatly contributed to starting a fruitful dialogue between mathematically oriented economists and game theorists, on the one hand, and structurally oriented development economists, on the other. Neo-institutional economists have extended the scope of economics and widened the range of topics which it is permissible and legitimate for economists to deal with. At the same time, they have added to development economics some of the methodological rigidity of traditional economics (Toye, 1993). The neo-institutional analyses have especially contributed to putting high on the agenda the exploration of 'opportunism', that is research regarding rationally self-interested behaviour in circumstances where transaction costs are high, where information is deficient, and where uncertainty prevails. These conditions probably have a stronger impact in most Third World countries than in highly industrialised societies, although even here they have a considerable impact upon economic performance.

CHAPTER 18

State or Market?

The question regarding the respective roles of the state and the market in the development process has been debated continuously since the end of the 1940s. Previous chapters have repeatedly dealt with the issue as part of the presentation and discussion of both the economic and the political theories and the strategies derived from them. This chapter will briefly recapitulate the main positions and then move on to review the intense discussion on the subject which began around 1980 and continues into the 1990s.

There are great variations in how different countries, during different periods of time, have arranged the interactions between state and market, as is evident from the earlier chapters. These variations – surprisingly – have not played any central role in the more recent debate, where the views have often been presented as being in favour of *either* an interventionist state and a mixed economy, *or* a non-interventionist state and a free-market economy. It has been largely a debate about a state-managed versus a market-led development strategy. This is reflected in the first sections of the present chapter where this debate is reviewed without going very much into the dissimilarities prevailing in the Third World. Subsequently, however, a more differentiating approach will be applied.

As a starting point it is deemed appropriate to describe briefly the state-managed development model, because this is the one which preoccupied most of the research within development studies from the 1950s until the end of the 1970s. This is also the model that had the greatest impact upon the development strategies pursued by a majority of Third World countries during the same period. We shall try to summarise the rationale behind this model, particularly in the way it has been formulated in development economics. Afterwards, we shall look at a number of the problems and weaknesses of this model, which have been emphasised continuously in the theoretical debates. A separate section follows examining the resurrection of neo-classical economics in development research and its far-reaching propositions regarding the effectuation of a market-led development model.

After having contrasted the two models in their pure forms, we shall introduce more nuanced approaches which look at the social embeddedness of markets and search for more complex interrelations between market and state. The chapter ends with a section on the political economy of the reform process with particular emphasis on the political feasibility of carrying through the changes in economic policy that neo-classical and other theories have proposed since the end of the 1980s. In this connection, it is necessary to consider the marked differences among the countries of the Third World.

It should be borne in mind that the distribution of roles and functions between state and market is only one aspect of a more comprehensive problematique where questions concerning political decentralisation, popular participation and people-managed development also come in. These themes are taken up in Part V of the book.

The rationale behind state-managed development

In a simplified representation, the state-managed development model can be characterised by two central elements. One is a state-building strategy that aims at anchoring the state in the surrounding society. It is a strategy that tries to extend the state institutions so that they reach down and out to the citizens (cf. Chapter 12). The other element is a state-managed development effort which involves the use of the state bureaucracy as an engine of growth and development, and as a central planning and allocation mechanism (cf. Chapter 16).

The rationale behind this model has been formulated in many different ways. Basically, the arguments in favour of extensive state interventions have centred around the fundamental economic structures of backward societies, their undeveloped markets and the absence of a sufficiently strong entrepreneurial class.

The principal argument has stated that under the existing conditions, Third World countries would not be capable of initiating a sustainable and self-reinforcing growth process unless the state intervened and co-ordinated the development efforts. At the same time, there was an implied assumption behind the whole argument that the state could and would act as a rational actor to the benefit of the society as a whole, that is in the interest of the common good. Pushed to extremes, it could be formulated as three simple propositions: the economists should advise; the politicians should decide; and the government officials should implement the correct economic policies.

Instead of repeating the more specific arguments embodied in the various theories in favour of state interventions, we shall briefly look at the main arguments in support of different types of state intervention.

At least five types of state interventions may be identified:

1. Procurement of general judicial and institutional preconditions for production and exchange of commodities and services, including a legal framework for enforcing property rights, contracts, etc.
2. Macro-economic policies such as fiscal, income, and exchange rate policies.
3. Procurement of material infrastructure, including roads and railways, and provision of public services in areas like education and health.

4. Operational controls over private-sector companies.
5. The state's direct participation in the production of goods and services.

In the theoretical debates, there has been disagreement on the state's role in all these five areas, though it is the market-replacing types of interventions – (3), (4) and (5) – that have given rise to most of the serious controversies. Disagreement concerning the first two types of interventions has been limited to nuances in the perception of how much the state should intervene.

The principal reason why the state should participate actively in the procurement of material and social infrastructure has focused on the notion that these necessary preconditions for economic growth and social progress would not be produced by the private sector. Similarly, the direct participation of the state in certain production sectors has been based on the argument that private capital would not be forthcoming in a number of strategic areas. The more specific reasons could vary. One could be that the rate of profit which could be realised would be considerably below the prevailing average. A second reason could be that the amount of capital required would be too large for any single private enterprise, or at least for any domestic firm. A third reason could be that the gestation period would be too long compared with alternative investments. Finally, the risks involved could be prohibitive for private entrepreneurs.

As regards the operational controls over private-sector companies, these interventions have been justified by, *inter alia*, the need to create a better balance between economic sectors; dispersal of growth and income opportunities geographically and in social terms; or the wish to counteract foreign control or economic power concentration.

However, it is not these reasons that are in focus in this chapter, and so they are not discussed further here. Instead, attention shall be drawn to the criticism of the state-managed model. This criticism has been pursued partly with reference to empirical evidence, partly with reference to general economic, especially neo-classical theory. Both types of criticism will be briefly reviewed.

Neo-classical criticism of the state: Bhagwati, Little and Bauer

The World Bank has played a central role in the experience-based criticism by continuously emphasising the negative economic effects of extensive state interventions (for example in the annual *World Development Reports*). However, there is also a copious amount of empirical literature from other sources concerning the pros and cons of state interventions in a large number of individual countries (for example Little, Scitovsky and Scott, 1970).

Regarding the involvement of the state in the procurement of material infrastructure, the establishment and running of communication systems and with respect to provision of public services like electricity and water supply, the World Bank and others have emphasised that the parastatals and public enterprises generally have a poor performance record. They have functioned ineffectively and inefficiently. Most of the states in the developing countries have not had either the necessary financial resources or sufficient administrative and technical capacity to handle the tasks. This has created problems for the private sector which, in turn, has had to establish parallel structures and supplies itself. For example, many companies have had to install backup diesel generators because of frequent power cuts.

Operational controls over private-sector enterprises have been criticised as being expensive solutions to short-term problems. Government controls which have interfered directly with the economic functioning of private enterprises, including their investment priorities, have often proved costly, ineffective, and even counter-productive in the sense that they have brought about the opposite effect to that intended. The most common long-term impact, perhaps, has been undesirable side effects, where a control has had the desired effect, but only accompanied by unwanted consequences of a different kind. Protection of indigenous industries, for instance, may make good sense in the short term, while in the long term the outcome has in many cases been unwanted side effects in the form of uncompetitive industries manufacturing at costs far above world market prices.

Finally, with regard to the state's direct participation in the productive sector, the criticism has particularly emphasised low capacity utilisation and overemployment in public industrial undertakings. As a result, cost-effectiveness has been low, often to the extent that the public sector undertakings have made losses even in areas where private companies have been able to earn substantial profits. For governments with an increasing deficit on their public accounts, this has been deemed unacceptable.

From the point of view of neo-classical economic theory, general observations such as the above have been interpreted as empirical confirmation of how unfavourable the effects are when the state interferes with the private sector and the play of free-market forces.

This point of view is in no way new. It can be traced all the way back to the first formulations of the neo-classical paradigm and to the later criticism of Keynes's conceptions of the appropriateness of relatively extensive state interventions (cf. Chapter 2). However, the view was advanced with still greater force towards the end of the 1970s, and around 1980, it became generally accepted among the decision makers in the OECD countries and in the World Bank and the International Monetary Fund. This political breakthrough was facilitated by the changes of government in the USA, the UK, and West Germany (Reagan, Thatcher and Kohl) at almost the same time. In all three countries, the road was thus paved for a change of the leading financial advisers in favour of monetarists and micro-economists with roots in the neo-classical paradigm. So widespread was this change that one could describe it as a 'change of guard' with respect to the management of the capitalist world economy (Svendsen, 1990). John Toye has described it as 'a counter-revolution in development theory and policy' (Toye, 1987).

The representatives of this counter-revolution were, among others, *Deepak Lal* (1983), *Bela Balassa* (1982), *J. N. Bhagwati* (1982) and *Ian Little* (1982) as well as to some extent *P. T. Bauer* (1984).

The principal thesis advanced by these neo-classical economists was that free competition and market mechanisms, in all countries and under all circumstances, would bring about a more optimal allocation of production factors and a more optimal distribution of commodities, than a regulated economy with administrative control and central planning. They recognised that there were market failures and that these were more extensive in most of the developing countries than in the OECD countries. But they rejected the idea that special theories or strategies were required for the developing countries (cf. Chapter 4). In addition, they claimed that the market failures were insignificant in comparison to the consequences of government failures, which they saw as being the most serious problem facing economic progress in the backward countries.

The Indian economist, Deepak Lal, based on empirical studies made in the 1960s and 1970s, directed his criticism against essentially all forms of state intervention in industrial activities and trade (Lal, 1983). He asserted that these interventions, instead of promoting, had limited and distorted economic development. Lal did not deny that, under certain circumstances, positive results could be achieved if dogmatic state control was replaced by a rational form of state control. However, he was sure that such rational forms of control would, at the same time, imply a considerable reduction of the economic interventions of the states.

In another context, Lal argued that if the government for some reason – as in the case of India – insisted on trying to influence development through economic planning, then this planning should, in order to achieve the intended impact, be based on realistic prices and not just on purely political priorities (Lal, 1980).

Another Indian economist, Jagdish Bhagwati, stated essentially the same views (Bhagwati and Desai, 1970), but in addition developed a special term taken over from new political economy about '*direct unproductive profit-seeking behaviour*', so-called DUP-behaviour (Bhagwati, 1982). The reasoning behind this concept was that economic actors, under all circumstances, would aim at profit maximisation. This would be socially desirable, provided it happened under free market conditions where the sum of the many individual actions added up to an optimal utilisation of society's resources. Essentially, this was a restatement of the traditional 'invisible hand' hypothesis: that the self-seeking actions of a multitude of individuals would be amalgamated into the common good. Conversely, it was not socially desirable when this profit-maximising behaviour was aimed at exploiting the scarcity that was created by market-distorting state interventions.

When a government, for instance, introduced restrictions on industrial activity or imports, and demanded that producers and importers should obtain special licences or permits from the authorities before they could do anything, then many resources would be misdirected into totally unproductive efforts to acquire such licences and permits. The competition in order to acquire gains of this sort from the government, Bhagwati termed DUP-behaviour. The producers and importers would further, as part of their rent-seeking behaviour, try to acquire extra licences and permits, because these could be traded or used to prevent competitors from entering particular areas of industry or trade. Bhagwati concluded that, irrespective of the possible genuine intentions on the part of political authorities, this type of state interference with the economic functioning of private enterprises would create strong incentives for rent-seeking behaviour and – even when there were market failures – make everything worse by shifting resources from productive and output-producing activities to unproductive activities.

The British economist, Ian Little, put great emphasis in his analyses on demonstrating how a micro-economic approach, which relied on profit and growth maximisation at firm level, would produce better results than state interventions, because the latter by necessity were based on highly insufficient information. Little and several other neo-classical economists further emphasised that, because of the self-seeking behaviour of state employees, there was often a significant discrepancy between the official policies and their actual implementation.

By emphasising corruption, nepotism, and other forms of self-seeking behaviour, and stressing how the 'common-good state' was, in reality, controlled by external and internal special interests, the neo-classical economists adopted conceptions similar to those contained in the new political economy approaches (cf. Chapter 17). But they differed from these by asserting that governments in general had very little positive impact and often lacked the capacity effectively to implement even their own policies.

Summing up the various neo-classical contributions, at least four major causes of government failures may be identified:

1. self-seeking and calculating politicians and other actors, who form co-alitions to control the allocation of resources in accordance with their own narrow interests;
2. corrupt behaviour among politicians and government officials;
3. lack of, or absence of, competent administrators with the necessary understanding of economics and business operations; and
4. general lack of knowledge about the private sector and its way of functioning.

The neo-classical economists often applied, in their extensive analyses, an ideal-type construction of a perfect market with unrestricted competition and evaluated the developing countries in relation to this by indicating the respects in which, and the extent to which, these countries differed from the ideal-type model. This method resulted in quite interesting and thought-provoking empirical studies which commanded, and rightly so, respect among many development researchers throughout the 1980s.

On the other hand, the neo-classical economists' strategic recommendations caused immediate and intense criticism from both economists and other development researchers. As has already been implied, they proposed that the economic role of the state should be minimised: the state should be 'rolled back'. Instead, it should be left to the price mechanisms in competitive markets to decide what should be produced and in what quantities. The overriding consideration was to get the prices right, because the market would then take care of the dynamics, the growth and the structural trans-formation of the backward economies. In comparison with the Keynesian-inspired development economics of the previous decades, the neo-classical economists shifted the whole focus from 'getting the policies right' to 'getting the prices right'.

More specifically, the neo-classical strategy in the 1980s involved a com-bination of the following elements:

1. All distorting interventions in the pricing mechanisms should be abolished in order to achieve maximisation of growth and development.
2. Foreign trade should be liberalised to remove the incentives for inward-looking economic behaviour and to replace them with incentives for outward-looking and export-oriented economic activity.
3. The public sector should be reduced in size through privatisation of public undertakings and the relinquishment of as many economic tasks as possible to private companies.

During the 1980s, the neo-classical economists had considerable influence on the international development debate, and their recommendations were generally accepted by the International Monetary Fund and the World Bank, in addition to many bilateral donor organisations. The World Bank also incorporated many of the recommendations into the conditions for several structural adjustment loans to countries in the Third World. In this manner, the Bank took an active part in pressuring several governments into pursuing neo-classical policies.

Towards the end of the decade, the neo-classical counter-revolution, however, was gradually forced on to the retreat, both in the theoretical debates and in the management of international development co-operation. The counter-revolution came increasingly to be perceived as a reaction that had gone too far in its criticism of the previously so dominant state-managed development model (Killick, 1989). Instead, a more balanced approach emerged between the state-managed and the market-led model – a com-promise which came to set the agenda for the international debate and development efforts of the 1990s.

It is interesting to note in passing, how the World Bank commenced the 1980s with an almost uncritical promotion of the neo-classical propositions regarding rolling back the boundaries of the state, but ended the decade with an emphasis on the need for capacity building within state structures. This was followed, in the *World Development Report* of 1991, by a nuanced discussion about the best and most feasible distribution of labour between state and market.

Market and state: a question of division of labour

The recent debates on market and state have not been confined to two-sided confrontations between neo-classical economists and others. Many more conceptions and propositions have been advanced. Before going on with the direct criticism of the neo-classicists and the attempts to outline a framework for a more open approach, it may therefore be appropriate to look briefly at a few contributions outside the main streams of thought.

The Belgian economic historian *Jean-Philippe Platteau* has questioned the notion that the market can be grafted with guaranteed success on to any society at any time (Platteau, 1993). He has argued instead that the foundations of the market are shaky and that the market mechanism can only function smoothly when embedded into an appropriate social structure. Emphasis is put on two crucial preconditions: the pervasive incidence of abstract, impersonal relationships; and the existence of generalised morality, particularly in the form of honesty.

Generally speaking, none of these preconditions is present in the industrially most backward societies in Africa and Asia, where exchange of commodities and services takes place in several segmented markets and other systems without any price mechanism. Furthermore, these societies are characterised by economic behaviour that varies greatly depending on whether the exchange is made with others from the in-group, with whom affinities are shared, or with outsiders, that is all others. The members of one's own group cannot be cheated. However, cheating is both permitted and encouraged when it comes to others, including foreign businesspeople or tourists, who on this basis are charged higher prices than the members of the in-group. Under circumstances like these, markets function very differently from what is anticipated in economic theory; and relying exclusively upon the market mechanism may therefore produce unanticipated results.

Another economist, *Jerome Davis*, with inspiration from new institutional economics, has studied other preconditions for the effective functioning of markets, particularly in the form of commodity exchanges (Davis, 1993). Among the preconditions noted by Davis may be mentioned access to finance, transferability and standardisation of contracts, and the existence of risk-spreading organisations. But several other institutional prerequisites must be in place for a market to function. In addition, Davis has drawn attention to the fact that markets can be costly to establish and run, mainly because market clearing involves considerable transaction and information costs.

Neo-structuralist economists have extended the criticism of the market as a universal remedy to economic problems to the broader field which characterised the earlier debates between neo-classicists and structuralists (cf. Chapter 6). The neo-structuralists to some degree recognise the perfect market with free competition as a standard against which one should evaluate specific economic structures, but they add to this a number of other standards, particularly regarding the social distribution of incomes and growth. Moreover, they are concerned with who decides about the development priorities in the private sector and who exercises the strongest influence on state policies (Salazar-Xirinach, 1993). The neo-structuralists have, in comparison with Prebisch and the other earlier Latin American structuralists, recognised the necessity of rolling back the state in certain areas, but their development strategy still promotes a far more actively intervening state than the one the neo-classicists imagine as the optimal.

Neither these nor other recent theories on market and state will be examined further in this connection. Instead, we shall look a little closer at how the direct criticism of the neo-classical economists has resulted in a more balanced approach with an outline of options available to the decision makers in developing countries (Toye, 1987; Killick, 1989; Streeten, 1993). This could provide also a framework for an understanding of the continued debate on state–market relations in the 1990s.

Current thinking about the state has exposed the neo-classical dichotomy – state *or* market, public *or* private – as false in two respects. First, there is no clear borderline. Between the 'pure' cases of public and private enterprises there are in most countries several types of overlapping ventures like jointly-owned companies; public companies with hired-in private sector management; private firms operating publicly licensed franchises; co-operatives; etc. Second, markets require a legal and regulatory framework which only governments can provide. Legal entitlements and liabilities are just as important as the market system of commodity exchange. To this could be added that neither the state nor the market in the developing countries functions in agreement with the assumptions and the hypotheses of the theories (Stiglitz, in: Meier, 1989: pp. 101ff.).

Against this background, the central issue becomes more complex than just choosing between state or market. Positively formulated, the overriding concern is to determine the most appropriate division of labour between the two with a further view to avoiding or compensating for both state and market failures.

When considering the desirable role of the state, there are essentially two different issues involved, according to the British economist *Tony Killick* (Killick, 1989):

1. How large should the state be in relation to total economic activity?
2. What types of policy instruments should the state employ?

There is hardly any doubt that the vast majority of developing countries could improve their economic performance by introducing so-called market-oriented or market-friendly reforms. But this need not result in a reduction of the size of the state. In general, market-oriented reforms are likely in practice to alter, rather than reduce the demands on public policy and public institutions.

The point is that the absolute size of the public sector and the quantity of state interventions are less important than the way in which the state acts and the kinds of relationship it establishes with the private sector. Based on this understanding, it becomes important to examine government interventions with a view to determining which should be continued unchanged, commercialised, privatised, delegated to local authorities, or stopped altogether.

In the assessment of state interventions from this point of view, a distinction can be made between purely economic considerations, on the one hand, and considerations regarding the politically possible, on the other. The question is, in other words, what is economically feasible and what is politically feasible. The question is further, what is economically and politically feasible *at a given time*. Recent analyses have strongly pointed to the need for continuous adaptation to changing circumstances, particularly to extract maximum benefits from the world market.

From the point of view of economic feasibility, the key task is to establish a working relationship between the state and the private sector. Following contemporary conventional thinking on this issue, as proposed also by World Bank economists, states should do less in those areas where markets work properly; they should do more where markets cannot be relied upon. To the extent that policy interventions are necessary, they should work with or through the market forces rather than against them.

From the point of view of political feasibility, the task is to find out whether sufficient support can be mobilised for the proposed policy reforms.

Market-friendly reforms

In this section we shall ignore what is politically feasible and consider the distribution of labour between the state and the private sector only from an economic point of view. This allows us to identify some of the options that, in principle, are available to the decision makers in the developing countries. We shall look at such options in relation to provision of public services and in relation to deregulation and promotion of private sector development. These are some of the most debated subjects in the development policy debates in the 1990s.

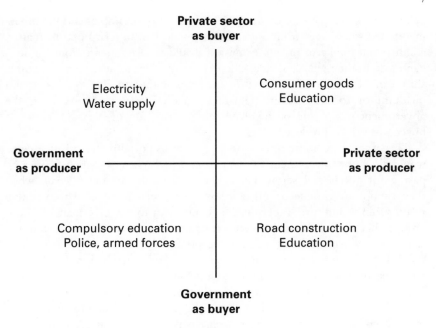

Figure 18.1 Government and private sector as buyer and producer of public services

With respect to provision of public services, it is characteristic that contemporary studies have adopted central elements proposed by the neo-classical economists, but modified these so as to fit into the new framework. A major point is that the administrative capabilities and capacities of governments in developing countries are severely strained by the weight of their numerous activities. When this observation is combined with the general experience concerning state provision of many public services, it appears warranted to ask whether improvements benefiting economic development can be attained by moving to the private sector the responsibility for some of the public services. This would entail a revised division of responsibilities and labour between the two sectors.

In order to place this crucial question in its proper perspective, it may prove useful to consider how the government as well as the private sector can act as a *buyer* or *producer* of public services, or as both. This can be illustrated by the matrix shown in Figure 18.1 (based on Roth, 1987).

The two top quadrants represent the private sector as buyer, and the bottom quadrants represent the public sector as buyer. The quadrants to the right represent the private sector as producer, and those to the left the government as producer. Examples of goods and services falling into the various quadrants are given in the figure. Thus, electricity may be produced by government and bought by the private sector. Roads may be constructed by the private sector but paid for by the government. These examples and the others mentioned would vary from one country to another. In terms of this matrix, a shift from public to private provision would involve a shift from the left-hand side to the right-hand side. The important point to note here is that this shift can be attained in two different ways, either to the top right-hand quadrant or to the bottom right-hand quadrant. In the latter case, the government would still be involved in the provision of services, but as a buyer instead of producer.

This way of establishing a working relationship with the private sector would allow the government to compensate for any major market failures by paying for goods and services of great importance to society, even when they cannot be produced and sold on a commercial basis. This working relationship would further permit the government to buy on behalf of social groups that do not have the necessary purchasing power, and thus at the same time provide a safety net for the poor.

This more complex approach to the issue of privatisation is what the more recent theoretical contributions propose. They further note that privatisation cannot be justified as an end in itself, but must be seen as a means to achieve other objectives, including a more cost-efficient procurement of infrastructure or services to the citizens. It is apparent that the outcome of a privatisation drive depends on whether the resources and skills are available to run the enterprises concerned. Public inefficiency should not simply be replaced with private inefficiency. The outcome also depends on whether the required legal framework and other extra-firm conditions, including a competitive environment, are in place (Streeten, 1994: pp. 37ff.).

Regarding deregulation and promotion of the development of the private sector, it should first be noted that governments can choose between two extreme types of policy and from among a whole range of combinations of the two. The two extremes are: (a) policies operated primarily through market forces; and (b) policies of control and command operated under government administration whereby goods and services are produced in accordance with politically determined priorities and procedures, thus replacing to some extent the market mechanisms. In some of the analyses undertaken by the neoclassical economists, a clear distinction between these two types of policy was not drawn. It is a distinction, however, which since the beginning of the 1990s has been almost universally incorporated into the literature. This applies to the theoretical analyses as well as to the strategic recommendations.

In the literature on the causes of South Korea's, Taiwan's and other Far Eastern countries' successful economic development, it is thus also no longer claimed that the key to their success is simply the absence of state regulations and interventions. Rather, it is proposed that the secret is the specific nature of these regulations and interventions. The next section takes a closer look at the Far Eastern experiences and how they have influenced theory building.

The East Asian miracles

Since 1960, eight high-performing East and South-East Asian economies have grown more than twice as fast as the rest of the countries in the region, roughly three times as fast as Latin America and South Asia, and five times faster than Sub-Saharan Africa (World Bank, 1993b). These Far Eastern experiences and the interpretations of them have played such an important role for general theory construction concerning the role of the state that there is reason to look a little closer at the different views. At least three can be identified: the pure neo-classical view; the revisionist view; and the so-called functional approach.

Adherents of the *neo-classical view* stress the high-performing Asian countries' success in getting 'the basics right'. They assert that the states have refrained from interfering with price formation, foreign trade and the economic functioning of private enterprises. At the same time, they note that the governments in these countries have been active when it comes to providing a stable macro-economic environment and a reliable legal framework, and political incentives for export-oriented industrial development. In addition, the governments have actively invested in education and health (see Chen, 1979; Wolf, 1988).

This interpretation has been strongly criticised by *'revisionists'* like *Alice Amsden* and *Robert Wade*. They argue that the states in South Korea and Taiwan, in particular, have intervened to a such extent that they have 'governed the markets' in critical ways and consciously manipulated prices to promote selective sector development. The 'revisionists' contend that the East Asian governments have consistently and deliberately remedied market failures and altered the incentive structure to boost industries that would not otherwise have thrived (Amsden, 1989; Wade, 1990).

Particularly, the capital markets have not conformed to the neo-classical model. They have been controlled by the governments by means of both interest rate policies and direct control measures. In the case of South Korea, the government has issued direct instructions to the banks and guided investments by selective credit policies. The prioritised sectors and industries have been offered so-called 'policy-loans' carrying interest rates far below the normal market rate. They have also received both administrative and technical support from the state. Furthermore, the authorities in South Korea have systematically intervened in the market competition between the companies and forced upon them a co-ordination of their utilisation of scarce resources. So-called 'contests' have been organised by the government in order to avoid 'unnecessary' competition among national companies. And finally, over a long period, there have existed tight import controls and several restrictions on foreign investors.

The overall picture emerging from the case of South Korea – and also from the case of Taiwan with only a slightly different composition of the policy instruments – is one of a high degree of state interventionism. But – and this is an important but – the interventionism noted in the two East Asian and other high-performing economies has been different from state interventionism in South Asia and Africa. In the former cases, the emphasis has been on providing a policy framework for competition, growth and export, while in the latter cases it has been on restrictions and control. Also, when the Far Eastern authorities have forced the companies into some form of co-ordination, it has happened through economic 'contests' among firms with a view to combining the benefits from co-operation and competition.

The third view, the *functional approach* to explaining the high growth rates in some Asian economies, has been formulated by a group of researchers and employees of the World Bank (World Bank, 1993b). Based on an extensive investigation of the Far Eastern high-growth countries they have reached conclusions which combine some of the views expressed by the revisionists with some of those promulgated earlier by the neo-classical economists.

Like the revisionists they recognise that contests with the state as 'referee' in important respects have worked just as well, or even better, than free-market competition, but they emphasise that the preconditions for this are hardly ever found in other developing countries. This applies, in particular, to the competence and independence of the civil service. In addition, they note that the Far Eastern governments' mode of intervening has, as a whole, been primarily market friendly. Only in exceptional cases have the governments tried to bypass or substitute the market mechanisms.

The whole approach is far less dogmatic than that which characterised World Bank studies in the 1980s. The functional theory outlined in the summary report, *The East Asian Miracle*, is of such quality that it deserves to be considered carefully in the 1990s' discussions on the state–market relationships. It is therefore briefly reviewed in the following paragraphs.

Figure 18.2 portrays in a simplified form the functional approach to understanding growth in the high-performing Asian economies. The figure shows the interaction among: (a) two sets of policy choices; (b) two methods of competitive discipline; (c) three central functions of economic management; and (d) the outcomes in terms of growth and income distribution. The solid lines with arrows indicate how policy choices contributed to outcomes via attainment of the three growth functions. Many policies contributed simultaneously to two or even three functions. High investments in human capital, for instance, contributed both to accumulation and to productivity-based increase of competitiveness. Openness to foreign technology was another major vehicle for productivity-based catching up.

The double-arrows indicate numerous self-reinforcing feedbacks. For example, rapid growth and relatively equal income distributions contributed to accumulation by increasing savings rates and generating larger and more effective investments in human capital.

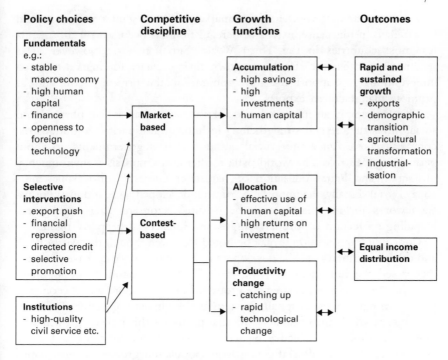

Policy choices	Competitive discipline	Growth functions	Outcomes

Fundamentals
e.g.:
- stable macroeconomy
- high human capital
- finance
- openness to foreign technology

Market-based

Accumulation
- high savings
- high investments
- human capital

Rapid and sustained growth
- exports
- demographic transition
- agricultural transformation
- industrialisation

Selective interventions
- export push
- financial repression
- directed credit
- selective promotion

Contest-based

Allocation
- effective use of human capital
- high returns on investment

Equal income distribution

Institutions
- high-quality civil service etc.

Productivity change
- catching up
- rapid technological change

Figure 18.2 A functional approach to growth
Source: World Bank, 1993b: p. 88 (simplified)

The policies listed as fundamentals affected the attainment of growth functions primarily through market-based mechanisms of competitive discipline. The selective interventions went beyond that by altering the market incentives by providing, for instance, special incentives for manufactured exports or performance-based subsidised credit.

Some of the selective interventions in reality guided and in some cases even bypassed markets, but, according to the functional theory, these interventions made sense within a neo-classical framework because they addressed particular market failures and were limited so as not to interfere too much with the competitive environment and the functioning of private enterprises. The World Bank report describes the mix of policies pursued as well-adapted to changing circumstances and priorities, in contrast to the policies pursued by most other developing countries which have been characterised either as lacking purposeful direction or as rigid continuations of demonstrably unsuccessful measures.

The refinement and sophistication of the analyses contained in this functional approach has, along with other recent theoretical contributions, penetrated into some of the strategic recommendations of the World Bank and other international organisations in the 1990s. The prevailing point of view is now that control-oriented and market-substituting interventions should be avoided. In this sense, extensive deregulation has been put on the agenda for most countries in the Third World. Simultaneously, however, it is recommended that the states strengthen their capacity for market-oriented interventions to support the development of the private sector and to promote manufactured exports.

This may imply an increased role for the state in areas like physical and social infrastructure and strengthening technological capacities and industrial competitiveness. Again the crucial question is how governments go about performing their role. The World Bank furthermore emphasises environmental protection and better utilisation of natural resources (World Bank, 1991, 1992, 1993a). Finally, the importance of well-developed legal and institutional frameworks for the market and the private sector are often highlighted, including protection of property rights and intellectual property rights.

Concluding this section it may be noted that even though the World Bank and other contributors to the development debate of the 1990s have generally recognised the importance of the state for socio-economic development, most of the views promulgated are grounded in assumptions about economic growth within a private capitalist system as the ultimate objective. The roles of the state are defined primarily by what promotes this type of growth, and only as a subsidiary objective by what is required to compensate for the associated marginalisation affecting large population groups in most Third World societies.

Adherents of the concept of human development as the superior goal have attacked exactly this implicit prioritisation. One of them, *Paul Streeten*, has proposed as an alternative a normative theory focusing on the ideal role of the state and the measures required for making the market more people friendly, that is more geared to benefit the population as a whole, rather than just the producers and the consumers with buying power (Streeten, 1993, 1994). Some of his views will be discussed in Part V of this book.

The political feasibility of economic reforms

The issue of political feasibility has already been introduced above. It is now appropriate to deal more explicitly with this aspect, which has been attracting considerably more attention among mainstream development economists and decision makers within international development agencies since the late 1980s.

As noted earlier in this chapter, the basic conceptions which influenced mainstream economics for many years viewed the state as a rational actor, guided by the common interests of all its citizens. The state could act irrationally when the amalgamated preferences of the citizens were not known but, in principle, the problem then was merely to work out the 'best' policies and the 'best' role for the state.

This is not the conception embodied in the current rethinking of the state among development economists and staff of international agencies like the World Bank and the UNDP. It is interesting to note that both these major agencies have recently addressed the whole issue of political feasibility and the nature of the state in explicit terms (World Bank, 1991: Ch. 6; UNDP, 1991). According to their (new) conception, which is more in keeping with political science concepts, the state is both an actor and an institutional framework for resolving conflicts of interest. As an actor, the state acts in accordance with the most powerful groups, possibly reflecting a compromise between their vital interests and those of other groups of society (cf. Chapter 16). It follows from this basic conception that the crucial question is not merely to work out the 'best' policies but rather to work out the 'best possible' policies within the framework of the existing power structure. The 'best' policies in the traditional, purely economic sense may be opposed to powerful interests and therefore not adopted or, if adopted because of external pressure, prevented from bringing about the intended effects.

This has been part of conventional wisdom for many years among political scientists in general – as well as among Marxist-inspired researchers. However, the interesting point here is that this line of reasoning is currently being integrated into the discussion of the feasibility of economic reform. Of particular relevance to the discussion of a framework for promoting private enterprise is an observation made by the World Bank according to which those who stand to lose from privatisation and deregulation are generally better organised and politically more powerful than those who stand to gain (World Bank, 1991: p. 104). Those who stand to lose are vested interests within government or, more specifically, politicians who augment their political support by means of distributing public resources and privileges; officials earning a decent living from applying discretionary controls; and managers and workers with secured employment in over-staffed public enterprises.

We have already, in an earlier chapter, discussed some of the reasons why so many African and Asian rulers chose the state-managed development model (Chapter 17), and there is no need to repeat the arguments here. The major point in the present context is to emphasise that historically as well as under contemporary conditions there are good – political – reasons for choosing and continuing the policies of government control and command, as seen from the perspective of the ruling groups in many developing countries. Consequently, the more market-oriented options discussed in the previous section may not be politically feasible.

They may be even less feasible in societies where such reforms carry with them a variety of communal implications. Ethnic communities that have wielded political power over the government apparatus, thus ensuring economic security for their own members, would not have an interest in promoting private enterprise if that resulted in a redistribution of economic benefits in favour of opposing ethnic groups (like the Chinese in Indonesia,

Malaysia and other countries, or the Indians in Fiji and Guyana). Aspects like these have so far not been taken into account in the market-friendly approach currently prescribed by the World Bank and other international agencies, but there is little doubt that in practice they play important roles in several countries (cf. Bowie, 1991).

Noting that the most desirable market-oriented reforms, as seen from an economic perspective, in many cases cannot be implemented because of the prevailing political power structure has important implications for the theoretical approach to the issue. In this lies a clear incentive always to combine the economic analysis with an investigation of the political setting – an incentive to work with the political economy of economic reforms. The World Bank and UNDP have taken the first few steps in this direction. Some of the prominent development economists, for example *Anne O. Kreuger*, have gone considerably further and have, through studies of coalition formation for and against economic reforms, contributed to a concrete explanation of the development-impeding policies which have been pursued in a number of developing countries (Kreuger, 1993; cf. also Haggard and Kaufman, 1992).

CHAPTER 19

Development and Security

The preceding chapters make it clear that the theories within development studies are rich in conceptions and analyses regarding the role of the state in relation to the economic processes, both internally in the individual developing countries and externally in relation to foreign trade and other international transactions. Earlier, in Part III of the book, we saw a similar wealth and multiplicity regarding theories on the state and the political processes. This is not the case with the subject area of the present chapter. On the contrary, the whole theme must be introduced by stating that development research has generally ignored security aspects in the attempts to analyse and explain the behaviour of states and the outcomes of development processes. There are a few development researchers who have tried to integrate these aspects in a more systematic manner (for example Hettne, 1986), but otherwise it has been left to another research tradition within peace and conflict research to establish the causal and other interlinkages between security issues and development issues.

We shall not try to review the theory formation within peace and conflict research of particular relevance for establishing these interlinkages but confine ourselves to scattered observations on how, from the perspective of development studies, one could put security issues and matters of security policy on the research agenda.

First, the relevance of also considering the security problems in connection with studies of development processes will be considered, especially in relation to the 'choice' of development strategy. This involves looking at the security role of the state in conjunction with its development-promoting functions. Next, we shall look at the interaction between development and security by focusing on how development and transformation processes may function as, respectively, conflict-generating and peace-promoting processes. This is followed by a brief discussion of how security policies may affect societal development. Specific attention will be given in this context to questions concerning how armament and disarmament are likely to affect economic growth and development in a wider sense. The chapter is concluded with reflections on the implications of the ending of the Cold War for the countries of the Third World.

The three-dimensional state

Seen in a broader perspective, most of the conceptions of the state in development research can be characterised as two-dimensional. The state is studied from the point of view of its interactions with, on the one hand, the socio-economic processes, and on the other, the political and cultural processes. The Thai political scientist *Chai-Anan Samudavanija* has summed up the fundamental role of the state in relation to the socio-economic processes as one of promoting *development* (D) in some form or other. In relation to the political and cultural processes the major role of the state is to encourage and regulate *participation* (P) of the citizens in the decision-making processes (Chai-Anan, 1991). However, Chai-Anan is of the opinion that the most important role of the state is, in reality, to ensure *security* (S) for itself and for the country. Thus a third dimension is added to the conception of the state.

Chai-Anan has further pointed out that the states of the developing countries today are under massive pressure to deal with all three tasks at the same time. They all have to function as S-states to survive as independent entities. But they are simultaneously under pressure from both their own citizens and the industrialised countries to function as D- and P-states, moreover where the emphasis concerning the latter dimension is on demands for democratisation and, consequently, a relatively open and extensive public participation in the decision-making processes (cf. Chapter 13).

In practice, not all the states in the Third World manage to handle all the three tasks. Many focus predominantly on security, others combine this with development or participation, and only a few can be characterised as SDP-states. One of Chai-Anan's interesting points in this connection is that the European rulers, during the period when they established the foundations for the modern states and built up their nations, could single-mindedly pursue their goal of state building and security creating arrangements. They were not under pressure to promote either socio-economic development or public participation, in the way that the rulers of the developing countries are today.

Using this three-dimensional conception of the societal roles of the state as a starting point we shall try to argue a little more for the appropriateness of also including the security dimension within the field of development research. The main point here is that, by ignoring the security aspects, there is a danger of producing significant distortions in the presentation of the factors which affect the formulation of development policies because security considerations, in practice, often play important and sometimes decisive roles in the organisation of governments' development efforts.

Most countries in the Third World face both internal and external security problems of significant scope. The internal security problems originate chiefly from the heterogeneity of the population with respect to religion, ethnicity and language. Uneven development with concentrations of growth, progress and privilege in small geographical and social enclaves may also contribute to creating security problems for many states, because the segments of the population not benefiting and excluded often rise in revolt. In the many cases where socio-economic conflicts coincide with religious, ethnic or linguistic lines of division, serious threats to the security of the state and its territorial integrity frequently arise.

In development research, internal security problems have sometimes been treated as problems of authority and legitimacy (for example in Jackson and Rosberg, 1982a, 1982b; Hawthorn, 1991). In this connection it has been highlighted as typical of many developing countries, especially in Africa, that their governments have not established effective authority over all their territory, and often their exercise of power has been regarded as non-legitimate by large groups of the population. In such circumstances, governments have been forced to give very high priority to the reinforcement of state security and territorial integrity – to the detriment of both development initiatives and promotion of public participation in political decision making. Conversely, the governments in countries without any serious internal security problems have been able to give higher priority to these efforts – provided that external threats have not obstructed this kind of prioritisation.

The external security problems often stem from other states' quest for power and more specifically from demands concerning the alteration of the borders which the colonial powers, in their era, established without much consideration of existing lines of division in the populations or traditional territorial claims. The external security problems were in many regions considerably intensified by the East–West confrontation and the super-powers' attempts to secure influence and control over their own supply routes and access to vital resources.

To this may be added the combination of security problems and economic decline which normally follow in the wake of natural disasters and extensive environmental damage.

The point is that all these conditions are likely to affect the formulation of development strategies of individual states. For the most influential decision makers, security considerations presumably take precedence over other considerations when they perceive serious internal or external threats. General development concerns of an economic and social character typically come second and are thus assessed in the light of the security policies. This probably applies in particular to the many countries where the armed forces either directly control government power or play a significant role as one of the most powerful political organisations in the society. However, it also applies to countries with more democratic forms of regime such as India, for example (cf. the discussion of India's situation in the section on disarmament and development below).

The impact of security considerations on the formulation of development strategies can be traced in many other areas, such as the physical location of, and control over, strategically important industries; special priority to defence-related resource exploitation and industrial companies; the pattern of physical infrastructure development; and technology policy. Moreover there is, of course, the whole issue of military armament and the associated biased resource allocations to the detriment of development efforts in the civil sector.

In continuation of these general reflections on the impact of security considerations upon development policies, it is logical to raise the question of whether socio-economic development, in a more specifically determined sense, is liable to reduce the internal and external security problems, and thereby reduce the need for a military build-up and the use of coercion in attempts to solve these problems. The question may be asked in general, but it has to be stressed that universally valid answers cannot be provided, because circumstances in different societies and at different times vary too much. Furthermore, the issue has not received much attention from development researchers and thus very few theoretical propositions have been elaborated on the possible causal relationships.

Development as a conflict-generating process

Seen in a longer historical perspective, it may initially be noted that development in the sense of economic growth and industrialisation has often acted as a conflict-generating process. Industrial development in Europe was thus associated with great tensions and occasional wars between those states and large trading companies who strove for control over raw materials, supply routes, territories and labour. The colonisation of most of the Third World can be seen in such a perspective. The wars were fought both in the colonial areas and in Europe.

The division of Europe in the twentieth century, and the associated development in the East of fundamentally different economic and political structures, for a long period generated conflicts – again both in Europe and in the Third World.

Looking at the impact of growth-oriented and market-controlled development in the Third World, the picture is less unambiguous. There is little doubt, however, that the socially biased distribution of development benefits in many countries has acted to create conflict – especially where economic inequalities and conflicts have coincided with (or could be interpreted as) religious, ethnic or linguistic conflicts. There are many examples of excluded, marginalised and poor population groups revolting exactly in conjunction with a period of economic prosperity. This was the case, for instance, with the Bengalis in East Pakistan up to 1971, and with the Tamils in Sri Lanka from 1979 onwards. In other cases, some better-off population groups have revolted and demanded further privileges or even political separation from the majority of less-prosperous fellow citizens. Examples of this are the

Ibos' attempt to establish their own Biafra in the 1960s, and the Punjabis' efforts to establish their own homeland in India from the mid-1980s.

It is not only uneven development within developing countries that has created conflicts. The same is true in a number of cases where the economic differences between neighbouring countries have been deepened. This has led to tensions, and sometimes pressures from the poorer countries to obtain a share of the increasing prosperity of their neighbours. Both Syria's military interventions in the Lebanon and Iraq's temporary occupation of Kuwait contained such elements.

Although a number of cases can be identified where economic development has caused or compounded military confrontations, it should be stressed that the above observations concern certain specific patterns of development and special circumstances. There are other examples, in other countries and at other times, where even an extremely biased distribution of wealth and incomes has not resulted in open and extensive conflicts. A similar argument applies if attention is shifted from the internal conditions to the interrelations between different countries. Hence, it is not warranted to draw any firm and general conclusions concerning the conflict-generating potential of socio-economic development patterns.

However, a few general observations may be proposed if we look at the subject matter from a slightly different perspective where the principal focus is on the recurring *crises* in the development of most societies.

Many social science researchers throughout the twentieth century have paid attention to both long and short waves, especially in the Western societies' economic development. But today it is a far more widespread conception that social development all over the world and in all dimensions runs through periods of prosperity and progress and other periods character-ised by decline and crisis. The nature of these crises has altered radically over time. Furthermore, they manifest themselves in dissimilar ways in different societies (Hettne, 1990: Ch. 1).

The period since the beginning of the 1970s has in several crucial respects been characterised by crises – not only with respect to the economy, the wearing down of the environment and the exhaustion of non-renewable natural resources, but also with regard to political and cultural conditions in the broadest sense (Binder et al., 1986). It might be asserted that the crisis-like course is mostly global as regards the economic and ecological conditions. However, at the same time it is noteworthy how far-reaching global inter-dependence has also become when it concerns political events and cultural manifestations – which is perhaps most clearly illustrated by the global impact of the Islamic revival, especially in the Arab world and Iran. The effects filter into the Western industrial countries and Eastern Europe mainly through economic mechanisms, but it would be insupportable for that reason to reduce the decisive forces to economic phenomena. On the contrary, the political strengthening of Islam and of the countries where Islam is an important and critical political force, illustrates how political and cultural factors impact upon both the internal conditions and the concerned societies' international position.

The Islamic revival – especially the strengthening of the more fundamentalist movements – in large parts of the Arab world and Iran has created crises and upheavals in several of the societies concerned. It has also led to radical changes in both the prevailing conception of development and the policies pursued in these societies. Other regions of the Third World have over the same period experienced crises of other types. The Swedish researcher *Björn Hettne* has pointed to some of the basic patterns by stating that the most striking sign of crisis and at the same time the most prominent development problem in Latin America is the debt burden. Likewise, the most serious problems in Sub-Saharan Africa are insufficient food supply and the widespread environmental degradation. South Asia faces mainly intensive ethnic and linguistic conflicts which threaten both the security of the states and economic progress (Hettne, 1990: Ch. 1).

Summary statements like these of course conceal the real-world multiplicity, which Hettne himself has also emphasised. They are included here only to illustrate that the countries of the Third World face fundamentally different security problems. The multiplicity could further be emphasised with reference to the relatively highly industrialised Far Eastern countries, especially South Korea and Taiwan, and the ways in which their governments have managed, with American aid, to handle massive security problems and at the same time have been able to support and promote considerable economic progress (cf. Chapter 18). Thus is also emphasised the need for a differentiated approach in any closer analysis of the nature of the development processes and their presumed effects on the security situation.

Development as a peace-promoting process

The greater interdependence referred to above does not only imply that instability and crisis-like situations can multiply throughout large parts of the world. It also contains the seeds for less tension-filled and fruitful international co-operation. Much indicates that the greatly increased international interaction – economic, political, social and cultural – which is also a result of the recent decade's socio-economic development, can form a fertile ground for a trust-creating and peace-creating process.

This applies especially to the relationship between East and West, where the process is further facilitated by the radical changes and reforms in Eastern Europe and Russia – changes and reforms which to a high degree have involved a transformation of these societies towards greater similarity with the Western market economies. It is noteworthy that a structural change of this kind has penetrated so rapidly and extensively in the former Communist societies, which previously were only to a very small extent objects of direct

Western efforts in this respect, whereas the developing countries have often tried to resist Western influence and attempted to follow other development paths with strong elements of their own political and cultural heritage.

Crucial to the question of the peace-promoting aspects of the development process, however, is not primarily whether the many different societies in the world converge towards greater similarity. It is probably more important whether the increased interdependence, the continuously more intense trans-national and international interactions, also bring about increased mutual understanding and acceptance – of the differences, the otherness of other societies.

This does not seem to be the consequence in all cases. On the contrary, extended interactions have often been associated with sharpened conflicts and xenophobia among the citizens and the decision makers in both the Third World and the industrialised countries. None the less, with some reservation it may be asserted that, in a longer-term perspective, the intensified international interactions at all levels – together with the international efforts at co-ordinating development initiatives – are likely to promote peace. Of special importance in this connection are probably the more permanent international fora, including the United Nations and the Conference on Security and Co-operation in Europe, where representatives from different countries can exchange views. But also *ad hoc* initiatives may have positive impacts upon both the international conditions of trust and the global development efforts. Examples include the work of the Brandt Commission and the Brundtland Commission.

Neither the permanent nor the temporary arrangements for the promotion of international security and development can, however, be credited with any great penetrating power in very critical situations such as, for example, that following Iraq's military occupation of Kuwait in 1990. In this case, none of the established international mechanisms could prevent a war which, regardless of its geographical limitation, has had decisive influence on many aspects of North–South and South–South relations.

In addition, it must be acknowledged that the international arrangements have had only modest significance for the promotion of social equality, poverty eradication, ecologically sustainable development, national self-determination and public participation. Goals like these seem utopian in the foreseeable future, though this does not render them unimportant. On the contrary, such goals, by the force of their visionary content, may inspire contemporary debates and expose the limitations in ongoing development co-operation, both in the developing countries and at the international level.

After this discussion of the potential impact of socio-economic and international political developments upon the security situation, we shall try to assess the possible causal interrelationships from a different perspective by asking whether extensive disarmament can be presumed to lead to economic progress. First we shall refer very briefly to some general propositions regarding this issue. Subsequently, the specific case of India will be reviewed in order to draw attention to the types of conditions which more specifically have to be considered in a detailed account of the subject.

Disarmament and development

The literature contains many different propositions regarding the relationship between, on the one hand, armament and disarmament, and on the other hand, societal development. Disregarding the position that there is no direct relationship, one extreme point of view is that military armament promotes economic growth, while disarmament will often remove some of the driving force behind a growth process. The opposite extreme position is that armament involves a diversion of resources which could otherwise have been used in a more immediate manner and with far better results to further socio-economic growth and development. The concluding document adopted at the United Nations special conference on the relationship between disarmament and development in 1987 aligned itself closely with this latter conception. Armament was not totally deprived of a growth-promoting impact under all circumstances, but it was emphasised that military expenses would generally have a less positive effect on economic growth than comparable civil investments. Therefore, it would be advantageous to disarm and move resources from military use to use in the civil sector. In particular, this would be the case for the many poor countries who import most of the supplies for their armed forces. The document emphasised that the arms race devoured far too great a share of the world's human, financial natural and technological resources and thus put a heavy burden on the economy of all countries (United Nations, 1987).

This general description of the impact of disarmament can be adapted to the conditions in South Asia, where the conflict and the arms race between India and Pakistan have dominated the political security situation. It has been documented for both these countries that armament has implied considerable socio-economic costs. There is no agreement concerning the extent or the precise character of these costs. Among the prevailing conceptions, however, none appears to argue that armament in this region has contributed decisively to the economic progress, let alone socially broad-based development, of either India or Pakistan. The military sector in both countries, on the contrary, has strengthened the tendencies towards sporadic growth in geographical and social enclaves, from where there have been very few spread effects on the rest of society. In India's case, it should be noted that even though close linkages have been established between the armed forces and domestic defence industries, this has not had any positive effects for the vast majority of the population.

In the light of this, it may be asked whether a gradual disarmament – provided this became politically feasible – could contribute definitively to macro-economic growth and possibly also promote social equality and human development. No firm answers can be given to the question, but it is possible to point to some interlinkages which indicate that the whole matter may be a bit more complicated than is often assumed in the popular literature and the United Nations' resolutions.

The point is that even though armament in India, originally, was motivated primarily by security policy considerations, it has since then become part of a more comprehensive development strategy. Defence-related production is thus today an essential precondition for many of the backward and forward linkages between the country's different economic sectors and branches of industry. Since the mid-1960s, India has built a steadily expanding defence industry which has prompted an increased demand for capital goods and basic products predominantly produced in India. In this way, the defence industry has functioned as a growth engine for substantial parts of the civil sector.

Of course, in principle, this demand could have been brought about by corresponding investments in the civil sector. Furthermore, based on the conception that the two sectors compete for scarce resources, it must be noted that these resources could probably have been used more advantage-ously in the civil sector. Defence-related production in India is extremely capital intensive, technology intensive and import demanding – and therefore, in important respects, in conflict with the factor endowment of the country. Many other reasons could be given in support of a transfer of resources from the military to the civil sector, including that such a conversion would free up the skills of highly qualified researchers who presently work in military institutions for use in civil projects.

However, the interesting point that closer investigations lead to is that the Indian defence industries do add important dynamics to the country's eco-nomy, because they have a multiplier effect on other domestic industries and at the same time account for large export incomes. The attractive alternative would logically be to use the resources for building civil-sector industries with similar effects, but especially with regard to earning export incomes this has already proved to be difficult. In other words, it is unlikely that India, as a matter of course, would be able to switch over to non-military products which to the same extent could be sold in the world market. The result could therefore be the loss of a considerable export income, as well as the loss of many jobs for the unskilled – losses that India would find very difficult to handle. Since, in addition, domestic demand for arms and other military equipment is probably a precondition for production with economies of scale – and thereby for competitive unit prices – it can be difficult to argue for extensive disarmament based on narrow economic considerations. Formulated a little differently, the Indian armed forces' purchase of the products from the national defence industries is probably a necessary precondition for the international competitiveness of these products – and this competitiveness is important for Indian industry in general.

As noted, firm conclusions cannot be drawn; our knowledge of the causal interrelationships is insufficient. Besides, any conclusion would depend on how different development objectives are prioritised. What one may derive from considerations such as the above is the need, as also emphasised by the United Nations conference referred to earlier, to carry out more thorough empirical analyses of how best to link disarmament and military conversion to economic growth and societal development in a broader sense.

The developing countries in the international system after the Cold War

Issues concerning the possibility of disarmament and its potential impact upon socio-economic development have, for the Third World as a whole, become of more immediate interest since the end of the so-called Cold War, chiefly because this change has removed important parts of the international driving force behind armament. Although no general and decisive scaling down of regional conflicts and antagonisms between the developing countries can be observed, the ending of the Cold War is probably so profound a change in the international system that it deserves some reflection on the possible lasting effects. *Barry Buzan* is one of the researchers who has tried to give a systematic and comprehensive account of the consequences of the new global security situation for the developing countries (Buzan, 1991a, 1991b), but several other authors have recently contributed to identifying the changes brought about by the ending of the Cold War (cf. Holm and Sørensen, 1995).

Buzan claims that the centre–periphery approach captures much of what remains constant from the past and is, at the same time, a useful framework within which to consider the impact of the changes in the centre on the security of the periphery. He then goes on to identify a number of defining features for the new pattern of great-power relations after the Cold War. Three features are particularly noteworthy. The first is the change from a bi-polar power structure to a multi-polar structure, where not only the USA and Russia are poles of power. Japan and the European Community are also poles on account of their economic power position.

The second new feature is a considerably lower degree of ideological rivalry and conflict. Buzan states in this connection that the history of the twentieth century in a historical perspective might well be seen as an era of wars between great powers about the right economic ideology. The first round of war, starting in 1914, gave birth to Fascist and Communist states that challenged the capitalist West. The second round saw Western and Communist powers combining in 1941 to eliminate Fascism. The third round, the Cold War, which was fought in a different manner with focus on the arms race, technological innovation, economic growth and societal attractive-ness, ended peacefully in 1989 with the collapse of the Communist states in the face of a decisively superior Western performance. Western market capitalism and political pluralism thus today command a broad consensus as the most effective and desirable form of political economy available – not without critics, but without any real alternatives.

The third trend, according to Buzan, is the emergence of a global dominance of a security community among the leading capitalist powers. This security community comprises all the leading capitalist powers in North America, Europe and Asia.

These three emerging features have important consequences for the peripheral societies. The demise of both power bi-polarity and ideological rivalry have removed many of the opportunities for the developing countries to play on the conflicts between the states of the centre. The developing countries can no longer count on massive military aid or maintenance of the level of economic aid, because they have lost much of their value as strategic assets in great-power rivalry. Buzan also mentions that the breakdown of the Communist regimes has considerably weakened part of the legitimacy of the one-party systems in many developing countries which, as a result, have come under further pressure from the Western countries to introduce political pluralism (cf. Chapter 13).

It can be added that several other researchers have noted the possibilities of a significant reduction of aid to the developing countries, not only because these countries are now of less value to the capitalist centre, but further because the former Communist countries in the North-East compete with the South for economic aid. Most development researchers have noted these prospects with regret, while others, such as the veteran *Keith Griffin*, have welcomed the changes. Griffin has done so on the basis that Western aid has not been particularly effective anyway, as seen from the point of view of the poor population groups. Aid has always predominantly been a product of the Cold War and was thus shaped by the strategic and political interests of the rich countries. This may not apply to aid from the Nordic countries (Denmark, Finland, Norway and Sweden) and certain other smaller countries, but overall Griffin sees no reason to worry about the possible demise of foreign aid (Griffin, 1991).

The above-mentioned prospects should also be seen in connection with the fact that the colonial era, for the large majority of countries in the periphery, now lies some generations in the past. Therefore, the rulers cannot in the same way as previously refer to foreign rule as the root cause of many of their problems, but must themselves take on the responsibility or find new scapegoats. A further consequence may be a general weakening of anti-Western ideologies which, according to Buzan, is counterbalanced by the widespread Islamic revival. Islam, in large parts of the Third World, has taken over the role played by Communism as the frame of reference for anti-Western movements.

Buzan's reflections are, as he has emphasised, speculative. There is not yet a basis for working out genuine theory about the consequences of the new structure in the international system, but there is no doubt that development research in the next decade must carefully consider the markedly changed global system and its implications for the developing countries. Buzan is pessimistic on behalf of these countries, which he consistently refers to as the periphery rather than the Third World. Although this may look like a promotion from third rank to second, the deeper reality is that the centre is now more dominant, and the periphery more subordinate, than at any time since decolonisation began.

PART V

Civil Society and
the Development Process

CHAPTER 20

Dimensions of Alternative Development

The chapters in this part of the book will shift attention away from the state, the market and the corporate economy and, instead, focus on *civil society* in the broad sense of the term. The core of civil society is the household, but the concept refers also to the social life of citizens within the households, and the interaction of households in the local community and in the various other forms of social organisations outside the formal political system and the corporate economy. The theories and debates reviewed in the present and the following chapters deal with patterns of organisation in civil society and their interrelations with economic and political development processes. Particular attention will be given to the impact of economic growth trajectories and patterns of political change upon different social groups.

In a certain sense, one might say that the chapters in this part of the book attempt to summarise propositions and strategies proposed by schools of thought that present themselves as basic alternatives to the comprehensive body of theory reviewed and discussed in previous parts of the book. Evidently, the theories and strategies dealt with so far constitute a very complex intellectual framework with several competing and to some extent mutually exclusive propositions. Thus, it is difficult to conceive of a set of alternative approaches in any strict sense.

But precisely by their focus on the social life of the individual citizens and civil society, the so-called alternative approaches and theories do set themselves apart from the hitherto dominant positions in the international development debates. Further, the alternative approaches are generally more explicitly normative than most mainstream theories. They deal with development not only in terms of causal relationships but also in terms of what kind of development is preferable, as seen from the viewpoint of various social groups, or from the perspective of equality, justice, self-reliance, environmental sustainability or cultural pluralism. A group of approaches often referred to as *Another Development* present themselves chiefly as normative, while other approaches, including those dealing with social distribution of growth or the formation of ethnic identities, combine normative concepts with causal theory (Hettne, 1990: Ch. 5, 1995: Ch. 4).

Alternative development theories have been subjected to considerable enrichment and further elaboration since the early 1980s. Moreover, these theories have achieved far greater importance in the academic debates as well as in international development co-operation.

The present chapter provides an overview of the different perspectives which characterise the alternative approaches, and delves into the theoretical heritage and the basic positions from which these approaches have been worked out *either* as further elaborations and additions, *or* as rejections of mainstream theories and strategies.

In the next chapter, theories and strategies which have largely focused on poverty, social inequality, basic needs and human development are looked at. This is followed, in Chapter 22, by a discussion of theories concerning the political economy of civil society. Chapter 23 focuses on a distinctive aspect of the politics of civil society, that is ethnic identities and conflicts. The concluding chapter in this part of the book looks at the – predominantly normative – theories of people-managed development.

It should be noted at the outset that in many regions of the Third World conceptions and ideologies of development have emerged as countervailing and very fundamental alternatives to 'Western' thinking. These include Mahatma Gandhi's social and political philosophy in an Indian context; Islamic fundamentalism in the Middle East, Iran, Malaysia and other countries; Islamic socialism in Pakistan and some Arab countries; the theories of Frantz Fanon and others on alienation and suppression; African socialism; and Mao's special variant of historical materialism.

There is no doubt that all these approaches, in different ways, have added to the understanding of development and, more importantly, have drawn attention to possible alternative patterns of societal transformation. Moreover, as strategies for action, they have decisively affected economic, political and social change in several countries. There is no doubt either that a more comprehensive and open dialogue between these approaches and the essentially Western-inspired theory formation and development debates would add to the latter significant new dimensions and useful insights. This has been shown by social anthropologists and many researchers within the humanities who have devoted themselves thoroughly to these Third World ideologies, theories and strategies, and in this manner achieved an understanding superior to that of social scientists as regards the cultural foundations and micro-level conditions for societal change. They have been able to grasp the importance and dynamics of national and local traditions and institutions.

Notwithstanding this acknowledgement of the Third World-based alternative approaches, they will not be subjected to further discussion in this book, chiefly because that would require a very considerable expansion of the exposition, but also because it would split up the presentation further and introduce totally different issues and debates. It follows from this statement that the present book does not claim to cover all types of theoretical contribution to understanding societal development. Rather, it should be seen as an attempt to review and discuss only those bodies of theory that can be understood within the framework of Western rationalism with roots in the philosophies of the European Enlightenment, and with its main emphasis on interpretation and explanation, rather than the normative and utopian. The book should further be regarded as a presentation that reflects the global economic and political dominance of the OECD countries at the theoretical level. Only sporadically does the exposition escape beyond these limitations.

Alternative development perspectives

It has already been implied in the introduction above that basically two types of alternative approach can be identified. The distinguishing characteristic of the first type is *a redefinition of the development goals*. The approaches belonging to this category, after having established different goals, deal extensively with how to measure and how to promote societal change towards such alternative goals. Proponents of this type of alternative approaches include *Amartya Sen, Dudley Seers, Paul Streeten, Mahbub ul Haq*, and other theorists who have rejected economic growth as an end in itself and, instead, emphasised welfare and human development with increased choices as the higher-order objectives (cf. Chapter 3). These theorists have at the same time turned their attention towards social inequality and poverty, and in doing so insisted on looking at 'development' as processes which may have very dissimilar meanings and implications for different social groups. They have not rejected the whole body of mainstream economic development theory, but rather tried to supplement it in certain essential respects. Something similar can be said to apply to Myrdal's societal theory, and to several of the other previously discussed schools of thought within development economics. The next chapter looks more closely at these forms of more limited alternative approach, including some which incorporate a gender dimension into the economic and social analyses.

The second type of alternative approach has not only disaggregated the development process and emphasised its dissimilar effects on different social groups, but has additionally shifted the whole perspective and focus towards civil society. They may, therefore, as a group be referred to as *theories of civil society*.

Some, predominantly normative, theories of civil society have gone as far as to revive romantic conceptions of local communities as sufficient bases and frameworks for human welfare. They believe that the state is part of the problem and should therefore be avoided as much as possible. They regard the establishment and strengthening of autonomous local communities as both a means to promote human well-being and as an end in itself (Korten, 1990).

John Friedmann, an American social scientist, has in one of the few comprehensive presentations of alternative development theories criticised such

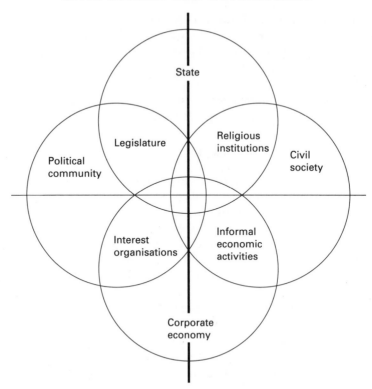

Figure 20.1 The four domains of social practice

romantic and utopian approaches for their exaggerated perceptions of the excellence and infallibility of people (Friedmann, 1992). He has further criticised them for a naive belief that alternative development can be created and sustained in small local communities and in consistent opposition to the state. Friedmann's point in this context is that although an alternative develop-ment must begin locally, it cannot end there. Without the state's collaboration, the lot of the poor cannot be significantly improved. Finally, Friedmann has distanced himself from this type of alternative approach, because it assumes conflict-free and homogenous human communities, whereas the real world is rife with conflicts of interest, inequalities of all kinds, subordination of women, etc.

We shall not discuss further these local community-centred alternative approaches in their more extreme forms, though we will, in Chapter 24, discuss the particular variant that may be described as a normative theory of people-managed development. Otherwise, attention will be focused on em-pirically grounded and more explanation-oriented alternative approaches, of which Friedmann himself is one of the outstanding proponents.

The perspective in Friedmann's analyses can be described with the help of Figure 20.1 which – in a simplified form – depicts various domains of social practice and their various degrees of institutionalisation (after Friedmann, 1992: p. 27, with adjustments). Figure 20.1 shows four overlapping domains of social practice: the state, the corporate economy, the political community and civil society. Each domain has a core of institutions that shape the behaviour within the respective spheres. In the case of the state, it is the bureaucracy and judicial institutions; for the corporate economy it is the corporation and the market; for the political community it is autonomous political organisations and social movements; and finally in the case of civil society the core institution is the household. The figure further shows how different types of institutions and activities may be seen as combining or interlinking the four domains of practice. For instance, a legislature may be seen as combining the political community with the state.

The strongly drawn vertical line indicates that it is the axis linking the state and the corporate economy which typically dominates and sets the agenda for the development process in the Third World – as well as in the industrial countries of the First World and in the former centrally planned economies.

A similar dominance can be identified in the international development debates up until now, in the sense that they have centred mainly around the corporate economy and the state, and around the interrelationships between these two domains of practice. What Friedmann and other proponents of alternative theories of civil society try to do in this context is to change the agenda and shift the primary attention to the horizontal axis passing through civil society and the political community.

Friedmann's perspective furthermore comprises analyses of both poverty problems and social inequality, including inequality between men and women. Friedmann has also tried to integrate an environmental perspective into his theory construction. Similar perspectives are found in most of the literature concerning alternative development.

Theoretical origins and emergence of alternative development theories

The redefinition of the goals of development and the accompanying focus on social aspects of the development process and its results can, in the long-term perspective, be traced back to *John Stuart Mill* (1806–1873) and to the social liberalism of the nineteenth century.

In a shorter time perspective, the roots must be searched for in the economic development debate of the 1960s and early 1970s. The British economist *Dudley Seers* was one of the scholars whose name became closely associated with the efforts to redefine development. In a speech in 1969, he posed for the first time three pertinent questions which have since then often been used as reference points for much of the debate about alternative development. Quoted from an article published a few years later, the crucial points were:

> The questions to ask about a country's development are therefore: What has been happening to poverty? What has been happening to unemployment? What has been happening to inequality? If all three of these have become less severe, then beyond doubt there has been a period of development for the country concerned. If one or two of these central problems have been growing worse, and especially if all three have, it would be strange to call the result 'development', even if per capita income had soared. (Seers, 1972)

Since Seers summed up this development conception as an alternative to the narrow focus on economic growth, several important contributions have been made to analyse and explain development with emphases on poverty, unemployment and inequality. The next chapter reviews a selection of these contributions.

With respect to the theories of civil society, their theoretical heritage may, in the long-term perspective, be traced back to conservative romanticism and utopian socialism, which were both normative reactions against the emerging nineteenth-century capitalist society and the accompanying centralisation and institutionalisation of state power (Hettne, 1990: Ch. 5). These two ideologies, each in its particular way, promulgated ideas about a better society based on community in the sense referred to by the more precise German word *gemeinschaft*, not on society as *gesellschaft*. Conservative romanticism wanted to preserve what were seen as the more human-friendly local communities of the past. Utopian socialism wanted to introduce such communities to replace alienating capitalism.

This basic preoccupation with, and positive assessment of, small local communities – outside the reach of the state and the corporate, capitalist economy – can be identified in many of the contemporary alternative development conceptions and theories. Other roots can be traced back to variants of populism, such as the ideology of the Narodniks in Russia, or to the early anti-capitalist peasant movements in Asia.

It should be added that in Western political philosophy there is a long tradition of constructing concepts and theories with an emphasis on civil society. This tradition dates all the way back to the Greek city states. It played a central role for philosophers such as Hegel and the young Marx. However, there is no need in the present context to delve into these theoretical origins. It should suffice to note that most present-day notions of civil society resemble the conception proposed by Antonio Gramsci. Contrary to previous conceptions of civil society as essentially everything outside the domain of the state, Gramsci in the twentieth century introduced a distinction between the state, the basic economic structures and civil society (for an introduction to Western thinking on civil society, see Cohen and Arato, 1992).

In a shorter time perspective, the theoretical heritage can be traced back to anthropological studies, and more specifically to the Hungarian-born *Karl Polanyi*'s theory of different forms of economic and social integration and distribution (Polanyi, 1957). For Polanyi, the market system was only one among several forms of integration and distribution. Other mechanisms for distributing products and services were based on reciprocity, or on various religious or political principles for sharing burdens and benefits. Particularly the notions of reciprocal exchange have inspired recent theory formation and studies of exchange processes in civil society – within households and the informal social networks. This has also been a major source of inspiration for Göran Hydén and others who have elaborated concepts like the 'economy of affection' or the 'moral economy' to capture the essence of social inter-relations and forms of integration in peasant economies (cf. Chapter 17).

In the literature on alternative development, certain central events are often noted as being particularly important for the emergence and con-solidation of a new agenda for development. Among the earliest such important events was a conference in Stockholm in 1972 on Human Environ-ment, which led to the establishment of the United Nations' environmental organisation UNEP. Two years later there followed a seminar in Cocoyoc, Mexico, organised by UNEP in collaboration with UNCTAD. It was attended by outstanding experts from all parts of the world, including Mahbul ul Haq and Samir Amin, to mention but two. The concluding declaration of the Cocoyoc seminar brought together two major strands of the alternative movement: those who had argued that highest priority should be given to satisfying the basic needs for food, water and shelter, and those who were primarily concerned about the destruction of the environment and exhaustion of non-renewable natural resources.

Both aspects were, a few years later at a seminar organised by the Inter-national Foundation for Development Alternatives (IFDA), linked more explicitly to notions of citizens' responsibilities, and to their autonomous power and capacity for influencing development independently of the state and the corporate economy. IFDA termed this approach the 'Third System Project' for the purpose of underlining how it was different from mainstream development thinking. The IFDA approach focused on people and people's power, as distinct from 'conventional' analyses that focus on either the state and politics – the first system – or the corporate economy and the market – the second system. As mentioned earlier, Chapter 22 looks at some of the more recent alternative theories with a focus on civil society and other aspects of the 'third system'.

CHAPTER 21

Poverty and Social Development

The earliest economic growth and development theories paid little attention to social inequality. They did not regard inequality as being decisive for the course and patterns of economic growth and transformation. Nor did they regard the social implications of the growth processes as a central issue. Both these themes, however, received more and more attention in the international development debate from the beginning of the 1960s onwards (cf. Part II).

On one hand, it was debated whether a high or a low degree of inequality with respect to the distribution of income was most conducive to rapid and sustained economic growth. The main argument for a high degree of inequality was that high-income groups had the highest propensity to save, and therefore were the most important source of capital formation. Poor people could not contribute in this respect, not even with increasing incomes because most of the increase would be spent on food and other basic necessities. Opposing this contention, other researchers propagated the view that the most essential barrier to growth was not lack of capital, but insufficient domestic demand. Consequently, priority should be given to increasing this demand through income increases also for the poor as well as high-income groups. As the poor, especially in agriculture, were more productive than the rich, and because poor people in general would demand goods that were domestically produced while the rich would to a higher degree demand imported products, a case could be built for making income distribution more equal.

On the other hand, it was debated whether economic growth led to greater or lesser social inequality. One strand of thought claimed that growth would typically lead to greater inequality in the early stages and up to a certain point, after which continued growth would lead to a decline in the degree of inequality because the incomes of poorer groups would then tend to grow faster than the average. This view thus implied a hypothesis about a delayed trickling-down of the growth results to the poor in a society. The other major view was that economic growth would only trickle down to resource-weak groups under very exceptional conditions.

It was this second view which, in the 1960s and 1970s, appeared the most convincing. This could be attributed mainly to better statistical coverage with social indicators and disaggregated information about different income groups. The new statistics supported the assertion that there was very little trickling-down – even after long periods of growth. The data revealed that aggregate growth in most developing countries had predominantly been associated with income increases for the already affluent social groups, typically the 10–40 per cent of the population with the highest incomes, depending on the specific character of the growth process.

Knowledge about these tendencies prompted many development researchers to pay much more attention to inequality issues and to the problems of poverty in the developing countries. They began to study the whole process of interaction between, on the one hand, income and resource distribution and, on the other, the patterns of economic growth and transformation. At the same time, international organisations like the ILO, and later the World Bank and many others, incorporated poverty assessment in their analyses and poverty alleviation in their development strategies.

At first, there was a widespread tendency among both the researchers and the international organisations to look at the poor as passive target groups who, with assistance from external development agents such as the state, the donor organisations and others, should be helped out of their economic misery. But gradually the understanding grew that the poor were also independent actors, who possessed a tremendous potential for helping both themselves and the societies in which they lived. The changing perceptions over time may, somewhat simplified, be described in the following manner. First, the poor were almost invisible in the statistics as well as in theory formation. Then they became visible as a passive category of clients that had to be assisted by others. Finally, in the third stage, they appeared as visible *and* as living, active human beings, who mostly took care of themselves without external support.

Parallel to these shifts in perception, corresponding shifts occurred in the formulation of strategies – away from macro-economic growth strategies with no attention to poor target groups; via socially diversified development strategies with built-in poverty alleviation measures; towards combinations where only the poorest are seen as passive receivers of aid, while the majority of them are supported as producers who make a net contribution to aggregate growth. As a corollary to these changes, there has been a move away from the simple and one-dimensional income measures of poverty and development towards composite sets of indicators for welfare and quality of life.

It is noteworthy that similar basic trends can be observed with respect to research and strategies that focus on women and gender relations, as described later in this chapter. Before addressing this topic we shall, in the following sections, look into the basic needs approach, human development conceptions and strategies, and certain biases concerning how poverty is perceived by many researchers and most policy makers.

Poverty and the basic needs approach

The strategy known today as the basic needs strategy was first formulated by the ILO, the United Nation's international labour organisation, in the mid-1970s (ILO, 1976). Important inputs were provided earlier, however, by several researchers, including a group of economists from the World Bank and the highly regarded Institute for Development Studies in Sussex, which in 1974 published the work *Redistribution with Growth* (Chenery et al., 1974). The main thrust of this work was a continued commitment to growth in industry and other modern sectors, but combined with special measures aimed at assisting the 40 poorest per cent in each of the developing countries.

The ILO did not reject the need for growth in the modern sectors but argued – on the basis of studies commissioned by the organisation in Kenya and other poor countries in the early 1970s (ILO, 1972) – that growth apparently did not lead to substantial expansion of employment opportunities and increased incomes for the poor. Therefore, comprehensive measures targeted at the poor and unemployed were required – measures that involved a diffusion of capital and other resources, instead of the concentration to which mainstream economic theories had given priority.

The fundamental ideas in the basic needs strategy have since been taken over and further elaborated by many development researchers and several international organisations, including the World Bank, as well as by the Nordic aid agencies and other bilateral aid organisations. None of the organisations or agencies, however, has adopted the strategy as the core of its approach. Rather, they have added poverty and basic needs considerations to their mainly growth-oriented strategies.

The basic needs strategy has not emerged from a comprehensive and coherent theory; nor has it been developed into one set of measures. The strategy, rather, should be seen as a category comprising several different approaches and specific measures that reflect considerable differences regarding emphases and priorities (Hunt, 1989: Ch. 9; Streeten et al., 1982). Some of them put emphasis on creating employment as the major means to increase incomes of the poor. Others emphasise the need for extending public services and especially note the importance of primary education and health care. Some of the strategies are presented as adjuncts to, and modifications of, growth-oriented approaches, while others are proposed as substitutes for mainstream thinking.

Disregarding the finer nuances, however, it is possible to point to a core of the basic needs approach as being attempts to provide opportunities for the full physical, mental and social development of the human personality (Streeten et al., 1982: Ch. 1). Moreover, three types of basic needs tend to recur in most of the formulations, and a particular mode of reasoning in favour of the basic needs strategies may also be extracted. There is a general consensus that basic needs include, first, the individual human beings' and

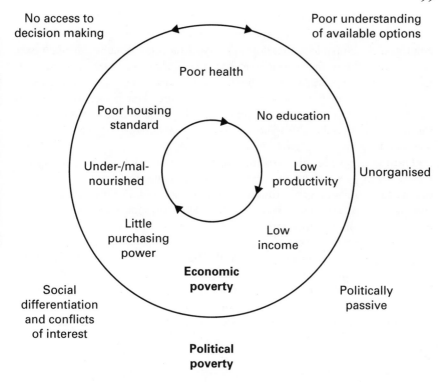

No access to
decision making

Poor understanding
of available options

Poor health

Poor housing
standard

No education

Under-/mal-
nourished

Low
productivity

Unorganised

Little
purchasing
power

Low
income

**Economic
poverty**

Social
differentiation
and conflicts
of interest

Politically
passive

**Political
poverty**

Figure 21.1 The vicious circles of economic and political poverty

the families' need for food, shelter, clothes and other necessities of daily life; secondly, access to public services such as drinking water, sanitation, health and education; thirdly, access to participate in, and exert influence on, decision making both in the local community and in national politics. The basic mode of reasoning in support of the basic needs strategy can be summarised in the following way.

Genuine economic development implies not only growth, but also persistent and measurable progress and social improvements for the poor and resource-weak groups in a society. This progress and the improvements concern not only incomes, but all aspects of the poverty complex. In this connection it is emphasised that being poor in a developing country is not just synonymous with inferior purchasing power – there is a whole range of other symptoms associated with poverty, as illustrated in Figure 21.1.

The poor are under- and malnourished; they live in miserable housing conditions and have bad sanitary and hygienic conditions, etc. All these conditions make the poor very susceptible to disease. Their general health is also far worse than that of the rest of the population. In addition, the poor lack even the most elementary education. As a result of bad health conditions and inadequate education, the poor are generally less productive than the rest of the population. For the same reasons, they are poorly paid when employed and unable to exploit the opportunities available through self-employment. Thus, they continue to have very little income and, consequently, their purchasing power remains highly inadequate. They are, in other words, 'screwed down' in poverty and conditions where their basic needs are not satisfied. This whole process is repeated continuously and the situation of the poor can thus be characterised as a vicious circle – a poverty circle, as illustrated by the inner circle in Figure 21.1.

The many people who are trapped in the poverty circle are the last to benefit from growth and they rarely experience any real improvements as a direct result of aggregate growth. During periods of decline and economic recession, they are the first to be hit. They do not have the necessary economic resources to change the mechanisms that keep them in deep poverty. In addition, according to some of the proponents of the basic needs strategy, the poor do not have the necessary political resources to do anything decisive about their own situation.

In spite of their large numbers, poor people have very few opportunities to influence and affect decision making within the political system, even in a democracy; and they have no access at all to the important centres of power within the corporate economy. Further, poor people are divided into several distinct social groups that often view each other with animosity. Although they share the basic symptoms of poverty, their living conditions are very dissimilar. Many are landless rural labourers, while others have small plots of land. Some of them run trade and service businesses in the villages or in the larger towns, others are street vendors or day labourers. Some are healthy; some are chronically ill (typically up to 10 per cent in the poorest developing countries). To this are added the differences in the situation of men and women, and divisions by ethnic affiliation, language, religion, etc.

The combined outcome is a considerable social differentiation which makes it difficult for the poor to act collectively and to organise themselves. The difficulties are compounded by the lack of education and the often associated poor understanding of the options for action available. The result is a low degree of organisation and political passivity. Finally, it could be added that the state in most economically backward countries is organised so as to exclude the large numbers of poor people from influencing decision making, mainly because meeting their demands would imply serious threats to the powerful elites who control the state.

The complex of conditions that tend, in a mutually reinforcing manner, to keep economically poor people also in political poverty is depicted in Figure 21.1 by the outer circle. Unlike the symptoms of economic poverty, where the predominance of a circular causation is assumed, we have indicated that the conditions reproducing political poverty and exclusion interact with each other in a multidirectional manner. This may actually apply to the conditions referred to in the inner circle, too, but there is a tendency in the literature to treat economic poverty in terms of a vicious circle or even a vicious spiral.

Under the circumstances outlined above – and this is ultimately the central point in the basic needs approach – a special development strategy for the poor must be worked out. Special arrangements must be made for, and in co-operation with, this target group if it is to break out of poverty and exclusion and achieve decisive improvements. At the same time, the strategy embodies the moral imperative that everybody should, first and foremost, contribute to satisfying the basic needs of all human beings in the world and that this should be given priority over further welfare improvements among the rich of the developing countries, as well as in the affluent industrialised countries.

Normative elements of this kind characterise much of the literature on basic needs. However, it should be noted that many of the researchers who designate first priority to meeting basic needs argue, at the same time, that the rich by helping the poor would also help themselves. Helping the poor would contribute to aggregate growth both directly and indirectly, primarily because an increase in the purchasing power of the poor would 'trickle up' in the shape of increased demand. Moreover, investing in the poor would give a high rate of return because inexpensive productivity improvements among poor producers would create considerable additional growth. The latter point has been elaborated particularly in relation to women, who often play vital roles in production in Asia and Africa, notably in the rural areas.

The basic needs strategy figured prominently in the international development debate in the latter half of the 1970s. During the same period, many aid agencies incorporated some of the core elements of the strategy into their project and programme designs, as indicated earlier. Not very many governments in the Third World, however, embraced the basic needs approach. Most decision makers tended to look upon the strategy with suspicion, as an invention of the North they could not afford. This position was reinforced gradually during the 1980s, as the implications of the debt crisis and adverse international economic conditions in general were felt in more and more poor countries. 'The change of guard', which brought neo-classical economists into prominence in some of the large OECD countries and the World Bank around 1980, accentuated the trend (cf. Chapter 18).

The centre stage, during most of the 1980s, was therefore captured by the debates on the state and the market and by the strategies of macro-economic structural adjustment programmes. It is worth noting, though, that the poverty focus and the priority to basic needs were preserved by many researchers and some international organisations, including UNICEF (Cornia, Jolly and Stewart, 1987).

Towards the end of the 1980s, the poverty focus reappeared on the international agenda for development, partly due to pressure from organisations like UNICEF and UNDP, partly because numerous studies had documented the detrimental social implications of most of the structural adjustment programmes. Even the World Bank revisited its previous poverty programmes and came forward with clear formulations on the need for addressing poverty in a direct manner, rather than through macro-economic measures. The revised strategy proposed by the Bank comprised three main elements: (a) productive use of the poor's most abundant asset, that is labour, through the introduction of more labour-intensive technologies and other strategies for creating better opportunities for employment; (b) improved access to basic social services, including primary health care, family planning, nutrition and primary education; and (c) direct assistance to those worst off, who cannot be reached with the other programme elements (World Bank, 1990).

The focus on eradication of poverty in the international debate was further reinforced by the World Summit for Social Development held in Copenhagen in 1995. It is interesting that the programme of action adopted at this meeting made reference to both the economic and the political aspects of poverty. It stated that the eradication of poverty requires universal access to economic opportunities, which will promote sustainable livelihood and basic social services as well as special efforts to facilitate access to opportunities and services for the disadvantaged. But it further stressed that people living in poverty must be empowered through organisation and participation in all aspects of political, economic and social life – and, in particular, in the planning and implementation of policies that affect them. The document made explicit reference to the importance of involving the poor themselves in the elaboration of detailed strategies that should build on their own experiences, livelihood systems and survival strategies.

Several researchers have contributed to evolving more specific strategies for poverty eradication. We shall conclude the present section by briefly taking note of the ideas proposed by *Michael Lipton* and *Simon Maxwell*. Based to some extent on Lipton's earlier studies of the causes of poverty (cf. Chapter 10), they have emphasised three central elements in such a strategy.

The first is a commitment to labour-intensive production aimed at increasing the assets, employment and incomes of the poor. The main argument for this is that a realisation of the potential abilities and the potential entrepreneurship of the poor will often be the cheapest, fastest and most reliable path to growth. The second element consists of providing access to basic social services for as many poor people as possible, as a necessary precondition for releasing their potential. The third element is the creation of a safety net for the poor, including food security and social security in general, as a guard against setbacks and to give these people the security which is yet another precondition for releasing their creative potential (Lipton and Maxwell, 1992).

Although the World Bank, as indicated above, has in recent years incorporated important aspects of a poverty-focused approach, neither its analyses nor its policies and practices can be seen as representing alternative approaches to development. In this respect, the emphases and priorities recently proposed by UNDP come much closer to challenging mainstream thinking. The following section looks at some aspects of UNDP's approach to human development.

Social welfare and sustainable human development

With inspiration from earlier alternative theories within development economics, and under the leadership of the Pakistani-born economist *Mahbub ul Haq*, a group of scholars prepared for the UNDP the first comprehensive report on human development in 1990 (UNDP, 1990). They defined development as a process of enlarging people's choices in a much broader sense than proposed by mainstream economists (cf. Chapter 3). According to Haq, the defining difference between the economic growth and the human development schools is that the first focuses exclusively on the expansion of only one choice – income – while the second embraces the enlargement of all human choices – whether economic, social, cultural or political (Haq, 1995: Ch. 2).

It could be argued that an increase in income would enlarge all other choices as well. But this is exactly what Haq and others have questioned by asserting that the causal link between expanding income and expanding human choices depends on the quality and distribution of economic growth, not only on the quantity of such growth. They have argued that a link between income growth and human welfare has to be created consciously through public policies that aim at providing services and opportunities as equitably as possible to all citizens. This cannot be left to the market mechanisms, because these are essentially very unfriendly to the poor, to the weak, and to the vulnerable (Haq, 1995: Ch. 12).

Rejecting the automatic link, however, should not be taken to imply any rejection of the importance of economic growth, according to Haq. He very carefully tries to balance the argument by pointing, on the one hand, to the need for growth in poor societies to reduce mass poverty and, on the other, to the fact that the distribution of growth and the manner in which available resources are being utilised often matter more to the poor than aggregate growth of national income and production.

The human development school at first drew attention primarily to the choices in three essential areas: the opportunity to lead a long and healthy life; the opportunity to acquire knowledge; and the opportunity to have access to the resources needed for a decent standard of living. To these were later added several other dimensions and aspects, and the name of the concept itself was changed from 'human development' to 'sustainable human development' in order to highlight the importance of sustaining all forms of capital and resources – physical, human, financial and environmental – as a precondition for also meeting the needs of future generations.

The UNDP reports, which have been published annually since 1990, present accounts of human development in both developing countries and industrialised countries. These accounts are based on an index with three central components: (a) the average real income per capita, adjusted downwards for the rich countries by using the purchasing power of a country's currency (that is the number of units of a particular currency required to purchase the same representative basket of goods and services that a US dollar would buy in the USA); (b) the average life expectancy; and (c) adult literacy combined with real access to education at various levels (UNDP, 1995: pp. 134ff.).

The concept of human development has gradually been extended into basically all areas of societal development. To the original focus on the missing link between income and welfare has been added particular concern for the provision of social infrastructure and services that are made available on an equal basis to all citizens; special emphasis on gender equality; and equal opportunities for participation in political and economic decision making. The latter requires both an enabling legal and institutional framework, and empowerment of citizens and civil society organisations so that they become capable of reaching up to the authorities. Some of the adherents of the concept have furthermore put special emphasis on the environmental and natural resources aspects of sustainability.

As a reflection of the emphasis on gender, recent UNDP reports have included indicators for measuring gender equality. The 1995 report, in particular, focused on this issue (UNDP, 1995).

UNDP's work on human development contains some attempts at identifying causal relationships and obstacles to the enhancement of welfare and the enlargement of opportunities and choices on an equitable basis. Strategies for overcoming these obstacles are also discussed. In these respects, UNDP's studies may be regarded as contributing to theory formation concerning the preconditions for, and obstacles to, particular patterns of development. But beyond that, most of the studies undertaken or commissioned by the organisation are purely descriptive and normative, rather than explanatory. They are based on moral standards which are used as ideal-type models to describe the generally low levels of human development achieved throughout the Third World.

The same moral standards are applied as part of an appeal to governments in both recipient countries and donor countries to engage in new forms of development co-operation that are more conducive to promoting sustainable human development with particular emphasis on equality. Similar approaches dominate much of the literature on human development in general (for example *Journal of Development Planning*, 1989; Max-Neef, 1991; Haq, 1995).

These observations in no way imply a dissociation from the endeavours of placing human development at the top of the policy agenda, but they explain why, in the present context where the primary concern is with theory formation, the presentation and discussion is restricted to this broad outline of concepts and ideas.

Unobserved poverty: Chambers

The literature on poverty, basic needs and human development generally assumes that decision makers and those responsible for implementing poverty alleviation measures have a fair amount of knowledge about the problems involved. This has been challenged, however, very forcefully by *Robert Chambers*, who has come to the conclusion that efforts to counter poverty, particularly in rural areas, are undermined from the outset by a lack of perception as to the nature and scale of the problem on the part of those whose task it is to alleviate poverty (Chambers, 1983). According to Chambers, neither policy makers nor the professional staff have a proper understanding of rural poverty. With few exceptions all these people live in urban areas. Their direct rural experience is therefore limited to brief and hurried visits, which exhibit six major 'biases' against contact with and learning from poor people in the countryside.

The first bias is spatial – towards easily accessible areas close to towns and roads. Chambers's point here is that because the areas most frequently visited are easily accessible they are also less impoverished than the hinterland. The second is a bias towards places where there are projects and where initiatives have been successful. The third bias is towards individuals who are better off and healthy, men rather than women, users of services and adopters of practices rather than non-users and non-adopters. The fourth bias is seasonal: most visits take place during the dry season, when travel is relatively easy – and when poverty is less visible than during the wet period before the harvest. The fifth bias is what Chambers terms diplomatic, that is a bias against seeking out the poorest of the poor and against seeking out those who are chronically ill or physically or mentally handicapped. The sixth and final bias is professional, a tendency for development workers to focus narrowly on the concerns of their own specialisation, rather than trying to understand the holism of poverty.

As a result of these biases, rural poverty is 'underperceived'. Only the conditions of the less poor are properly understood. Those of the majority of poor people are little known and far less understood. Or to quote Chambers:

> The prosperity after harvest of a male farmer on a project beside a main road close to a capital city may colour the perceptions of a succession of officials and dignitaries. The plight of a poor widow starving and sick in the wet season in a remote and inaccessible area may never in any way impinge on the consciousness of anyone outside her own community. (Chambers, 1983: p. 24)

The further implication of the biases described is that most poverty eradication strategies are primarily directed towards the less poor. Chambers acknowledges that there are exceptions. There are government programmes, NGOs and research projects that seek out the poorest people in the poorest areas; but the overall tendency is to focus on the less poor. With this as his starting point, Chambers has done extensive research on what he calls 'integrated rural poverty' and worked out strategies on how to learn from the poor themselves and how to collaborate with them on more equal terms. It will take us beyond the scope of this book to review Chambers's analyses and recommendations, but it should be noted that he has made a very substantial contribution in this field.

A note on gender and development

It is a distinctive feature of most of the development research that focuses on poverty and social inequality that it also pays attention to the, often very dissimilar, implications of growth and development patterns on women and men. This applies, as mentioned above, to UNDP's analyses which in recent years have included more and more information on the gender-specific effects of both development courses and different strategies. The same applies, albeit to a lesser extent, to the analyses of the World Bank and to much independent research which can hardly be regarded as alternative or a counter-point to mainstream thinking. Thus, it appears that the endeavour of making women visible, initiated by gender researchers in the 1960s and 1970s, has been successful in the sense that the agenda for development is today strongly influenced by gender considerations.

This has not brought about, however, any basic changes in mainstream theory formation within social science development research, particularly not within economics. Gender research remains, therefore, outside and to some extent even opposed to mainstream thinking. Women have become more visible in the statistics, as have men. Women are often singled out as being a category that is affected in a particular manner by development policies, by structural adjustment programmes or by societal changes in a broader sense. But investigation into the life and work of women has not been widely accepted as a necessary and integrated part of social science research. Further, the priority now given by gender researchers to the structure and dynamics of gender relations, rather than just to women as a category, has not yet had any discernible impact upon mainstream development research. Similarly, the shift among gender researchers from studying women as recipient and passive clients to trying to understand their roles as active citizens has not been reflected in much of the mainstream theory formation. In all these respects, one has to search for substantive and elaborated contributions outside the dominant schools of thought.

A review of the rich and often empirically grounded literature on 'women in development' and 'gender and development' is beyond the scope of the present book. A proper coverage would require at least a couple of chapters (cf. Stølen and Vaa, 1991; Young, 1993). Instead, we shall limit ourselves to looking briefly at the different perspectives and changing emphases which have characterised analyses and theory formation concerning women and gender relations.

As mentioned in the introduction to this chapter, women's studies have changed focus over time in a manner similar to the changes in the perception of the poor. Initially, the emphasis was on making women visible, mainly as a passive category of clients that had to be assisted by others through special development efforts. This later changed to a perception of women as living, active human beings, who as producers and in other roles mostly take care of themselves without external support.

Using a distinction suggested by *Eva Rathgeber*, overall trends in research on women and gender could be described with reference to two main positions – Women in Development (WID) and Gender and Development (GAD) – where the first coincides with the approach adopted by many governments and international organisations (including the World Bank and UNDP), and the latter with recent elaborations and changes proposed by researchers (Rathgeber, 1990; Young, 1993: Ch. 8).

The WID approach focuses solely on women, and attributes the inferior status and social position of women chiefly to their exclusion from the spheres of the state and the corporate economy. Proponents of the WID approach were among the first to point to women's invisibility and to the lack of data on their conditions of living and activities. They argued that women in general were excluded from development processes and that they did not benefit from economic growth unless the whole process was shaped with a view to improving the conditions of women in particular. The core of the strategy for change implied a 'mainstreaming' of women – integration of women into the mainstream of economic, political and social life. They should be ensured greater access to services, a wide range of occupations and positions of power. Women should be treated on equal terms with men.

The WID approach has been criticised by *Kate Young* and other researchers belonging to the competing school of thought, the GAD school (Young, 1993). They have argued that by focusing exclusively on women, the WID analyses fail to understand how gender relations work, and how they impact upon women in civil society and within the household. They have further criticised the WID approach for giving far too much attention to the public spheres, the state and the corporate economy, and to equity strategies that aim too much at making women behave in the same ways as men.

The alternative GAD perspective that they have suggested is constructed around a set of key propositions, some of which are the following: that women are actually incorporated into the development process but in very different ways; that women are not a homogeneous category but are divided by class, colour and creed; that the totality of women's and men's lives

should be the focus of analyses, not merely their productive, or their repro-
ductive activities; and that women are not passive, nor marginal, but active
subjects of societal processes. The GAD approach implies less emphasis on
what could be termed static comparative analyses of gender inequalities, and
more emphasis on studying the structures and processes that give rise to
women's disadvantages. It implies analyses of culturally specific forms of
social inequalities and divisions, with a further view to understanding how
gender is related to, and interlocked with, other forms of inequality and
social hierarchies.

Proponents of the GAD approach often do acknowledge that the previous
focus on women as a social category and the accompanying impact studies
were probably necessary in the initial stages. But they argue, at the same
time, that a genuine understanding of the gender problematique depends on
holistic analyses of the social and cultural systems, where the gender identities
are created and reproduced, and where conflicts between men and women
are fought on different levels. With this broadening of the analytical perspective – and the corresponding conceptual framework elaborated by GAD
researchers – their approach ought to be taken much more seriously into
consideration by mainstream development researchers.

CHAPTER 22

The Political Economy of
Civil Society

Chapter 21 discussed approaches which have opposed or added to mainstream thinking by focusing on the social implications and human dimensions of macro-economic processes of change. The present chapter is concerned with a different type of alternative approach and theory, more preoccupied with the political economy of civil society itself. The perspective applied here has already been briefly introduced (cf. Chapter 20). Before coming to the theoretical propositions evolved within that perspective, it may be useful to look at the kind of criticism of macro-economic theory that is found in the literature on the political economy of civil society. This criticism often serves to justify the alternative focus (Friedmann, 1992).

Some of the critical points raised by proponents of a civil society approach resemble criticism that has been formulated earlier by economists who otherwise adhere to one of the schools of thought discussed in other parts of this book. This is the case with respect to two principal points. First, national income accounts do not reveal how income is distributed either socially or territorially. As a result, they do not indicate how aggregate growth affects different groups of people or different regions in a country. Because of the focus on these aggregate figures and the information they provide on macro-economic performance and balances or imbalances, the theories using them as central inputs tend to treat countries as far more homogeneous and economically integrated than in reality they are.

Second, conventional measures of economic growth are often misleading and do not present an accurate picture of the total production of a society. Specifically, three major types of productive activities are not accurately reflected in national accounts statistics, that is subsistence activities in agriculture, forestry and fisheries; activities in the so-called informal sector, including some illegal activities; and household production activities. It can also be added that conventional measures of national income do not count the costs of environmental destruction or the consumption of non-renewable natural resources or non-durable sources of energy.

These and some other points of criticism formulated by proponents of an alternative development do not, strictly speaking, represent a break with the analyses and debates within mainstream development economics, where several efforts have been made to incorporate distributive dimensions, informal economic activities and environmental aspects in particular into theory construction – although these efforts cannot be said to have advanced very far. Where the alternative approaches do break more radically with mainstream thinking is in defining the household not merely as a unit of consumption, but also as an important unit of production (Friedmann, 1992: Ch. 3). Even this proposition, however, has to some extent been encompassed by development economics, particularly in theories concerning agriculture and natural resource management (cf. Chapters 10 and 11).

In relation to mainstream political science theory formation it is even more difficult to identify clear lines of demarcation, partly because the conceptual frameworks here are less stringent than those of development economics, but also because political scientists have generally paid more attention than economists to informal activities and civil society. An important difference may be noted, however, in the sense that the alternative approaches, in contrast to mainstream political science studies, do not use the state, the formal political processes, or the macro-political power struggles between classes or nationally organised interest groups as their starting point. Their point of departure is, instead, the autonomous organisation of citizens, and their focus is on the local community. They try to bring out sharply the human actors, their self-perceptions, and the cultural and social forms and practices which provide the framework for group formation, organisation and collective action (Frederiksen, 1990).

In the following sections, we shall look at selected fragments of theory concerning civil society institutions and processes. No attempt is made to cover the whole range of available theories. Rather, the focus is on a few contributions that we believe can complement the picture of Third World societies painted by the theories presented in the other parts of the present book. An important implication of this selectivity is that the comprehensive and rich body of theory in social anthropology about the social institutions of civil society, including the household, is essentially left out of consideration – but with an added recommendation that the present account be supplemented with such types of studies (cf. for example, Joekes and Kabeer, 1991).

Households and the whole-economy model: Friedmann

Some of the theorists who have contributed to working out conceptual frameworks and theories which can supplement development economics approaches are *Karl Polanyi* (Polanyi, 1977) and *John Friedmann* (Friedmann, 1992). Common to them is the basic contention that economic relations and economic activity are deeply embedded in the matrix of social and cultural relations. They further assume that the specific character of these societal

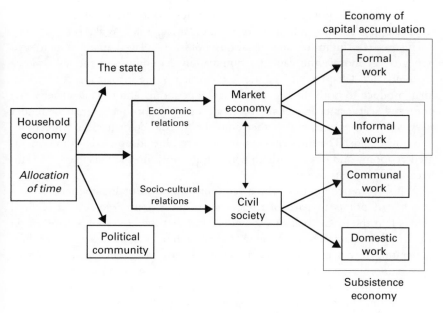

Figure 22.1 The whole-economy model
Source: Friedmann, 1992: p. 50 (simplified)

relations are more important determinants of human behaviour than the incentive structures proposed by mainstream economists, that is utility and profit maximisation.

In order to understand economic processes, therefore, it is necessary to probe into the socio-cultural institutions of civil society, the most important of which is the household. Both Polanyi and Friedmann regard the household as the basic organising unit of civil society, through which the individual relates to society, and through which non-market and market relations are articulated. The household performs these essential functions by, as Friedmann puts it, continuously solving the problem of allocating the time of its individual members to different tasks, spheres of life, and domains of social practice (cf. Figure 20.1, p. 292). Time is perceived in this context as the basic resource of the household in relation to material and social reproduction.

Households are, in the real world, not free to choose how to allocate time. They are constrained by the necessities of producing a livelihood for their members. This puts poor households in a very different position from that of rich households. The latter can choose from a wide range of options and allocate considerable time to its members to engage in market-economic activities and in politics and the sphere of the state. In contrast, the poor households have to concentrate on productive work, which in their case mainly means household work and informal economic activity outside the market economy. Figure 22.1 provides an outline of the model Friedmann uses to place the households in what he refers to as the whole economy in a developing country (cf. also Guyer and Peters, 1987; Wilk, 1989).

Figure 22.1 indicates how the households are placed in relation to two types of economy: the capital accumulation economy and the subsistence economy (cf. Chapter 8). The area of overlap is the informal sector, which may produce to both the organised market economy and to civil society. The informal sector is characterised by small units that produce, repair or render services to other sectors, to other units within the sector itself, or directly to the households. The lines of demarcation are blurred upwards to the organised economy and downwards to community work (in the village or the slum area) and domestic work.

With reference to this whole-economy model, Friedmann underlines a number of points of particular relevance to poor households. A very central one is that the model helps us to understand that the households' production of livelihood implies a merging of economic activities and other life-generating forces and activities. It helps to show that considerable parts of the economic activities are not geared to limitless accumulation, but to creating a livelihood for the producers and their households. This is done both within the households themselves and by allocation of a part of the time of the members to community work and other informal work outside the household.

From this it follows that consumption as an activity cannot meaningfully be separated from production, as in neo-classical economics. Rather, consumption is merged with, and largely indistinguishable from other household activities. As producers of their own life and livelihood, households are viewed as proactive and capable of pursuing their own interests, again unlike in neo-classical economics where their role consists primarily of consumption and biological reproduction of labour.

These propositions resemble the actor conceptions and theories found in much of the more recent literature on both women and poor peasants (and slum dwellers), who are attributed with abilities and capacities to process social experiences and exploit the opportunities available as part of their survival strategies. Poor and resource-weak households may not always succeed, of course, in achieving a decent level of living, but the point is that they are generally capable of making the best possible out of the situation they live in.

This should be the starting point from which research is then conducted into external constraints and factors that limit the freedom of action of the poor (cf. Chapter 21; Stølen and Vaa, 1991; Jazairy et al., 1992: Ch. 2). The implied recognition of the space for action, even poor people's action, corresponds essentially to the perspectives proposed earlier in abstract social science theories by authors like Pierre Bourdieu and Anthony Giddens. The latter, in particular, insisted that although poor men and women were not free to make their lives as they would wish, they would in most cases be able autonomously to shape the conditions in which they found themselves (Giddens, 1977).

As actors, households form locally limited units that enter into wider spheres of activity, often through social networks where interactions are based on mutual trust, reciprocal exchange and social obligations – altogether different from the forms of interaction in the market economy. Friedmann emphasises that it is often the women who play the dominant roles in these interactions.

The model of the whole economy provides a framework for an alternative development theory with emphasis on the interdependencies which exist between the rationality of economic reasoning and the moral relations embedded in kinship, friendship and neighbourhood. It provides a framework for studying and understanding how households interact with each other as well as with the corporate economy and the sphere of the state. As such, the model may be used to view some of the mainstream theories as relevant but confined in their analytical perspective to only selected aspects of the totality of societal structures and relations.

The informal sector and jobless growth

The informal sector referred to above has been incorporated not only into theories of civil society and its institutions; specific attention has also been given to the informal sector in more conventional, but at the same time pioneering analyses. As in the case of the basic needs approach, ILO played a prominent role in this connection by showing, on the basis of empirical investigations, how growth in the organised economy contributed very little to absorbing the rapidly growing workforce in many developing countries (ILO, 1972, 1976).

Mainstream approaches within development research have indeed paid some attention to the informal sector but, until the 1970s, mainly as a sector and a segment of society that was bound progressively to disappear as a result of economic growth and structural transformation. The various modernisation theories perceived the informal sector as part of the traditional society which should be developed and replaced by modern institutions and practices. The Neo-Marxist approaches perceived it basically in a similar way, based on the expectation that the sector, in the course of time, would become integrated into capitalist production and the market economy.

As it gradually became evident that these expectations were not fulfilled in the vast majority of developing countries – on the contrary, they experienced greater growth in informal employment than in formal – interest grew in reaching an understanding of this process. In connection with this, interest also grew in investigating the salient features of the informal sector and its own dynamics. This increased interest in the informal sector has primarily manifested itself in the form of a large number of empirical and largely descriptive studies. But various theories have also been proposed that attempt to explain why the sector has continued to grow in many countries in Asia and Africa. One of these explanations simply points to the fact that the labour force in the countries concerned has grown much more rapidly than the number of jobs in the organised economy and the public sector. An increasing number of people have therefore been forced into seeking their livelihood in the informal sector, which has thus become an important target for their survival strategies.

It may be added that these strategies have often been combined with other measures when households in Asian and African societies have tried to secure for themselves a decent standard of living. Permanent salaried employment has been the most important source of income for only a minority of families. Combinations of subsistence production, petty commodity production, small-scale trading, services, and other forms of unregistered, informal activities have become more important sources of income for a fast growing number of households (Kongstad and Mønsted, 1980).

Other types of explanation have paid more attention to the economic functions of the informal sector in relation to the formal economy. The so-called network theories point out, in this connection, the interdependent relationships between the large companies, on the one hand, and networks of small-scale producers of commodities and services, on the other. The productivity and low costs of the large companies often depend on the possibilities of getting supplies from producers and service providers in the informal sector.

In 1993, UNDP took up the problems concerning the informal sector, partly on the basis of studies earlier commissioned by the ILO, partly on the basis of independent research undertaken on the subject of employment and unemployment. UNDP pointed out that the growth rate of employment, after around 1960, had consistently lagged behind that of output. This applied to OECD countries, where output increases had in some cases even been accompanied by falls in employment. And it applied to the developing countries as whole, where the growth in employment during the period from 1960 to 1987 was less than half the aggregate economic growth rates (UNDP, 1993: Ch. 3). These trends revealed what the organisation and many researchers have characterised as *jobless growth* – as growth that did not generate employment.

The authors of the UNDP report on human development noted four main reasons for this discrepancy between growth of production and employment growth. First, the stagnating population growth in the OECD countries had prompted the enterprises there to develop more labour-saving technologies, which were subsequently transferred to the developing countries through the transnational corporations. Second, this tendency was strengthened by the increased costs of labour in the highly industrialised countries. Third, military research and development, which has generally been extremely capital intensive, had reinforced the trend. Fourth, the increased capital- and technology-intensity of production has been supported by the existing and very unequal income distribution, where around 20 per cent of the world's population have enough purchasing power to secure for themselves over 80 per cent of the total production.

Because of the magnitude of jobless growth, a considerable and increasing number of people have been forced to search for their livelihood outside the formal economy of accumulation. Evidently, those employed in the organised economy have been able, by means of their comparatively high incomes, to contribute to the maintenance of other members of their households, but it is equally clear that these contributions have not been sufficient to cope with population growth in most poor countries. Therefore, the burden on the informal sector – and on the household economy – of providing a livelihood for millions of people has continuously increased.

Taking note of these facts, *Paul Streeten* has argued for giving much more attention to job creation, including self-employment, in the small-scale and informal sectors (Streeten, 1994). In addition to being an important source of income for many poor people, these sectors embody a considerable potential for contributing to the total production of many societies. In order to work out more specific strategies, however, much more knowledge about the various parts of the small-scale and informal sectors is required.

According to Streeten, the informal sector comprises at least four distinct groups in terms of employment conditions: (a) the self-employed, who sometimes use the unpaid labour of members of their families; (b) the casual workers, hired on a day-to-day basis; (c) the workers employed on a regular basis by small-scale firms which are not regulated or taxed by the authorities; and (d) the 'outworkers', those who work in their homes under a putting-out system. To achieve an intended impact it will be necessary to adapt specific job-creation strategies to these various forms and conditions of employment.

Streeten makes the interesting observation that the activities in parts of the informal sector are anti-cyclical, that is growing with a decline in aggregate demand, and declining with its growth. This phenomenon is to some extent related to the largely supply-driven employment of the informal sector. It absorbs fairly easily additional entrants, whereas in the formal, private sector employment is chiefly demand-driven. Therefore, when aggregate demand declines, formal employment tends to follow suit. This need not be the case with informal employment which often actually increases during recessions, thus providing a safety net for many poor people. The 'informalised' workers may not continue to receive incomes at the same levels as before, but at least they have access to resources – and may avoid the sense of worthlessness and alienation which frequently overcomes the unemployed.

The strategies proposed by Streeten simultaneously to exploit the anti-cyclical features of the informal sector and its potential for contributing to overall growth centre around the possible complementarities between small-scale enterprises and large-scale firms. With reference to the successful combination of the two in the case of Japan, Streeten argues in favour of adopting a similar approach in many poor countries, but in such a manner that specific conditions and opportunities are taken into account. A blueprint for developing the informal sector is not available.

Citizen resistance: Bailey and Scott

Friedmann in the study earlier referred to (Friedmann, 1992) emphasises the autonomy of civil society institutions, and the freedom of people to act, including their opportunities for producing, co-operating and engaging in collective action without any outside help. Not least in his many exemplifying descriptions of social movements in Latin America is this emphasis identifiable. Nevertheless, Friedmann's contribution to theory formation is primarily an effort to relate the political economy of the households, and the local community, to the organised economy and the state. This can be seen as a strength in relation to mainstream development research, because in this manner he enters into a fruitful dialogue with the predominant theories and analytical approaches. But at the same time, Friedmann plays down some of the features which are otherwise among the distinguishing characteristics of alternative development thinking (as well as of many anthropological approaches), especially their strong emphasis on the local communities' own history and *resistance* against the rulers who dominate at the macro-level.

An early example of studies with this emphasis was *F. G. Bailey*'s work on Orissa in India from 1963, where he described how the peasants in the villages tended to react with animosity towards and resistance against people coming from outside, whether police officers, politicians, development workers or trade unionists. Regardless of their promises, they were all seen by the peasants as people one should avoid getting too much involved with, because they could not be trusted. It was better to stick to the local patrons whom the peasants knew – even though these patrons suppressed and exploited them (Bailey, 1963).

Since Bailey made these observations, a whole body of literature has appeared about the resistance forms adopted by peasants, but also more generally about the resistance forms among social groups in civil society. *James Scott*'s study from 1985, *Weapons of the Weak: Everyday Forms of Peasant Resistance*, deserves a special mention in this context. The study describes how poor people in a Malaysian village perceive, and act within, the wider societal framework within which they live. Scott makes a distinction between three levels: the first level where the macro-economic and political processes for the peasants are given but distant and only vaguely recognised frameworks for their daily lives. The second level comprises the directly perceived interventions from the surrounding society, including government interventions.

The third level consists of local events and conditions in the individual villages as they are perceived and experienced directly by the peasants.

Scott portrays the villagers' daily lives and their 'own' history, and shows how they resist interventions from the state and the actors of the corporate economy. The forms of resistance are, as Scott emphasises, low-profile techniques, partly hidden from others and characterised by 'foot-dragging evasions' and passivity, rather than open rejection or struggle (Scott, 1985; cf. also Scott, 1990). But these forms of resistance are none the less effective means for households and local communities who, for one reason or another, do not want to adopt centrally decided norms and priorities in their daily lives; who do not want to be further integrated into the society of the rulers; or – as in Scott's study – do not want to be incorporated into capitalist production patterns and class relations.

The general propositions that may be extracted from Scott's and similar studies are necessarily of a different nature from those arrived at in macro-economic and macro-political research. Because of the focus on individual villages and their unique features, and because of the extent to which the researchers' subjective perceptions and interpretations shape the analyses and conclusions, the outcome is rarely a theory with general propositions that can be tested in other settings. Rather, these local-level studies of village life and forms of resistance, in addition to revealing specific relations and patterns of behaviour, generate a certain perspective and methodological principles. These, in turn, may be very valuable additions to macro-oriented studies.

There is no doubt that the understanding of the development dynamics in a specific society will be considerably enhanced if macro-level studies of structures and institutions are combined with investigations of the daily life of real people and of the motives and constraints which shape their behaviour. This observation is also relevant for the considerations on politics as discourse, which we shall look at in the next section.

Politics as discourse

It is significant that most theories concerning politics and political development in the Third World build on concepts and modes of reasoning which have been taken from the mainstream political science of the West. This undoubtedly entails a danger of misinterpretations and inadequate explanations, because political life in different societies is lived and experienced according to particular traditions and forms of understanding. Politics and political behaviour are so closely related to specific conditions that a deeper understanding demands detailed insight, not merely into the dominant mode of perceiving and thinking in a society, but also into the several individual local communities' and the individual socio-cultural groups' own frames of understanding and the manner in which they attach meaning to political behaviour.

This is part of what the so-called discourse analysis seeks to capture. We shall end this chapter with a few observations on this approach.

It should be noted from the outset that discourse analysis constitutes a method and an approach to the study of politics, rather than a coherent theory. Proponents of discourse analyses are sceptical about the possibility of working out a general theory of political conditions and political development in different societies. The observations below, accordingly, confine themselves to a few methodological points which, in turn, may indicate some limitations of mainstream political science approaches.

Discourse means language use which is rule-bound and expresses coherent forms of knowledge. *Michel Foucault*'s ground-breaking studies from the 1960s and the 1970s on the interrelation between knowledge and power in social institutions, such as prisons and mental hospitals, shifted attention from the linguistic sign to the interlinkages between that to which the sign refers and the linguistic expression (Foucault, 1980). A certain language usage constitutes authority in itself and exercises power. The privileging and 'naturalisation' of certain linguistic, legal, social and scientific discourses is a normative process which excludes what is seen to be deviant. From this perspective, different language uses and discursive knowledge systems in themselves structure the distribution of power in a society and the access of different social groups to that power.

When the term discourse is applied in relation to politics, it may be seen as a further elaboration and refinement of the concept of ideology, and as a radical critique of that concept's notion of 'false consciousness'. Different discourses are linked to the possibility of possessing and exercising power, and are neither false nor true.

In a social sciences perspective, discourse analysis is a tool to gain greater insight into the political culture of a society or a particular social grouping. The analysis will look for discourses or discursive practices in social institutions, and traces of institutional forms and social practices in discourses. Its raw materials are texts in the broad sense or, to put it differently, sign systems. Discourse analysis may capture historically conditioned mentalities of importance to the political identity and mode of action of particular social groups. These groups may be defined by nation, ethnicity or religion; they may be constituted on the basis of gender or class.

Discourses may also be a part of a wider system of thought that sets the basic conditions for access to and construction of knowledge – the conditions for achieving understanding of reality. An example is *Edward Said*'s influential work from 1978 on orientalism, in which he analysed how the Western conception and construction of the 'Orient' came to impact upon science, art and culture in India and the Middle East (Said, 1978).

Discourses are always composite, and discourse analysis is a carefully argued interpretation rather than an exhaustive, verifiable characterisation. When discourse analysis is used in the social sciences, the substantiation of the conclusions arrived at rests on an account of the complex and often vaguely articulated relationship between the discourse, or the system of signs, and the social conditions to which it refers.

Politics of identity and politicisation of identity are fields of great importance in many areas of the Third World, as well as in the former Communist countries and parts of Western Europe. Discourse analysis may be useful in this context, because it can capture the linguistic articulation of ethnic and other identities which is a central precondition for their politicisation (cf. Hansen, 1991). The analysis seeks to unravel relations between power and powerlessness, forms of understanding and linguistic articulation, that is phenomena which are seen to precede social mobilisation and the emergence of organisations and institutions.

Research into politics as discursive practices occurs in the border zone between the humanities and the social sciences, and may contribute to new theoretical insights in the area of identity politics. The next chapter looks into identity formation and politicisation partly from this perspective, partly from other perspectives elaborated within political science.

CHAPTER 23

Ethnic Identities, Nationality and Conflict

Civil society interacts with the state and the corporate economy in many ways. Some of these modes of interaction have to do with the citizens' perceptions of where they belong. In this respect, most countries in the Third World are quite complex and very different from the highly industrialised societies. Even though in Western Europe and other OECD countries some struggles do occur over the demarcation of the political community and the state's territory – for example Basque separatism in Spain – it is a fundamental characteristic of these countries that there is a high degree of congruence between state and nation. Furthermore, in the case of the European nation-states, nationalist ideologies historically became popular before the formation of the states within well-defined borders. Thus, the spreading of nationalist ideologies, and the perceptions of political and cultural affiliations and community preceded the formation of the state. The population in each of the nation-states sensed some kind of common identity and a common sense of belonging, prior to the formation of territorially defined states.

The course of development in most of the Third World has been very different from this pattern. Here, the sequencing has often been the reverse: the formation of states prior to the consolidation of nations. An important part of this process took place in the colonial era, when external powers established themselves as states within territories that were rarely demarcated either in accordance with objective attributes of the populations (such as, for example, language), or in accordance with the inhabitants' perceptions of affiliation and community. It was therefore a central task both for these states and for the growing nationalist movements that wanted to take over from the colonial rulers, to create nations which were congruent with the territorially united populations. Most post-colonial states in reality faced the same task – and still do. *John Saul* has described the principal task of the post-colonial states, notably in Africa, as one of creating the national foundations for themselves (Saul, 1974). Theories of political development often refer to this endeavour as 'nation building'.

The main point is that, in many cases, what emerged in the Third World were *state-nations*, rather than nation-states. Similarly, the kind of ideology that came to dominate in many countries could be referred to as *state nationalism*, rather than popular nationalism with a strong foundation in civil society and the political community (Stavenhagen, 1990; cf. also Figure 20.1). The lack of initial congruence between states and nations in many Third World countries has placed a considerable burden on their political systems and has often negatively impacted upon economic and social development, chiefly by diverting resources from development efforts to conflicts between states and their people, or to border disputes between states (cf. Chapter 19).

The basic relationship between society and state, however, varies considerably from one country to another. At least four different categories can be identified. One category consists of countries such as Singapore and Thailand, where there is a high degree of congruence between nation and state, and where the legitimacy of the state is solidly grounded in the perceptions of the majority of the population as belonging to exactly the political community which is governed by the concerned state.

A second category comprises countries where large parts of the population perceive the state as a distant and alien institution. This applies to many African countries, where large numbers of peasants in subsistence agriculture regard themselves only to a very limited extent as citizens belonging to a larger political community, and for whom the local community or smaller ethnic groupings make up a far more important frame of reference for their identity.

A third category consists of countries, mainly in South and South-East Asia, where large ethnic communities co-exist within the same state territory, but without having strong feelings about belonging to the same nation. Finally, in contrast to such multi-ethnic societies a fourth category encompasses the Arab countries, where the nation-state relationship is more or less the reverse, in the sense that here the states have demarcated territories which unite only smaller parts of what many see as the Arab nation.

This chapter looks at different theoretical conceptions of nationality and ethnic identity, and how they are formed and achieve political and economic significance. The first section introduces some of the basic notions about nationalism and ethnic identities. Then follows a brief outline of selected theories concerning the fundamental characteristics of such collective identities and their origin. The third section discusses, in general terms, why and how ethnic identities are politicised, while the fourth section provides an illustration of this process with examples taken from India. The chapter is concluded with a few observations on the impact of ethnicity upon the formulation and implementation of development strategies.

Nationalism and ethnic identities

The terms 'nation', 'nationalism' and 'nationality' are used in the literature with very varied meanings. Many of the conceptions may be covered by defining *nationalism* as a collective and widespread feeling of identification and solidarity with a certain limited group of people – a nation. Nationality then refers to this perceived affiliation. Nationalism may be predominantly positive, but will often be accompanied by a negative perception of dissimilarity in relation to, and possibly hostility towards, one or more outgroups, that is it may be turned against other nations.

As mentioned above, several states in the Third World were established with territories that comprised either a multitude of nations or only a part of a nation in terms of the definition of the word adopted here. In both cases, the legitimacy of the states was weakened, because they were not regarded as indisputable representatives of particular nations.

Christopher Clapham has argued that, due to the lack of congruence between nation and state, a distinguishing feature of the post-colonial states just after independence was a combination of power and fragility (Clapham, 1985: Ch. 3). They were powerful on account of their well-organised civil and military bureaucracies, which they took over from the colonial rulers. But they were at the same time fragile, because these bureaucracies had to exercise their power in societies which were not integrated political communities. It was therefore of great importance for these bureaucracies and the new political rulers to initiate an integration process – a nation-building process.

This national consolidation and integration process can be seen as an extension of the state-building efforts discussed elsewhere in the book (cf. Chapter 12). State building aims at securing territorial integrity, if necessary by force. This also implies achieving international recognition as a sovereign state. Further, state building aims at creating institutional capacity within the state apparatuses to handle both political and economic development tasks. In comparison, the main purpose of nation building is to integrate the population of a certain territory into a cohesive unit. National consolidation and integration imply the creation of community and collective solidarity in the population – the creation of a national feeling sufficiently widespread and sufficiently strong to unite the vast majority of the population within the same political community.

This nation-building project has not succeeded in all the countries of the Third World, especially not in large parts of Africa or in South and South-East Asia. In many countries, large population groups do not recognise the political community which has been forced upon them by the state. This applies, for example, to the Tamils in Sri Lanka and the Sikhs in the Punjab, India. Other population groups do recognise the sovereignty and legitimacy of the state, but at the same time perceive themselves as disfavoured minorities or even as suppressed people. Examples are the Sindhis in Pakistan and the tribal peoples in the Chittagong Hill Tracts in Bangladesh.

Many of the Sri Lankan Tamils, and some of the Sikhs in the Punjab, demand full independence and the establishment of their own state, corresponding to what they perceive as their nation. Others have more limited demands about political equality and a larger share in economic benefits and privileges. These differences are reflected in theory formation as a plurality of concepts which try to capture different population groups' dissimilar relations to the state and the territorially constructed community. Some theorists, in this connection, apply a distinction between nationalities and ethnic groups. Nationalities are then often defined by their demands for a separate state, while ethnic groups are defined as those that limit their demands to improvements and rearrangements within an existing state.

Other theorists, while essentially making a similar distinction, have tried to introduce a dynamic perspective by conceptualising ethnicity and nationality as part of an open and complex process of identity formation. The conceptualisation proposed by *Paul Brass* appears particularly interesting here (Brass, 1991: Chs 1–2). Brass distinguishes between *ethnic groups* or categories, *ethnic communities* and *nationalities*.

Ethnic groups are categories of people with common, objective characteristics such as language or religion. The population of any society may, in principle, be divided into such categories, although linguistic and other cultural distinctions may overlap and blur the boundaries. When an ethnic group starts to organise and act collectively against other groups or against the state, Brass refers to this process as *ethnic transformation*, the result of which may be the creation of an ethnic community – that is a clearly identifiable group with a common ideology based on a multiplicity of symbols and attributes which have been brought into congruence with each other. An ethnic community that additionally demands political autonomy or, at the extreme, its own separate state, according to Brass, has evolved into a nationality.

Using this conceptual framework, Brass has worked out a theory concerning the conditions under which ethnic groups undergo the processes of transformation leading to subjective self-consciousness as ethnic communities and political significance as nationalities. Before taking a look at this theory, the following section reviews briefly the very different conceptions of ethnicity and nationalism found in the literature.

Origins of collective identities and nationalism

The literature on identity formation contains many different conceptions and definitions of ethnicity and nationalism, but the discussion can be centred around two fundamentally different positions. These may subsequently be subjected to further refinement.

According to the first position, ethnic and national identities are constituted by common objective characteristics, such as language, race and religion. These identities are in a sense pre-existing – based on some kind of primordial identification and loyalty. This conception of identity formation is to some extent associated with the normative view that the unity of people with shared characteristics, and their separation from other people with different characteristics, are 'natural' phenomena that should be accepted as facts of life.

Proponents of these views include scholars like *Clifford Geertz* (Geertz, 1963). The views have also influenced the scholars who, during the 1990s, have proposed development strategies under the heading of 'ethnodevelopment' – that is strategies which take into account the fact that, in many Third World countries, the 'people' consist neither of individuals nor of nations, but of ethnic categories in Brass's terminology (cf. Hettne, 1990: Ch. 5).

To the extent that ethnic and national identities become politically significant or begin to impact upon the economic processes they can, from this main point of view, be seen as manifestations of and interventions from the structures and institutions of civil society.

In contrast to this approach, researchers such as *Ernest Gellner* (Gellner, 1983), *Hobsbawm* (Hobsbawm, 1991), *Brass* and, in Scandinavia, *Blom Hansen* (Hansen, 1996) represent the second fundamental position. They see ethnicity and nationality as phenomena which are socially and ideologically constructed, and perhaps even politically manipulated by elites fighting for control over resources and privileges.

According to this conception, language, religion and territorial affinity only acquire their special importance if and when they are used as a basis for awareness creation and social mobilisation. Collective identities are, in other words, what people make of them. They are in no way pre-given, primordial identities; on the contrary they are feelings of community and solidarity which have evolved in social processes and are therefore context-dependent. Expressed differently, collective identities like ethnicity and nationalism are ideological constructions of the relationships between the state, civil society and individual actors. Hobsbawm, in this connection, stresses that ethnic and national communities typically base their unity on creative history writing, which contains a good deal of inventions and imaginings with added notions of common cultural inheritance, common heroes, common norms and customs, and so on.

This second position is associated with the basic normative idea that ethnicity and nationalism are – if not downright 'unnatural', then at least something that should be explained and justified in a different context.

Turning to the nuances in the various conceptions, it is possible to identify a whole range of propositions regarding the significance of the so-called objective characteristics. These propositions have been formulated in response to questions like: Why are notions of ethnicity and nationality so important for people? What kinds of dynamics are involved when ethnicity and nationality are socially and culturally constructed and the objective characteristics turned into perceived and experienced primordial attachments among large numbers of people?

By applying an approach along these lines, the Norwegian anthropologist

Frederik Barth, in a now classic analysis of ethnic lines of division, has tried to amalgamate the two basic positions referred to above (Barth, 1969). He argued that ethnic identity is not pre-given, but chosen, voluntary and constructed, invented and imagined. However, at a later stage, ethnic identity may be perceived as given, absolute and fixed by people with certain common characteristics (Lindholm, 1993). In a long-term perspective it may be of interest to investigate when, how, by whom, and under what conditions existing ethnic communities were constructed. But in a contemporary per-spective, the central questions are how ethnic boundaries of a particular community are maintained and how people organise themselves and interact with other ethnic groups and the state.

As implied above, it follows from the first main position that ethnic communities and nationalities have an indisputable right to be recognised as autonomous entities with an associated right to decide on their own develop-ment priorities. The second position, on the other hand, does not endow a priori any ethnic category with special status or rights of any kind. Brass extends this position a step further by arguing that ethnic communities and nationalities should be perceived mainly as political movements created by elites who, through the manipulation of symbols, have tried to muster as much support as possible for their own narrow interests. This brings us to his theory of the politicisation of ethnic identities.

Politicisation of ethnic identities: Brass

Brass's theory about the formation, persistence and transformation of ethnic identities and nationalities focuses on competing elites from different ethnic categories and their struggles for control over new opportunities in the modern segments of developing societies (Brass, 1991). Brass, like most other political scientists, assumes that elites will always seek to maximise their share of power and control over resources in a society. He then argues that mobilisation of support for elite claims on the basis of ethnic and national identities have proven to be one of the most effective means for achieving these goals.

In his analyses of India, which he uses as his main case for elaborating the more general theoretical propositions, Brass starts by identifying the origins and differentiation of elites as a consequence of the economic and political modernisation processes. The second step is to find out how the competing elites go about building support for their claims. He notes that an important tool in this connection is symbol-manipulation aimed at con-structing ethnic communities around each of the elites. The point is that the many potential ethnic communities – the ethnic categories – in India and several other developing countries only become politicised and start acting as separate entities if and when an elite perceive a self-interest in appealing for support on the basis of ethnic characteristics.

Based on his studies, Brass concludes that elite competition, however, only constitutes a necessary precondition for the symbol-manipulation that is involved in communal mobilisation, not a sufficient precondition. At least three other preconditions need to be present before elite competition and symbol-manipulation can result in successful communal mobilisation and ethnic transformation from category to community. The first precondition is the existence of the means to communicate the selected symbols of identity to other social classes within the ethnic groups concerned. The means necessary to promote such inter-class communication include the availability of mass media, standardisation of the local language, and the existence of books in the local language. The second precondition is the existence of a socially mobilised population to whom the symbols may be communicated. The third precondition is the absence of intense class cleavages within the ethnic groups which might prevent the elites from building multi-class support.

Brass further argues that the second phase in ethnic transformation – the transformation of ethnic communities into nationalities – will only take place if the demands of a particular movement go beyond the narrow interests of the elites and are articulated on behalf of the community as a whole. A second important precondition at this stage is that a certain organisation succeeds in achieving a special status and can claim to represent the entire ethnic community, internally *vis-à-vis* community members and externally *vis-à-vis* other communities and the state. Brass strongly emphasises that nationalism manifests itself as a result of contradictions and conflicts of interest, and not merely as a positive feeling of solidarity with an in-group.

There is no doubt that Brass has drawn attention to important aspects of identity formation and politicisation of ethnicity by emphasising the role of elite competition. Many examples may be cited of elites and their organised representatives having played vital and decisive roles in the politicisation of ethnicity. On the other hand, it may be appropriate to see the process as more dialectic – as a process where elites, so to speak, try to mobilise around certain socio-cultural characteristics, but where the citizens also have certain choices. Identity formation may be considered as a multiplicity of processes leading to different competing identities, rather than a linear process resulting – or not resulting – in the formation of a particular ethnic community and its transformation to a nationalist movement (cf. Jha, 1989). One of these identities may prevail under certain conditions, while other identities may prevail under different conditions. One can thus very well imagine that Muslim and Hindu workers join hands on a Monday in pursuit of higher wages and better working conditions and, yet, on a Friday fight each other over religious issues. In this sense, there is a 'choice', a situational and context-dependent choice, of political identities.

Consequently, identity formation is not only constructed from above. It is not only dependent on the appeal of the elites and the efficiency with which they manipulate the symbols, although Brass may be correct in pointing to the special importance of elite manipulation in determining which ethnic groups come to assert themselves as political communities and nationalities. But the potential followers' perceptions of their situation and the options available to them are likely to have a strong impact on the outcome as well. In this connection a simple hypothesis could be proposed to the effect that elite-manipulation will be more effective and successful in relation to people who themselves experience competition and conflict with other people belonging to different ethnic categories. The combination of these perspectives may be illustrated with a case from India: the Sikh separatist movement.

Politicisation of the Sikh community:
an illustration

The emergence of a separatist movement among the Sikhs in the Punjab in India can be used to illustrate politicisation of an ethnic identity, in a process characterised by both elite action and the presence of particularly favourable conditions for mass mobilisation.

The Sikhs have for more than four centuries constituted a separate religious community with their own rituals, their own religious teachings and their own social norms. For a brief period from the end of the eighteenth century and up till 1849, the Sikhs ruled in their own empire under Maharaja Ranjit Singh, and thus appeared as a separate nation. But otherwise the Sikhs, until the 1880s, have been perceived as merely a distinctive minority with its own interpretation of Hinduism.

It was only after the growth of strong Hindu renaissance movements, which aimed at purifying the religious community and getting rid of all 'alien' elements, that the Sikhs reacted with similar efforts. Since then, the Sikhs' feeling of mutual solidarity and their perception of being different from other religious communities have been emphasised and strengthened in different ways. Rituals and customs have been taken more seriously and ascribed higher importance. In addition, after the First World War, more attention was given to Sikh shrines, the so-called *gurudwaras* (temples). One particular movement demanded that these temples should be ruled by the Sikhs themselves and not by either the authorities or the priests, who until then had controlled the shrines through inheritance. After several years of struggle, the British colonial power recognised the Sikhs' right to full control over the temples and, in 1925, a special committee of Sikhs was established to exercise this control. All adult Sikhs have since been able to participate in the election of the members of this committee. Together with the high-priests, the committee came to function as a uniting organisational framework which held the Sikhs together as a religious community.

The events accompanying the division of British India into the two independent states, India and Pakistan, strengthened the cohesiveness of the

Sikh community and their sense of being different from other religious communities, especially the Muslims. At the time of partition, the new border was drawn right across the province where the majority of the Sikhs lived. The many Sikhs who after partition were in Pakistan had to flee to India after violent clashes with the Muslims. In contrast, the Muslims fled from the Indian Punjab to Pakistan. The result was a strong concentration of Sikhs in the present-day Indian Punjab.

Even though the common religious identity through these traumatic experiences was also, to some extent, transformed into a social and political communality, it is noteworthy that the political demands of the Sikhs in independent India were essentially limited to demands for local self-government within a Punjab state with boundaries drawn in such a way that the Sikhs obtained a clear political majority. A small minority did claim an independent state for the Sikhs, a Khalistan, but this minority had no political power during the first decades after India's independence.

This changed towards the end of the 1970s, when the separatists increased their political influence considerably, chiefly because the Congress Party at that time intervened and in reality supported the separatists. Indira Gandhi and her Congress Party, while in opposition at the federal level during the period 1977–80, pursued a quite effective 'divide-and-rule' strategy. Every disagreement within the other parties was exploited in order to create the greatest possible disunity. In the Punjab, the strategy implied that the Congress Party did not confine itself to exploiting the traditional factional disagreements within the Sikhs' largest party, *Akali Dal*, but in addition supported religious fanatics and extremists among the Sikhs. This included the youth organisation, *Dal Khalsa*, which from its founding in 1978 demanded an independent Sikh state outside the Indian federation. Among those who received assistance from the Congress Party during this period was Bhindranwale, who later became one of the most prominent leaders of the Sikh extremists.

The overall purpose of the strategy was to split the ruling Janata Coalition so that the Congress Party could regain government power at the centre, but the result in the case of the Punjab was primarily a significant weakening of the traditional factions within *Akali Dal* which, in turn, left more room for the Sikh extremists in the politics of the state. The reasons why this could happen in the Punjab probably had to do with fundamental economic and social changes which had brought about a particularly fertile ground for religious agitation.

In comparison with other Indian states, the Punjab is a prosperous state. The population here have experienced considerable economic progress since the mid-1960s, mainly due to the green revolution in agriculture. Paradoxically, it is exactly because of this economic progress that dissatisfaction among the Sikhs started to grow during the 1970s and 1980s. Sikh peasants increasingly felt that they did not benefit in proportion to their substantial contribution to growth in agricultural production. The main reason was the low level of prices they could secure for their produce.

Similar perceptions thrived among peasants throughout India. This was part of the background for the increased conflict over the entire development strategy pursued by the central government. But where this conflict in the rest of India led to confrontations between rural and urban interests, the conflict in the Punjab was given an extra dimension. Here, nearly all peasants were Sikhs, while the traders and buyers were predominantly Hindus. Similarly, the people from whom the peasants had to buy fertilisers and other inputs for agricultural production were also Hindus. Under these circumstances, it was 'natural' for the Sikh peasants to perceive the conflict of interests concerning the prices also as a conflict between the two religious communities. Or, to put it differently, it was convenient for them to present the conflict in this way in order to bring about a closing of their own ranks and to build support from other Sikhs.

In the cities, where the Hindus constituted a majority in most of the Punjab, the two religious communities clashed in competition for jobs and promotions. Essentially the new feature here was a growing number of young Sikhs with a higher education but without a job. It was not difficult under these conditions for the religious and political agitators to convince this group that it was the Hindus who took the jobs to which the Sikhs were entitled. Other areas could be cited where economic conflicts of interest coincided with – or could be interpreted as coinciding with – religious differences. But those stated are sufficient to illustrate the fertile ground which, towards the end of the 1970s, was created for an appeal to the Sikh identity and for a political mobilisation based on that identity. The new situation was effectively exploited by *Dal Khalsa* and the militant student federation, who succeeded in politicising a considerable segment of the Sikh community in support of an independent state.

The Congress Party, after returning to power in 1980, changed its strategy and began suppressing the Sikh separatists. Subsequent developments, however, are of no special interest in the present context, where the main point has been to illustrate how a number of factors can interact to bring about the transformation of an ethnic category, first, into an ethnic community, and second, into a nationalist movement that demands political independence.

Ethnicity and development strategies

We have so far focused on identity formation within potential ethnic communities. There are, however, other important issues relating to ethnicity. We shall end this chapter by briefly drawing attention to two further such issues, namely the favourable treatment of certain ethnic groups by means of biased development strategies and the ethnicisation of international politics (Hettne, 1986).

Strictly speaking, the considerations relating to these issues do not amount to independent contributions to theory formation. They merely emphasise that ethnic aspects are important and should be incorporated into development research.

Regarding the favouring of certain ethnic groups – and the concomitant disfavouring of others – the main point is that government policies are often biased in ethnic terms, and that this should be considered in any analysis of development policies and strategies. According to one type of reasoning, predominantly moral and normative, all ethnic categories and communities in a society should have a share – proportionate to their size – of the political power and the benefits accruing from economic development. This position is sometimes referred to as the alternative theory of ethno-development.

Another type of reasoning, with a more prominent element of causal theory, would assert that a systematic disfavouring of certain groups will eventually lead to a unification and politicisation of these groups in opposition to the government. Such policies would contribute to transforming ethnic categories from being passive non-beneficiaries to being active political adversaries who might threaten political stability and the survival of the government concerned. To be able to understand and possibly predict such intensification of conflicts it will be useful to investigate possible biases based on the interests of ethnic categories and communities.

Regarding the ethnicisation of international politics, this is mainly a hypothesis which on the basis of an increasing number of case studies claims that ethnic conflicts will often take on international dimensions. When ethnic communities and nationalities are met with suppression and rejection of their demands from the state and other groups, they will often seek international support for their claims – in neighbouring countries or further afield. The relationships between the state concerned and other countries are thus likely to be influenced by the ethnic conflicts. Many instances of this tendency have occurred during the last decades; just to mention one example: the Tamil rebellion against the central government in Sri Lanka and its consequences for the relationship between Sri Lanka and India.

The causal relationship, though, may also be the reverse, as when governments perceive an interest in supporting ethnic groups in other countries in order to weaken these politically and military. Pakistan's support of the Sikh separatists in the Indian Punjab, and of the Muslims in Indian-held parts of Kashmir, are cited as examples of this.

The overall conclusion that emerges from the above observations concerning ethnic identities and nationalities is that these are important phenomena that should be taken much more into consideration within mainstream development studies and theory formation.

CHAPTER 24

People-managed Development

The majority of the theories which have been presented in the previous chapters are primarily contemplative and explanatory. They describe and interpret what has happened, and what is about to happen, in the Third World. They try to explain changes which have taken place, as well as unchanged reproduction of existing societal conditions. It is, however, also an essential component in many development theories that they, explicitly or implicitly, argue for change. The theories often concern themselves quite extensively with how the existing conditions can be changed in accordance with certain more precisely defined development goals. In keeping with this, we have throughout the book included references to the various development strategies which have been proposed on the basis of the different theories and their conceptions of what development is, or ought to be. We have noted that the recommendations on strategy vary considerably with regard to means and method, and with respect to the degree of detail in the directives for action.

What is remarkable, though, is the extent to which the hundreds of proponents of the several theories agree on *who* should implement the strategies. On this point, the overwhelming majority envisage that this has to be left to existing authorities or large organisations of some kind or another: Third World governments; the World Bank, the International Monetary Fund or other international organisations; bilateral donor organisations; or large corporations and other private companies. Mainstream thinking is characterised by a strikingly high degree of consensus when it comes to identifying or choosing the types of main actors in the development process. The overall preference is clearly for existing bureaucratic organisations, public or private. Very few theories emphasise the role of people, the role of the individual citizens, men and women, as independent actors. Class theories do focus on people, but generally in a very abstract sense, and mostly within a structuralist framework that assigns little freedom of action to the individual. Theories of people's participation do envisage that people can, and should, play a role in development planning and implementation, but again there is a tendency to reduce individual citizens to actors with only a marginal influence and subordinate roles. Only some of the so-called alternative theories reviewed in the present part of the book, including particularly those focusing on women and gender, expect and recommend that development efforts can and should rely to a significant extent on people as both an end and a means of societal development.

The focus on, and preference for, bureaucratic organisations as the principal actors and vehicles of development can be seen as a reflection of reality, and especially of the distribution of power obtaining in Third World societies and the international system. Nevertheless, this chapter, as an attempt to supplement and criticise mainstream thinking, will focus on theories and strategies that take ordinary citizens as their starting point. In several respects these theories can be viewed as extensions and elaborations of the theories of public participation (cf. Chapter 16), but they go much further in their formulation of what they themselves characterise as alternative development strategies with emphasis on the human dimension. Moreover, they strongly disassociate themselves from any form of bureaucratic and centralised control over the development process. Their strategy can be characterised as *people-managed development* – as development which starts with and is controlled by civil society, and thus as development which reduces the importance of the corporate capitalist economy and the state.

Theories of people-managed development do not claim that people have, so far, played more prominent roles in aggregate societal development than described in mainstream theories. But they claim, on the one hand, that people have effectively managed their own development at the micro-level to a significantly higher degree than is recognised in mainstream thinking, and on the other, that people *ought* to play much more prominent roles even at the macro-level, because that is the only way genuine progress and improvements can be attained.

One of the outstanding representatives of people-managed development is the American social scientist and development consultant, *Guy Gran*. He has, with his major work *Development by People*, laid the foundations for a comprehensive strategy of people-managed mass development (Gran, 1983). Other proponents with slightly different emphases include John Friedmann (cf. Chapter 22), and *David Korten* (Korten, 1980, 1990). *Robert Chambers* can also be counted in this group (Chambers, 1983). In addition, UNDP's *Human Development Report 1993* can be seen as incorporating core features of the people-managed development strategy (UNDP, 1993). The same applies to Mahbub ul Haq's recent reflections on human development (Haq, 1995).

Friedmann elaborated his normative theory on inclusive democracy on the basis of a more extensive theory about civil society. His main interest was to identify conditions that excluded poor people from decision making and prevented them from getting a fair share of society's resources. The strategy Friedmann proposed centred around empowerment of the poor and devolution of powers to local authorities which should, at the same time, be made accountable to the majority of their citizens – that is the poor people in their areas of jurisdiction (Friedmann, 1992: Ch. 5).

Korten's starting point was primarily the role of the NGOs and their opportunities for strengthening resource-weak groups and securing better living conditions for them. Korten, in his more recent works, has increasingly incorporated an environmental dimension in his analyses. He underlines, in this connection, the need for a shift from growth-oriented to people-centred development strategies. This shift implies giving first priority to the fulfilment of the basic needs of the poor which, in turn, requires that the rich in the world reduce their consumption to a sustainable level.

Chambers's contribution to people-managed development, what he referred to as 'reversals in management', was elaborated in connection with his critical assessment of development work in the rural areas. At the core of the strategy proposed by Chambers was a reversal of the learning processes. Rather than simply applying the knowledge acquired through conventional education, development workers should try to learn directly from the rural people, try to understand their knowledge systems and elicit their technical knowledge. Similarly, the whole system of governance should be reversed. Authoritarian and hierarchical structures and procedures should be replaced by arrangements which shifted power and initiative downwards and outwards (Chambers, 1983, Ch. 8).

In the following sections, it is mainly Gran's ideas and propositions which are presented, but with reference to contributions from other researchers involved in the debate on people-managed development.

Criticism of bureaucratic governance: Gran

Guy Gran arrives at his alternative development strategy on the basis of an extensive criticism of both theory and practice in development co-operation, in which he participated as a consultant for the World Bank. The criticism of the existing theories at the abstract level adds little, if anything, decisively new to the preceding discussions of mainstream theories. More interesting is Gran's detailed demonstration of how wrong it can go in practice, when the development efforts are based on conventional macro-economic theories (Gran, 1983: Chs 3–5).

Based on this criticism, Gran argues that human development in the Third World is impeded by three major problems. The first is the strong concentration of power within government bureaucracies and large private corporations. The second problem is the narrow economic considerations these bureaucratic organisations use as a basis for their decisions and mode of functioning. The third major problem is the exclusion mechanisms which work through both the state and the market, and whose impact is a marginalisation and exclusion of the vast majority of poor people from the economic and political community.

Gran believes much of the misery in the world can be traced back to the distinct and narrow interests of the economic and political elites, and to their modes of acting. He emphasises the form of organisation generally preferred by the elites, that is the bureaucratic form, as a principal problem in itself. Bureaucratic organisations operate from the top downwards, they are control oriented and worry so much about security that they become impenetrable and closed to the rest of society. Gran further notes, like several of the Marxist-inspired theorists, that bureaucratic organisations are incapable of motivating people outside these organisations and generally unsuited to mobilising human resources in a society.

International organisations like the World Bank and official bilateral aid agencies are selected as targets for particular criticism by Gran. One of the major problems with these bureaucratic organisations is that their staff and leading decision makers are separated both institutionally and culturally from the people they try to assist through international development co-operation. In this respect they do not, in principle, occupy positions different from those of top bureaucrats and politicians in developing countries, but the gulf between these officials and the people they aim to assist is so much wider that, in practice, the results are often more disastrous. Gran mentions, in this connection, many examples of how lack of knowledge – or lack of understanding – of local conditions on the part of aid agency staff has resulted in projects that have failed miserably.

The reasons why aid organisations have often acted inadequately or incorrectly are many. Sometimes the organisations have simply pursued objectives with little relation to development concerns in the Third World, as when the primary objective has been to assist private enterprises from the rich countries to penetrate the economies of the poor countries. Other, and generally more important, reasons have to do with the fact that neither staff nor decision makers have the time or opportunity to become properly acquainted with the local conditions. This is not due to lack of will, according to Gran, but chiefly a result of the way in which bureaucratic organisations work. The predominant part of the information flows within such organisations consists of internal papers prepared according to specific procedures that rarely provide much room for 'deviating' cases or for the immense complexity of societal realities. In fact, there is rarely room for anything but the purely economic data.

Another element in the explanation is that staff and decision makers have largely had incorrect or at best insufficient training in relation to the tasks they deal with. Their background is mainly experience from the industrialised countries, and professionally their training lies generally within neo-classical economics and law. A particular problem highlighted by Gran in this connection is that the people who take the most crucial decisions have typically been trained many years ago, and have not in the meantime had the opportunity of systematically getting acquainted with the more recent elaborations of theory. Their frame of understanding, therefore, consists of mainly old and now rejected theories – especially narrow macro-economic theories. It is interesting to note the similarities here with Robert Chambers's criticism of decision makers and professional staff for 'under-perceiving' the nature and extent of rural poverty, because of fundamental biases in their approach, and because of their own educational background and training (cf. Chapter 21).

While Chambers's focused and elaborate criticism has lost little of its relevance and validity, one might raise the question whether Gran's more sweeping statements have. Gran, in his main work on the subject, did stress that his criticism was aimed primarily at the World Bank and USAID, the aid department of the American Government. And he did emphasise that a number of specialised United Nations agencies were different from these two organisations, because they took into account the local conditions, involved the local population, kept their staff up to date with the results of recent development research, and applied conceptual frameworks that were much broader in scope than the conventional macro-economic models. The same could be said to apply to some of the official bilateral aid agencies, like those in the Nordic countries. The point it is necessary to make here, however, is that even with these qualifications Gran's criticism is less valid today than when it was first formulated in the early 1980s. Most multilateral as well as bilateral development agencies have since then tried to broaden their perspectives and adjust their strategies more to national and local circumstances, to some extent in collaboration with representatives of the population in Third World countries.

Gran's criticism may thus have to be softened a little with regard to contemporary multilateral and inter-governmental development co-operation but, in comparison with the ideal strategy that he has proposed, there is still a very long way to go. Pursuing Gran's version of people-managed development would imply a very significant decrease in all types of official development co-operation. Instead, much more emphasis would be given to non-state popular organisations and aid from people to people. More importantly, development managed by people themselves in the Third World would imply a reduced role for international organisations and governments of the rich countries in development endeavours.

Mass development through people's participation

The fundamental assumption in Gran's development strategy is that no government will use the necessary resources on mass development and mass welfare unless the poor population majority is sufficiently powerful to force such a policy upon the government. Therefore, the strategy above all aims at empowering the poor and deprived social groups.

The first decisive element in the strategy is to make the many people who do not belong to the economic and political elites aware of their situation and their possibilities. The process of awareness creation Gran refers to as *conscientisation.* He defines this, in accordance with the Brazilian *Paolo Freire* (cf. Freire, 1990), as a process through which people – not as passive recipients but as knowing and active citizens – achieve a deeper understanding of the social reality which shapes their lives and of their capacity to transform that reality.

The second element in the strategy is a breaking down of the many barriers that obstruct people's participation and prevent the poor, in particular, from exerting their influence on decision making and allocation of resources. The further aim is to organise the poor and deprived citizens. Not every kind of organisation can be used in this connection. As implied in Gran's general criticism of bureaucratic forms of organisation, these cannot be used to attain genuine empowerment of the poor; they will not release the human potential and the initiative which is found among the suppressed. At the same time, this form of organisation has a tendency to exclude large social groups from participation and influence.

The idea, therefore, is not to organise people into large, hierarchical, and closed organisations. What Gran suggests, instead, are small 'base organisations' with a flat or horizontal decision-making structure, open membership and decision-making procedures geared to ensure consensus. The base organisations should have as their principal task the conscientisation and education of the members with a further view to enabling them to fulfil their roles as active and socially responsible citizens. In addition, the base organisations should, on the one hand, manage the local human and physical resources in accordance with local priorities, and on the other, articulate and promote local demands and interests in relation to the authorities and the rest of society.

The third element in the strategy is to reorganise the local communities in such a way that the citizens gain equal access to opportunities to influence decisions affecting their conditions of life. Gran believes that this goal can best be achieved by reorganising the local communities into relatively small units. Each of these should be entitled to deal with a wide range of issues and resources pertaining to their members' livelihood. The assumption implicit here is that the best results are obtained when the local organisations can prioritise across many different issues and areas. Only in this way can they reach balanced decisions on how to make the best use of the scarce resources available to satisfy the many different basic human needs.

In a long-term perspective, it is possible to trace some of the ideas embodied in Gran's propositions and recommendations all the way back to Jean-Jacque Rosseau (1712–1778) and his conceptions of direct democracy in small local communities (Sabine, 1961: Ch. 28). In a shorter time perspective, a certain resemblance can be noticed with the romantic ideas in some of the alternative development theories mentioned earlier (cf. Chapter 20). It follows from this observation that the criticism directed against such conceptions is also relevant *via-à-vis* Gran's strategy. In the present context it is deemed particularly relevant to draw attention to the difficulties in establishing base organisations across class distinctions, gender and perceived ethnic affiliations. Furthermore, there is reason to highlight the problems encountered when trying to organise poor people, who are subordinate to and dependent upon local patrons. Gran does not deal explicitly with either these or other related constraints and difficulties.

Decentralisation and people-managed development

If small local organisations of the kind Gran envisages are to achieve decisive influence on the life conditions of their members and citizens in general, it presupposes, in almost all developing countries, radical decentralisation or, more specifically, a considerable devolution of authority (cf. Chapter 15). The situation obtaining in the large majority of countries is presently character-ised by a high degree of centralisation. Most important decisions are taken at the central level and close to the top of the bureaucratic and political hierarchies. This prevents locally organised groups from exerting any influence. Therefore, people-managed development as envisaged by Gran requires that many more decision-making powers are transferred to local authorities and even beyond that, to citizen organisations within the local communities.

Gran's suggestions are far-reaching on this point, and it is only reluctantly that he acknowledges that there are certain limits to decentralisation and devolution. He does note, though, that a number of development problems cannot appropriately be solved locally. Moreover, there will be a continued need for co-ordinating the development efforts at higher levels, especially at national level. Hence, there will be a need for involving provincial authorities and especially national authorities. But – and this is the most important point here – these authorities, under the envisaged new conditions, will function in societies where demands are articulated and aggregated by a large number of well-organised citizen groups.

The reasoning behind the propositions regarding people participation and decentralisation is essentially that the combination of these two strategies is likely to release dormant forces and resources, which can be used in the overall development efforts. Gran believes that increased influence for citizens on their own livelihood conditions will stimulate, more than anything else, their willingness to take greater responsibility and make self-sacrifices – to the benefit of socially broad-based development.

The long-term goal of this development strategy is to initiate and sustain a process through which basic human needs are satisfied to increasing degrees. In this connection, Gran underlines that the needs are not just material, but also social, political and cultural – and seen as far more necessary than in conventional versions of the basic needs strategy. Thus, what is at stake is not confined to food, habitat and so on but also self-respect, and recognition and acknowledgement as human beings. An important point here is that the prioritisation among the various needs cannot be decided a priori or by outsiders. Which needs are to be satisfied first, and to what extent, have to be decided through the people's participation. Hence, participation is not just a means to an end in the development process; it is a goal in itself – a goal which is inseparably related to and at the same level as other development goals.

Development catalysts

Gran's strong emphasis on the poor and weak population groups' self-organisation, self-management and self-rule raises the question of whether the whole process can be initiated by the concerned groups themselves. The answer is no. On the contrary, Gran argues, there are so many external obstacles and internalised values impeding poor people from acting collectively and taking responsibility for their own conditions that there is normally a critical need for a catalyst – one or more persons who can take the initiative and facilitate the processes of self-organisation and keep them going until they become sustainable. A large proportion of Gran's work is devoted to these catalysts and their role in community development. It is extensively discussed how to select them, how they should be trained, and how they should subsequently function in the local communities. Only a few main points can be brought out here.

Gran believes that the most appropriate procedure is to choose members of the local 'target' groups and train them before sending them back to their villages or local communities in urban areas. The training should be both technical and social, where the main emphasis is on community organisation and community development.

This procedure, however, can often be difficult to apply in practice. It may therefore be necessary to use an alternative approach, where the development catalysts are recruited from other segments of society or from other countries, including the industrialised countries. What is important here is the kind of role these 'outsiders' take upon themselves. They should not act as managers or experts, but rather as facilitators, mediators or brokers. Therefore, Gran prefers non-government development workers to government-employed experts and advisers. He further notes that NGOs in the industrialised countries are better suited than the official aid agencies to fulfil these tasks, the main reasons being that the NGOs are generally less bureaucratic, more geared to work at the grass roots level, more flexible in their mode of operating, and more prepared to support the poor and weak population groups *vis-à-vis* the local and national authorities.

Gran's views on the need for catalysts to support the self-organisation of poor people are found in much of the literature on the subject, but many authors – both researchers and practitioners with first-hand experience from development co-operation – reject Gran's positive assessment of what external development agents can achieve. Chambers, especially, claims that people from the rich industrialised countries are generally unable to play decisive roles. According to him, development workers from foreign countries may be of some assistance to communities and local organisations, but they remain external to the conflicts and change processes in the poor countries.

David Korten previously promulgated a similar view, partly based on empirical investigations which indicated that the vast majority of the best functioning and most effective voluntary organisations in Asia relied much more on their own charismatic leaders and the efforts of their own members and followers, than on any external development catalysts.

In a more recent study, Korten has introduced a basic distinction between different types of voluntary organisation which includes a more elaborate analysis of the roles played by external agents (Korten, 1990: Ch. 9). The most important distinction here is between what he terms 'third-party' organisations, that is those basing their social legitimacy on the premise that they exist to serve the needs of third parties – persons who are not them-selves members of the organisations – and 'first-party' organisations. The latter, also referred to as genuine people's organisations, possess three defining characteristics:

1. They are mutual benefit associations that base their legitimacy on the ability to serve their own members' interests.
2. They have a democratic structure that gives members ultimate authority over their leaders.
3. They are self-reliant in that their continued existence is not dependent on outside initiative or funding.

It follows from this that external catalysts are expected to play only a very marginal role in relation to first-party organisations, while they may perform important functions in relation to third-party organisations. Korten mentions, as examples of first-party organisations, self-reliant co-operatives, labour unions and political interest groups. He believes that these types of organ-isation embody much more potential than international NGOs or official donor agencies for promoting the interests of poor population groups in the Third World.

Without necessarily questioning this latter point, and without going into any detail concerning the matter, it is worthwhile to note here that external catalysts can play very important roles even in relation to first-party organisa-tions. This came out very clearly in an international evaluation of ILO's assistance to trade unions under the workers' education programme, where initial inputs from foreign trade unionists and workers' educators could be identified as very critical preconditions for subsequent strengthening of the unions in most of the 14 countries studied (Martinussen, 1991d).

Global consciousness and accountability

Gran's analyses and strategies for people-centred development are not convincing in all respects. His criticism of all forms of bureaucracy as major obstacles to social and human progress appears too far-reaching and one-sided. Moreover, it is not evident why the forms of organisation proposed by Gran to replace bureaucratic hierarchies should, under all circumstances, be the best and most effective vehicles of development. There is little doubt that his 'base organisations' may often contribute to empowering poor people, but they may also be turned into a local power base for the better-off household members, for the best educated and most articulate, for male members, etc. Can the base organisations, with their universal mandate, really take care of all the interests of the different member groups? Will there not, in the foreseeable future, continue to be a need for separate organisations to cater for the special interests of poor women – or of landless rural labourers, who sell their labour to both rich and poor peasants?

Regardless of these and other objections to Gran, he and other proponents of people-managed development strategies should be credited for having added important new dimensions to the debate on structure and agency in societal transformation processes. They have placed the conscious human being centre stage, as an actor with options and opportunities for influencing the course of development and change. Each individual actor may not be capable of achieving much, but as a part of collective efforts he or she may bring about a visible impact. In this manner, development issues and problems facing millions of poor people in the Third World can be made more relevant to ordinary citizens, even within a theoretical framework. At the same time, the underlining of the potential roles of the development catalysts from the industrialised countries implies an appeal for global consciousness and responsibility among citizens in that part of the world.

Most important, though, is the claim that a people-managed development strategy will be the best for the great majority of the poor and suppressed population groups in the Third World. Gran, Korten and others are very optimistic in their assessment of what can be achieved through joint efforts in accordance with the prescribed strategy. Gran summarises his position on this point by saying that the present, miserable world order has been created by people; therefore it can also be changed to something better by – other – people.

This, unfortunately, is not particularly convincing. It is worth trying but, in order to achieve an impact, any kind of collective action has to take into consideration the kinds of challenge and opposition faced. The theory of people-managed development contains a much-needed supplementary emphasis on people's opportunities for acting collectively, and a much-needed discussion of how to bring about local solutions to global problems. But the theory cannot replace the accumulated insights into the structures, processes and power relations that constitute the context of human action – and which, in various forms, have been conceptualised within the mainstream theories of development and underdevelopment reviewed in the present book.

Moreover, even though Gran and Korten in their discussion of strategy take into account the need for intermediary organisations that can link the base and community organisations with the larger society and the global system, they both essentially promulgate a 'small-is-beautiful' approach to the whole problem. A polemical criticism to this approach has been summed up in just one sentence: 'Small may be beautiful, but it may also be insignificant'.

The reasoning embodied in this brief statement has stimulated many of the recent strategy discussions among development researchers and practitioners within the international NGO community to focus more on how to replicate and scale up development efforts in local communities. Small community projects and other small-scale efforts are not rejected, but they are increasingly seen as only one type of intervention among several others, and there is an increasing awareness of the need to integrate these into much more comprehensive macro-economic and macro-political strategies (Drabekk, 1987; Korten, 1990: Ch. 10 and Part IV).

Local political mobilisation similarly continues to be accepted, but again within a broader framework where this endeavour is seen as part of large-scale mobilisation within national movements. The end goal is not only to articulate demands for local reforms and local improvements, but rather to do so with a further view to bringing about national and global reforms (Friedmann, 1992: Ch. 7).

The previously all-dominating state-managed and market-led development models are in this way more directly confronted with an alternative people-managed, civil-society-based development model.

It is doubtful, considering the structural limitations and the power relations revealed in the analyses and theories presented in this book, whether any radical changes will occur in the general balance between these models of development in the Third World. Nevertheless, it appears warranted to conclude that there is, in many countries of the Third World, notably in Asia and Latin America, a trend towards a stronger manifestation of civil-society dynamics. These dynamics have to be given more attention not merely at the fringe of mainstream thinking, but much closer to the core of future development research and theory formation.

PART VI

Theory Construction in Development Research

CHAPTER 25

A Critical Assessment of Development Theories

In the previous 24 chapters, I have attempted to present an overview of theory formation within development studies – or rather of the aspects of the theory formation with which I am familiar, and which I regard as significant from one perspective or another. The criteria for selection are listed in the preface.

A summary of the theories presented is not of interest in this context, as the presentation in itself is a summary of the existing rich and varied theory formation in this area. Rather, the purpose of this final chapter is the more limited one of uncovering and describing some essential characteristics of the theory construction in general and therefore less precise terms. Initially, I will dwell on a theoretical and methodological critique; on changes which have manifested themselves as shifts in analytical and geographical objects of study; and on some of the conditions which have been particularly influential in theory building. The latter two areas of focus are concerned with a discussion of issues which have been addressed throughout the presentation, whereas we have not previously placed the discussions in a theory of science perspective.

Where previously emphasis was placed on accounting for the views and reasoning of others, albeit with my own comments, I will in the following primarily be presenting my own reflections on the nature and weaknesses of the theory construction. The grounds for assessing theory construction are explicit as well as implicit ideal-typical conceptions of what constitutes good-quality social science.

Characteristics of theory construction in development research

In presenting the many different theories I have grouped these into a small number of categories. In doing so, I have made a number of discretionary assessments concerning their mutual kinship or lack of it. It has not always been self-evident to which category a given theory belongs. This is due to the fact that much of the theory construction in development studies has been introduced with no explicit considerations concerning basic ontological, epistemological and methodological positions. I perceive this as a serious shortcoming. To elaborate this point, I will begin by outlining what I regard as the minimum requirements of a good social science theory.

It must be demanded of a theory that its ontological and epistemological assumptions are explicitly stated. This implies an indication of the fundamental conceptions of reality, of the nature of society, and of how this reality can be analysed and comprehended. In relation to these central issues there are crucial differences between, say, liberalist approaches, which rest on methodological individualism, and Marxist or other structuralist approaches.

Further, it is required of a theory that the normative premises and political priorities it embodies are thoroughly exposed. Moreover, the concepts and theoretical propositions elaborated within the framework in question should be compatible with the basic assumptions, and should of course feature a high degree of logical consistency and precision. This does not preclude piecing together elements from the different conceptual frameworks and theories, but it implies that such eclecticism should be carried out meticulously and with an understanding of the fact that not all elements can be matched, because they rest on dissimilar ontological and epistemological assumptions. For example, an application of the class concept, which involves defining class as a group of individuals, is incompatible with a Marxian class concept and the associated mode of explanation.

In addition, it must be demanded of a good theory that it demarcates its sphere of applicability or defines the circumstances under which it is assumed to be valid. Finally, it must in principle be possible to submit the propositions regarding reality to falsification tests, while it is at the same time understood that the abstract theory elements – without empirical content (as for example the abstract mode-of-production concept) – can be judged solely on the basis of their applicability and utility in bringing forth propositions about real societal phenomena and changes in these.

Only a few theories within the field of development research lived up to these demands in the 1950s and 1960s, and in this respect no decisive changes have occurred since then. Development research has on the whole been concerned primarily with reaching empirically based generalisations, often with the further goal of providing strategy recommendations. At no point in time has there been a widespread attempt to reflect more thoroughly on foundations in the history of ideas or the history of social science theory; nor have development theorists paid much attention to how their contributions related to basic assumptions within the theory of science.

With respect to indicating the realm of applicability and validity, few of the classical theories of the 1950s and 1960s contained any explicit considerations. In this regard, however, a shift can be observed away from implicit claims of universal validity for all Third World countries towards more differentiated theories which take into account the dissimilar conditions and structures of these countries. I shall return to this point later.

The central concern in the present context is to emphasise the tendency – in this case a continuous one – to link development research to strategies, to political stance and action, rather than regard such research as part of a cumulative process of testing the underlying positions in the theory of science and the applicability of abstract theories of culture and society. Corresponding to this, development research has not been particularly concerned with criticism or generation of theory that lies substantially outside its own subject area. To put it rather bluntly, I would maintain that quite a considerable part of development research has been characterised by limited methodological and theoretical awareness and thus by an insufficient reflection on its own assumptions.

In my view, this constitutes part of what has rendered development research relatively easy prey to external influences, whether these be currents within the established disciplines of study or changed political priorities in the area of international development co-operation. This point will also be elaborated further.

Before doing so, however, there is another characteristic of development research and the associated theory formation which demands attention and comment in the light of the minimum requirements outlined above. This concerns the handling of normative elements, of values and valuations that interfere with research priorities and procedures. Interferences of this kind are not specific to development research. It is currently widely acknowledged within the social sciences that the value orientation of the individual social scientists, as well as values and interests in the surrounding society, manifest themselves in all phases of the research process and thus influence theory building at all levels. Based on this recognition, social scientists like Arnold Brecht and Gunnar Myrdal have attempted to develop methodological principles – known under the designation 'scientific value relativism' – in order to prevent valuations and values from producing a *bias* in description, interpretation and explanation. In this context bias is, among other things, the manipulation of data for the purpose of substantiating preconceived opinions with a normative content. One of the most important principles of scientific value relativism is the above-mentioned requirement of providing an explicit indication of the value orientation of the researcher. The fundamental idea is that the social scientist, by accounting more fully for his or her own preferences and for the values and research policy priorities which may have affected the approach and procedures adopted, allows other social scientists the option of being wary of bias-generating influences.

Looking back at the theory building of the first decades after the Second World War, it is remarkable how little influence considerations of this kind have had within the field of development research. On the contrary, it was characteristic of the literature of the time, with Myrdal as a significant exception, that it treated development problems as though they were objective and value-free. This applied notably to modernisation theories – economic, sociological and political science theories (for example Rostow and Almond). This is so much more conspicuous, owing to the fact that development theories are constituted to such a great extent around certain development goals and the processes leading to these goals – or away from them. Hence, the values feature prominently from the very outset, because development goals obviously cannot be established in a value-free manner or independent of particular interests.

It is worth adding that the setting and prioritisation of goals influence not only the choice of approach and the course followed in drawing inferences and organising the findings, but are also crucial in determining possible types of development strategies. Moreover, the establishing of goals exerts considerable influence on the relationships between industrialised countries and developing countries within international development co-operation. If the goal, as it is in modernisation theories, is to deconstruct the so-called traditional institutions and structures and replace them with Western ones, then it is 'natural' to involve Western experts and to grant them a prominent role in the development process. Correspondingly, notions maintaining that method and theory based on experience from industrialised countries can be applied unmodified in developing countries, as claimed by some neo-classical economists, grant a central position to social scientists and experts knowledgeable in this area, while at the same time assigning less importance to Third World scholars.

It was not so much these consequences of the value orientations which were the first objects of criticism in the late 1960s and early 1970s. This tendency did not manifest itself until later. Rather, the early criticism focused more directly on the definitions of development as change towards an ever greater similarity with modern Western industrialised societies. This criticism came from several camps. The neo-Marxist dependency theories and the Soviet Marxism of the time rejected, each in its own way, both the value premises and the evolutionist perception of the development process. But there were only a few attempts within these traditions to make their own value premises explicit, just as there was no question of a break with the ethnocentric notions that we – the North-western or North-eastern social scientists – are capable of defining 'development' for Third World societies, their populations and social classes from the outside.

The first advances towards such a more fundamental break can be traced far back within social anthropology, but they did not penetrate other areas of development research until the end of the 1970s with theories of alternative development (another development). Especially in the approaches that can be grouped under the heading 'people-managed development', there is a clear emphasis on the fact that development goals cannot be set by the social scientist (or by any other outsider), but must be based on an investigation of wants, priorities and goals in the society or societal group, whose conditions and history are of interest to the social scientist.

This does not preclude a concurrent analysis and assessment of the situation and the course of development on the basis of the researcher's own perception of the appropriate goals. But it undoubtedly tightens attention on the value premises, including the ethnocentric and culture-specific values, if the researcher continuously attempts to separate his or her own understanding of development from that of others. At the same time, a platform is established for a more detailed and critical consideration of advantages and disadvantages associated with a massive input of experts from industrialised countries and the transfer of Western experiences and institutions to the countries in the Third World.

Over the last 25 years, the debate among development theorists has indeed focused more generally on the value premises embodied in goal determination and perhaps particularly on the role of these premises in the elaboration of development strategies. But there continues to be a widespread tendency to allow personal values and preferences, as well as the research policy priorities and special interests which are integral to theory construction, to appear to be considerably more objective than they are. I find this to be an unfortunate and not particularly respectable tendency within development research.

This is not rendered less unfortunate by the fact that the tendency gained momentum in the 1980s concurrently with the strengthening of the counter-revolutionary economists. The most prominent representatives of this group have had a marked propensity to present their own value-laden judgements concerning economic development, and the strategy suggestions that follow from these, as objective and value-free. On the other hand, they have made it clear that Keynesianism, Marxist-inspired development theory, and other theories advocating active state intervention in the development process are all either subjective in their assessments, bound by special interests – or at best have misunderstood the dynamics of the development process.

During the 1990s, the counter-revolution has been on the retreat among economists. But this has not crucially weakened the tendency of advocates in the debate to contrast the standpoints as correct or incorrect, true or false. It is precisely this simple opposition which obscures the importance of the value premises and special interests in framing development theory.

After this brief discussion of the role of values and the way in which they have been handled, there is a third characteristic of theory construction which deserves particular attention. This pertains to the perspectives applied and, in connection with these, both the level of aggregation or abstraction and the postulated realms of applicability and validity.

In these respects, it was characteristic of non-anthropological theory construction in the 1950s and 1960s that it predominantly applied a very broad perspective, demonstrated a high level of aggregation or abstraction, and postulated validity for developing countries, Third World countries or peripheral societies in general. Primary focus was on the 'big' questions and macro-phenomena in a theory construction that attempted to expose the basic character of processes of development and underdevelopment, and the determinants of these processes.

A clear preponderance of theories focused on economic conditions, not only within development economics where this was to be expected, but also within the Marxist and neo-Marxist traditions. Moreover, there was a prevailing tendency to devote attention *either* to internal conditions in specific developing countries *or* to external relations, notably the dependency on the world market and industrialised countries.

Appreciable changes have taken place in all these respects over the last 25 years. These changes are the focus of attention below. But rather than proceed directly to an overview of the principal tendencies, as in the above discussion, I will attempt here to reflect concurrently on the determinants of importance to choice of approach and theory construction.

External factors influencing the construction of development theories

It has already been mentioned that, in my view, development research is relatively easily influenced from 'the outside' – by conditions and currents external to its subject area and outside its own theoretical and methodological traditions. One of the reasons for this is the noted weakness of its methodological and theoretical awareness and anchoring. Other particulars of development research, which presumably work towards the same effect, are its strong emphasis on empirical studies as well as its action-orientation and multidisciplinarity. In addition, the whole unresolved question emerges of whether development research can meaningfully and productively be isolated as a distinctive field of study. Granted that it may be isolated in this manner, the second question arises concerning the demarcation of such a field. These are all circumstances which reduce the theoretical and methodo-logical discussion within development research to just one among several determinants of method elaboration and theory construction.

Obviously, it is not possible in the context of this final chapter to account more precisely for the manner in which the different determinants have influenced development research. What I can do is merely to indicate some of the types of determinants and, with the help of a few examples, seek to illustrate how they have manifested themselves.

In an enumeration of the determinants, it is appropriate to commence with a reminder that the whole advance of non-anthropological research regarding developing countries and their positions within the international political-economic system was occasioned to a great extent by political decolonisation in a progressively increasing number of countries in Asia, the Middle East and Africa from the end of the 1940s and onwards. This decolonisation proceeded on a course parallel to a bipolarisation in inter-national politics and the intense efforts associated with this tendency, stemming mainly from the Western powers, to secure allies and influence in the new states.

Looking at the period of approximately the last 20 years, it is clear that here, too, considerable influence on development research can be traced to super-power interests and foreign-policy orientations. But precisely on this last count, the radical changes that have taken place in the international system since 1989 may pave the way for research which, at least, is less dependent on interests and priorities determined by the super-powers' international security policies than was the case previously. On the other hand, one can easily imagine further intensification of influences from the economic interests of the affluent countries. But most conspicuous of all is probably the force with which an increased knowledge about specific circumstances in developing countries, as well as about the actual changes in these circumstances, manifested itself in the theory building of the late 1970s onwards.

The enhanced knowledge about the conditions obtaining in developing countries, revealed in a rapidly increasing number of empirical studies, disclosed so varied and multifarious a picture that all theories claiming validity for Third World countries as a whole necessarily had to be questioned. It proved particularly impossible to perceive developing countries as one large group of societies with homogeneous economic structures, development conditions and potentials. This was the case regardless of whether these societies were described as peripheral, underdeveloped, dual economies or satellites.

When the economic dimension is given prominence here, it is not to suggest that the differences in this regard were found greater than where political and cultural conditions were concerned. On the contrary, the point is simply that economic theory construction previously went much further than the others with respect to explicit or implicit claims of uniformity.

Beyond providing greater insights into Third World conditions in general, research over the past 20 years has uncovered significant real changes. These concern, first, the further differentiation among developing countries regarding their conditions and possibilities. Secondly, they concern changes in the international system of decisive importance to the development prospects of various categories of countries in the Third World. The rise in oil prices in 1973 and again in 1979 were among the events that revealed the differentiation which had already occurred, as well as giving the process further impetus.

The increased differentiation, which could already be observed in 1973, could be traced back to a complicated interplay of a number of factors such as the resource endowment and economic conditions in the individual countries, heterogeneous social structures, marked differences in the various countries' policies and their implementation, as well as the very different positions of the developing countries within the international system. In regard to the latter, there is probably good reason to emphasise that the reallocation of international investments and the transnationalisation of the growth processes of the industrialised countries benefited only a small number of developing countries. The remaining countries were left to compete on highly unequal terms in the global market with both the highly industrialised societies and their transnational corporations, and the few newly industrialised countries which during a brief but critical period of time were able to benefit from the so-called new international division of labour, thus creating an internal basis for export-oriented industrial development.

For these and a number of other reasons, the developing countries were very differently prepared for handling the recession in the world economy and the increasing protectionism introduced by the industrialised countries throughout the 1980s. At the same time many African countries, which were among the poorest to begin with, were further subjected to setbacks – partially due to adverse climatic conditions, primarily drought, but which moreover could be traced back to internal political and social conditions as well.

One last factor to be mentioned here – of significance for the increased disparity between the developing countries – is the military interventions of the super-powers and regional or internal conflicts, which forced a number of states to stake so much on armaments that their economic and social development possibilities were markedly limited.

Attention can be drawn – and should be in an actual analysis – to several more factors that have contributed to increasing the differences between the many countries in the Third World, as has been done throughout the book. The purpose, however, in this particular context is the more limited one of establishing that the actual tendencies towards differentiation have exerted great influence on theory construction within development research and have forced it in the direction of a corresponding differentiation. It no longer constitutes good practice to claim universal validity for proposed theories, exceptions being some neo-classical schools of thought among economists and perhaps also the so-called world-system theorists.

This, however, does not imply that development research today is characterised by meticulous and explicit statements concerning the limitations of validity or the conditions under which the given generalisations are presumed to be valid. Rather, the change manifests itself in the form of theories that are elaborated with reference to delimited regions and types of developing countries (for example East Africa or high-performing economies in the Far East). The question remains whether this kind of differentiation is a useful and productive one when it is combined to such a limited extent with comparative or generalising research objectives. The differentiation in theory construction is clearly necessary, but fragmentation into disparate and unrelated theoretical propositions concerning specific societies or regions is not concordant with the efforts of good social science to identify general trends and patterns of correlations.

In some of the more recent contributions to theory building considerably more attention has been paid to cultural aspects, their complexity and diversity, and to the ways in which culture-specific conditions and certain historical circumstances manifest themselves in the development process and in the elaboration of development strategies. As a further consequence of this, many non-anthropological development researchers have increased their attention to middle-level theory construction, focusing on phenomena between structures and individual actors.

Some have gone in the direction of the type of detailed studies which also characterise traditional social anthropology, with emphasis being placed on the investigation and description of local societal phenomena at the micro-level. The so-called studies of everyday life are among these. Others, comprising a somewhat larger group of development researchers, have elaborated what in a wider sense may be termed sector-oriented theories within international development studies. The goal here is theory construction pertaining to sectors which may be delimited by economic, social, political, as well as cultural criteria. To this category of theory construction belong theories of the informal sector, theories of peasant economies, theories of rural development, and the like. Theories of people's participation and of the role of transnational corporations in the development process may also be included in this group.

It is apparent that with respect to method, these varied forms of sector-oriented theories have no appreciable kinship. What justifies grouping these theories together is solely their shared attempt to break with the previously predominant tendency to focus on societal formations in their entirety as the central units of analysis. Instead, they focus their attention on delimited sub-components which, in turn, are usually studied comparatively in several societies, or with a generalising aim in instances where only few societies and societal segments are involved.

Furthermore, this sort of middle-level theory construction often reflects a transnational or international perspective. Evidently, this applies particularly to theories about the role of transnational corporations in the Third World, but the tendency recurs in many other contexts. The sector-oriented theories have hereby contributed to a greater understanding of the links between societal sub-components across national borders. They have drawn attention to the way in which sectors and geographically delimited enclaves are frequently more closely linked to corresponding sectors in the industrialised countries than to other segments of the national economy. In this respect, sector-oriented theories have complemented macro-level theories on external relations between states and entire societal formations.

Regardless of what one might think of the individual theories that have been advanced, there can hardly be any doubt that in an overall assessment the theoretical upheaval within development research over the last 10 to 15 years should be welcomed. It is basically commendable how rapidly and meticulously development researchers in general have reacted to the changing tendencies and new insights into the conditions in the Third World. On the other hand, it has to be admitted that development studies as a subject area, for reasons outlined previously, continues to be characterised by a lack of internal consistency, a high degree of eclecticism that is not always productive, and 'fashion' trends in theory construction and in the areas of focus.

It was claimed above that theory construction is influenced not only by change tendencies in the Third World, but also by changes in the international system. This influence is nevertheless not very distinct as of yet. The situation seems to be that the radical changes in the global system, following the collapse of the centrally planned economies in the Soviet Union and Eastern Europe and the end of the Cold War, are clearly acknowledged without yet having resulted in comprehensive and systematic attempts at adjusting relevant theories in accordance with these changes.

Stronger efforts have been made recently to undertake a critical reconstruction of the 1970s' theories of transnationalisation and internationalisation of capital, the new international division of labour, etc., aiming to assess more specifically the extent of their validity. One of the endeavours in this context is an extension of the general considerations concerning differentiation and involves, among other aspects, attempts at finding out why developing countries have been affected in such different manners by the movement and localisation of capital. Another effort is to a greater extent concerned with ascertaining whether the patterns discerned earlier in the international movement of capital still prevail. In this connection, the question has also been raised of whether the development strategies that previously brought about good results in the newly industrialised countries, such as South Korea and Taiwan, would be at all appropriate in the prevailing international circumstances of the 1990s.

In the further account of determinants of theory construction, the next type to be addressed is the influence that stems from results of specific development activities. At the centre of attention here is the feedback from the application of development strategies that previous theory construction indicated as the most relevant and adequate with respect to reaching certain objectives. This *feedback* comes from different places. Most important are the results provided by various governments' development efforts, viewed in relation to market-led development processes. However, theory building has also been influenced to a great extent by international development co-operation, and the successes and failures achieved in this area. In addition, most recently we find a lesser but increasing influence from observed effects of development efforts executed by other agents in the Third World, among these local popular democratic organisations and NGOs in a broader sense.

At a high level of aggregation and abstraction, the recurrent common feature that economic growth was limited to small geographic enclaves – to certain narrowly delimited sectors and to small, already affluent, societal groups – contributed to creating special problems for liberalist theory construction during the 1970s. This feature corresponded poorly to the expectations of modernisation theory. At the same time, classical dependency theories were faced with great difficulty in explaining the comprehensive industrialisation which was in fact taking place in parts of the Third World. Circumstances like these contributed to speeding up the aforementioned differentiation in theory building. But at a lower level of abstraction they also led to an intense debate regarding the utility and applicability of different development strategies under dissimilar conditions.

At these lower levels of abstraction it was perhaps currents within international development co-operation, in particular, which came to influence development research and its theory construction the most. I am thinking here, among other things, of the influence wielded by proposals focusing on basic needs strategies, starting in the middle of the 1970s and again in the early 1990s. I am thinking further of the increased importance given to people's participation in development co-operation. Yet another example is the increased priority assigned to women by most international as well as national aid agencies. In all these three areas, the original strategy proposals were in general theoretically ill-founded. They did not emerge from a comprehensive and substantial theory formation within the field of development research. Nor do I think it is possible to claim that such theory construction has yet come forth as the result of the introduction of strategies with the specific aims of alleviating poverty, mobilising people or improving women's conditions. Granted, comprehensive empirical research has been initiated and effected in all three areas as a response to the introduction of the new accentuations in the strategy debate. But aside from the marked influence in quantitative terms, the most remarkable aspect appears to be just how ill-prepared development research has been, methodically and theoretically, to assimilate and integrate (or reject) such influences from practical development co-operation.

This also manifests itself, albeit in a somewhat different way, in connection with the introduction of environmental concerns in the course of the 1980s. Again it must be accepted as meritorious that development researchers also reacted with rapidity and flexibility to this new current – in this case even including responding to altered research priorities in other fields such as the natural sciences. However, the methodical and theoretical weaknesses of this response are less commendable.

The environmental problems have been acknowledged as cross- and multidisciplinary. But this is precisely one of the pertinent characteristics of the subject area which has not yet manifested itself in integrated theories about causes of environmental degradation, resource depletion or pollution. In addition, there has been a tendency to incorporate the environmental problem complex as an isolated subject area of development research, separate from other development problems both in the context of analysis and of theory formation. Also in this respect, the response resembles the situation in the other areas which have been strongly influenced by international development co-operation.

The last type of determinant which shall be touched on briefly here is the influence from the debate regarding method and theory within the conventional social science disciplines. This influence can in part be identified in the form of development researchers taking over new methods, concepts and research priorities. It may further be observed in the way that altered conceptions and accentuations in the social sciences, notably economics, manifest themselves in the industrialised countries' policies *vis-à-vis* developing countries, either directly or indirectly through international organisations such as the World Bank and the International Monetary Fund. These changes have had a strong impact upon the research priorities among development researchers.

The counter-revolution among economists, which has already been mentioned, may be used to illustrate both processes, as we have touched on in discussions previously in the book. In the academic debate, the viewpoints which are today perceived as counter-revolutionary go all the way back to the 1940s and the criticism of Keynes in the early post-war period. The criticism was primarily directed at Keynes's notions of the appropriateness of relatively comprehensive state intervention seeking to promote economic development. On the basis of micro-economic theory, the critics instead claimed that better results would be attained if market mechanisms were allowed to work unhindered. Another type of criticism came from the so-called monetarists, primarily in the United States, for whom Keynes's theories were completely inadequate or simply mistaken, particularly where the discussion of inflation problems was concerned.

However, neither of these two currents gained decisive importance until the end of the 1970s and then not so much by virtue of their intellectually convincing argumentation as due to altered political circumstances. The doctrines of the blessings of the free market and the merits of monetarism had been assumed as a political-economic programme by a number of right-wing parties in Western Europe and in the United States. When these parties came to power in 1979–80 in the UK, the United States and West Germany, the anti-Keynesian currents penetrated both domestic policy and attitudes towards how developing countries ought to prioritise in *their* economic policies. By virtue of the three countries' strong positions in international aid co-operation, including in institutions like the International Monetary Fund and the World Bank, a continually increasing number of developing countries were forced to adjust their economic policies in accordance with the new currents.

These changes entailed a challenge for development research on the whole that exponents of both the previously predominant liberalist and neo-Marxist theories were unprepared for. The general impression was that existing theory within the field of development research was poorly equipped either to integrate or to reject the impact of monetarism and micro-economic theory. Only in most recent years has a more thorough debate and criticism of the counter-revolutionary economists, and the development strategies they have recommended for Third World countries, gained momentum.

Concluding remarks

I shall not attempt to formulate a genuine conclusion based on the considerations presented here. They possess in themselves a concluding character and, as presented above, they can only be perceived as unsupported claims. In return, I hope of course that the views presented will appear reasonably plausible to other scholars of development research – or stimulate counter-argument and debate. There is a need for a far more comprehensive debate and careful reflection on the theory of science positions (implicitly) adopted by development research and on its methodological principles. There is an equally strong need for a more thorough discussion of the determinants of theory construction, including a need to identify those influences which on the premises of the theories advanced must be perceived as irrelevant external influences or as biases resulting from dominant values or interests.

Lastly, I would have liked to advance a possible outline of the course development research and theory construction is taking. However, after careful consideration I would rather pronounce myself incapable of presenting such a qualified and substantiated scenario. Instead, this chapter will close with summarising emphasis on the fact that the present situation is characterised, on the one hand, by an advanced and productive dialogue between competing and conflicting theories of development in the Third World. On the other hand, the field is characterised by powerful attempts to revive mono-disciplinary approaches, principally within economics. In this context, the book at hand may be seen as a contribution to achieving an overview of the varied and rich debate and the bodies of theory available, and at the same time as a reminder to those favouring monodisciplinary approaches that it is not possible to grasp the complexities of the Third World that way.

Bibliography

(The year mentioned in brackets after the publisher refers to the year when the book or article first appeared.)

Alam, Muhammad M., Ahmed S. Huque and Kirsten Westergaard, 1994, *Development through Decentralization in Bangladesh. Evidence and Perspective*, Dhaka, University Press.

Alavi, Hamza, 1972, 'The State in Postcolonial Societies: Pakistan and Bangladesh', *New Left Review*, No. 74.

Alavi, Hamza, 1982, 'State and Class Under Peripheral Capitalism'. In: H. Alavi and T. Shanin (eds), *Introduction to the Sociology of Developing Societies*, London, Macmillan, 1982.

Almond, Gabriel and J. Coleman (eds) 1960, *The Politics of the Developing Areas*, Princeton, NJ, Princeton University Press.

Almond, Gabriel and B. Powell, 1966, *Comparative Politics: a Developmental Approach*, Boston, Little, Brown & Co.

Amin, Samir, 1974, *Accumulation on a World Scale*, New York, Monthly Review Press (1970).

Amin, Samir, 1976, *Unequal Development*, Sussex, Harvester Press (1973).

Amin, Samir, 1992a, 'A World in Chaos'. In: H. Lindholm (ed.), 1992.

Amin, Samir, 1992b, *Empire of Chaos*, New York, Monthly Review Press.

Amsden, Alice H., 1989, *Asia's Next Giant: South Korea and Late Industrialization*, New York, Oxford University Press.

Anderson, Perry, 1979, *Lineages of the Absolutist State*, London, Verso.

Apter, David E., 1965, *The Politics of Modernization*, Chicago, IL, University of Chicago Press.

Apter, David E., 1987, *Rethinking Development. Modernization, Dependency and Postmodern Politics*, Newbury Park, CA, Sage Publications.

Arnfred, Signe and A. Weis Bentzon (eds), 1990, *The Language of Development Studies*, Copenhagen, New Social Science Monographs.

Bagchi, Amiya Kumar, 1982, *The Political Economy of Underdevelopment*, Cambridge, Cambridge University Press.

Bailey, F. G., 1963, *Politics and Social Change: Orissa in 1959*, London, Oxford University Press.

Balassa, Bela, 1982, *Development Strategies in Semi-Industrial Economies*, Baltimore, MD, Johns Hopkins University Press.

Banuri, Tariq, Göran Hydén, Calestous Juma and Marcia Rivera, 1995, *Sustainable Human Development. From Concept to Operation: A Guide for the Practitioner*, New York, UNDP. A discussion paper.

Baran, Paul, 1957, *The Political Economy of Growth*, New York, Monthly Review Press.

Baran, Paul and P. M. Sweezy, 1968, *Monopoly Capital. An Essay on the American Economic and Social Order*, Harmondsworth, Penguin.

Bardhan, Pranab, 1984, *Land Labor and Rural Poverty*, New York, Columbia University Press.

Bardhan, Pranab (ed.), 1989, *The Economic Theory of Agrarian Institutions*, Oxford, Oxford University Press.

Bardhan, Pranab, 1992, 'A Political-Economy Perspective on Development'. In: Jalan, 1992.

Barth, Fredrik, 1969, *Ethnic Groups and Boundaries. The Social Organization of Cultural Difference*, London, George Allen & Unwin.

Bates, Robert H., 1981, *Markets and States in Tropical Africa: The Political Basis of Agricultural Policies*, Berkeley, CA, University of California Press.

Bates, Robert H. (ed.), 1988, *Toward a Political Economy of Development. A Rational Choice Perspective*, Berkeley, CA, University of California Press.

Bauer, P. T., 1981, *Equality, the Third World, and Economic Delusion*, Cambridge, MA, Harvard University Press.

Bauer, P. T., 1984, *Reality and Rhetoric. Studies in the Economics of Development*, London, Weidenfeld and Nicolson.

Bayart, Jean-François, 1991, 'Finishing with the Idea of the Third World: The Concept of the Political Trajectory'. In: Manor, 1991.

Bayart, Jean-François, 1993, *The State in Africa. The Politics of the Belly*, London, Longman (French edn 1989).

Belshaw, Derycke, Piers Blaikie and Michael Stocking, 1991, 'Identifying Key Land Degradation Issues and Applied Research Priorities'. In: Winpenny, 1991.

Berry, R. A. and W. R. Cline, 1979, *Agrarian Structure and Productivity in Developing Countries*, Baltimore, MD, Johns Hopkins University Press.

Berry, S., 1993, 'Understanding Agricultural Policy in Africa: The Contributions of Robert Bates', *World Development*, Vol. 21, No. 6.

Bhagwati, J. N., 1982, 'Directly Unproductive Profit-Seeking (DUP) Activities', *Journal of Political Economy*, 90, October.

Bhagwati, J. N. and P. Desai, 1970, *India. Planning for Industrialization*, London, Oxford University Press for the OECD.

Bharadwaj, Krishna and Sudipta Kaviraj, 1989, *Perspectives on Capitalism. Marx, Keynes, Schumpeter and Weber*, New Delhi, Sage Publications.

Bienen, H., J. Parks, and J. Riedinger, 1990, 'Decentralization in Nepal', *World Development*, Vol. 18, No. 1.

Binder, Leonard et al. (eds), 1968, *Crises in Political Development*, Princeton, NJ, Princeton University Press.

Binder, Leonard et al. (eds), 1986, *Crisis and Sequences in Political Development*, Princeton, NJ, Princeton University Press.

Bista, Dor Bahadur, 1991, *Fatalism and Development. Nepal's Struggle for Modernization*, Hyderabad, Orient Longman.

Blaikie, Piers, 1985, *The Political Economy of Soil Erosion in Developing Countries*, Harlow, Longman Development Studies.

Blaikie, Piers and Harold Brookfield (eds), 1987, *Land Degradation and Society*, London, Methuen.

Boserup, Ester, 1965, *The Conditions of Agricultural Growth. The Economics of Agrarian Change under Population Pressure*, London, George Allen & Unwin.

Boserup, Ester, 1970, *Women's Role in Economic Development*, London, George Allen & Unwin.

Boserup, Ester, 1981, *Population and Technological Change. A Study of Long-term Trends*, Chicago, IL, University of Chicago Press.

Bowie, Alasdair, 1991, *Crossing the Industrial Divide. Society and the Politics of Economic Transformation in Malaysia*, New York, Columbia University Press.

Brandt Commission, 1980, *North South: A Programme for Survival*, London, Pan Books.

Brandt Commission, 1983, *Common Crisis. North South: Co-operation for World Recovery*, London, Pan Books.

Brass, Paul, 1991, *Ethnicity and Nationalism. Theory and Comparison*, New Delhi, Sage Publications.

Bromley, Daniel W., 1989, 'Property Relations and Economic Development – the Other Land Reform', *World Development*, Vol. 17, No. 6.

Brundtland, Gro Harlem et al., 1987, *Our Common Future*, Oxford, World Commission on Environment and Development, Oxford University Press.

Bruun, Hans Henrik, 1972, *Science, Values and Politics in Max Weber's Methodology*, Copenhagen, Munksgaard.

Burris, Val, 1987, 'The Neo-Marxist Synthesis of Marx and Weber on Class'. In: Wiley, 1987.

Buzan, Barry, 1991a, 'New Patterns of Global Security in the Twenty-first Century', *International Affairs*, Vol. 67, No. 3.

Buzan, Barry, 1991b, *People, States and Fear. An Agenda for International Security Studies in the Post-Cold War Era*, London, Harvester Wheatsheaf.

Caldwell, John C., 1982, *Theory of Fertility Decline*, London, Academic Press.

Cardoso, F. H., 1972, 'Dependency and Development in Latin America', *New Left Review*, No. 74.

Cardoso, F. H. and Faletto, 1979, *Dependency and Development in Latin America*, Berkeley, CA, University of California Press (1971).

Chai-Anan Samudavanija, 1991, 'The Three-Dimensional State'. In: Manor, 1991.

Chambers, Robert, 1983, *Rural Development. Putting the Last First*, New York, John Wiley.

Cheema, G. and D. A. Rondinelli (eds), 1983, *Decentralization and Development. Policy Implementation in Developing Countries*, Beverly Hills, CA, Sage Publications.

Chen, Edward K. Y., 1979, *Hypergrowth in Asian Economies: A Comparative Survey of Hong Kong, Japan, Korea, Singapore and Taiwan*, London, Macmillan.

Chenery, Hollis et al., 1974, *Redistribution with Growth*, London, Oxford University Press.

Chenery, Hollis, S. Robinson and M. Syrquin, 1986, *Industrialization and Growth*, New York, Oxford University Press.

Chenery, Hollis and T. N. Srinivasan (eds), 1988, *Handbook of Development Economics*, Vol. I, Amsterdam, Horth Holland.

Chenery, Hollis and T. N. Srinivasan (eds), 1989, *Handbook of Development Economics*, Vol. II, Amsterdam, Horth Holland.

Chenery, Hollis and M. Syrquin, 1975, *Patterns of Development, 1950–1970*, London, Oxford University Press.

Clapham, Christopher, 1985, *Third World Politics. An Introduction*, London, Croom Helm.

Clark, Gordon L. and Michael Dear, 1984, *State Apparatus. Structures and Language of Legitimacy*, Boston, MA, Allen & Unwin.

Cleaver, H. M., 1972, 'The Contradictions of the Green Revolution', *Monthly Review*, Vol. 24, No. 2.

Cliffe, L., 1987, 'The Debate on African Peasantries', *Development and Change*, Vol. 18, No. 4.

Coase, Ronald H., 1937, 'The Nature of the Firm', *Economica*, Vol. IV.

Coase, Ronald H., 1960, 'The Problem of Social Cost', *Journal of Law and Economics*, Vol. 3, pp. 1–44.

Cohen, Jean L. and A. Arato, 1992, *Civil Society and Political Theory*, Cambridge, MA, MIT Press.

Coleman, James S. (ed.), 1965, *Education and Political Development*. Princeton, NJ, Princeton University Press.

Coleman, James S., 1976, 'Modernization: Political Aspects', *International Encyclopedia of the Social Sciences*, Vol. 10, New York, Collier, Macmillan.

Corbridge, Stuart, 1990, 'Post Marxism and Development Studies: Beyond the Impasse', *World Development*, Vol. 18, No. 5.

Cornia, G. A., R. Jolly and F. Stewart (eds), 1987, *Adjustment with a Human Face. Protecting the Vulnerable and Promoting Growth*, Oxford, Clarendon Press.

Dahl, Robert A., 1971, *Polyarchy: Participation and Opposition*, New Haven, CT, Yale University Press.

Dandekar, V. M. and N. Rath, 1971, 'Poverty in India I–II', *Economic and Political Weekly*, 2 and 9 Jan.

Davis, Jerome, 1993, 'On the Role of Markets in Economic Development: The New Institutional Economic Transactions Approach Defined'. In: Martinussen, 1993a.

Deger, Saadet, 1992, 'Military Expenditure and Economic Development: Issues and Debates'. In: Lamb, 1992.

Diamond, L., S. M. Lipset and J. J. Linz (eds), 1988, *Democracy in Developing Countries*, Boulder, CO, Westview Press.

Dickens, Peter, 1992, *Society and Nature. Towards a Green Social Theory*, Hertfordshire, Harvester Wheatsheaf.

Drabek, Anne Gordon (ed.), 1987, 'Development Alternatives: The Challenge for NGOs', *World Development*, Vol. 15, Supplement.

Dunning, John H., 1988, *Explaining International Production*, London, Unwin Hyman.

Easton, David, 1953, *The Political System*, New York, Alfred Knopf.

Easton, David, 1965, *A Systems Analysis of Political Life*, New York, John Wiley & Sons.

Ehrlich, Paul R., 1968, *The Population Bomb*, New York, Balantine Books.

Ehrlich, Paul R. and Anne H. Ehrlich, 1990, *The Population Explosion*, New York, Simon and Schuster.

Emmanuel, Arghiri, 1972, *Unequal Exchange. A Study of the Imperialism of Trade*, New York, Monthly Review Press (1969).

Evans, Peter B., 1989, 'Predatory, Developmental and Other Apparatuses: A Comparative Political Economy Perspective on the Third World State', *Sociological Forum*, Vol. 4, No. 4.

FAO, 1981, *Promotion of Self-help Organisations of the Rural Poor in Africa*, Rome.

Ferdinand, K. and M. Mozaffari (eds), 1988, *Islam, State and Society*, London, Curzon Press.

Forster-Carter, A., 1973, 'Neo-Marxist Approaches to Development and Underdevelopment', *Journal of Contemporary Asia*, Vol. 3, No. 1.

Forster-Carter, A., 1987. 'Knowing What They Mean?'. In: J. Clammer (ed.), *Beyond the New Economic Anthropology*, London, Macmillan

Foucault, Michel, 1980, *Power and Knowledge*, Worcester, Harvester Press.

Frank, Andre Gunder, 1967, *Capitalism and Underdevelopment in Latin America: Historical Studies of Chile and Brazil*, New York, Monthly Review Press.

Frank, Andre Gunder, 1981, *Crisis in the Third World*, London, Heinemann.

Frederiksen, Bodil Folke, 1990, 'Development Studies from Below: A View from the Humanities'. In: Arnfred and Bentzon 1990.

Freire, Paolo, 1990, *Pedagogy of the Oppressed*, London, Penguin (1972).

Friedmann, John, 1992, *Empowerment. The Politics of Alternative Development*, Cambridge, MA, Blackwell.

Fröbel, F., J. Heinrichs, and O. Kreye, 1980, *The New International Division of Labour*, Cambridge, Cambridge University Press (1977).

Furtado, C., 1965, *Development and Underdevelopment*, Berkeley, CA, University of California Press.

Ganapathy, R. S. et al., 1985, *Public Policy and Policy Analyses in India*. New Delhi, Sage Publications.

Geertz, Clifford, 1963, 'The Integrative Revolution'. In: C. Geertz (ed.), *Old Societies and New States*, New York, Free Press.

Gellner, Ernest, 1983, *Nations and Nationalism*, Oxford, Basil Blackwell.

George, Susan, 1988, *A Fate Worse than Debt*, London, Pelican Books.

Giddens, Anthony, 1977, *Studies in Social and Political Theory*, London, Hutchinson.

Giddens, Anthony, 1989, *Sociology*, Cambridge, Polity Press and Basil Blackwell.

Gill, G. J., 1991, *Seasonality and Agriculture in the Developing World. A Problem of the Poor and Powerless*, Cambridge, Cambridge University Press.

Gran, Guy, 1983, *Development by People. Citizen Construction of a Just World*, New York, Praeger.

Griffin, Keith, 1979, *The Political Economy of Agrarian Change*, London, Macmillan.

Griffin, K., 1991, 'Foreign Aid after the Cold War', *Development and Change*, Vol. 22, No. 4.

Grindle, Merilee S. and John W. Thomas, 1990, 'After the Decision: Implementing Policy Reforms in Developing Countries', *World Development*, Vol. 18, No. 8

Grindle, Merilee S. and John W. Thomas, 1991, *Public Choices and Policy Change: The Political Economy of Reform in Developing Countries*, Baltimore, MD, Johns Hopkins University Press.

Gusfield, J., 1976, 'Tradition and Modernity: Misplaced Polarities in the Study of Social Change', *American Journal of Sociology*, Vol. 72, January.

Guyer, Jane I. and P. E. Peters (eds), 1987, 'Conceptualizing the Household: Issues of Theory and Policy in Africa', *Development and Change*, Special Issue, Vol. 18, No. 2.

Haggard, Stephen and Robert F. Kaufman (eds), 1992, *The Politics of Economic Adjustment*, Princeton, Princeton University Press.

Hansen, Thomas Blom, 1991, *Politics and Ideology in Developing Societies. An Exploratory Essay*, Aalborg, Aalborg University.

Hansen, Thomas Blom, 1996, *The Safron Wave* (forthcoming).

Haq, Mahbub ul, 1995, *Reflections on Human Development*, New York, Oxford University Press.

Hardin, Garett, 1968, 'The Tragedy of the Commons', *Science*, Vol. 162, pp. 1243–8.

Harris, Nigel, 1987, *The End of the Third World. Newly Industrialising Countries and the Decline of an Ideology*, Harmondsworth, Penguin (1986).

Hasan, Zoya, S. N. Jha and R. Khan (eds), 1989, *The State, Political Processes and Identity. Reflections on Modern India*, New Delhi, Sage Publications.

Hastrup, Kirsten, 1990, 'Udvikling eller historie – antropologiens bidrag til en ny verden' (Development or history – the contribution of anthropology to a new world, in Danish), *Den Ny Verden*, 23. årg. nr 1.

Hawthorn, G., 1991, 'Waiting for a Text: Comparing Third World Politics'. In: Manor, 1991.

Hayami, Y. and V. Ruttan, 1985, *Agricultural Development: An International Perspective*, Baltimore, MD, Johns Hopkins University Press (1971).

Helleiner, G. K., 1989, 'Transnational Corporations and Direct Foreign Investment'. In: H. Chenery and T. N. Srinivasan, 1989 (Vol. II).

Hettne, Björn, 1986, *Approaches to the Study of Peace and Development*, Göteborg, PADRIGU Papers.

Hettne, Björn, 1989. *The Globalization of Development Theory and the Future of Development Theory*, Gothenburg, PADRIGU Papers.

Hettne, Björn, 1990, *Development Theory and the Three Worlds*, Essex, Longman.

Hettne, Björn, 1995, *Development Theory and the Three Worlds: Towards an International Political Economy of Development* (revised edn of Hettne, 1990), Essex, Longman.

Hirschman, A. O., 1958, *The Strategy of Economic Development*, New Haven, CT, Yale University Press.

Hirschman, A. O., 1981, *Essays in Trespassing: Economics to Politics and Beyond*, Cambridge, Cambridge University Press.

Hobsbawm, E. J. and T. Ranger (eds), 1983, *The Invention of Tradition*, Cambridge, Cambridge University Press.

Hobsbawm, E. J., 1991, *Nations and Nationalism since 1780: Programme, Myth, Reality*, Cambridge, Cambridge University Press.

Holm, H. H. and G. Sørensen (eds), 1995, *Whose World Order. Uneven Globalization and the End of the Cold War*, Boulder, CO, Westview Press.

Hunt, Diana, 1989, *Economic Theories of Development: An Analysis of Competing Paradigms*, New York, Harvester Wheatsheaf.

Huntington, Samuel, 1968, *Political Order in Changing Societies*, New Haven, CT., Yale University Press.

Huntington, Samuel and J. M. Nelson, 1976, *No Easy Choice. Political Participation in Developing Countries*, Cambridge, MA, Harvard University Press.

Hydén, Göran, 1983, *No Shortcuts to Progress. African Development Management in Perspective*, London, Heinemann.

Hydén, Göran, 1986, 'The Anomaly of the African Peasantry', *Development and Change*, Vol. 17, No. 2.

Hydén, Göran and M. Bratton (eds), 1992, *Governance and Politics in Africa*, Boulder, CO, Rienner.

Hymer, Stephen, 1976, *The International Operations of National Firms: A Study of Direct Foreign Investment*, Cambridge, MA, MIT Press.

IDS Bulletin, 1988, 'Ajustment and the State: The Problem of Administration Reform', *IDS Bulletin*, Vol. 19, No. 4.

ILO, 1972, *Employment, Incomes and Equality: a Strategy for Increasing Productive Employment in Kenya*, Geneva, ILO.

ILO, 1976, *Employment, Growth and Basic Needs: A One-World Problem*, Geneva, ILO.

ILO, 1978, *Popular Participation in Decision-making and the Basic Needs Approach to Development*, Geneva, ILO.

Jackson, R. H. and C. G. Rosberg, 1982a, *Personal Rule in Black Africa. Prince, Autocrat, Prophet, Tyrant*. Berkeley, CA, University of California Press.

Jackson, R. H. and C. G. Rosberg, 1982b, 'Why Africa's Weak States Persist: The Empirical and the Juridical in Statehood', *World Politics*, Vol. XXXV, No. 1.

Jalan, Bimal, 1992, *The Indian Economy: Problems and Prospects*, New Delhi, Viking.

Jazairy, Idriss, M. Alamgir and T. Panuccio, 1992, *The State of World Rural Poverty. An Inquiry into its Causes and Consequences*, Published for the International Fund for Agricultural Development by New York University Press.

Jha, S. N., 1989, 'Dynamic View of Identity Formation: An Agenda for Research'. In: Hasan et al., 1989.

Joekes, Susan and Naila Kabeer (eds), 1991, 'Researching the Household: Methodological and Empirical Issues', *IDS Bulletin*, Vol. 22, No. 1.

Johnson, Chalmers, 1982, *MITI and the Japanese Miracle. The Growth of Industrial Policy, 1925–75*, Stanford, CA, Stanford University Press.

Johnston, B. F. and J. Mellor, 1961, 'The Role of Agriculture in Economic Development', *American Economic Review*, Sept.

Journal of Development Planning, 1989, 'Human Development in the 1980s and Beyond', *Journal of Development Planning* (Special Issue), No. 19.

Kasfir, Nelson, 1986, 'Are African Peasants Self-Sufficient?', *Development and Change*, Vol. 17, No. 2.

Kaviraj, Sudipta, 1989, 'On Political Explanation in Marxism'. In: Bharadwaj and Kaviraj, 1989.

Kaviraj, Sudipta, 1991, 'On State, Society and Discourse in India'. In: Manor, 1991.

Kay, Cristóbal, 1989, *Latin American Theories of Development and Underdevelopment*, London, Routledge.

Kay, G., 1975, *Development and Underdevelopment: A Marxist Analysis*, London, Macmillan.

Keynes, John Maynard, 1973, *The General Theory of Employment, Interest and Money*, London, Macmillan (1936).

Killick, Tony, 1989, *A Reaction Too Far. Economic Theory and the Role of the State in Developing Countries*, London, Overseas Development Institute.

Kohli, Atul, 1991, *Democracy and Discontent. India's Growing Crisis of Governability*, Cambridge, Cambridge University Press.

Kongstad, Per and M. Mønsted, 1980, *Family, Labour and Trade in Western Kenya*, Uppsala, Scandinavian Institute of African Studies.

Korten, David C., 1980, 'Community Organization and Rural Development: A Learning Process Approach', *Public Administrative Review*, Vol. 40, No. 5.

Korten, David C., 1990, *Getting to the 21st Century. Voluntary Action and the Global Agenda*, West Hartford, CT, Kumarian Press.

Krueger, Anne O., 1974, 'The Political Economy of the Rent-Seeking Society', *The American Economic Review*, Vol. 64, No. 3.

Krueger, Anne O., 1993, *Political Economy of Policy Reform in Developing Countries*, Cambridge, MA, The MIT Press.

Kuhn, Thomas, 1972, *The Structure of Scientific Revolutions* (2nd edn), Chicago, IL, University of Chicago Press.

Kuznets, Simon, 1955, 'Economic Growth and Income Inequality', *American Economic Review*, March.

Kuznets, Simon, 1966, *Modern Economic Growth*, New Haven, CT, Yale University Press.

Lal, Deepak, 1980, *Prices for Planning. Toward the Reform of Indian Planning*, London, Heinemann.

Lal, Deepak, 1983, *The Poverty of 'Development Economics'*, London, Institute of Economic Affairs.

Lall, Sanjaya and Paul Streeten, 1977, *Foreign Investment, Transnationals and Developing Countries*, London, Macmillan.

Lamb, Geoffrey (ed.), 1992, *Military Expenditure and Economic Development. A Symposium on Research Issues*, Washington, DC, The World Bank (Discussion Paper No. 185).

Langdon, S. and M. Godfrey, 1976, 'Partners in Underdevelopment: The Transnationalization Thesis in a Kenyan Context', *Journal of Commonwealth Politics*, March.

LaPalombara, J. (ed.), 1963, *Bureaucracy and Political Development*. Princeton, NJ, Princeton University Press.

LaPalombara, J. and M. Weiner (eds), 1966, *Political Parties and Political Development*, Princeton, NJ, Princeton University Press.

Lappé, F. M. and J. Collins, 1979, *World Hunger. Ten Myths*, Washington, DC, Institute for Food and Development Policy.

Lappé, F. M. and R. Schurman, 1989, *Taking Population Seriously*, London, Earthscan Publications.

Lauridsen, Laurids S., 1991, 'The Debate on the Developmental State'. In: Martinussen, 1991a.

Lauridsen, Laurids S. (ed.), 1993, *Bringing Institutions Back in. The Role of Institutions in Civil Society, State and Economy*, Roskilde, International Development Studies.

Laursen, Karsten, 1984, 'Global interdependens' (Global interdependence, in Danish), *Den Ny Verden*, 18. årg. nr 3.

Laursen, Karsten, 1987, *Udviklingsøkonomi* (Development economics, in Danish), Copenhagen, Nyt Nordisk Forlag Arnold Busck.

Laursen, Karsten, 1990, 'Udviklingsprocessens struktur' (The structure of the development process, in Danish), *Den Ny Verden*, 23. årg. nr 1.

Lawry, Steven W., 1989, *Politique de tenure et gestion des ressources naturelles en Afrique de l'ouest sahélienne*, Madison, Land Tenure Center.

Lerner, Daniel, 1958, *The Passing of Traditional Societies: Modernizing the Middle East*, New York, The Free Press.

Lewis, Arthur, 1954, 'Economic Development with Unlimited Supplies Labour', *Manchester School of Economic and Social Studies*, Vol. 22, No. 2. Genoptrykt i: Agarwala, A. and S. Singh (eds), *The Economics of Underdevelopment*, London, Oxford University Press, 1958.

Lewis, Arthur, 1955, *The Theory of Economic Growth*, London, Allen and Unwin.

Liddle, R. William, 1992, 'The Politics of Development Policy', *World Development*, Vol. 20, No. 6.

Liebenstein, H., 1989, 'Organizational Economics and Institutions as Missing Elements in Economic Development Analysis'. In: *World Development*, 1989.

Lindholm, H. (ed.), 1992, *Approaches to the Study of International Political Economy*, Gothenburg, PADRIGU.

Lindholm, H., 1993, 'Introduction: A Conceptual Discussion'. In: H. Lindholm, (ed.), *Ethnicity and Nationalism. Formation of Identity and Dynamics of Conflict in the 1990s*, Göteborg, Nordnes.

Lipset, S. M., 1959, 'Some Social Requisites of Democracy: Economic Development and Political Legitimacy', *American Political Science Review*, Vol. 53, No. 1.

Lipton, Michael, 1977, *Why Poor People Stay Poor. Urban Bias in World Development*, London, Temple Smith.

Lipton, Michael, 1991, 'A Note on Poverty and Sustainability', *IDS Bulletin*, Vol. 22, No. 4.

Lipton, Michael, 1993, 'Urban Bias: Of Consequences, Classes and Causality'. In: Varshney, 1993.

Lipton, Michael and Simon Maxwell, 1992, *The New Poverty Agenda: An Overview*, Sussex, Institute of Development Studies (Discussion Paper 306).

Lisk, Frankley (ed.), 1985, *Popular Participation in Planning for Basic Needs. Concepts, Methods and Practices*, Aldershot, Gower. Prepared for the ILO.

Little, I. M. D., 1982, *Economic Development. Theory, Policy and International Relations*, New York, Basic Books.

Little, I. M. D., T. Scitovsky and M. Scott, 1970, *Industry and Trade in Some Developing Countries. A Comparative Study*, London, Oxford University Press for the OECD.

Löwith, Karl, 1982, *Max Weber and Karl Marx*, London, George Allan and Unwin (1932).

Mamdani, Mahmoud, 1972, *The Myth of Population Control. Family, Caste and Class in an Indian Village*, New York, Monthly Review Press.

Manor, J. (ed.), 1991, *Rethinking Third World Politics*, London, Longman.

Marshall, Alfred, 1920, *Principles of Economics*, London, Macmillan (1890).

Martinussen, John, 1980, *Staten i perifere og post-koloniale samfund: Indien og Pakistan* (The state in peripheral and post-colonial societies: India and Pakistan, Vols I–IV, in Danish, with an English summary), Århus, Politica.

Martinussen, John, 1988, *Transnational Corporations in a Developing Country: The Indian Experience*, New Delhi, Sage Publications.

Martinussen, John (ed.), 1991a, *Development Theory and the Role of the State in Third World Countries*, Roskilde, International Development Studies.

Martinussen, John, 1991b, 'Theories of the State'. In: Martinussen, 1991a.

Martinussen, John, 1991c, 'Policy Process and Regime Forms'. In: Martinussen, 1991a.

Martinussen, John (ed.), 1991d, *ILO/Danida Assisted Workers' Education Projects. Synthesis Report*, Copenhagen, Danida.

Martinussen, John, 1992, 'Regulation of TNC Activities in a Third World Country: The Indian Experience'. In: H. Lindholm (ed.), 1992.

Martinussen, John (ed.), 1993, *New Institutional Economics and Development Theory*, Roskilde, International Development Studies.

Martinussen, John, 1994, 'Marx and Weber and the Understanding of Politics within Development Studies'. In: Martinussen (ed.), *The Theoretical Heritage from Marx and Weber in Development Studies*, Roskilde, International Development Studies.

Martinussen, John, 1995, *Democracy, Competition and Choice: Emerging Local Self-Government in Nepal*, New Delhi, Sage Publications.

Marx, Karl, 1957–58, *Grundrisse der Kritik der politischen Ökonomie*, Frankfurt, Europäische Verlagsanstalt.

Marx, Karl, 1969, *Resultate des Unmittelbaren Produktionsprozesses*, Frankfurt, Verlag Neue Kritik (originally written in the 1860s).

Marx, Karl, 1972, *Das Kapital*, Berlin, Dietz Verlag (1867–1894).

Marx, Karl and F. Engels, 1972, *On Colonialism. Articles from the New York Tribune and Other Writings*, New York, International Publishers.

Max-Neef, M. A., 1991, *Human Scale Development. Conception, Application and Further Reflections*, New York, Apex Press.

Meadows, D. H, D. L. Meadows and J. Randers and W. W. Behrens, 1972, *The Limits to Growth*, New York, Universe Books.

Meadows, D. H, D. L. Meadows, J. Randers, 1992, *Beyond the Limits. Global Collapse or a Sustainable Future*, London, Earthscan Publications.

Meier, Gerald M., 1989, *Leading Issues in Economic Development*, New York, Oxford University Press.

Meier, Gerald M. and Dudley Seers (eds), 1984, *Pioneers in Development*, New York, Oxford University Press for the World Bank.

Meillassoux, C., 1970, 'A Class Analysis of the Bureaucratic Process in Mali', *Journal of Development Studies*, Vol. 16.

Mellor, John, 1986, 'Agriculture on the Road to Industrialisation'. In: J. P. Lewis and V. Kallab (eds), *Development Strategies Reconsidered*, Washington, DC, Overseas Development Council.

Mill, John Stuart, 1852, *Principles of Political Economy*, London, Parker (1848).

Mjøset, Lars, 1993, 'Comparative Typologies of Development Patterns: The Menzel/ Senghass Framework'. In: L. S. Lauridsen (ed.), 1993.

Moore, Barrington, 1966, *Social Origins of Dictatorship and Democracy. Lord and Peasant in the Making of the Modern World*, Harmondsworth, Penguin.

Moore, Mick (ed.), 1993, 'Good Government?', *IDS Bulletin*, Vol. 24, No. 1.

Moser, C. O. N., 1991, 'Gender Planning in the Third World: Meeting Practical and Strategic Gender Needs'. In: Wallace and March, 1991.

Myrdal, Gunnar, 1956, 'Trade as a Mechanism of International Inequality'. In: Meier, 1989, pp. 385ff.

Myrdal, Gunnar, 1959, *Value in Social Theory*, New York, Harper and Brothers. Ed. Paul Streeten.

Myrdal, Gunnar, 1968, *Asian Drama. An Inquiry into the Poverty of Nations*, Harmondsworth, Penguin.

Myrdal, Gunnar, 1970, *The Challenge of World Poverty. A World Anti-Poverty Programme in Outline*, Harmondsworth, Penguin.

Nabli, M. K. and J. B. Nugent, 1989, 'The New Institutional Economics and Its Applicability to Development'. In: *World Development*, 1989.

Nordlinger, Eric, 1988, 'The Return to the State: Critiques', *American Political Science Review*, Vol. 82, No. 3.

North, Douglass C., 1990, *Institutions, Institutional Change and Economic Performance*, Cambridge, Cambridge University Press.

Nurkse, Ragnar, 1953, *Problems of Capital Formation in Underdeveloped Countries*, Oxford, Blackwell.

Olsen, Gorm Rye, 1994, *Political Power and Economic Change in the Arab World. A Comparison of Egypt, Iraq, and Saudi Arabia*, Copenhagen, Centre for Development Research.

Oman, Charles, 1994, *Globalisation and Regionalisation: The Challenges for Developing Countries*, Paris, OECD.

Oman, Charles P. and G. Wignaraja, 1991, *The Postwar Evolution of Development Thinking*, London, Macmillan.

Ostrom, Elinor, 1990, *Governing the Commons: The Evolution of Institutions for Collective Action*, Cambridge, Cambridge University Press.

Palma, G., 1978, 'Dependency: A Formal Theory of Underdevelopment or a Methodology for the Analysis of Concrete Situations of Underdevelopment?', *World Development*, Vol. 6. In: Meier, 1989, pp. 105ff.

Parsons, Talcott, 1937, *The Structure of Social Action*, New York, McGraw-Hill.

Platteau, Jean-Philippe, 1993, 'The Free Market is Not Readily Transferable: Reflections on the Links Between Market, Social Relations and Moral Norms'. In: Martinussen, 1993a.

Polanyi, Karl, 1957, *The Great Transformation*, Boston, MA, Beacon Press.

Polanyi, Karl, 1977, *The Livelihood of Man* (ed. Harry W. Pearson), New York, Academic Press.

Popkin, S. L., 1988, 'Public Choice and Peasant Organization'. In: Bates, 1988.

Porter, M. E., 1990, *The Competitive Advantage of Nations*, London, Macmillan.

Poulantzas, Nicos, 1973, *Political Power and Social Classes*, London, New Left Books (1968).

Poulantzas, Nicos, 1978, *State, Power, Socialism*, London, New Left Books (1978).

Prebisch, Raúl, 1950, *Economic Survey of Latin America, 1949*, New York, United Nations (authored by Prebisch).

Prebisch, Raúl, 1984, 'Five Stages in my Thinking on Development'. In: Meier and Seers, 1984.

Przeworski, Adam, 1990, *The State and the Economy under Capitalism*, London, Harwood.

Pye, L. W. (ed.), 1963, *Communication and Political Development*, Princeton, NJ, Princeton University Press.

Pye, Lucien W., 1966, *Aspects of Political Development*, Boston, MA, Little, Brown & Co.

Pye, Lucien W. and S. Verba (eds), 1965, *Political Culture and Political Development*, Princeton, NJ, Princeton University Press.

Randall, V. and R. Theobald, 1985, *Political Change and Underdevelopment. A Critical Introduction to Third World Politics*, London, Macmillan.

Rathgeber, Eva M., 1990, 'WID, WAD, GAD: Trends in Research and Practice', *Journal of Developing Areas*, Vol. 24, No. 4.

Ravnborg, Helle Munk and Hans-Otto Sano, 1994, *The Poverty Objective in Development Assistance*, Copenhagen, Centre for Development Research.

Redclift, Michael, 1987, *Sustainable Development: Exploring the Contradictions*, London, Methuen.

Ricardo, David, 1911, *The Principles of Political Economy and Taxation*, London, Dent (1817).

Riggs, Fred W., 1981, 'The Rise and Fall of Political Development'. In: *The Handbook of Political Behaviour*, S. C. Long (ed.), New York, Plenum Press.

Riggs, Fred W., 1984, 'Development'. In: Giovanni Sartori (ed.), *Social Science Concepts. A Systematic Analysis*, Beverly Hills, CA, Sage Publications.

Robertson, A. F., 1984, *People and the State. An Anthropology of Planned Development*, Cambridge, Cambridge University Press.

Roemer, John E., 1982, *A General Theory of Exploitation and Class*, Cambridge, MA, Harvard University Press.

Roemer, John E., 1988, *Free to Lose. An Introduction to Marxist Economic Philosophy*, Cambridge, MA, Harvard University Press.

Rondinelli, Dennis, J. McCullough and R. Johnson, 1989, 'Analyzing Decentralization Policies in Developing Countries. A Political-Economy Framework', *Development and Change*, Vol. 20.

Rosdolsky, Roman, 1972, *Zur Entstehungsgeschicte des Marxschen 'Kapital'*, Frankfurt, Europäische Verlagsanstalt.

Rosenstein-Rodan, Paul, 1943, 'Problems of Industrialisation of Eastern and South-Eastern Europe', *Economic Journal*, June–Sept. In: Meier, 1989, pp. 279ff.

Rosenstein-Rodan, Paul, 1957, 'Notes on the "Big Push"'. In: Meier, 1989, pp. 281ff.

Rosenstein-Rodan, Paul, 1984, 'Natura Facit Saltum: Analysis of the Disequilibrium Growth Process'. In: Meier and Seers, 1984.

Rosenthal, Irwin I. J., 1965, *Islam in the Modern National State*, Cambridge, Cambridge University Press.

Rostow, W. W., 1960, *The Stages of Growth*, Cambridge, Cambridge University Press.

Rostow, W. W., 1978, *The World Economy: History and Prospects*, Austin, University of Texas Press.

Rostow, W. W., 1980, *Why the Poor Get Richer and the Rich Slow Down*, Austin, University of Texas Press.

Roth, G. 1968, 'Personal Rulership, Patrimonialism and Empire-Building in the New States', *World Politics*, Vol. 20, pp. 194–206.

Roth, G., 1987, *The Private Provision of Public Services in Developing Countries*, New York, Oxford University Press, Published for the World Bank.

Roy, P., 1981, 'Transition in Agriculture: Emperical Indicators and Results', *Journal of Peasant Studies*, Vol. 8, No. 2.

Rudolph, L. and S. Rudolph, 1967, *The Modernity of Tradition: Political Development In India*, Chicago, IL, Chicago University Press.

Sabine, George H., 1961, *A History of Political Theory*, London, Harrap (3rd edn) (1937).

Sachs, I., 1974, 'Ecodevelopment', *Ceres*, Vol. 17, No. 4.

Said, Edward W., 1978, *Orientalism*, New York, NY, Pantheon Books.

Salazar-Xirinachs, J. M., 1993, 'The Role of the State and the Market in Economic Development'. In: Sunkel, 1993.

Samuelson, Paul A., 1967, *Economics. An Introductory Analysis*, New York, McGraw-Hill (7th edn).

Sandbrook, Richard, 1985, *The Politics of Economic Stagnation in Tropical Africa*, Cambridge University Press.

Sandbrook, Richard, 1986, 'The State and Economic Stagnation in Tropical Africa', *World Development*, Vol. 14, No. 3.

Saul, John, 1974, 'The State in Post-Colonial Society: Tanzania', *Socialist Register 1974*.

Saul, John 1979, *The State and Revolution in Eastern Africa*, London, Heinemann.

Schultz, T. W., 1964, *Transforming Traditional Agriculture*, New Haven, CT, Yale University Press.

Schumpeter, Joseph A., 1934, *The Theory of Economic Development*, Cambridge, MA, Harvard University Press (German edn, 1912).

Schumpeter, Joseph A., 1947, *Capitalism, Socialism, and Democracy*, London, George Allen & Unwin.

Scott, James C., 1985, *Weapons of the Weak: Everyday Forms of Peasant Resistance*, New Haven, CT, Yale University Press.

Scott, James C., 1990, *Domination and the Art of Resistance: Hidden Transcripts*, New Haven, CT, Yale University Press.

Seers, Dudley, 1972, 'What are We Trying to Measure?', *Journal of Development Studies*, April.

Sen, Amartya, 1988, 'The Concept of Development'. In: Chenery and Srinivasan, 1988.

Senghass, D., 1985, *The European Experience. A Historical Critique of Development Theory*, Dover, Berg Publishers (1982).

Shanin, T. 1982, 'Class, State and Revolution'. In: *Introduction to the sociology of 'Developing Countries'*, H. Alavi and T. Shanin (eds), London, Macmillan.

Shiva, V., 1991, *The Violence of the Green Revolution*, London, Zed Press.

Shivji, I. G., 1976, *Class Struggles in Tanzania*, London, Heinemann.

Silverman, Jerry M., 1992, *Public Sector Decentralization. Economic Policy and Sector Investment Programs*, Washington, DC, The World Bank (Technical Paper, No. 188).

Singer, Hans, 1984, 'The Terms of Trade Controversy and the Evolution of Soft Financing: Early Years in the UN'. In: Meier and Seers, 1984.

Singh, Yogendra, 1989, 'Relevance of Max Weber for the Understanding of Indian Reality'. In: Bharadwaj and Kaviraj, 1989.

Smith, Adam, 1974, *Wealth of Nations*, Pelican Books (1776).

Solodovnikov, V. G. and V. Bogoslovsky, 1975, *Non-Capitalist Development: An Historical Outline*, Moscow, Progress Publishers.

Sonntag, Heinz Rudolf, 1973: 'Die Staat des unterentwickelten Kapitalismus', *Kursbuch 31* (Berlin, May).

Sørensen, Georg, 1993, *Democracy and Democratization*, Boulder, CO, Westview Press.

South Report, 1990, *The Challenge to the South. The Report of the South Commission*, Oxford, Oxford University Press.

Stavenhagen, Rodolfo, 1990, *The Ethnic Question. Conflicts, Development and Human Rights*, Tokyo, United Nations University Press.

Stetting, Lauge, K. E. Svendsen and E. Yndgaard (eds), 1993, *Global Change and Transformation. Economic Essays in Honor of Karsten Laursen*, København, Handelshøjskolens Forlag.

Stiglitz, J. E., 1989, 'Markets, Market Failures and Development', *The American Economic Review*, Vol. 79, No. 2.

Stølen, Kristi Anne and Mariken Vaa (eds), 1991, *Gender and Change in Developing Countries*, Oslo, Norwegian University Press.

Streeten, Paul P. et al., 1982, *First Things First. Meeting Basic Human Needs in Developing Countries*, Published for the World Bank by Oxford University Press (1981).

Streeten, Paul P., 1984, 'Development Dichotomies'. In: Meier and Seers, 1984.

Streeten, Paul P., 1993, 'Markets and States: Against Minimalism', *World Development*, Vol. 21, No. 8.

Streeten, Paul P., 1994, *Strategies for Human Development. Global Poverty and Unemployment*, Copenhagen, Handelshøjskolens Forlag/Munksgaard International Publishers.

Sunkel, Osvaldo (ed.), 1993, *Development from Within. Towards a Neostructuralist Approach for Latin America*, Boulder, CO., Lynne Rienner.

Svendsen, Knud Erik, 1990, 'Udviklingsøkonomi, økonomisk politik og politisk økonomi', (Development economics, economic policy, and political economy, in Danish), *Den Ny Verden*, 23. årg., nr. 1.

Syrquin, Moshe, 1988, 'Patterns of Structural Change'. In: Chenery and Srinivasan, 1988.

Timmer, C. Peter, 1988, 'The Agricultural Transformation'. In: Chenry and Srinivasan, 1988.

Todaro, Michael P., 1971, *Development Planning: Models and Methods*, Nairobi, Oxford University Press.

Todaro, Michael P., 1982, *Economics for a Developing World*, Essex, Longman.

Törnquist, Olle, 1984, *Dilemmas of Third World Communism. The Destruction of the PKI in Indonesia*, London, Zed Books.

Toye, John, 1987, *Dilemmas of Development. Reflections on the Counter-Revolution in Development Theory and Policy*, Oxford, Basil Blackwell.

Toye, John, 1993, 'The New Institutional Economics and its Implications for Development Theory'. In: Martinussen, 1993a.

Tsurumi, Y., 1984, *Multinational Management. Business Strategy and Government Policy*, Cambridge, MA, Ballinger.

UNCTAD, 1994 (Division on Transnational Corporations and Investment), *World Investment Report. Transnational Corporations, Employment and the Workplace*, New York.

UNCTC, 1992 (Transnational Corporations and Management Division), *World Investment Report 1992. Transnational Corporations as Engines of Growth*, New York.

UNDP, 1990, *Human Development Report 1990*, New York, Oxford University Press.

UNDP, 1991, *Human Development Report 1991*, New York, Oxford University Press.

UNDP, 1992, *Human Development Report 1992*, New York, Oxford University Press.

UNDP, 1993, *Human Development Report 1993*, New York, Oxford University Press.

UNDP, 1994, *Human Development Report 1994*, New York, Oxford University Press.

UNDP, 1995, *Human Development Report 1995*, New York, Oxford University Press.

United Nations, 1987, *International Conference on the Relationship Between Disarmament and Development*, New York.

United Nations, 1988, *The United Nations and Disarmament. A Short History*, New York.

UNRISD, 1981–83, *Dialogue About Participation. No. 1–3*, Geneva.

Uphoff, N. T., J. Cohen and A. A. Goldsmith, 1979, *Feasibility and Application of Rural Development Participation: A State of the Art Paper*, New York, Cornell University (Monograph Series No. 3).

Vandergeest, Peter and F. H. Buttel, 1988, 'Marx, Weber, and Development Sociology: Beyond the Impasse', *World Development*, Vol. 16, No. 6.

Varshney, Ashutosh (ed.), 1993, 'Beyond Urban Bias', *Journal of Development Studies*, Special Issue, Vol. 29, No. 4.

Vernon, Raymond, 1973, *Sovereignty at Bay: The Multinational Spread of US Enterprises*, Harmondsworth, Penguin (1971).

Vernon, Raymond, 1977, *Storm over the Multinationals: The Real Issues*, Cambridge, MA, Harvard University Press.

Vernon, Raymond, 1979, 'The Product Cycle Hypothesis in a New International Environment', *Oxford Bulletin of Economics and Statistiscs*, Vol. 41, No. 4.

Viotti, P. R. and Kauppi, M. V., 1993, *International Relations Theory. Realism, Pluralism, Globalism*, New York, Macmillan.

Wade, Robert, 1988, *Village Republics: Economic Conditions for Collective Action in South India*, Cambridge, Cambridge University Press.

Wade, Robert, 1990, *Governing the Market: Economic Theory and the Role of the Government in East Asian Industrialization*, Princeton, NJ, Princeton University Press.

Wallace, T. and C. March (eds), 1991, *Changing Perceptions. Writings on Gender and Development*, Oxford, Oxfam.

Wallerstein, Immanuel, 1974, *The Modern World System, Capitalist Agriculture and the Origins of the European World Economy in the Sixteenth Century*, New York, Academic Press.

Wallerstein, Immamuel, 1979, *The Capitalist World Economy*, Cambridge, Cambridge University Press.

Wallerstein, Immanuel, 1980, *The Modern World System II. Mercantilism and the Consolidation of the European World Economy, 1600–1750*, New York, Academic Press.

Walras, L., 1954, *Elements of Pure Economics*, London, George Allen & Unwin (1926).

Ward, R. and D. Rustov, 1964, *Political Modernization in Japan and Turkey*, Princeton, NJ, Princeton University Press.

Warren, Bill, 1973, 'Imperialism and Capitalist Industrialization', *New Left Review*, No. 81.

Warren, Bill, 1980, *Imperialism: Pioneer of Capitalism*, London, New Left Books and Verso.

Weber, Max, 1958, *Religion of India: The Sociology of Hinduism and Buddhism*, New York, Free Press (1920–21).

Weber, Max, 1965, *The Protestant Ethic and the Spirit of Capitalism*, London.

Webster, Neil, 1990, *Panchayat Raj and the Decentralisation of Development Planning in West Bengal: A Case Study*, Copenhagen, Centre for Development Research.

Weiss, John, 1988, *Industry in Developing Countries. Theory, Policy and Evidence*, London, Routledge.

Wiley, Norbert (ed.), 1987, *The Marx–Weber Debate*, Newbury Park, CA, Sage Publications.

Wilk, Richard, 1989, *The Household Economy: Reconsidering the Domestic Mode of Production*, Boulder, CO, Westview Press.

Williamson, O. E., 1986, *Economic Organization. Firms, Markets and Policy Control*, Hertfordshire, Wheatsheaf.

Wilson, Fiona, 1993, *Reflections on Gender as an Inter-disciplinary Study*, København, Center for Udviklingsforskning (Working Papers 93.2).

Winpenny, James Thomas (ed.), 1991, *Development Research: The Environmental Challenge*, London, Overseas Development Institute.

Wolf, Charles, 1988, *Markets or Governments: Choosing between Imperfect Alternatives*, Cambridge, MA, MIT Press.

World Bank, 1980, *World Development Report 1980*, Oxford, Oxford University Press for the World Bank.

World Bank, 1990, *World Development Report 1990*, Oxford, Oxford University Press for the World Bank.

World Bank, 1991, *World Development Report 1991*, Oxford, Oxford University Press for the World Bank.

World Bank, 1992, *World Development Report 1992*, Oxford, Oxford University Press for the World Bank.

World Bank, 1993a, *World Development Report 1993*, Oxford, Oxford University Press for the World Bank.

World Bank, 1993b, *The East Asian Miracle. Economic Growth and Public Policy*, Oxford, Oxford University Press for the World Bank.

World Bank, 1994, *Adjustment in Africa. Reforms, Results, and the Road Ahead*, Oxford, Oxford University Press.

World Development, 1989, 'The Role of Institutions in Economic Development', *World Development*, Special Issue.

Worsley, Peter, 1984, *The Three Worlds. Culture and World Development*, London, Weidenfeld & Nicolson.

Wright, Erik Ohlin, 1978, *Class, Crisis, and the State*, London, New Left Books.

Wright, Erik Ohlin, 1985, *Classes*, London, New Left Books.

Young, Kate, 1993, *Planning Development with Women. Making a World of Difference*, London, Macmillan.

Zolberg, A., 1966, *Creating Political Order: The Party States of West Africa*, Chicago, IL, Chicago University Press.

Name Index

Subject Index